Human Resource Development

Today and Tomorrow

Human Resource Development

Today and Tomorrow

by

Ronald R. Sims

INFORMATION AGE
PUBLISHING

Greenwich, Connecticut 06830 • www.infoagepub.com

Library of Congress Cataloging-in-Publication Data

Sims, Ronald R.
  Human resource development : today and tomorrow / by Ronald R. Sims.
     p. cm.
  Includes bibliographical references.
  ISBN 1-59311-487-7 (pbk.) – ISBN 1-59311-488-5 (hardcover)
  1. Personnel management. I. Title.
  HF5549.S59244 2006
  658.3'124–dc22
                                                                    2006005235

Copyright © 2006 Information Age Publishing Inc.

All rights reserved. No part of this publication may be reproduced, stored in a retrieval system, or transmitted, in any form or by any means, electronic, mechanical, photocopying, microfilming, recording or otherwise, without written permission from the publisher.

Printed in the United States of America

CONTENTS

Preface . . . . *vii*

1. Introduction to HRD *1*

2. Maximizing Learning Outcomes in Human Resource Development: The Role of Learning and Learning Styles. *25*

3. Assessing HRD Needs *55*

4. Designing Effective HRD Initiatives *83*

5. Training Methods: Implementing HRD Initiatives *113*

6. Evaluating HRD Initiatives *139*

7. Employee Socialization and Orientation *177*

8. HRD and Career Management and Development. *205*

9. Management Development *241*

10. HRD, Organizational Change and Development *275*

11. HRD: Bridging Today and Tomorrow *303*

References *319*

PREFACE

HRD professionals are increasingly finding themselves welcomed at the strategic table in their organizations. This is because they have continued to find ways to assist their organizations in not only surviving, but thriving in our increasingly global world. HRD professionals continue to recognize the importance of employee knowledge, skills and motivation to organizational success. This recognition has opened many doors as organizational leaders accept the fact that human resource development (HRD) initiatives can be used to ensure that organization members have what it takes to successfully meet the demands that confront them and their organizations. Challenges like globalization and an increasingly diverse workforce along with a much more complex and competitive environment makes it more difficult to ensure that organizations will succeed. To help their organizations meet these challenges HRD professionals have had to constantly search for ways to increase the success of their HRD efforts. And, while they have been successful to some extent, they must continue to find ways to meet and exceed the expectation that HRD can more often than not add value to the organization.

This book is written with the belief that HRD professionals will continue to learn, change and find ways to reinvent themselves and the profession individually and collectively as we move further into the 21st century. A major point of this book is that HRD will continue to become more and more important to organizational success. And, as calls for accountability and bottom line impact continue to rise, HRD professionals will be proactive in demonstrating their value to the organization.

The primary audience for this book is practicing HRM and HRD professionals, and other organizational leaders. The book provides tested and proven ideas important to demonstrating the value of HRD. From a practical viewpoint, it is based on actual experience, a strong research base, and accepted practices presented in an easy to read form.

A second target audience is students of HRD and HRM who are preparing for careers in this important field. This book will help them develop a solid foundation to the study of HRD practices that are key to HRD success regardless of the type of organization.

A third target audience is managers or leaders at all levels of an organization who are increasingly expected to take on HRD responsibilities while also partnering with HRD professionals. It offers these individuals a firsthand look at what they should expect of their HRD functions or areas and how they can encourage HRD professionals in their organizations to be accountable' strategic partners in helping the organization achieve its success by getting the most out of its human capital.

OUTLINE OF THE BOOK

Chapter 1 provides a current look at human resource development and its ever changing role and the accompanying challenges in organizations who are increasingly recognizing HRD professionals as valued strategic partners in their efforts to survive and thrive in the 21st century. Chapter 2 discusses those considerations important to maximizing learning outcomes in HRD initiatives. Chapter 3 focuses on assessing the importance of needs assessment to the HRD process. Chapter 4 covers what HRD professionals should do to design effective HRD initiatives.

Chapter 5 describes a number of training methods that can be used to implement HRD initiatives. Chapter 6 emphasizes the importance of assessing HRD initiatives as a critical means of communicating the impact of such efforts in helping organizations achieve their objectives.

Chapters 7 through 10 provide a look at specific HRD applications with Chapter 7 discussing employee socialization and orientation; Chapter 8 focuses on HRD and career management and development; Chapter 9 discusses management development, and Chapter 10 emphasizes the important role HRD professionals should play in organization change and development efforts. Finally, Chapter 11 provides a concluding look at HRD today and the need for the field and HRD professionals to continue to look for ways to continuously learn, change and reinvent themselves if they are to receive the respect and support from organizational leaders in the years to come.

ACKNOWLEDGMENTS

As always, a very special thank you goes to Herrington Bryce who continues to serve as a colleague, mentor, and valued friend. The administrative support of the School of Business Administration at the College of William and Mary is also acknowledged.

As with every previous endeavor, I owe much to my wife Serbrenia and our daughters, Nandi, Dangaia, and Sieya, who provide encouragement, support, patience, and assistance while I am immersed in research and attached to a computer.

CHAPTER 1

INTRODUCTION TO HRD

INTRODUCTION

The field of Human Resource Development (HRD) continues to go through a process of discovery and transformation. And, as Dilworth (2003) has recently noted "the quest for the essence of HRD and how to deliver it is intensifying." There still is no single point of view or predominant framework and the field continues to be a mosaic of multiple perspectives, in some cases only loosely arrayed: It can still be described as emergent, dynamic, and modeled by the contexts, circumstances, and cultures in which it occurs. It is our contention that such a view of HRD is healthy and needed if the field is to continue to grow and develop as it attempts to meet the diverse needs of an increasingly demanding global world. In our view, a mosaic of multiple perspectives should be viewed as strengths of the field of HRD, and not as an "Achilles' heel."

In the field of HRD, there has been a debate on whether performance or learning is most important for the field (Ying, 2004; R.A Swanson, 1995; Watkins & Marsick, 1995). The performance view argues that the purpose of HRD is to improve organizational performance (Swanson & Arnold, 1996), whereas the learning view contends that HRD should develop individuals who ultimately contribute to organizational prosperity (Bierema, 1996). Nevertheless, all seem to agree that learning should be a vital component of HRD practice (learning will be the focus of Chapter 2). A more recent conception of HRD views the field as including learning, performance, and change (Gilley & Maycunich, 2000). This recent view of HRD as "the process of facilitating organizational learning, performance, and change through organized interventions and initiatives, and management actions for the purpose of enhancing an organization's performance, capacity, capability, competitive readiness and renewal" (Gilley & Maycunich, 2000, p. 6) forms the bases of our definition of HRD. That is, HRD is defined as "strategically-driven (i.e., systematic and planned) activities designed to improve current and future organizational learning, performance and change."

This chapter first provides a brief look at HRD and its link to other human resource management (HRM) activities. The chapter then discusses the strategic importance of HRD.

The chapter also discusses the roles, skills and competencies of HRD professionals. We then discuss several critical challenges facing HRD professionals. Finally, the chapter offers a strategic approach to HRD as a natural beginning for HRD in any organization.

HUMAN RESOURCE DEVELOPMENT AND OTHER HUMAN RESOURCE MANAGEMENT ACTIVITIES

In the early 1980s, the field of personnel management shifted its emphasis as personnel departments renamed themselves "human resources departments." In some instances this change was cosmetic, but in many cases the change in language marked a subtle shift, from a function that essentially handled staffing and related administrative activities to a function that essentially handled staffing and related administrative activities to a function that focused on the development of people as a resource to the organization (Yorks, 2005).

This shift in roles put into practice what Miles had, much earlier, described as the distinction between a human relations and a human resources perspective (Miles, 1965). Miles argued that most employees are capable of contributing more to the organization than traditional management practices allow. Management's task is to create work situations that permit employees to contribute as broad a range of their talents as possible to the organization's goals. Work should be developmental. Following this line of reasoning, training and development, and especially management and organization development, in many ways become the standard barriers of the new HRM department (Miles, 1965; Yorks, 2005).

HRD has its roots in training and development, which in turn has traditionally been one of several HRM functions. It has been suggested that the guiding principle of HRM can be expressed as positioning the right people to achieve the highest possible performance in order to meet strategic goals (Yorks, 2005). Further, successfully putting this principle into practice involves asking and answering questions such as "What kinds of people do we need, that is, what knowledge, skills, and abilities do we seek? How do we best position them in the organization once they are employed? How do we motivate and retain these employees? What systems will manage them effectively?

The guiding principle of HRD can be expressed as preparing and continually developing people and learning systems to achieve the highest possible performance in order to meet strategic goals (Yorks, 2005). Successfully executing this principle in practice involves asking and answering questions such as "What kind of learning and development do members of the organization need? How do we allocate learning opportunities among employees? How do we keep track of our employees' various and individual competencies and capabilities? How do we manage the knowledge and the social and intellectual capital of the organization?

In most organizations, training or HRD is part of a larger HRM department. HRM encompasses those activities designed to provide for and coordinate the human resources of an organization. How the HRM function is carried out varies from organization to organization. Some organizations have a centralized HRM department with highly specialized staff, but in other organizations, the HRM function is decentralized and conducted throughout the organization. Coordination and synchronization of HRM and HRD activities are necessary regardless of how an organization structures its HRM functions.

HRM functions can be divided into primary and secondary functions. Primary functions are directly involved with obtaining, maintaining, and developing employees. Primary functions include: human resource planning, equal employment opportunity, staffing (recruitment and selection), compensation and benefits, employee (labor) relations, health, safety, and security, and human resource development. Secondary functions either provide support for general management activities or are involved in determining or changing the structure of the organization. Secondary functions include: organization/job design, performance management and performance appraisal systems, research and information systems.

The objectives of specific HRD activities vary greatly (i.e., changing or improving the knowledge, skills, and attitudes of individuals; career development efforts intended to assist individuals through a series of career stages; and organization) development efforts to enhance the effectiveness of an organization. The differing objectives, in turn, often determine which other aspects of the broader HRM system should be more tightly integrated with a particular HRD activity. Clearly, if the objective is socializing new hires, the HRD activity should be coordinated with recruitment activities. Because HRD for new hires often includes a discussion of important company policies, the content of the training, for example, is likely to reflect the organization's entire set of HRM practices.

When the objective of HRD is improving job performance, the HRD activity should be designed using job analysis information about what is required to do the work. If the objective is developing employees for future promotion and advancement, the activities should be aligned with the selection criteria used when hiring people into those higher-level positions. If the objective of HRD is to create a culture of change, it may be appropriate to link performance evaluations and rewards to completion of the HRD activities.

Because there are so many possible objectives of HRD, all of the HRM functional areas are integrated with HRD efforts in various ways. However, any particular HRD program is likely to require very close alignment with other HRM activities as evident in the interdependency of the HRM and HRD questions introduced earlier. The answer to questions like "What kind of people do we need?" and "Can we successfully recruit such people?" influences what kind of training and development is required. Often retaining highly talented people depends on how organizations allocate learning and development opportunities. HRD and HRM professionals must ensure that there is a maximum coordination among the overlapping sectors of HRD and HRM functions.

STRATEGIC IMPORTANCE OF HRD

The strategic importance of HRD to organizational performance has been increasingly underscored (Werner & DeSimone, 2006; Chermack, Lynham, & Ruona, 2003; Swanson & Holton, 2001; Brockbank, 1999). In today's intensely competitive and global marketplace, maintaining a competitive advantage by becoming a low-cost leader or a differentiator puts a heavy premium on having a highly committed or competent workforce. Competitive advantage lies not just in differentiating a product or service or in becoming the low-cost leader but in also being able to tap the organization's special skills or core competencies and rapidly respond to customers' needs and competitor's moves. In other words competitive advantage lies in management's ability to consolidate organization-wide technologies and production and service skills into competencies that empower individual organization's to adapt quickly to changing opportunities.

In a growing number of organizations human resources are now viewed as a source of competitive advantage. There is greater recognition that distinctive competencies are obtained through highly developed employee skills, distinctive organizational cultures, management processes and systems. This is in contrast to the traditional emphasis on transferable resources such as equipment. Increasingly it is being recognized that competitive advantage can be obtained with a high quality workforce that enables organizations to compete on the basis of market responsiveness, product and service quality, differentiated products and technological innovation.

Strategic human resource management (SHRM) can be defined as 'the linking of human resources with strategic goals and objectives in order to improve business performance and develop organizational culture that foster innovation and flexibility'. SHRM means accepting the HRM function as a strategic partner in the formulation of the organization's strategies as well as in the implementation of those strategies through HRM activities such as recruiting, selecting, training, developing and rewarding personnel. Whereas SHRM recognizes HRM's partnership role in the strategizing process, the term "HRM Strategies" refers to specific HRM courses of action the organization plans to pursue to achieve its aims.

HRM can play a role in environmental scanning (i.e., identifying and analyzing external opportunities and threats that may be crucial to the organization's success). Similarly HRM is in a unique position to supply competitive intelligence that may be useful in the strategic planning process. HRM also participates in the strategy formulation process by supplying information regarding the organization's internal strengths and weaknesses. The strengths and weaknesses of an organization's human resources can have a determining effect on the viability of the organization's strategic options.

By design the perspective demands that HRM managers and HRD professionals become strategic partners in business operations playing prospective roles rather then being passive players reacting to the requirements of other organizational functions. Strategic HRM managers and HRD professionals need to continue the change in their mindset from seeing themselves as relationship professionals to resource professionals knowing how to utilize the full potential of their human resources.

The new breed of HRM managers and HRD professionals need to continue to understand and know how to measure the monetary impact of their actions, so as to be able to demonstrate the value-added contributions of their functions. HRD professionals become strategic partners when they participate in the process of defining organizational strategy, when they ask questions that move strategy to action and when they design HRD practices that align with the business strategy. By fulfilling this role, HRD professionals increase the capacity of a business to execute its strategies.

The primary actions of the strategic HRD professional translate organizational strategies into HRD priorities. For example, in any organizational setting, whether corporate, functional, business unit or product line a strategy exists either explicitly in the formal process or document or implicitly through a shared agenda on priorities. As strategic partners, HRD professionals should be able to identify the HRD practices that make the strategy happen. The process of identifying these HRD priorities is much easier when HRD is a strategic partner and its efforts are strategically integrated within the organization as HRD professionals prospectively conduct organizational diagnoses (i.e., processes through which they audit their organizations to determine its human resource strengths and weaknesses).

Translating organizational strategies into HRD practices helps an organization in three ways. First, the organization can adapt to change because the time from the conception to the execution of a strategy is shortened. Second, the organization can better meet customer demands because its customer service strategies have been translated into specific policies and practices. Third, the organization can achieve financial performance through its more effective execution of strategy.

In brief, a strategic perspective of HRD that requires simultaneous consideration of both external (organization strategy) and internal (consistency) requirement leads to superior performance of the organization. This performance advantage is achieved by:

1. Marshaling human resources that support the organizational strategy and implementing the chosen strategy, efficiently and effectively.
2. Utilizing the full potential of the human resources to the organization's advantage.
3. Leveraging other resources such as physical assets and capital to complement and augment the human resources-based advantage.

HRD professionals have made some progress in moving toward a more "strategically integrated HRD" (Werner & DeSimone, 2006; Rothwell & Kazanas, 2004; Gilley & Maycunich, 1998; Littlefield & Welch, 1996, pp. 11–12). In particular, HRD can demonstrate its strategic capability in three primary ways: (1) directly participating in their organization's strategic management process as suggested above, (2) providing education and training to line managers in the concepts and methods of strategic management and planning, and (3) providing training to all employees that is aligned with the goals and strategies of the organization (Torraco & Swanson, 1995).

First, HRD professionals should contribute information, ideas, and recommendations during strategy formulation and ensure that the organization's HRD strategy is consistent with the overall strategy. The HRD strategy should offer answers to questions like: Are the organization's HRD objectives, strategies, policies, and programs clearly stated? Are all HRD activities consistent with the organization's vision, mission, objectives, policies, and internal and external environment? How well is the HRD area performing in terms of improving the fit between the individual employee and the job?

Are appropriate concepts and techniques being used to evaluate and improve organizational learning and performance?

The second strategic role for HRD professionals is to provide education and training programs that support effective strategic management. Training to help line managers develop a global perspective is essential for organization's to succeed in a highly competitive environment. Management education efforts also place emphasis on strategic management issues. Organizational leaders are increasingly exposing their managers to separate courses (or portions of courses) that emphasize SHRM issues and how these relate to their strategies and outcomes.

Finally, HRD professionals must continue to improve their ability to demonstrate that all their HRD efforts are clearly linked to the goals and strategies of the organization. There is every indication that organizations will continue to expect HRD professionals to demonstrate that their efforts are contributing to the viability and financial success of the organization. The growing emphasis on strategic HRD is part of this movement to build a stronger business case for HRD programs and interventions (Phillips, 1996a). We will take another look at strategic HRD later in this chapter by way of introducing a strategic HRD model.

THE ROLES, SKILLS AND COMPETENCIES OF HRD PROFESSIONALS

As an integral part of today's learning organizations HRD professionals must perform a wide variety of roles. And the role of HRD within "learning organizations" is becoming clearer, despite the fact that there are still many uncertainties for HRD professionals, especially with regard to the question of how to bring their new roles into practice. This section discusses some of the suggested roles, skills and competencies for HRD professionals.

In her article on HRD competencies and future trends in HRD Pat McLagan (1996) identified the following nine important roles for HRD practitioners to perform:

1. *HRM strategic advisor.* In this role the issues and trends concerning an organization's external and internal people are brought to the attention of the strategic decision makers
2. *HRM systems designer and developer.* This role involves designing and preparing HRM systems for implementation so that HRM systems and actions are mutually reinforcing and have maximum impact on organizational performance, development and endurance.
3. *Organization change consultant.* This role means facilitating the development and implementation of strategies for transforming organizations.

4. *Organization design consultant.* This role involves identifying the work required to fulfill organizational strategies. It also involves organizing the work so that it makes efficient and effective use of resources.
5. *Learning program specialist.* In this role learning needs are identified to design and develop structured learning programs and materials in a variety of media formats for self-study and workshop or electronic delivery.
6. *Instructor/facilitator.* This is an increasingly difficult role. In it information is presented, structural learning experiences are lead and group discussions and group processes facilitated.
7. *Individual development and career consultant.* This role involves helping people assess their competencies, values and goals so they can identify, plan, and implement development actions.
8. *Performance consultant.* This role means assisting a group or individuals to add value in the workplace. It's a coaching and consulting role in which HRD people perform both analytical and systems-design work.
9. *Researcher.* This role involves assessing HRD practices and programs and their impact empirically. It also means communicating results so that the organization and its people accelerate their change and development.

As part of former President Clinton's National Performance Review initiative, the President's Management Council chaired by former Vice President Al Gore formed the Human Resource Development (HRD) Council in an effort to develop strategies, policies, and programs that support individual and organizational performance across the federal government (HRD Council, 1997). The HRD Council suggested that HRD contributes to the business of the agency by performing the following roles:

1. *Clarifying business goals.* Using their knowledge of the organization's business, HRD professionals work with leaders and managers to clarify the business of the agency.
2. *Consulting on performance improvement.* HRD, in moving beyond its traditional training role, works with organizational clients to diagnose performance problems and anticipate issues before they become "problems."
3. *Promoting systems thinking and a future orientation.* The role of the HRD professional is to constantly stay abreast of new methods and ideas for helping organizations define their ideal future and assess present performance against it.

4. *Building coalitions.* Improved performance organization-wide requires HRD to build coalitions with others who influence the resources and environment of the organization, such as managers, labor representatives, strategic planners, and specialists in personnel, information resource management, facilities, and procurement.
5. *Facilitating workplace learning.* The role of the HRD individual as learning facilitator includes helping individuals move through the process of acquiring new knowledge and capabilities. Facilitating workplace learning means ensuring that, as changes take place in the organization's technologies, systems, environment, and programs, learning opportunities are integrated where needed.
6. *Integrating people and technology.* HRD has a key role to integrate the use of technology for learning into the business practices of the agency. HRD assists in planning, implementing, and utilizing technology—for learning and workforce improvement.
7. *Brokering talent and services.* HRD professionals provide a variety of learning services and support systems. In addition to providing these services directly, they serve as brokers and talent scouts—reviewing and acquiring external programs.
8. *Modeling high-performance behaviors.* HRD professionals must see themselves as change agents. As such, they must demonstrate the personal, interpersonal, and professional competencies they encourage and help develop in others.

The HRD Council also developed a list of competencies organized in three levels to show a development pattern for HRD practitioners: entry level, or "contributor" to solutions; mid-level, or "integrator" of solutions; and senior level, or "strategist" of solutions. At each level, the competencies listed in the technical and leadership/managerial categories are those that the HRD practitioner should master when at that level. It is assumed that HRD professionals will be working to develop all the competencies throughout their career (see Table 1.1).

According to Swanson and Holton (2001), HRD roles can span the organization such as the chief learning organization officer, director of organizational effectiveness, or director of executive development. They can also fit within a subunit such as a manager of sales training, HRD coordinator (at a particular company location), or bank teller training specialist.

Table 1.1. HRD Council Task Force HRD Competencies

	Technical	Leadership/Managerial
Senior Level Strategist	Strategic HR Practices HR Systems Succession Planning Organizational Performance Outcome Measures	Vision Federal Legislative Process Financial Management Budget Business Process Reengineering Leveraging Resources External Awareness
Mid-Level Integrator	Organizational Development Diagnosis Performance Intervention Group Facilitation Coaching and Mentoring Team Performance Instructional Technology Contracting/Purchasing Cost Benefit Analysis	Marketing Program Evaluation Strategic Planning Systems Thinking Program/Project Management Change Management Negotiating Priority Management
Entry Level Contributor	Performance Analysis Learning Systems Career Development Concepts Instructional Systems Development HRD Rules and Regulations Presentation Platform Skills	Organizational Knowledge Customer Orientation Ethics Teamwork Communication Creative Thinking Problem Solving Self-Development Information Technology

Rao (2005) has suggested that some of the responsibilities of HRD professionals known as chief knowledge officers (CKOs) and chief learning officers (CLOs) include:

- Strategic planning at the highest levels of the company.
- Ability to integrate diverse groups and work across all functions; develop the culture; build awareness of knowledge management or organizational learning.
- Design and implement a knowledge and/or learning infrastructure to tie together corporate databases, employees' tacit knowledge and paper files.
- Consulting activities, organizational effectiveness.
- Work closely with CEOs.

Dave Ulrich and others (1999) recently outlined the following four skills for HRD professionals (Chief Learning Officers-CLOs):

1. The CLO knows, appreciates and influences business strategy including customer relationships and financial performance.
2. Understands the nuances of making change and applies the change.
3. Understands the essence of information and knowledge management and creates an organization in which learning occurs.
4. Maintains focus on training and development, but is sensitive to the entire array of HRM practices.

Responsibility for building next generation leaders rests with the CLOs and CKOs. The CLOs and CKOs perform multiple roles like that of a consultant, entrepreneur, technologist, environmentalist, and a champion of knowledge and learning (Ulrich et al., 1999; Rao, 2005). Rao and Ulrich also note that the roles and responsibilities are gradually evolving. It is in many cases a strategic as well as a possible informal role for HRD professionals. Competencies required for HRD professionals include:

- Visionary outlook;
- Strong people orientation and interpersonal skills;
- Familiarity with technology and best practice studies;
- Experience or capability in strategic thinking;
- Familiarity with knowledge management tools or the newest learning methodologies;
- Strong customer service orientation;
- High level of flexibility.

Others have suggested that HRD professionals must redefine their role based on the recognition that as organizations change their systems, processes and strategic goals, they too must change. That is, HRD professionals must become the architect of organizational change. With this in mind, the primary purpose of HRD professionals in organizations is no longer limited to the training of individuals. Instead, it must be about teaching organizations to "learn how to learn" (Harewood, 2005).

Werner and DeSimone recently noted that an HRD professional must perform a wide variety of functional roles. A functional role is a specific set of tasks and expected outputs for a particular job, for example, classroom trainer or instructional designer. To carry out these various roles, HRD professionals need to possess many different skills or competencies (Werner & DeSimone, 2006). Berenthal et al. described three stages of "foundational competencies needed by all HRD professionals.

Foundational competencies are depicted as falling into three areas of expertise that are supported by technology: personal (demonstrating, adaptability, modeling personal development), interpersonal (building trust, communicating effectively, influencing stakeholders, leveraging diversity, networking and partnering), and business/management (analyzing needs, proposing solutions, applying business acumen, driving results, planning and implementing, assignments, thinking strategically) (Berenthal et al., 2004). HRD professionals then make use of these foundational competencies as they develop areas of expertise. These areas of expertise fall in the category of workplace learning and performance roles and include: designing learning, improving human performance, delivering training, measuring and evaluating, facilitating organizational change, managing the learning function, coaching, managing organizational knowledge, and career planning and talent management. The four highest roles HRD professionals form are: learning strategist, business partner, project manager, and professional specialist (Berenthal et al., 2004; Werner & DeSimone, 2006; Davis, Naughton, & Rothwell, 2004). The learning strategist is involved in the high-level decision making concerning how HRD initiatives will support the goals and strategies of the organization. The business partners work together with managers and others in determining how the HRD initiative will be implemented and evaluated. The project manager is involved with the day-to-day planning, funding, and monitoring of HRD initiatives, whereas the professional specialist adds her or his expertise in particular areas, for example, designing, developing, delivering, and evaluating the HRD initiative (Berenthal et al., 2004; Davis et al., 2004).

Yorks has recently suggested that "although there are various ways in which HRD competencies can be grouped and defined, generally the skill sets required for HRD work fall into two categories: program development and consulting. Additionally, moving into more senior roles requires a broad understanding of both, although, generally, the expertise of an HRD professional is more soundly grounded in one or the other" (Yorks, 2005). Yorks offers the following skills and competencies that HRD professionals need if they are going to be adaptable to the changing needs of their organizations and provide HRD leadership to the strategically-driven organization:

1. Learning and Leadership Development Competencies (Program Development):
   - Classroom facilitation and presentation capabilities.
   - Knowledge and application of adult learning theory, including learning styles, learning contexts, and a variety of learning methods such as accelerated learning and action learning.
   - Needs analysis and program assessment.
   - Curriculum design.
2. HRM Consultant Competencies Supporting HRM Generalists and Business Unit Managers:
   - Understanding and executing the consulting process.

- HRM "literacy" in the various HRM disciplines, including learning and development, organizational development and effectiveness, compensation, staffing, policy and strategy, executive sourcing and succession planning, and diversity and affirmative action.
- Business/product knowledge.
- Project management team dynamics, including the capability of building a cohesive team.
- Coaching and development.
- Diagnosis and problem solving (Yorks, 2005).

Probably the most critical role (and competency) that HRD professionals must play in the future is the relationship building aspect of HRD work. Continuing to involve managers at all levels of the organization in decision-making, implementation and evaluation of HRD initiatives is an increasingly important aspect of this role. Although HRD professionals already recognize that this is their main responsibility, they must continue to work on building active partnerships with managers in the future. After all, HRD professionals need the input of managers if they are to successfully identify learning needs, stimulate and support informal learning, and ensure the continuous learning of employees at all levels of the organization. In the end, the most important role for HRD professionals is to establish the credibility of HRD initiatives and processes as tools for leading in today's challenging environment.

CHALLENGES FOR HRD PROFESSIONALS AND THEIR ORGANIZATIONS

The environment faced by organizations and their HRD professionals is a challenging one. Demographics are changing in the workforce, particularly with the increase in the diversity of employees and the aging of the workforce in many countries. Competing in a global economy has shifted from trade and investment to the integration of operations, management, and strategic alliances, which has significantly affected the requirements for developing globally competent employees. Also, the introduction of many new technologies that require more educated and trained workers and the need to find and develop qualified workers for the growing number of skilled jobs of all types. Failure to successfully close the skills gap through retraining and other HRD efforts will ensure that organizations will not be able to compete in an increasingly sophisticated market. All of these forces contribute to the challenge to build human capital in organizations. HRD professionals and others in their organizations must increasingly develop strategies for ensuring superior knowledge, skills, experience and lifelong learning within their workforce. All of these factors are combining to put more pressure for organizations and HRD professionals to continually increase the "collective value" of an organization's workforce. Each of these challenges (1) changing workforce demographics and diversity, (2) competing in a global environment, (3) technological changes, (4) eliminating the employee skills gap, and (5) developing human capital-lifelong learning and organizational learning and their potential impact on HRD will be briefly discussed in the following sections.

Changing Workforce Demographics and Diversity

There is no doubt that the American workforce has changed in dramatic ways. Two decades ago the American workforce was predominantly white and male. In the 1970s, non-Hispanic white males represented about 68% of the workforce. By 2006, white males will represent less than 40% of the workforce (Work-Family Roundtable, 1995). More recent forecasts by the U.S. Bureau of Labor Statistics project that the total U.S. labor force will consist of only 35% white, non-Hispanic males (Toossi, 2004). Almost half of the new entrants for the years 2002–2012 will be women.

These same projections also predict that white, non-Hispanic males will comprise fewer than one-third of new labor force entrants for the years 2002–2012 (Toossi, 2004, p. 53). In addition to the possibility of having differing educational backgrounds, immigrant employees are likely to have language and cultural differences. Organizations must begin now to successfully integrate these people into their workforces.

Almost everyone has heard the phrase "the graying of America." By the year 2012, the average age of employees will climb to 41.4 from 40.0 in 2012 (Toossi, 2004, p. 54). The change will be accompanied by a significant drop in the number of employees from 25 to 39 years. In 2002, 56.3% of the labor force was 40 or older, by 2012, almost 60% of the labor force will be in this age category. This age increase and drop in the younger labor pool will have a mixed effect. The older workforce will likely be more experienced, reliable, and stable, but possibly less adaptable to change and retraining.

The increasingly diverse workforce has several implications for HRD professionals. First, organizations need to address ethnic, racial, and other prejudices that may persist, as well as cultural insensitivity and language differences. Second, with the increasing number of women in the workforce, organizations should continue to provide developmental opportunities that will prepare women for advancement into the senior ranks and provide safeguards against sexual harassment. Third, the aging of the workforce highlights the importance of creating HRD programs that recognize and address the learning-related needs of both younger and older workers.

Competing in a Global Environment

Another dimension of diversity is related to the increasing globalization of many organizations. As organizations become more global, diversity must be defined in global and not just Western terms (Ivancevich & Gilbert, 2000). Defining diversity in global terms means looking at all people and everything that make them different from one another, as well as the things that make them similar. Differentiating factors often go beyond race and language and may include such things as values and customs. Diversity in an increasingly global world means that HRD professionals must develop a global-local balance as discussed below.

Today's organizations are increasingly confronted with the challenge of having HRM policies and processes in place that embody a global culture yet recognize local differences. Global capabilities as well as local cultural sensitivity to employees, customers, and patterns will be increasingly critical to the success of the organization. The challenge for HRD is to find and maintain the global–local balance, constantly assisting the organization in adapting to changing business, social, economic, and political conditions (Marquardt & Berger, 2003; Wellens & Rioux, 2000).

To be successful in the global arena organizations must have workable strategies for sharing learning across their locations and operational groupings. HRD needs to work through the organization to facilitate shared knowledge and innovation. Marquardt and Berger (2003) recently pointed out that although proponents of organizational learning and knowledge management have noted these needs for some time, most organizations are far from achieving successful implementation of information-sharing systems and cross-culturally driven innovation. The global-local balancing act also involves the need for members of the organization to feel that they belong to a global enterprise and yet feel accountable for their contributions in a more local sense (Ulrich & Smallwood, 2002).

HRD professionals can expand on the following traditional roles to enhance their organization's globalization efforts:

- preparing employees for overseas assignments; include cross-cultural training, expatriation and repatriation support, language training;
- building global teams and enhancing their ability to work virtually across time and distance;
- creating systems for continuous quality improvement to meet global customer expectations; developing cross-cultural communication skills;

- developing abilities in learning how to learn through action learning processes; and
- building capabilities in knowledge management and technology systems (Marquardt, 1998; Marquardt & Reynolds, 1994).

HRD professionals must also do a better job of ensuring that global HRD preparation is an ongoing, proactive process made up of a variety of learning opportunities. For example, consideration should be given to the timing of cross-cultural development. Marquardt and Berger suggest that in many cases currently, training is not undertaken until shortly before a person must deal with or travel to another culture. A crash course in culture and language is destined to be superficial and not provide the nuances and sensitivity needed to be effective (Marquardt & Berger, 2003).

Technological Changes

The much heralded "information age" has arrived swiftly (Ivancevich, 2001; Bassi, Benson, & Cheney, 1996). Its arrival has impacted jobs, the way business is conducted, and the need for more knowledge workers. The trends of the technology revolution are recognizable as the following:

1. *Growth in the knowledge needs.* World trade is growing more than three times faster in knowledge-intensive goods and services such as biomedicine, robotics, and engineering.
2. *Shift in human competencies.* Some predict that by 2015 almost all net employment growth will be in knowledge workers.
3. *Global market connection.* Technology is dissolving borders and creating an interconnected marketplace.
4. *Business streamlining.* Easy-to-use communication, electronic mail, electronic conferencing, and databases are creating instantaneous dissemination of data to make better decisions to geographically dispersed workers.
5. *Rapid response.* Technology permits quick communications, which allows faster decision making.
6. *Quicker innovation.* Teams of marketing, engineering, and production personnel working in parallel with computer provided files, data, and information develop products faster. Every stage—product conception design, development, and manufacturing—is accredited through the use of electronic technology resources.
7. *Quality improvement.* The concept of building quality into the entire process of making, marketing, and servicing is enhanced by computer monitoring systems and through robotics.

8. *Industrial Revolution.* Prior to the Industrial Revolution most people worked either close to or in their homes. However, mass production technologies changed this and people began to travel to work locations or factories. Today, with increased computer technology, there is a move for many to work from their homes, or engage in what is referred to as telework or telecommuting. More and more frequently, companies are using telecommuting. Options range from allowing employees to work at home one day a week to running entire projects, or even organizations, through electronic communication with employees all over the country or even on different continents working closely together, yet never meeting face to face.

Given forces like knowledge creation and information technology, and the sheer magnitude of change, it is only rational that HRD will continue to be different as we move further into the twenty-first century. HRD professionals will need to constantly reassess their role in more technologically sophisticated organizations. For example, Swanson and Holton (2001) suggest that the twenty-first century challenge for HRD is to engage in high-tech means of developing and unleashing human expertise coming from the demand to do HRD work better, faster, and cheaper. HRD will continue to face the challenge of quickly applying technology to the task of developing and unleashing human expertise to the task of improving its own and the organization's operations.

Eliminating the Skills Gap

For organizations to compete successfully in a global economy and address the reality that technologically-drive work increasingly requires more education and more skills, they must hire educated workers who can effectively perform the work in knowledge-intensive jobs. The idea of a skills gap—a mismatch between skills learned in school or possessed by an employee talent pool—and those required in the jobs created by today's economy—will continue to receive a lot of attention from organizations and their HRD professionals. Today's workplace requires workers with higher, more generic skills, such as problem solving, decision-making, communication, and teamwork. Schools in the United States are not perceived to be producing students with these skills. For example, even though the United States has one of the highest standards of living in the world, reports have suggested that between 25 and 40% of hourly employees have some basic skills deficiency (Werner & DeSimone, 2006). The result, it is argued, is a skills gap that threatens American productivity and competitiveness.

Two great concerns of employers today are finding good workers and training them. The difference between the skills needed on the job and those possessed by the applicants, the skills-gap, is of real concern to HRM and HRD professionals and their organizations looking to hire competent employees. Organizations need reliable, responsible workers who can solve problems and who have the social skills and attitudes to work together with other workers. While organizations would prefer to hire people who are trained and ready to go to work, they are usually willing to provide the specialized, job-specific training necessary for those lacking such skills. And this is increasingly difficult given the skills gap.

The skills gap will continue to pose challenges for organizations in the United States. For example, how can trainees learn how to operate new equipment if they cannot read and comprehend operating manuals? Further, how can new employees be taught to manipulate computer-controlled machines if they do not understand basic math? (Werner & DeSimone, 2006). Obviously, those organizations that want to be competitive in a global environment have a vested interest in education reform.

Other countries have educational systems that do a better job of teaching students the basic skills needed by most employers. Among other things, countries like Germany emphasize vocational education and school-to-work transition programs, so that school-age children can begin apprenticeship programs as part of their formal education. Since there is every indication that there will continue to be a growing number of jobs which require more education and higher levels of language, math, and reasoning skills than current ones, HRD professionals will have to help their organizations develop strategic HRD planning models that carefully weigh deficiencies in skills and shortage of skills.

The skills gap must be faced head on by HRD professionals and their organizations. HRD professionals must help their organizations develop world-class HRD efforts to train and develop employees who can move beyond the skills gap to be productive employees.

Developing Human Capital: Lifelong Learning and Organizational Learning

While the skills gap poses particular challenges for HRD professionals it is but one component of the broader challenge related to developing human capital. The idea that organizations "compete through people" highlights the fact that success increasingly depends on an organization's ability to manage human capital. The term "human capital" describes the economic value of KSAs. Although the value of the assets may not show up directly on an organization's balance sheet, it nevertheless has tremendous impact on an organization's performance.

Human capital is intangible and elusive and cannot be managed the way organizations manage jobs, products, and technologies. One of the reasons for this is that the employees, *not* the organization, own their own human capital. If valued employees leave an organization they take their human capital with them, and any investment the organization has made in training and developing those people is lost.

To build human capital in organizations, HRD professionals and other managers must increasingly develop strategies for ensuring superior knowledge, skills, and experience within their workforce. HRD professionals must develop learning activities that complement the organization's staffing practices to provide skill enhancement, particularly in areas that cannot be transferred to another organization if an employee should leave. In addition, HRD professionals must make sure that employees have opportunities for development on the job. The most highly valued intelligence will most likely be associated with competencies and capabilities that are learned from experience and are not easily taught. Consequently, HRD professionals have to do a good job of working with their organization's managers to provide developmental assignments to employees and making certain that job duties and requirements are flexible enough to allow for growth and learning.

Beyond the need to invest in employee development, HRD professionals have to work with their organizations to find ways of utilizing the knowledge that currently exists. Too often, employees have skills that go unused. Efforts to empower employees and encourage their participation and involvement more fully utilize the human capital available (Huang, 1998; Fusaro, 1998, p. 24; Bontis, 1996; Bowles & Hammond, 1996) and contribute to an environment in which employees are more likely to continue the learning process throughout their careers.

The need for lifelong learning requires organizations to make an ongoing investment in HRD. Lifelong learning can mean different things to different employees. For example, for managers lifelong learning may include attending management seminars that address new management approaches. To professional employees, this learning may mean taking advantage of continuing education opportunities. To semiskilled employees, it may involve more rudimentary skills training to help them to build their competencies.

The challenge for HRD professionals is to provide a full range of learning opportunities for all kinds of employees. Whether it is building human capital or lifelong learning opportunities, HRD professionals must ensure that their organizations find ways for all employees to learn and develop, regardless of their knowledge, skill or ability level.

A commitment to building human capital and lifelong learning means that HRD professionals are also helping their organizations to learn, adapt and change. That is, HRD professionals are addressing the challenge of helping their organization to become a learning organization. HRD professionals will continue to have to meet the challenge of facilitating the transition of traditional training programs to an emphasis on learning principles and tactics, on how learning relates to performance, and more important, on the relationship between learning and fundamental change (Argyris, 1994). To do this, HRD professionals must develop a solid understanding of learning theory and be able to devise tools that enhance individual development.

In the end, HRD professionals must not lose sight of the fact that creativity, once a trait avoided by employers, is now prized among employers who are trying to create the empowered, high-performance workforce needed for competitiveness in today's marketplace. Employees with these skills are in demand and will continue to be considered valuable human capital assets to organizations.

A STRATEGIC APPROACH TO HRD

As will be highlighted at various points throughout this book today's HRD efforts must take place within an overall framework for workforce learning and development which directly contributes to the organization achieving its vision, mission and strategic agenda in an increasingly global and competitive environment. As Figure 1.1 indicates, such a perspective forms explicit connections between HRM and HRD policies and practices and the organization's vision, mission and strategic agenda. The premise behind a strategic approach to HRD is that learning and development decisions that "fit" the organization's conditions positively impact learning, performance and change.

A strategic approach to HRD begins with the relationship between the organization's mission, strategic agenda, and its human resource development (HRD) needs. Current and future HRM/workforce requirements are derived from a clear and widely shared understanding of what the organization does and how it does it (including the forward thinking about what the organization needs to do in the future). A strategic approach continues with an assessment of the current capacity of its workforce—what are the composition and core competencies, knowledge, skills, abilities and other characteristics (KSAOCs) of current employees? From this assessment, areas of special need and/or continuous upgrading can be identified, and appropriate HRD delivered to those in need of it. But, a strategic approach to HRD does not conclude here. Organizations must take steps to ensure

Introduction to HRD 21

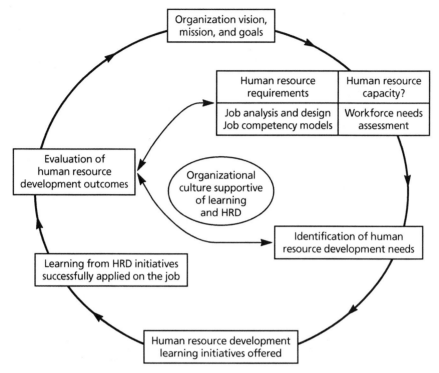

Figure 1.1. A model of strategic human resource development.

that the competencies learned and KSAOCs enhanced by HRD initiatives are indeed applied on the job. And, an evaluation system needs to be put in place that can examine the extent to which the competencies and KSAOCs targeted by HRD do indeed productively advance the mission of the organization. Finally, the organization needs a culture that fundamentally supports ongoing learning as part of the work role of every employee and its own success.

Discussions with most members of an organizations senior leadership would indicate their agreement that such a strategic approach to HRD is important to an organization's success. However, the real test of their commitment to such an approach is the extent to which they are willing to insist that there be a linkage, a common thread, between any HRD efforts and the organizations commitment to becoming and sustaining itself as a learning organization. A linkage that consistently stresses the organization's mission, goals, objectives, and strategies can result in a culture of HRD and institutionalized learning.

Senior leadership and a culture that support ongoing or lifelong learning and HRD initiatives are a key to successful HRD in any organization.

Clearly, improvements in HRD in particular will only make a marginal contribution toward increased employee and organizational performance and change if cultural barriers to sound HRD reinforcement exist in the organization. If HRD is to truly add value to an organization senior leadership *must* recognize that nothing short of a constant reengineering of the HRD system will enable them to meet the challenges ahead like those discussed earlier in this chapter.

Clearly, for HRD to be successful it must be inextricably woven into the clarity of the organization's mission, its HRM systems and its culture. All key stakeholders must work toward the development of a strategic HRD plan. One way the organization can begin this process is by stepping back, and working to answer this question, "*If we were designing HRD from the ground up, today, what would it look like?*"

To do this effectively, a number of issues need to be examined and/or clarified:

1. What are the core areas of human resource capacity that form the heart of the organization's ability to carry out its mission, today? Tomorrow? Within each of these core capacity areas, (a) what are the priorities? and (b) where will the organization get the highest return on its investment, and where will it get the lowest?
2. Where in the organization is it appropriate to locate responsibility for and to commit resources for *each* of these areas?
3. What kinds of alternatives, variations and flexibilities in substance and delivery system are required in each of these areas? What obstacles and opportunities currently exist to achieving this flexibility?
4. What HRD and non-HRD resources and delivery systems exist that have yet to be fully tapped?
5. What opportunities exist to address multiple (across work units, etc.) HRD needs, thus, allowing the pooling of HRD resources across the organization (regionally, nationally and globally) to be more cost-effective and conserve HRD dollars? (This is especially viable with the development of so many new technologies for delivering HRD, which has resulted in increased audience capacity, little additional cost, and more opportunities to do just-in-time HRD.)

Once the areas of priority for HRD and non-HRD have been confirmed, the HRD professionals and their organization can embark on a more detailed process to identify or analyze HRD needs as discussed in Chapter 3.

CONCLUSION

HRD in many organizations has been given a place at the strategic table. HRD professionals are expected to be instrumental in setting up learning processes that are in line with the strategic policy and, moreover, ensuring that this is done in a cost conscious and effective manner. Knowledge productivity and the distribution of knowledge have become important activities as knowledge has become the "capital" of the organization. HRD is a critical part of an organization's efforts to make employees competent and keep them so. The remainder of this book offers a closer look at the HRD process that HRD professionals should use to continue making contributions to the achievement of organizational objectives.

CHAPTER 2

MAXIMIZING LEARNING OUTCOMES IN HUMAN RESOURCE DEVELOPMENT

The Role of Learning and Learning Styles

> *An organization's commitment and capacity for learning can be no greater than that of its members*
>
> —Senge (1990)

INTRODUCTION

The competitive pressure facing organizations today require employees whose knowledge and ideas are current, and whose skills and abilities can deliver results. As organizations compete and change, human resource development (HRD) becomes even more critical than before. Employees who must adapt to the many changes facing organizations must be trained and developed continually in order to maintain and update their capabilities. Also, managers must have HRD to enhance their leadership skills and abilities. In a number of situations, employers have documented that effective HRD produces productivity gains that more than offset the cost of the HRD. However, despite these situations organizations continue to raise expectations that their investment in HRD pays off in ways that maximize the learning of "all" its employees. There is every indication that organizations will increasingly hold HRD professionals accountable for their employee's continual learning.

Learning is a vital aspect of all HRD efforts. Whether you are training a plumber's apprentice to use a welding torch, conducting a workshop to teach managers how to use progressive discipline more effectively, trying to get automotive workers to understand and follow new safety procedures, or promoting career development among an organization's employees, the goal is to change behavior, knowledge, or attitudes *through learning*. Supervisors and HRD professionals who understand the learning process and how to create an environment that facilitates learning, can design and implement more effective and accountable HRD interventions. In fact, with the recent growth of corporate universities and other learning centers, there is a new position within the top leadership of many large organizations, namely, *chief learning officer* (CLO) (Werner & DeSimone, 2006). This is more than a renaming of the senior HRD professional's position. Such an individual must emphasize both individual and organizational (strategic) objectives, and be able to make effective use of different forms of learning delivery.

The purpose of this chapter is to discuss those considerations important to maximizing learning outcomes in HRD initiatives for "all" organizational employees. More specifically, the chapter first discusses learning and types of learning. Next, the chapter focuses on several issues critical to maximizing learning followed by a discussion of how adults learn. The chapter then revisits the concept of learning and learning principles along with transfer of training. Finally, the chapter focuses on the importance of recognizing individual differences (learning styles) and learning strategies in the learning process.

WHAT IS LEARNING?

Learning is one of the most important individual and team processes that occur in organizations today and, of course in HRD efforts. So, what is learning? And, how do we know that learning has taken place? These are two important, yet complicated, questions. One researcher and adult learning theorist writes about levels of learning but equivocates and declines to define it, writing: "The word learning undoubtedly denotes change of some kind. To say what kind of change is a delicate matter" (Bateson, 1972, p. B23). In declining to define learning per se, Bateson identifies the defining characteristic of learning: it involves personal change, change that is stimulated through reacting to some encounter and not just a function of natural processes of maturation (Knowles, 1990; Hilgard & Bower, 1966). This change may take place in any of a number of domains, including motor skills, intellectual skills, knowledge content, cognitive strategies, awareness, or attitudes. With this in mind, we are defining learning as a relatively permanent change in behavior, cognition, or affect that occurs as a result of one's interaction with the environment. Several aspects of this definition are important. First, the focus of learning is change, by either acquiring something new (like skill in completing safety audits) or modifying something that already exists (like an accountant becoming more accurate in conducting audits). Second, the change must be long lasting before we can say learning has really occurred. For example, if a computer technician can recall the steps needed to repair a computer's hard drive on the third day of a training program but cannot remember them a week later back on the job, learning has not occurred. Third, the focus of learning can include behavior, cognitions, affect, or any combination of the three. Learning outcomes can be skill based (climbing a utility pole), cognitive (procedures for applying for a grant), or affective (becoming more safety conscious). Finally, learning results from an individual's interaction with the environment and learning does not include behavior changes attributable to physical maturation or a temporary condition (such as fatigue or drugs).

Levels and Types of Learning

A number of theorists and researchers have advanced our thinking about learning differentiating among levels or types of learning (Mezirow, 1991; Knowles, 1990; Cell, 1984; Argyris & Schon, 1982; Bateson, 1972). The distinctions among types of learning are important when considering the differences between basic manual skills training, such as keyboard skills, interpersonal skills, such as active listening, and learning that requires a significant reframing of past experience (Yorks, 2005).

Cell's Typology of Learning. Edward Cell idehtifies four types of learning: response learning, situation learning, transsituation learning, and transcendent learning. "Response leaning"—is a change in the way we are prepared to respond in a particular situation. Response learning is studied by behaviorists in psychology and includes rote learning and what Skinner has called "operant conditioning" (Skinner, 1953; Yorks, 2005). Behavioral modeling training, where supervisors learn to respond with a prepared set of answers when disciplining an employee for attendance or lateness, is an example of response learning. Certain kinds of sales and customer service training also involve response learning, such as specific techniques for handling certain customer objections. This kind of learning can also require the learner to apply a sequence of skills, or to match response to varying complex contingencies in situations such as selecting a certain negotiating tactic from many possibilities in the midst of a contentious negotiation.

"Situation learning," which involves a change in how a person organizes her or his understanding of a situation, a "change in ability to do response learning (Cell, 1984), is the second kind of learning identified by Cell. According to Cell response learning is dependent on situation learning, since how we interpret a situation shapes our response to it. What management views as punishment may be experienced as positive reinforcement by a worker in a workplace where the workforce does not respect management. Punishment can enhance a worker's status, reinforcing an adversary role in a labor organizing campaign. Basic employee and management training in topics such as affirmative action and sexual harassment involve situation learning-recognizing or interpreting situations differently and making judgments about how to react appropriately. In some instances, the success of such programs may require what Mezirow (1991) describes as transformative learning (discussed below) on the part of some participants. Participants who basically respect other workers but are unaware of how their actions impact others may extend an existing meaning frame or learn a new one as they become aware of and reflect on their assumptions. Other program participants with strongly held gender, racial, or sex-based biases may be unlikely to modify these biases, although they may modify their behavior to avoid disciplinary penalties. In other words, response learning will follow the training or development experience (Yorks, 2005).

Transsituation learning—learning how to change our interpretations of a situation is Cell's third kind of learning (Cell, 1984). This is what many HRD professionals (and adult educators) refer to as "learning-to-learn" (see, Kolb, 1984; Sims, 1998). This kind of learning involves reflecting on our learning processes themselves and identifying and questioning the assumptions that we are making about a situation. What Cell refers to as transsituation learning requires learners to reflect on the processes that characterize their learning, using reflective inquiry practices for critical self-reflection on how they have engaged in testing their assumptions and attributions.

Transcendent learning—modifying or creating new concepts is Cell's fourth kind of learning. This kind of learning is described as providing "possibilities—new tools—for interpreting individual situations" (Cell, 1984). Terms such as "empowerment," "servant leadership," and "psychological contract" all change how we talk about leadership and management and have opened up new avenues of research and practice. Such concepts become tools for social transactions and are tools that can facilitate changes in points of view and habits of mind. The importance of language and especially new concepts has increasingly been understood to be critical to inspiring transformative change.

Mezirow's Transformative Dimensions of Adult Learning. Mezirow's transformative dimensions of adult learning are especially useful for thinking about the kinds of learning necessary for today's HRD professionals and other organizational members to learn and support transformational organizational change (Mezirow, 1991, 2000, p. 8). Mezirow along with other influences draws in part on Cell's typology, more specifically his work in the pragmatism of John Dewey and William James and the critical social theory of Jurgen Habermas, resulting in what can be considered a critical pragmatic lens on learning from experience (Habermas, 1984).

Drawing on the work of Habermas, Mezirow postulates that learning takes place within two domains (i.e., instrumental learning and communicative learning), each with its own purpose and logic. The first is the domain of instrumental learning—"learning to manipulate the environment or other people" in the service of accomplishing tasks or solving problems. Response learning is a form of instrumental learning, but so is any "learning what and how" directed toward controlling or acting on the environment. In organizations, this is the domain of performance improvement. The second is the domain of communicative learning— "learning what others mean when others communicate with one another in the service of sensemaking" (Mezirow, 2000). This is a form of situational learning in which people extend or change their frame of reference. In organizations, sensemaking is the domain in which meaning is attached to instrumental actions and thus provides the contextual framing for performance improvement initiatives (Yorks, 2005).

Each of these two domains has its own standards of validity. Instrumental learning holds to validity tests of facts, measurements, and outcomes. Communicative learning had more nuanced validity tests requiring the assessment that others make of the speaker's and each other's authenticity, truthfulness, and qualification as they test the meanings of experience. It is heavily influenced by, and in turn, shapes or transforms, the cultural context in which people act. Instrumental learning can be fostered through programmed instruction that involves the transfer of information through lectures and visual presentations, reinforced through practice and coaching. High-quality science, quality management in engineering programs, technical training, and supervisory development programs include these elements, with information followed by laboratory work, simulations, or role-playing. Pedagogical designs that are focused on instrumental learning combine learning methods that foster a combination of "learning what" and "learning how" (Yorks, 2005).

Communicative learning requires dialogue and discussion, often building on experience and making sense of data. This kind of learning most often involves people who socially construct their learning through these processes of meaning—construction. In the absence of open dialogue, learners make judgments about the validity of the message based on their assessment of the trustworthiness of the source. Communicative learning occurs when messages about the intent of corporate policy are communicated or when projects and interventions designed to help employees make sense of organizational changes are implemented. For example, team building involves elements of both instrumental and communicative learning as participants develop interpersonal skills and competence in group dynamics while also constructing common meaning out of their experiences together (Yorks, 2005; Mezirow, 2000).

Mezirow argues that all learning, in a sense, involves situational learning, agreeing with Cell that even changes in response learning are dependent on an elaborated or altered frame of reference. He defines learning as "the process of using a prior interpretation to construe a new or revised interpretation of the meaning of one's experience as a guide to future action" (Mezirow, 2000). This reinterpretation can occur in one of four ways:

- by elaborating an existing frame of reference,
- by learning new frames of reference,
- by transforming points of view, or
- by transforming habits of mind.

Mezirow defines a frame of reference as a perspective organized by the assumptions and expectations that filter how we perceive the world. Frames of reference have two dimensions: (1) habits of mind comprising a set of assumptions—broad, generalized, predispositions that guide our interpretations of events and experience, and (2) points-of-view, clusters of beliefs, feelings, attitudes, and judgment that commonly operate outside of our awareness but are expressions of our broader habit of mind (Mezirow, 2000).

Frames of reference shape our understanding of both instrumental and communicative domains of our experience. Some learning is basically additive in nature as when a person elaborates an existing frame of reference or adds a new frame of reference without changing the beliefs and presuppositions of existing ones. However, when a disorienting dilemma or a disconfirming experience challenges people's frames of reference, it can lead them to critically reflect on their beliefs and presuppositions, resulting in either a transformed point of view or a transformed habit of mind (Cell, 1984; Yorks, 2005).

According to Cell and Yorks, transformative learning can occur in either the instrumental or the communicative domain and can be epochal in nature—a sudden, reorienting insight—or incremental—the result of a progressive series of experiences that transform a person's point of view. At the societal level, fundamental paradigm shifts in science represent cultural transformations during the last third of the 20the century that involved communicative learning, including our understanding of race and the civil rights movement; changes in the role of women in society and feminism; and changes in attitudes toward labor organizations (Yorks, 2005; Cell, 1984).

Transformative learning almost always requires placing people in situations that put them outside their comfort zones, belying the notion that learning is always fun. Changes in strategic thinking often require assessing alternative points of view, leading to changed habits of mind as executives and mangers have to reframe their view of the marketplace.

Single-Loop, Double-Loop and Deuterolearning

Over the past few decades many organizations have realized that they must be able to develop the capacity to transfer knowledge across the organization by collaborating and sharing expertise and information that is unbounded by status, space, and time. This emphasis on continuous learning, changing, and adapting led to what is called a learning organization. A learning organization is an organization in which "everyone is engaged in identifying and solving problems, enabling the organization to continuously experiment, improve, and increase its capability" (Daft, 1997). This approach involves a shift in an organizational paradigm—or gamma B change—because employees are expected to continuously learn as they produce. Continuous learning involves reflecting on experience and information and incorporating the conclusions into our subsequent thinking, our response to situations, and our planned actions. Learning can occur on at least three levels: single- loop, double-loop, and deuterolearning.

Single-loop learning occurs when we detect error; our actions fail to produce the results we desire, and we adjust our tactics or strategies without challenging the assumptions that frame our understanding of the situation. Single-loop learning emphasizes the identification of problems and then taking corrective action (Nevis, DiBella, & Bould, 1995; Hodgetts, Luthans, & Lee, 1994). Double-loop learning requires us to question the assumptions core values, or "governing variables" which guide our actions and inform how we frame or interpret a situation (Argyris, 1994; Senge, 1990). Deuterolearning is directed at the learning process by improving how the organization performs single- and double-loop learning (Cummings & Worley, 1997).

Argyris (cited in Abernathy, 1999) makes the following point about learning:

> learning is to persist, managers and employees must look inward. In particular, they must learn how the very way they go about defining and solving

problems can be a source of problems in its own right. I have coined the terms single-loop and double-loop learning to capture a crucial distinction. To give a simple analogy: A thermostat that automatically turns on the heat whenever the temperature in a room drops below 68 degrees is a good example of single-loop learning. A thermostat that could ask, "Why am I set at 68 degrees?" and then explore whether or not some other temperature might more economically achieve the goal of heating the room would be engaging in double-loop learning. (p. 6)

Single-loop learning is commonplace in continuous improvement programs, because employees are taught to identify problems and correct them. This type of learning is still important in the day-to-day performance of a learning organization and is regularly incorporated in HRD initiatives. Double-loop learning is an integral part of the process of transforming points of view and habits-of-mind. Double-loop learning can be triggered informally by traumatic events and experiences that cause people to deeply question their assumptions or through a cumulative series of experiences that incrementally lead to people rethinking their premises. Double-loop learning represents a radical shift in the way employees learn, because it involves changing basic assumptions and core values about how they work. For example, an HRD professional may become frustrated when he finds out that several HRD programs were not well received by participants. Upon reflection, the HRD professional might realize that these programs were designed three years ago and have become outdated. Further, the HRD professional might realize that the practice of HRD staff members relying on their own intuition and knowledge of the organization to determine HRD needs is not sufficient in these changing times. The HRD professional surmises that if the HRD program is going to be effective in the future, the HRD design approach must be changed and updated. This realization should prompt the HRD professional to conduct a needs assessment and update the design. Deuterolearning, the highest level of learning, is essentially learning to learn. Returning to the example, deuterolearning will have taken place if the HRD professional encourages other staff members to view all of the organization's HRD programs as works-in-progress and adopt a mind-set of continually adapting programs to meet the organization's changing needs. More will be said about learning organizations in Chapter 10.

The discussion to this point on the distinctions among kinds of learning are important to HRD professionals because they both help bring into focus some of the various dimensions of learning and facilitate thinking about their implications for the design of learning events intended to better address the increased calls for accountable HRD. What kind of learning is a particular HRD program or learning intervention seeking to produce? What do we know about the factors that facilitate or inhibit this kind of learning? Different kinds of learning objectives require different HRD and different educational designs. Certain delivery formats work better than others for meeting some kind of learning objectives. Response learning can be achieved through very concrete behavior designs, whereas HRD that involves selecting from among a range of responses based on the specifics of the situation typically requires the development of inquiry practices that often can only be effectively learned through experiential learning designs, such as action learning. Although more conventional language and terminology typically must be used when talking with line managers and others in today's organizations, these basic distinctions become important in doing sophisticated HRD or learning needs assessments, in helping others to understand the limitations of various learning program designs, and ultimately in maximizing learning.

MAXIMIZING LEARNING IN HRD INITIATIVES

Our definition of learning and the discussion of levels of learning make it clear that people acquire and develop skills, knowledge, and change behavior as a result of an interaction between forces within the learner and in the environment. While there are various factors that have been shown to affect learning this section will focus on learner readiness.

Learner Readiness

For HRD to be successful, learners must be ready to learn (Welsch, 2002). Learner readiness means having the basic skills necessary for learning, the motivation to learn, and self-efficacy.

Ability to Learn
Learners must possess basic skills, such as fundamental reading and math proficiency, and sufficient cognitive abilities. Organizations may discover employees lack the requisite skills to comprehend their HRD effectively. Various organizations have found that a significant number of job applicants and current employees lack the reading, writing, and math skills needed to do the job.

Motivation to Learn
A person's desire to learn HRD content is referred to as "motivation to learn" and is influenced by multiple factors. For example, the extent to which an employee taking a course on selling office equipment is motivated to learn the course content might be influenced by personal career

interests, and values, individual development learning plan, and the positive value the employee places on completing the course. The employee's motivation level may also be influenced by the HRD professional's motivation and ability, co-workers' encouragement to do well, and physical classroom or learning environment, and the HRD methods. Regardless of what the motivation is, without it, the employee will not learn the material.

Self-Efficacy

Learners must also possess self-efficacy, which refers to a person's belief that she or he can successfully learn the HRD program content. For learners to be ready for and receptive to the HRD content, they must feel that it is possible for them to learn. For example, some employees' levels of self-efficacy diminish in technical-skill development programs when they do not feel adequately able to grasp the material. These perceptions may have nothing to do with their actual ability to learn, but rather reflect the way they see themselves and their abilities. HRD professionals must find appropriate ways to boost the confidence of program participants who are unsure of their learning abilities. For instance, people with a low level of belief that they can learn certain content may benefit from one-on-one HRD efforts.

Several researchers have focused on the learner's (or trainee's) readiness to learn and coined the phrase "trainability" (Noe, 1986; Maier, 1973). Trainability focuses on the trainee's readiness to learn and combines the trainee's level of ability and motivation with his or her perceptions of the work environment (Noe, 1986; Maier, 1973)). A simple formula to convey this is: Trainiability = f(Motivaton × Ability × Perceptions of the Work Environment). This formula illustrates that a learner must have both the motivation and the ability to learn; if either is lacking, learning will not occur. The equation also shows that a very high level of one cannot completely overcome a very low level of the other (Maier, 1973). In addition, if employees perceive little support in the work environment for learning new knowledge or skills, they will be less likely to learn and use them (Noe, 1986). Thus, it is important for HRD professionals to note that trainability is not just a function of the individual trainee, but also of the work environment in which the learner will be asked to use what was presented in the HRD interventions.

Trainability is extremely important in HRD. Placing employees in learning events they are not motivated to attend or are not prepared to do well in wastes time and resources. Learners with less ability take longer to learn, which can increase the length of the HRD period and the expense involved in conducting HRD. In fact, it is possible that such learners may never learn to the levels desired by the organization or may become what Martinez refers to as "resistant learners" (more will be said about resistant learners toward the end of this chapter) (Matinez, 2000).

A number of studies have shown the clear links between ability and learning (Gordon & Klieman, 1976; Downs, 1970; Gordon, 1955). The same is true for motivation (Hicks & Klimoski, 1987; Reber & Wallin, 1984; Eden & Ravid, 1982; Komaki, Heinzemann, Lawson, 1980), as well as for perceptions of the work environment (Peters, O'Connor, & Eulberg, 1985).

The notion of pretraining motivation has also been studied by researchers over the past decade or so (Werner, O'Leary-Kelly, Baldwin, & Wexley, 1994). Findings include:

- The way trainees perceive training (e.g., as remedial versus advanced, or as an unpleasant task versus an opportunity) affects levels of learning, perceptions of efficacy, anxiety and perceptions of fairness (Martocchio, 1992).
- The way in which individuals view their own ability (as a fixed entity or an acquirable skill) affects anxiety level, efficacy perceptions, and the learning of declarative (factual) knowledge (Martocchio, 1994).
- Experiencing negative events on the job prior to training increase trainees' motivation to learn and their performance in training (Smith-Jentsch, Jentsch, Payne, & Salas, 1996).
- A number of other factors have been found to increase individuals' motivation to participate in and learn from training. Factors investigated include involvement in decisions about training, perceptions that participation in training will lead to benefits (e.g., increased job performance and career advancement opportunities), and perceptions of support (Clark, Dobbins, & Ladd, 1993; Noe & Wild, 1998), or lack of obstacles to use what has been learned in the work environment (Mathieu, Tannenbaum, & Salas, 1983).
- Characteristics of the organization (e.g., policies and guidelines regarding training participation) have been linked to participation in developmental activities (Maurier & Tarulli, 1994).

These findings are useful in that they suggest ways in which organizations can increase the motivation to participate in and learn from HRD interventions. For example, to ensure that learners perceive the value of what is being presented or HRD learning events, they must see HRD as an opportunity, as a way to address a need they have, and as a way to achieve valued outcomes. Further, learners must perceive the organization and their immediate work environment as supporting participation in HRD and in using what has been learned.

Learner readiness is extremely important in HRD. Placing employees in programs they are not motivated to attend or are not prepared to do well in waste time and resources. Employees with less ability take longer to learn, which can increase the length of the HRD period and the expense involved in conducting HRD. In fact, it is possible that such employees may never learn to the levels desired by the organization.

Assessing employee's relevant abilities, motivation, and self-efficacy prior to HRD initiatives can be important in maximizing the chances that learning will occur. This approach to maximizing learning fits with Glaser's (1984) notion that knowing the initial state of the learner is an important part of effective HRD.

THE LEARNING (OR HRD) NEEDS OF ADULT LEARNERS

Finding better ways to maximize learning "matters" in today's organizations. Strong minds fuel strong organizations. Organizations must capitalize on the uniqueness of its employees and build systems to leverage the uniqueness. One way of leveraging this uniqueness is through the recognition that HRD must begin with an understanding of how adults learn and each adult's unique or individual way of learning.

Assumptions about Adult Learning

An understanding of how adults learn can assist in efforts to develop accountable-HRD strategies and models that will provide the necessary connections in the HRD process that will individualize, personalize, and give ownership of the learning and motivation for learning to the adult learner. Malcolm Knowles (1980) theory on adult learning increases our understanding of how to maximize learning and design more accountable HRD initiatives.

Knowles (1980) has postulated his adult learning principles and practices under the banner of andragogy. A discussion of Knowles's adult learning theory will help the reader understand its usefulness in enhancing and maximizing learning in HRD efforts.

Knowles argued that teaching adults requires using a unique set of learning techniques that are different from those developed with and for children. *Pedagogy* (ped-e-go-je) literally means the art and science of educating children and often is used as a synonym for teaching.[1]

More accurately, pedagogy embodies teacher-focused education. According to Knowles pedagogy is the term traditionally used for instructional methodology, and this has most often emphasized educating children and teenagers through high school. In the pedagogic model, teachers assume responsibility for making decisions about what will be learned, how it will be learned, and when it will be learned. Teachers direct learning. Building on the earlier work of Lindeman, Knowles asserted that adults require certain conditions to learn (Knowles, 1973). Knowles proposed an adult-oriented approach to learning that he called *andragogy* (and-re-go-je). He borrowed the term to define and explain the conditions.[2]

Table 2.1 highlights some assumptions about adult learning adapted from Knowles (1973).

Table 2.1. A Comparison of Pedagogy and Andragogy

Learning Criteria	*Pedagogy*	*Andragogy*
The individual's self concept	Dependent	Self-directed
The importance of life experience	Not important	Very important
The time frame for relevant application of learning	Postponed for later use	Must be immediately
The focus of learning	Centered on the person	Centered on solving a problem
The readiness for learning	Related to physical growth and emotional development	Related to tasks and skills required
The importance of peers in learning process	Little emphasis on peers as resources	Peers are considered important resources
The responsibility for responsible learning	Teacher is responsible	The learner is responsible while the teacher makes resources available and helps the learning process

Andragogy is based on four assumptions about differences between adults and children.

1. Adults are *self-directed*.
2. Adults have acquired a large amount of *knowledge and experience* that can be tapped as a resource for learning.
3. Adults show a greater *readiness to learn tasks that are relevant* to the roles they have assumed in life.
4. Adults are motivated to learn in order to solve problems or address needs, and they *expect to immediately apply what* they learn to these problems and needs (Knowles, 1970).

Based on the andragogic model five issues should be considered and addressed in adult learning (or HRD initiatives). They include (1) letting adult learners know why something is important to learn, (2), showing adult learners how to direct themselves through information, and (3) relating the topic to the adult learners' experiences. In addition, (4) adults will not learn until they are ready and motivated to learn. Often this (5) requires helping them overcome inhibitions, behaviors, and beliefs about learning.

Andragogical HRD interventions are designed with these factors in mind. These techniques include joint planning, self-diagnosis, formulation of learning objectives, a collaborative teaching process, and involvement of participants in the evaluation of success. Two examples illustrate how this approach has been applied. First, an andragogical approach was used to teach writing to adults. The program used fifteen strategies including the following (Sommer, 1989):

- Consider the audience (for instance, conduct a needs assessment).
- Remember that adults need to be self-determining.
- Use peer collaboration.
- Include assessment to enhance course content.
- Find clear applications for writing.
- Rely on students' experiences.
- Include students in evaluating writing.

A second example comes from an article (Caudron, 2000) discussing the difference between "how learners learn" and "how trainers teach." Caudron spells out a number of differences between traditional (student) and nontraditional (adult) learners. Some of the differences are as follows:

1. Traditional learners need motivation and they are not always sure why they are in training. Nontraditional learners are highly motivated and want to learn.
2. Traditional learners raise few questions and often have little real-world experience to connect to the training content. Nontraditional learners raise many questions in class, seek opportunities to analyze training content in terms of own experiences, and need to connect class materials to real-world experiences.
3. Traditional learners resist participation and expect to be told what to do and how to do it. Nontraditional learners want to participate, dislike being talked at and value discussions and projects.
4. Traditional learners are more future-oriented and don't expect to immediately apply what they learn in training. Nontraditional learners are concerned with immediate problems and solutions.
5. Traditional learners are likely to accept information that they are given. Nontraditional learners can and will verify information given in training.
6. Traditional learners have few specific expectations. Nontraditional learners often have preconceived expectations of training that the

instructor should try to identify if possible. If the training isn't what the participants expected, they are likely to consider it to be a failure (Caudron, 2000).

Although andragogy has intuitive appeal, there are also some major concerns. Critics argue that separating the learning process into two stages—child and adult learning—makes little sense. Rather, they see learning as a continuous process (Davenport & Davenport, 1985). In addition, other significant problems and weakness of the andragogical approach have been noted. Some of the issues raised include the rigidity of the paradigm, the extent to which learners are either children or adults in their approach to learning, the approach's lack of recognition of the differences among adult learners, and the reluctance of many HRD professionals to criticize the approach because it presents a socially desirable view of adults as learners (Newstrom & Lengnick-Hall, 1991).

Although Knowles has moderated some of his original claims, he continued to argue that andragogical techniques can be used to teach both adults and more traditional school-aged students (Knowles et al., 1984). Indeed, many of the recent trends in elementary and secondary education (e.g., group learning, writing based on students' experiences) seem remarkably similar to Knowles' suggestions for adult learning. Despite these criticisms Knowles seminal work helps us understand the need to be attentive to how adults learn. Unfortunately, andragogy usually is cited in the education literature as the way adults learn. Knowles himself concedes that most of andragogy's key assumptions apply equally to adults and children. The sole difference is that children have fewer experiences and preestablished beliefs than adults and thus have less to relate.[3]

Instead of simply abandoning the work of Knowles and others on adult learning it is important to build on their work as suggested in several recent reviews on understanding adult learning (Sleezer, 2004; Merriam & Caffarella, 1999; Kuchinke, 1999). For example, andragogy is presented as one approach to adult learning along with others by Merriam and Caffarella. In another vein, Newstrom and Lengnick-Hall developed a contingency model that assumes that "adult learners are a heterogeneous group requiring different approaches to HRD depending on individual differences across important characteristics" (Newstrom & Lengnick-Hall, 1991, p. 46). Based on their approach, Newstrom and Lengnick-Hall suggest that trainee differences should be actively considered in designing HRD initiatives, leading to learning efforts adapted to fit the characteristics of the participants. Newstrom and Lengnick-Hall (1991) propose assessing groups on a number of dimensions. Some of the dimensions are as follows:

1. *Instrumentality.* Degree to which the trainee is concerned with the immediate applicability of the concepts and skills being taught.
2. *Attention Span.* Length of time the trainee can focus attention before substantial attentiveness is diminished.
3. *Expectation Level.* Level of quality (process) and quantity (content) that the trainee requires from the trainer or the training.
4. *Absorption Level.* Pace at which the trainee expects and can accept new information.
5. *Topical Interest.* Degree to which the trainee can be expected to have personal (job-relevant) interest in the topic.
6. *Self-confidence.* Degree of trainee's independence and positive self-regard, thus requiring high or low levels of feedback, reinforcement, and success experiences.

This very much supports the emphasis in this chapter on the need to consider individual differences in HRD efforts if one is committed to better responding to accountability demands.

In today's information age, the implications of paying attention to adult learning theories in general, like Knowles, and more specifically on how individuals learn is critical to better responding to the calls for increased accountability in HRD efforts. Paying attention to the andragogical framework and other adult learning theories can make a difference in the way adult learning efforts are organized and operated as well as in the way organizations and their HRD professionals see their role in helping adults learn. Additionally, a focus on adult learning theory has helped HRD professionals move from an HRD professional-centered to adult learner-centered HRD initiatives. Postponing or suppressing this move will slow down the ability of an organization or its employees to learn and gain the necessary competitive advantage in today's global marketplace.

Principles of Learning

Whether HRD takes place on or off the job, employees are expected to learn and apply KSAs to benefit both the organization and the employees. Because HRD *is* learning, HRD professionals can benefit from understanding and applying certain principles of learning when designing and implementing organization-sponsored HRD initiatives (Sims, 1998). Also, because neglect or misapplication of principles of learning could easily result in HRD that fails to achieve results, it is important that HRD professionals become familiar with the underlying principles of learning (Sims, 1998).

According to Jackson and Schuler learning may not take place if the HRD intervention is not structured to facilitate learning even when the HRD technique is appropriate (Jackson & Schuler, 2003). Learning factors (principles) that will affect the learning of today's employees and the success of HRD learning interventions are: (1) setting the stage—provide clear task instructions and model appropriate behavior; (2) increasing learning during HRD—provide active participation, increase self-efficacy, match HRD techniques to participants' self-efficacy, provide opportunities for inactive mastery, ensure specific, timely, diagnostic, and practical feedback, and provide opportunities for trainees to practice new behaviors; and (3) maintaining performance—develop learning points to assist in knowledge retention, set specific goals, identify appropriate reinforcers, train and develop significant others in how to reinforce behavior, and teach participants self-management skills. These factors indicate that the environment must be made ready for learning to occur (Sims, 1998; Jackson & Schuler, 2003).

Although incorporating these principles of learning is desirable, there are still those HRD efforts that do not have them or are designed without consideration of individual learning differences, motivation, learning curves and plateaus, reinforcement, feedback, and goal setting. Nevertheless, application of these principles of learning can increase the potential learning that occurs during HRD as well as learning intervention effectiveness and benefits to an organization.

Transfer of Training

Transfer of training refers to the effective application of principles learned to what is required on the job. The transfer of training to the job is critically important to the success of HRD effects. As will be highlighted in more detail in the discussion of transfer of training in Chapter 6, transfer can take many forms (i.e., positive transfer, zero transfer, negative transfer, near transfer, far transfer). Positive transfer occurs when job performance is improved as a result of training. Zero transfer occurs when there is no change in job performance as a result of training. Negative transfer occurs when job performance is worse as a result of training. Near transfer has to do with the ability to directly apply on the job what has been learned in training, with little adjustment or modification, whereas far transfer has to do with expanding upon or using what was learned in training in new creative ways (Garavaglia, 1995). To maximize transfer, HRD professionals and managers can take several approaches:

1. *Feature identical elements.* Transfer of training to the job can be facilitated by having conditions in the HRD program come as close as possible to those on the job.
2. *Focus on general principles.* In those cases where jobs change or when the work environment cannot be matched exactly, HRD professionals often stress the general principles behind the training rather than focusing on rote behavior. This approach helps learners learn how to apply the main learning points to varying conditions on the job.
3. *Establish a climate for transfer.* In some cases, trained behavior is not implemented because old approaches and routines are still reinforced by other managers, peers, and employees. To prevent this kind of problem, the manager should ensure that the work environment supports, reinforces, and rewards the learner for applying the new skills or knowledge.
4. *Give employees transfer strategies.* Particularly in settings that are not conducive to transfer, HRD professionals and managers should also provide learners with strategies and tactics for dealing with their transfer environment. One approach, called relapse prevention (RP), teaches individuals how to anticipate and cope with the inevitable setbacks they will encounter back on the job-that is, a relapse into former behaviors. By identifying high-risk situations that jeopardize transfer and developing coping strategies, relapse prevention can help employees gain better control over maintaining learned behaviors (Haskell, 1998; Bennett, Lehman, & Forst, 1999; Gist & Stevens, 1998); Burke, 1997).

Another powerful link to accountable HRD efforts is an increased appreciation of and understanding on what is known about the types and levels of learning as discussed earlier, learning styles and how individuals learn (differences in learning strategies).

LEARNING STYLES AND STRATEGIES

We view learning as both a product and process. That is, when we describe learning in terms of the kind of learning an HRD initiative might be intended to produce—a change that may involve acquiring a body of knowledge, a set of skills or competencies, a new attitude, or a reframed perspective. We are, then, essentially treating learning as a noun—as an outcome or a product.

Learning also involves a process, as in *"He is learning."* As Knowles (1973) observes, learning is a process that is internal to and controlled by the learner. From the perspective of HRD in practice, it is important to understand learning as both process and product, both in continuous relationship with each other. Understanding how to work with learning processes to produce a given outcome is as important as being clear about the kind of learning that is needed. Understanding and attending to learning styles and strategies is one way of maximizing learning and producing learning outcomes that meet both the individual employee and organizations HRD needs and expectations.

Although individuals learn continually, they do learn and process information in different ways, and have preferences about how they learn. Thus, everyone has a learning style. We may not have realized this earlier in our learning careers because most of us attended schools and programs where teachers and HRD professionals delivered instruction in one way. Most educators and HRD professionals talked to us, and we answered their questions. We then took pencil- and paper-based tests. Schools taught one way and didn't help or encourage us to learn our unique styles. That was also most often the case when we participated in most school or HRD initiatives.

The idea that people learn differently is venerable and probably had its origin with the ancient Greeks (Wratcher, Morrison, Riley, & Scheirton, 1997). Most educators, regardless of what types of students they interact with, have for many years noticed that some students prefer certain methods of learning more than others. While it is now accepted in most educational settings that we do have unique styles of learning there exists a confusing array of definitions of learning style, a term often used interchangeably with cognitive style or learning ability. Prior to the mid-1970s, researchers experimented with cognitive style; their definitions were different, but all were concerned with how the mind actually processed information or was affected by individual perceptions. After the early 1970s other writers and researchers developed varied definitions, models, instruments, and techniques for assessing individual learning characteristics. In some ways those models have (and continue to) differed, but many revealed essential similarities and were mutually supportive (Sims & Sims, 1995).

How a person learns is the focus of the concept of learning style. Many have offered their own definitions of learning styles as evidenced by the following list:

1. The cognitive, affective, and physiological factors that serve as relatively stable indicators of how learners perceive, interact with, and respond to the learning environment (Keefe, 1979; L. Swanson, 1995).
2. The preference or predisposition of an individual to perceive and process information in a particular way or combination of ways (Sarasin, 1998).

3. The way each learner begins to concentrate on, process and remember new and difficult information (Dunn & Dunn, 1992).
4. The way that person begins to process, internalize and concentrate on new material (Gremli, 1996).
5. A "predisposition" to adopt a particular learning strategy (Pask, 1988).
6. The unique way of thinking and reasoning that characterizes an individual learner (Gordon & Butt, 2003).
7. Is identified by connecting perceptual pathways and states of consciousness.[4]
8. The different ways in which children and adults think and learn.[5]
9. The characteristic strengths and preferences in the ways students take in and process information.[6]
10. A person's highly individualized preferences and tendencies that influence his or her learning (Smith, 1982).
11. Attempts to explain learning variation between individuals in the way they approach learning tasks (Toye, 1989).
12. It is a reflection of one's choice of preferred functions for perception (how data are perceived or collected), and how these same data are judged and mentally processed, i.e., how the individual comes to conclusions about the meaning and importance of specific data (Silver & Hanson, 1986).
13. The complex manner in which, and conditions under which, learners most efficiently and most effectively perceive, process, store, and recall what they are attempting to learn (James & Blank, 1993).

The first definition by Keefe is probably the most accepted of the various definitions (as characteristic cognitive, affective, and psychological behaviors that serve as relatively stable indicators of how learners perceive, interact with, and respond to the learning environment) (Keefe, 1978).

Classifications of Learning Styles

There are also many different ways to classify learning styles. One way of classifying learning styles is into these general categories: perceptual modality, information processing, and personality patterns. The categories represent ways to focus on the HRD learner.

Perceptual modalities define biologically-based reactions to our physical environment and represent the way we most efficiently adopt data. HRD learners should learn their perception style so they can seek out information in the format they process most directly. HRD professionals should pay attention to modalities to ensure learning initiatives strike all physiologic levels.

Information processing distinguishes between the way we sense, think, solve problems, and remember information. Each of us has a preferred, consistent, distinct way of perceiving, organizing, and retaining information.

Personality patterns focus on attention, emotion, and values. Studying these differences allows HRD professionals to predict the way participants will react and feel about different situations.

For space sake, we will spend our time here on perceptual modalities (i.e., Gardners's [1993] grouping of modalities) and Kolb's (1984) experiential learning model and learning styles.

Perceptual Modality. Perceptual modality refers to the primary way our bodies take in information. Commonly, researchers identify auditory, visual, kinesthetic, and tactile styles. The field of *accelerated learning* also relies heavily on modality to explain how learners can process information faster.

Howard Gardner and Wayne James and Michael Galbraith have established another, overlapping way of grouping modalities. Both groupings assert that there are at least seven modalities or *intelligences* that link to our individual styles.

Gardner suggests humans can be (1) verbal-linguistic (sensitive to the meaning and order of words), (2) musical (sensitive to pitch, melody, rhythm, and tone), (3) logical-mathematical (able to handle chains of reasoning and recognize patterns and order), (4) spatial (perceive the world accurately and try to re-create or transform aspects of that world), (5) bodily-kinesthetic (able to use the body skillfully and handle objects adroitly), (6) interpersonal (understand people and relationships), or (7) intrapersonal (possess access to one's emotional life as a means to understand oneself and others) (Gardner, 1993).

James and Galbraith's seven primary perceptual preferences are (1) print (reading and writing), (2) visual (such as graphs and charts), (3) aural (auditory, i.e., listening), (4) interactive (discussing, asking questions), (5) tactile/manipulative (hands on approaches, such as touching), (6) kinesthic/psychomotor (role playing, physical activities), and (7) olfactory (association of ideas with smell or taste) (James & Galbraith, 1985).

While Gardner's work encourages us to think about modality in new and creative ways, a solid grasp of the core modalities applies immediately to everything we do.

Most people retain a dominant and an auxiliary learning modality. We usually rely on those modes to process information at an unconscious level, but we may be consciously aware of which modes we prefer. We access through our senses, but generally favor one. We process visually (by sight), auditorally (by sound), kinesthetically (by moving), and tactilly (by touch).

Visual learners prefer seeing what they are learning. Pictures and images help them understand ideas and information better than explanations. A drawing may help more than a discussion about the same. When someone explains something to a visual learner, he or she may create a mental picture of what the person talking describes.

If you are a visual learner, you may find it helpful to see the person speaking. You may watch a speaker talk, as well as listen to what he or she says.

Many people assume reading is a visual action. Though we see the words, most of us process the information by hearing ourselves say the words. As a result, researchers identify people who prefer to process by reading, auditory learners. Others label the readers "Print-oriented," aligning them closely with visual learners (Shelton, Shelton-Conan, & Fulghum-Nutters, 1992). Visual learners are more shape- and form-oriented. Print-oriented people depend more on words or numbers in their images.

Auditory learners also fall into two categories. Auditory learners prefer spoken messages. The less understood auditory learners need to hear their own voice to process the information. The more prevalent type, "Listeners," most likely did well in educational or learning settings. Out of educational or learning settings too, they remember things said to them and make the information their own. They may even carry on mental dialogues and determine how to continue by thinking back on the words of others.

Conversely, those who need to "talk it out" often find themselves talking to those around them. In a classroom HRD setting when the HRD professional is not asking questions, auditory-verbal processors (talkers) tend to mutter comments to themselves. They are not trying to be disruptive and may not even realize they need to talk. Some researchers go so far as to call these learners "Interactives" (Shelton et al., 1992).

While some auditory learners prefer to listen to both themselves and others, mounting evidence suggests the two types are distinct and separate (Marks-Tarlow, 1995). Kinesthetic learners want to sense the position and movement of what they are working on. Tactile learners want to touch. "Enough talking and looking," they may say. "Let's work with this stuff. Let's get our hands dirty already." Even if kinesthetic or tactile learners don't get much from the discussion or the written materials, they may catch up and exceed the learning expectations or objectives through various hands-on HRD initiatives. Often, they don't thrive in traditional HRD efforts because most traditional HRD efforts don't offer enough opportunity to move or touch.

Most assessments group kinesthetic and tactile styles together, though they mean different things. Their similarity is that both types perceive information through nerve ends in the skin, as well as organ through muscles, tendons, and joints.

Recently, Neil Fleming developed the VARK questionnaire, which he described as a scale measuring one's "preferences for taking in and putting out information in a learning context." This questionnaire is available online. The four preferences measured by this scale are visual (V), aural (A), read/write (R), and kinesthetic (K). These preferences correspond to items 1, 2, 3, and 6 in the list above from James and Galbraith. In his research to date, Fleming has found no differences in preferences between males and females. Differences have emerged between learners (who have a greater preference for the kinesthetic) and educators (who have a greater preference for reading and writing) (Fleming, 2001).

Other research suggests that the majority of adults have a preference for visual material. Females are more likely than males to assimilate information from all available sources, whereas males tend to focus on fewer information sources (Darley & Smith, 1995; Meyers-Levy, 1989). Further, similar to Fleming's findings concerning differences between students and teachers, it has been argued that people who grew up watching more television and movies and playing interactive computer games may have different perceptual preferences than previous generations, and may need to be trained in different ways (Zemke, Raines, & Filipczak, 1999; Caudron, 1997).

Perceptual preferences imply that HRD professionals should, if possible, tailor their material and techniques to match learner preferences. For example, a study of advanced safety training for truck drivers focused on individuals with aural versus kinesthetic preferences. Training was provided either by lecture (with visuals) or by a hand-on, simulation approach. Trainees with auditory preferences learned substantially more when taught via lecture, whereas those with kinesthetic preferences learned substantially more when taught via the hands-on approach. The reverse was also true, that is, when preferences and training method were mismatched, training achievement and trainee attitudes were significantly lower (Dunn & Ingham, 1995). Another implication of the research on perceptual preferences is that it would be desirable to train learners to increase their learning efficiencies by taking advantage of multiple perceptual channels.

Kolb's Experiential Learning Cycle and Learning Styles. While we perceive information through our senses, we assimilate it with our minds, emotions, and muscles. Without processing information at multiple levels, the brain would be overwhelmed with a mass of cognitive matter: information, data, and facts that may seem impossible to comprehend or learn (Vella, 1994).

Most learning involves more than cognitive material (idea and concepts). Kurt Lewin (1951) wrote that little substantive learning takes place without involving something of all three aspects. Learning also involves feeling things about the concepts (emotions) and doing something (action). These elements need not be distinctive. They can be, and often are, integrated.

According to Kolb (1984):

> learning is a process whereby knowledge is created through the transformation of experience. This definition emphasizes several critical aspects of the learning process as viewed from the experiential perspective. First is the emphasis on the process of adaptation and learning as opposed to content or outcomes. Second is that knowledge is a transformation process, being continuously created and recreated, not an independent entity to be acquired or transmitted. Third, learning transforms experience in both its objective and subjective forms. Finally, to understand learning, we must understand the nature of knowledge, and vice versa.

In the book *Experiential Learning,* Kolb (1984) describes learning as a four-step process. He identifies the steps as (1) watching and (2) thinking (mind), (3) feeling (emotion), and (4) doing (muscle). He draws primarily on the work of Dewey (who emphasized the need for learning to be grounded in experience), Lewin (who stressed the importance of a person's being active in learning), and Jean Piaget (who described intelligence as the result of the interaction of the person and the environment).

Kolb's learning cycle is an influential theory that highlights learning as a process. Because of the complex nature of the learning process, there are opportunities for individual differences and preferences to emerge. A learning style in Kolb's model, represents how individual choices made during the learning process affect what information is selected and how it is processed. Kolb (1984) illustrates the notion *of* learning styles by observing how people learn to play pool:

> Some people just step up and hit the ball without bothering to look very carefully at where their shot went unless it went in the pocket. Others seem to go through a great deal of analysis and measurement but seem a bit hesitant on the execution. Thus, there seem to be distinctive styles or strategies for learning and playing the game (p. 66).

Differences in learning styles can explain why some individuals are more comfortable and successful with some HRD approaches (e.g., role playing, lectures, and videotapes) than others. Similarly, learning styles differences among HRD professionals can also contribute to their preferences for certain HRD approaches over others.

Kolb theorizes that an individual's learning style is based on that person's preferred modes of learning. A mode of learning is the individual's orientation toward gathering and processing information during learning.

Kolb wrote that learners have immediate concrete experiences that allow us to reflect on new experience from different perspectives. From these reflective observations we engage in abstract conceptualization, creating generalizations or principles that integrate our observations into sound theories. Finally, we use these generalizations or theories as guides to further action. Active experimentation allows us to test what we learn in new, more complex situations. The result is another concrete experience, but this time at a more complex level.

According to Kolb's model, to be effective learners we must (1) perceive information, (2) reflect on how it will impact some aspect of our life, (3) compare how it fits into our own experiences, and (4) think about how this information offers new ways for us to act. We must realize that learning requires more than seeing, hearing, moving or touching alone. We must begin integrating our senses and thoughts with our actions and feelings. Overall, the Kolb model sees learning as a process of creatively resolving issues, continually improving, and, through the integration of thought and action, internalizing knowledge (Kolb, 1984; Sims, 1998).

Although the entire Kolb learning cycle is involved in the most challenging learning situations, most people favor parts of the cycle over others, giving rise to the notion of learning styles. Kolb argues that an individual's learning style often combines two modes of learning, such as abstract conceptualization and active experimentation (thinking and doing). Each learning style emphasizes some learning abilities and deemphasizes others. Kolb identifies four learning styles:

- *Divergent style*—derived from concrete experience (CE) and reflective observation (RO), with strengths in imaginative abilities and sensitivity to diverse perspectives;
- *Assimilation style*—derived from reflective observation and abstract conceptualization (AC), integrating diverse perspectives into explanatory frameworks;
- *Convergent style*—derived from abstract conceptualization and active experimentation (AE), with strengths in applying ideas to practice, and
- *Accommodative style*—derived from active experimentation, with strengths in doing things and learning through trial and error (Kolb, 1984; Sims, 1998).

Kolb theorizes that learning styles are developed as a result of life experiences, as well as hereditary influences. He notes that although individuals may have a dominant learning style, they may use other styles in particular situations. To help individuals identify their learning style, Kolb developed a questionnaire called the *Learning Style Inventory* (LSI). The LSI assesses an individual's orientation toward the four modes of the learning process

(CE, RO, AC, and AE). Scores also reflect the individual's tendencies toward abstractness over concreteness and action over reflection (Kolb, 1984; Sims, 1998).

Kolb's theory and the LSI can help HRD professionals, supervisors, and employees identify and appreciate different approaches to learning. As a result, interventions can be tailored to individual learning preferences in both traditional and nontraditional HRD initiatives. For example, the design of a HRD event that is classroom-based highlights the need for diverse instructional strategies. Also, consider the fact that a team at the University of Colorado at Colorado Springs developed a computer-based tutoring system that assesses an individual's learning style, using Kolb's theory, and adjust its presentation accordingly (Iurich, 1990; Sims, 1998).

Extending the notion of the need for diverse HRD strategies, and following Kolb's analysis, when HRD content runs counter to a learner's aptitude and/or self-image of her or his abilities, the "press" of learning can produce counterproductive defensiveness. This mismatch can be intensified even more if the design of the learning event is inconsistent with the style of the learner.

Kolb's research suggests that the learning demands of various professions and occupations tend to lead to certain career choices. The cumulative effect of these choices across a number of people is a correlation between learning styles and certain organizational functions. This effect has implications for team and organizational learning. In essence, such occupational selection can embed certain strengths and limitations in terms of the collective learning of a work group or of an occupation. The advantage of this state of affairs is the fit between learning strengths and occupational demands; the disadvantages are the potential blind spots for learning that inhibit generative team and organizational learning. In contrast, teams composed of diverse learning styles have the potential for arriving at innovative solutions to highly unstructured or very volatile problems, if they know how to take advantage of the diversity of perspectives and views that different styles often produce.

While of great benefit to increasing our understanding of learning and the learning process, it is also important to point out some limitations of Kolb's model. First, it fails to account for the difference between single- and double-loop learning. Taken at face value, it is essentially a single-loop model that postulates simple reflection. Double-loop learning requires what Mezirow (1991) describes as "premise reflection," seeking to bring into consciousness one's presuppositions and questioning existing attributions about one's experience. In reality, one may easily draw erroneous conclusions from reflection on the content of one's experience, leading to a closed cycle of dysfunctional learning. Premise reflection and publicly testing one's conclusions with others are specific methods for building double-loop learning, or critical reflection, into the learning process as forms of validity testing. Playing the Devil's advocate and intentionally testing assumptions through direct and open inquiry are two methods for validity testing in practice.

Second, although Kolb acknowledges the role of the affective dimension of human learning, his model is essentially based on the rational dimension of learning. Heron (1992) notes that Kolb's model "is really a model of experiential learning derived from scientific inquiry; we reflect on experience, generalize from these reflections, then test the implications of these generalizations through further experience" (p. 195). Acknowledging that this is one valid model for producing learning, Heron adds that it "is a highly intellectual account of experiential learning . . . in the tradition of Dewey, Piaget, and Kelly [that makes] the dubious assertion that 'the scientific method provides a means for describing the holistic integration of all human functions'" (p. 194).

Learning Strategies

Similar to Kolb's modes of learning, learning strategies represent the "behavior and thoughts a learner engages in during learning" (Weinstein & Mayer, 1986, p. 315). Learning strategies are the techniques learners use to rehearse, elaborate, organize, and/or comprehend new material as well as to influence self-motivation and feelings. Learning strategies can be grouped into various categories (examples of each are listed in parentheses):

- rehearsal strategies (e.g., repeating items in a list; underlining text in an article; copying notes).
- elaboration strategies (e.g., forming a mental image; taking notes, paraphrasing, or summarizing new material).
- organizational strategies (e.g., grouping or ordering information to be learned; outlining an article; creating a hierarchy of material).
- comprehension monitoring strategies (e.g., self-questioning)
- affective strategies (increasing alertness; relaxation; finding ways to reduce test anxiety (Weinstein & Mayer, 1986).

HRD professionals have applied learning strategies in learning-to-learn programs, which seek to provide learners with the skills necessary to learn effectively in any learning situation. Given the dynamic nature of organizations and the environment, there is now a greater pressure on individuals to learn throughout their lives. Learning-to-learn programs are aimed at enhancing the learning process and making individuals more independent. The programs emphasize selecting those learning strategies needed to cope effectively with the nature of the material and the demands of the learning situation. Clearly, if employees can acquire and become skilled in applying a variety of learning strategies, they will likely benefit more from both formal learning opportunities (such as HRD initiatives) as well as informal ones (such as a problem-solving meeting).

So, what is a learning style? Is it akin to a clothing style, i.e., something we each have a preference for, but which may change radically over our lives and which we can choose to alter? Or is it an attribute with which we are born and have great difficulty in changing? This is very difficult to say definitively, because studies have not followed people from their early learning experiences through to adulthood, measuring their styles along the way. However, what evidence exists suggests that good learners are ones who are reasonably flexible in their style, and that styles can indeed change in response to the learning situation.

CONCLUSION

As evidenced in this chapter "People learn in different ways." In order to be effective in discharging their responsibilities, HRD professionals need to understand what learning is and levels of learning. Understanding the learning process and how learning can be maximized by paying attention to the learners' readiness, principles of learning, and transfer of learning are critical issues in effective HRD design and delivery. Additionally, HRD professionals should be familiar with learning styles and learning strategies and how they contribute to maximizing learning in general, and enhanced learner learning in particular. With such understanding, there is a greater likelihood that HRD will increasingly be perceived as a contributor to individual and organizational learning.

NOTES

1. Pedagogy from the Greek word paid, meaning child, and agogus meaning leader of.
2. In the *Adult Learner*, Knowles states, Andragogy is not a new word. It was used in Germany as early as 1833 and has been used extensively during the last decade in Yugoslavia, France and Holland. It is also worth noting that in 1927, Martha Anderson and Eduard Lindeman used the term in a volume titled *Education through Experience*.
3. Andragogy, initially defined as "the art and science of helping adults learn," has taken on a broader meaning since Knowles' first edition. The term currently defines an alternative to pedagogy and refers to learner-focused education for people of all ages.

4. Kids & Schools, "*A Symphony of Learning Styles*," Retrieved May 16, 2000, from http://www.weac.org/kids/june96/styles.htm
5. Telecommunications for Remote Work and Learning, *Pedagogy: Learning styles: Preferences*, (Retreived May 16, 2000). http://www.cyg.net/~jblackmo/diglib/styl-d.html
6. R. M. Felder, *Matters of Style*, Retrieved May 16, 2000, from. http://www2.ncsu.edu/unity/lockers/users/f/felder/public/Papers/LS-Prism.htm

CHAPTER 3

ASSESSING HRD NEEDS

INTRODUCTION

HRD professionals, HRM staff and managers must stay alert to the kinds of training and HRD efforts that are needed, where they are needed, who needs them, and which methods will best deliver needed knowledge, skills and abilities (KSAs) to employees. In today's cost-conscious organizations, the effective assessment of training needs is critical to achieving support for the training intended to improve employee and organizational learning and performance. Needs assessment is the key to designing training programs that create the type of work force that the organization needs to compete in the marketplace; it also is essential to give employees the KSAs they need to successfully complete and compete for jobs within the organization. Without first identifying both organizational and individual learning objectives, HRD professionals will be hard pressed to prove the return-on-investment (ROI) needed to justify HRD funding.

The purpose of this chapter is to highlight the importance of needs assessment to successful HRD. The chapter first defines needs assessment and its purposes before turning to a discussion of four levels of assessment. Next, the chapter describes several methods for collecting and analyzing HRD needs assessment data. The chapter concludes by taking a brief look at how needs assessment information can be translated into training or HRD needs which then allow for the design of relevant learning interventions intended to address the various needs.

DEFINITION AND PURPOSES OF NEEDS ASSESSMENT

Needs assessment is a process by which an organization's HRD needs are identified and articulated. It is the starting point of the HRD and training process. An HRD needs assessment can identify:

- An organization's goals and its effectiveness in reaching these goals.
- Discrepancies or gaps between employees' skills and the skills required for effective current job performance.
- Discrepancies (gaps) between current skills and the skills needed to perform the job successfully in the future.
- The conditions under which the HRD activity will occur (Werner & DeSimone, 2006).

With this information, HRD professionals learn where and what kinds of programs or interventions are needed, who needs to be included in them, and whether there are currently roadblocks to their effectiveness. Criteria can then be established to guide the evaluation process. It is obvious, then, that needs assessment is critical for an effective HRD effort.

However, despite its importance, many organizations do not perform a needs analysis as frequently or as thoroughly as they might. If anything, the competitive pressures currently facing organizations have made it more difficult than ever to carry out a needs assessment (Gordon & Zemke, 2000; Zemke, 1998). Some of the reasons needs assessments are not conducted include:

1. A needs assessment can be a difficult, time-consuming process. Too frequently, managers lament that they simply don't have the time to conduct needs assessment. A complete needs analysis involves measuring a variety of factors at multiple levels of the organization.
2. Action is valued over research. Managers often decide to use their limited resources to develop, acquire, and deliver HRD programs rather than to do something they see as a preliminary activity.
3. Incorrect assumptions are made that a needs assessment is unnecessary because available information already specifies what an organization's needs are. Factors such as fads, demands from senior managers, and the temptation to copy the HRD programs of widely admired organizations or competitors often lead to such conclusions.
4. There is a lack of support for needs assessment. This can be caused by a lack of bottom-line justification, or by the HRD professional's inability to sell needs assessment to management. Documenting the assessment and its benefits, and using analogies from respected fields (e.g., engineering scoping, medical diagnosis) are two ways to build support for doing needs assessment (Rossett, 1999).

HRD professionals should make sure these factors are considered when promoting needs assessment. Although it is possible to improve the organization's effectiveness without accurate needs assessment information, the results are by no means guaranteed. If the limited available resources are spent on programs that don't solve the organization's problems or help it take advantage of opportunities, the effort is a failure and the resources are wasted. In addition, the original problems still demand solutions.

The Need for Ongoing Training Needs Assessment

An effective HRD program cannot develop haphazardly in response to problems as they arise. A strategic (and systematic) approach to developing training efforts requires that some type of needs assessment be conducted to compare the benefits of the efforts with the projected costs and determine the long-term implications of the program. When the need for training is in question or where there could be alternatives, the needs assessment step becomes essential. This step also focuses on the impact of adding to the HRD workload. A well organized and centralized HRD area anticipates needs, wards off crises, and eliminates duplication of services.

Proactive planning for HRD must always involve some—self-assessment by the HRD area (for example, by conducting an HRD audit), looking at future trends that may impact the organization and the HRD initiative, determining goals for the function, setting objectives, and developing training plans that are responsive to the current and future training needs of the organization given its strategic agenda. Proactive planning enables the HRD professional to be in a position of helping to make things happen in the organization as opposed to watching things happen. With proactive planning, HRD professionals view needs assessment as a tool to help the organization identify problems and opportunities that may be best addressed by either training or nontraining interventions or a combination of the two. The role of HRD needs assessment as viewed by proactive HRD professionals is to work with other members of the organization to ascertain the nature and extent of performance problems or learning opportunities and potential solutions.

DETERMINING TRAINING NEEDS

As noted earlier, needs assessment is a process by which an organization's HRD needs are identified and articulated. A needs assessment involves collecting information to determine whether a training need exists, and if so, the kind of training required to meet this need. This investigation also should address why the need exists. With this information, organizational leaders and HRD professionals can identify the knowledge, skills abilities and other characteristics (KSAOCs) to include when designing HRD initiatives.

HRD professionals can conduct the needs assessment using only trainers or HRD professionals, however, the better approach is to develop a task force or resource team that includes both training and nontraining personnel (i.e., line managers, senior leaders, other employees). Formally involving employees in the needs assessment and design of HRD initiatives offers several advantages: the HRD initiatives are more likely to address critical needs; employees will feel more ownership of HRD programs; and employees and the HRD professionals will share greater accountability for fulfilling the HRD objectives.

The first step of the process is to determine the best means for assessing needs: what levels of assessment should be undertaken, what information to collect, which audience to survey, and what tools to use for collecting and analyzing the data. Assessment of the need for training usually consists of four levels of assessments: strategic/organizational, job or task, person, and demographic. Training or other HRD needs might surface in any one of these broad areas.

Strategic/Organizational Needs Assessment

Organizational needs assessment begins with an assessment of the short- and long-term strategy and strategic business objectives of the organization. The intent of the organizational assessment is to better understand the characteristics of the organization to determine where HRD efforts are needed and the conditions within which they will be conducted. This type of analysis has also been referred to as a strategic analysis (Gupta, 1999). For example, some years ago, Scott Paper purchased a food service operation that suffered from low employee morale. An extensive needs assessment process resulted in the food service division implementing a succession planning and management development program. Within four years, product defects dropped dramatically, on-time delivery rates increased to 98%, and plant capacity was increased by 35%. The point to stress here is that the organizational analysis they conducted (as part of the overall needs assessment) provided the impetus for a successful HRD effort, as well as the content of the actual development program (Sahl, 1992).

The organizational needs assessment should result in the development of a clear statement of the goals to be achieved by the organization's HRD activities. At USA Bank, for example, the results of an employee survey led the company to conclude that it needed to improve its career development activities. The survey, which was conducted following a merger, revealed that employees felt pessimistic about their future prospects at the company. The company's Opportunity Knocks program was subsequently developed to respond to the concerns employees had expressed (Kiger, 2001).

The organizational needs assessment requires a broad or "whole system" view of the organization and what it is trying to accomplish. The organizational characteristics studied may include goals, and objectives, reward systems, planning systems, delegation, and control systems, and communication systems.

McGehee and Thayer (2001) propose that needs assessment should be undertaken at the organization level to determine where training initiatives should best be directed in the pursuance of organizational objectives. Possibly the most appropriate focus for this area is provided by Katz and Kahn (1978) who suggest that organizational effectiveness can be expressed in the following terms:

1. *Goal achievement*, measured in relation to product or service quality, increased output and productivity improvements.
2. *Increased resourcefulness*, through achievement of greater market share, the establishment of new markets, and increased employee versatility.
3. *Customer satisfaction*, resulting from the minimization of complaints, the maximizing of on-time deliveries, and an enhanced organizational (or functional) image.
4. *Internal process improvements*, arising from group cohesion, high standards of supervision, minimal departmental boundaries, and the establishment of realistic and tangible departmental objectives.

Consequently the *organizational assessment* focuses on identifying where within the organization training is needed and examines such broad factors as the organization's culture, mission, strategy, business climate, short- and long-term goals, structure and the trends likely to affect these objectives. Its purpose is to identify overall organizational needs or opportunities (and the extent to which training is or is not a solution) and the level of support for training.

An awareness of the organization's resources is particularly useful in establishing HRD needs. Obviously, the amount of money available is an important determinant of HRD efforts. In addition, knowledge of resources such as facilities, materials on hand, and the expertise within the organization also influence how HRD is conducted. Perhaps the organization lacks the resources needed to support a formal training initiative, or perhaps the organization's strategy emphasizes innovation. In both cases, the organizational assessment that reveals such information plays a major role in determining whether training will be offered and the type of training (or nontraining or combination of the two) that would be most appropriate. If a lack of resources prevents formal training, an alternative HRD initiative like mentoring or a special project assignment might be used. An environment that focuses on innovation may call for an HRD initiative that focuses on enhancing employees' creativity.

The available resources and constraints that need to be considered when designing HRD programs and activities are important to a thorough organization needs assessment especially when they force HRD professionals to find answers to questions like: Can employees be taken off their jobs to participate in training? If so, for how long? Will training needs differ across locations—for example, in different states or different countries? If computer-based technology is to be used to deliver HRD, do employees have access to the specific technology they will need? By addressing such questions, an organization needs assessment can help ensure that HRD activities are practical in a specific content.

A thorough needs assessment must include a look at *organization goals*. Areas where the organization is meeting its goals probably don't require HRD efforts, but should be monitored to ensure that opportunities for improvement and potential problems are identified early. Effective areas can be used as models, and as a source of ideas for how things can be done more effectively in other areas. Areas where goals are not being met should be examined further and targeted for HRD or other appropriate human resource management (HRM) or management efforts.

Unless HRD is analyzed against the backdrop of organizational objectives and strategies time and money may well be wasted on HRD initiatives that do not advance the cause of the organization. Employees may be trained in KSAOCs they already possess; the HRD budget may be squandered on "rest and recuperation" sessions, where employees are entertained but learn little in the way of required KSAOCs and their relationship to achieving important organizational results; or the budget may be spent on glittering hardware that meets the HRD area's needs but not the organizations.

A thorough needs assessment should also look at organizational maintenance, organizational efficiency, organizational culture and environmental constraints. *Organizational maintenance* aims at ensuring a steady supply of KSAOCs. If succession plans point out the need to develop leadership talent, HRD efforts may include transferring high potential employees through a variety of positions and locations to ensure broad exposure to a variety of responsibilities.

Organizational efficiency might include checking on the degree of goal or results achievement, the extent to which current employees are performing well enough to achieve organizational goals and specific results. There are a number of indicators: productivity, accidents, waste, labor costs, output, quality of product or service, employee performance, or various other organizational measures. Examination of the organization's strategic agenda, the results of HRD planning, and the major variance between the units' successes and failures can help determine the role HRD could play. The organization's goals and achievement of important expected results can be analyzed for an entire organization or for an organizational unit such as a department or division. Information on the goals, objectives and results can be used to identify the scope and content of the HRD efforts. For example, to meet the goal of increased sales, training in new product knowledge, customer service and new customer development may be needed.

Organizational culture includes the value system or philosophy of the organization. The climate within the organization is an important factor in HRD success. Like the assessment of efficiency indexes, it can help identify where HRD initiatives may be needed and provide criteria by which to evaluate the effectiveness of the initiatives that are implemented. HRD efforts can be designed to impart the organization's philosophy or values to employees.

If the climate is not conducive to HRD, designing and implementing a program will be difficult. For example, if managers and employees do not trust one another, employees may not participate fully and freely in an HRD program. Similarly, if problems exist between senior and middle management, as has happened in many organizations during restructuring, middle managers may resist or not fully cooperate in the HRD effort, seriously reducing HRD effectiveness.

Analyzing HRD needs at the organizational level, present problems and future challenges to be met through HRD efforts. For example, changes in the external environment may present an organization with new challenges. *Environmental constraints* include legal, social, political, and economic issues faced by the organization. Demand for certain types of HRD programs can be affected by these constraints. For example in 1998, the Supreme Court decided two significant cases concerning sexual harassment (Belton, 1998, p. 270). Unfortunately, in both cases, supervisory training concerning sexual harassment was inadequate or nonexistent.[1] To respond effectively to environmental challenges, employees will need training to deal with these changes. The comments of one HRD manager illustrate the impact of the external environment: "After the Americans with Disabilities Act in 1990, we had to train every interviewer in the HRM department. This training was needed to ensure that our interviewers would not ask questions that might violate federal laws. When managers in other departments heard of the training, they too wanted to sign up. We decided that since they interviewed recruits, they should also be trained.

What was to be a one-time seminar became a monthly session for nearly two years.

Knowledge of legal issues can ensure that the HRD effort is in compliance and will not itself be a source of problems. For example, equal employment opportunity goals should be considered when determining how people will be assigned to a training program, especially if the program is a prerequisite for entry into a particular job. Similarly, economic issues, such as increased competition, can also have an impact on HRD programs. If an organization decides to reduce staff as a part of a cost-cutting program, training may be necessary to ensure that the employees who remain will be able to perform the tasks that were performed by the laid-off workers (Werner & DeSimone, 2006).

It is essential to analyze the organization's external environment and internal climate. Trends in the strategic priorities of a business, judicial decisions, civil rights laws, union activity, productivity, turnover, absenteeism, and on-the-job employee behavior will provide relevant information at this level. The important question then becomes, "Will training produce changes in employee behavior that will contribute to the achievement of the organization's goals?"

Goldstein (1986, p. 3; Goldstein, Macey, & Prien, 2001) provides a list of questions to ask during an organizational analysis:

1. Are there any unspecified organizational goals that should be translated into training objectives or criteria?
2. Are the various levels in the organization committed to the training objectives?
3. Have the various levels of participating units in the organization been involved with developing the program, starting with the assessment of the desired end results of training?
4. Are key individuals in the organization ready to accept the behavior of the trainees, and also serve as models for the appropriate behavior?
5. Will trainees be rewarded on the job for the appropriate learned behavior?
6. Is training being used to overcome organizational problems or conflicts that actually require other types of solutions?
7. Is top management willing to commit the necessary resources to maintain the organization and work flow while individuals are being trained?

HRD professionals should recognize that a supportive training climate improves the chances that employees will successfully transfer what they learn from training programs to the job. Some indicators of a supportive training climate are the following:

1. Incentives are offered to encourage employees to participate in HRD activities.
2. Managers make it easy for their direct reports to attend HRD programs.
3. Employees encourage each other to practice newly learned skills, and do not ridicule each other.
4. Employees who successfully use their new competencies are recognized and rewarded with special assignments and promotions.
5. There are no hidden punishments for participating in HRD (e.g., HRD activities are not scheduled to conflict with other important events; participation doesn't limit access to overtime pay).
6. Managers and others who are effective providers of HRD are recognized and rewarded.

These conditions are most likely to be found in learning organizations.[2]

In summary, the critical first step is to relate HRD needs to the achievement of organizational goals. If HRD professionals cannot make that connection, the HRD initiative is probably unnecessary. However, if a training need, for example, does surface at the organizational level, a job/task assessment (more recently referred to as work operations assessment) is the next step.

Job/Task Analysis

Job/Task assessment information is a valuable source of data to establish training needs. It requires a careful examination of the work to be performed after training. It involves (1) a systematic collection of information that describes *how* work can be determined; (2) descriptions of how tasks are to be performed to meet the standards; and (3) the KSAOCs and competencies necessary for effective task performance. Job analyses, performance appraisals, interviews (with jobholders, supervisors, and senior leadership), and assessment of operating problems (quality reports and customer reports) all provide important inputs to the assessment of HRD needs.

Because the organizational needs assessment is too broad to spot detailed HRD needs for specific jobs, conducting job analyses during the work operations assessment is essential. A thorough job analysis with competency modeling provides the information required for job needs analysis. Several approaches to analyzing jobs identify HRD needs. Task assessment, work sampling, critical incident assessment, and task inventories in which employees indicate how frequently they carry out a particular activity and the importance of each activity to the job are all ways to analyze the HRD needs of a particular job. Job analysis is an examination of the job to be performed. It focuses on the duties and tasks of jobs throughout the organization to determine which jobs require training given the organization's strategic agenda and expected business results. Job analysis requires a careful examination of the job to be performed after training.

A recent and carefully conducted job analysis during the needs assessment should provide all the information needed to understand job requirements and their expected contribution to achieving specific business results. These duties and tasks are then used to identify the KSAOCs and competency levels required to perform the job adequately. Then this information is used to determine the kinds of training needed for the job. If training and development are intended to address future needs, future-oriented job analysis and competency modeling should be used for the needs analysis.

Before Gillette could introduce its MACH3 triple-blade razor to the public, it needed to introduce its employees to the new machines that they would be using to produce the razor. The process of conducting the organization and job analysis began approximately a year before the razor hit the shelves. The HRM Director assembled a cross-functional team with representatives from HRM, manufacturing and engineering. The charge was to identify the skilled-labor requirements for mechanics and operators and assess the current workforce against these requirements. The exercise provided a picture of the skills that would be needed to operate sophisticated control systems, automated parts handling systems, pneumatics, and hydraulics. It also alerted the company to the increased level of team skills that would be required by the new manufacturing system. Within the year, Gillette employees had completed some 20,000 hours of required training—enough to guarantee a successful launch of the company's new product (Hays, 1999; Calandra, 1999).

The following is an example of a job/task analysis from a utility company. HRD professionals were given the job of developing a training system in six months (Holton & Bailey, 1995). The purpose of the program was to identify tasks and KSAOCs that would serve as the basis for training program objectives and lesson plans.

The project involved identifying potential tasks for each job in the utility's electrical maintenance area. Procedures, equipment lists, and information provided by subject matter experts (SMEs) were used to generate the tasks. SMEs included managers, instructors, and senior technicians. The tasks were incorporated into a questionnaire administered to all technicians in the electrical maintenance department. The questionnaire included 550 tasks. Technicians were asked to rate each task on importance, difficulty, and frequency of performance. The rating scale included zero. A zero rating indicated that the technician rating the task had never performed the task. Technicians who rated a task zero were asked not to evaluate the task's difficulty and importance.

Customized software was used to analyze the ratings collected via the questionnaire. The primary requirement used to determine whether a task required training was its importance rating. A task rated "very important" was identified as one requiring training regardless of its frequency or difficulty. If a task was rated moderately important but difficult, it also was designated for training. Tasks rated unimportant, not difficult, and done infrequently were not designated for training.

The list of tasks designated for training was reviewed by the SMEs to determine if it accurately described job tasks. The result was a list of 487 tasks. For each of the 487 tasks, two SMEs identified the necessary KSAs and other factors required for performance that included information on working conditions, cues that initiate the task's start and end, performance standards, safety considerations, and necessary tools and equipment. All data were reviewed by plan technicians and members of the training department. More than 14,000 KSAs and other factors were clustered into common areas. An identification code was assigned to each group that linked groups to task and KSAs and other factors. These groups were then combined into clusters that represented qualification areas. That is, the task clusters related to linked tasks that the employees must be certified in to perform the job. The clusters were used to identify training lesson plans and course objectives, HRD professionals reviewed the clusters to identify prerequisite skills.

The job or task analysis used in the example included these four steps:

1. Select the job(s) to be analyzed.
2. Develop a preliminary list of tasks to be performed on the job by interviewing and observing expert employees and their managers and talking with others who have performed a task analysis.
3. Validate or confirm the preliminary tasks. This involves having a group of SMEs answer in a meeting or a written survey several questions regarding the tasks.
4. Identify the KSAs necessary to successfully perform each task.

Although there is no general agreement about the purpose of task analysis, there are differing views of how it should be accomplished. The approaches used by others (Campbell, 1988; Goldstein, 1991; Goldstein et al., 1981; McGehee & Thayer, 1961; Wexley & Latham, 1991a) can be combined into the following five-step process:

1. Develop an overall job description.
2. Identify the task.
   - Describe what should be done in the task.

- Describe what is actually done in the task.
3. Describe the KSAOCs needed to perform the job.
4. Identify the areas that can benefit from training.
5. Prioritize areas that can benefit from training.

Regardless of the steps in job or task analysis, HRD professionals must recognize that task analysis focuses on the job, rather than on the individual doing the job. Information from task analysis and organizational analysis gives a clear picture of the organization and the jobs that are performed within it, and knowledge of the two provides a sound foundation for planning and developing HRD efforts.

Person Analysis

After information about the job has been collected, the analysis shifts to the person. A person analysis identifies gaps between a person's current capabilities and those identified as necessary or desirable. Person analysis can be either narrow or broad in scope. The broader approach compares actual performance with the minimum acceptable standards of performance and can be used to determine training needs for the current job. The narrower approach compares an evaluation of employee proficiency on each required skill dimension with the proficiency level required for each skill. This approach is useful for identifying development needs for future jobs that will require a specific skill. Whether the focus is on performance of the job as a whole or on particular skill dimensions, several different approaches can be used to identify the training needs of individuals.

Often, a person assessment entails examining worker performance ratings, then identifying individual employees or groups of employees, who are weak in certain KSAOCs. Employee performance data, diagnostic ratings of employees by their supervisors, interviews, or tests can provide information on *actual* performance against which each employee can be compared to *desired* job performance standards.

Performance data (e.g., productivity, accidents, and customer complaints), as well as performance appraisal ratings, can provide evidence of performance deficiencies. Person analysis can also consist of work samples and job knowledge tests that measure performance capability and knowledge. Major advantages of such measures are that:

- they can be selected according to their strategic importance,
- they often are easily quantified, and
- when they show improvements, the value of training investments is readily apparent.

A major disadvantage is that such indicators reflect the past and may not be useful for anticipating future needs.

Someone who can observe the employee's performance on a regular basis is in the best position to conduct a person analysis. Most often the source of performance ratings is the supervisor, but a more complete picture of workers' strengths and weaknesses may be obtained by expanding the sources to include self-assessment by the individual employee and performance assessments by the employees' peers. Depending on the nature of an individual's work, customers in addition to direct reports may also be in a position along with peers can be used to identify person-level needs. In fact, an evaluation approach called 360-degree performance appraisal uses as many of these sources as possible to get a complete picture of an employee's performance.

Immediate supervisors play a particularly important role in person analysis. Not only are they in a position to observe employees performance, but it is also their responsibility to do so. Also, access to HRD programs in many organizations requires the supervisor's nomination and support. Many methods of person assessment require an effective supervisor to implement them properly.

Performance problems can come from numerous sources, many of which would not be affected by training. The only source of a performance problem that training can address is a deficiency that is under the trainee's control (Mager & Pipe, 1984). Because training focuses on changing the employee, it can improve performance only when the worker is the source of a performance deficiency. For example, sales training will improve sales only if poor sales techniques are the sources of the problem. If declining sales are due to a poor product, high prices, or a faltering economy, sales training is not going to help.

It is important to note that when we talk about the employee as the source of performance problems, we are not referring only to deficiencies in such hard areas as KSAOCs directly connected to the job. Sometimes the deficiencies occur in such soft areas as diversity and ethics and they, too, require training to correct. In any case, a gap between actual and desired performance, for example, may be filled by training or nontraining but a thorough needs assessment helps determine what kind of needs exist.

Job/task analysis has increasingly shifted from an emphasis on a fixed sequence of tasks to the more flexible sets of competencies required for superior performance. Organizations such as Case and Principal Financial Group have found that as jobs change toward teamwork, flexibility requires that employees adjust their behavior as needed. Competency assessment focuses on the sets of skills and knowledge employees need to be successful, particularly for decision-oriented and knowledge-intensive jobs. While HRD programs based on job/task assessments can become dated as work undergoes dynamic change, HRD programs based on competency assessment are more flexible and perhaps have more durability (Zemke & Zemke, 1999; Lochanski, 1997; McNerney & Brigins, 1995, p. 19; Lawler, 1994). The following is an approach HRD professionals can use to perform a competency assessment (McNerney & Brigins, 1995):

1. Clarify the purpose of the effort. Will you be using the competency model for HRD purposes only or for other purposes as well?
2. Clarify the target for the effort. Will you be constructing a competency model for the entire organization? For only part of it? For only one or several job categories, such as senior executives or middle managers?
3. Network with others in your industry and in the training field. Try to find a competency model that already has been developed. (Industry associations or professional societies may have developed models.)
4. Form a panel of exemplary performers within your organization from the group targeted for assessment and from the group to which they report (such as managers and executives).
5. Ask a panel of eight to twelve people in your organization to review the competency study (or studies) obtained from other sources and to prioritize the competencies as they apply to success in your organizational culture.
6. Verify the competency model and secure ownership of it by encouraging input from others, such as senior executives.

Self-Assessment of Training Needs

One especially fruitful approach to the identification of individual training needs is to combine behaviorally based performance-management systems with individual development plans (IDPs) derived from self-analysis. IDPs should include:

1. *Statement of aims*—desired changes in knowledge, skills, attitudes, values, or relationships with others.
2. *Definitions*—descriptions of areas of study, search, reflection, or testing, including lists of activities, experiences, or questions that can help achieve these aims.
3. *Ideas about priorities*—feelings of preference or urgency about what should be learned first.

Individuals often construct their own IDPs, with assistance, in career planning workshops, through structured exercises, in the practice of management by objectives, or in assessment centers. They provide a blueprint for self-development. Chapter 9 provides a more detailed discussion of IDPs used to develop managers.

This form of training needs assessment is growing in popularity. At Motorola, for example, top managers require the employee and his or her supervisor to identify what the business needs are for the department and the business, as well as the skill needs and deficiencies of the individual. Many major organizations allow managers to nominate themselves to attend short-term or company-sponsored training or educational programs. Self-assessment can be as formal as posting a list of company-sponsored courses and asking who wants to attend, or as formal as conducting surveys regarding training needs.

Surveys and workshops are convenient tools for self-assessment (Ford & Noe, 1987; Jackson & Schuler, 2003). At Colgate-Palmolive, high-potential employees are expected to conduct a self-assessment and use it to develop a career plan (Conner & Smith, 1998; Jackson & Schuler, 2003). The components of the activities are shown in Table 3.1.

Table 3.1. Components of a Took Kit for Individual Development

I. Overview of the Individual Development Process
- Assess individual competencies and values
- Define personal strengths, development needs, and options for career growth
- Identify developmental actions
- Craft individual development plan
- Meet with manager to decide a course of action (based on preceding analysis)
- Accept the challenge of implementing the plan

II. Worksheets for Individual Assessment
- Competency assessment worksheet: assesses strengths and weaknesses for a specified set of competencies
- Personal values survey: assesses preferences for types of work environments, work relationships, work tasks, lifestyle needs, and personal needs
- Development activities chart: describes on-the-job and off-the-job learning opportunities that can be used to develop needs, and personal needs
- Global training grid: lists all formal training programs offered by the company and explains how each relates to key competencies
- Individual development plan: developed by the employee, this describes specific development goals and a course of action to be taken to achieve the goals

III. Defining and Understanding Global Competencies

This section of the tool kit is like a dictionary. It lists all the competencies considered to be important for various types of jobs throughout the company and describes the meaning of each competency. This section serves as a reference guide and encourages people across the company to use a common set of terms when discussing competencies and career development issues.

Self-assessment is premised that employees, more than anyone else, are aware of their weaknesses and performance deficiencies. One drawback of self-assessment is that individuals may not be aware of their weaknesses, especially if the organization does a poor job of providing honest feedback during performance appraisals. Also, employees may be fearful of revealing their weaknesses and so may not accurately report their training needs. In both cases, reliance on self-assessment may result in individuals not receiving training, education or other development that's necessary for them to remain current in their field. On the other hand, employees who are forced to attend programs that they believe they don't need or that don't meet their personal training needs are likely to become dissatisfied with training or other HRD efforts and lack the motivation to learn and transfer competencies.

Career Planning Discussions

To assist employees in identifying their strengths and weaknesses, some organizations make sure that managers hold career planning discussions with employees. At Eli Lily, "high potentials" discuss their strengths and weaknesses with managers. Prior to the conversation, the manager holds conversations with other executives to get their input. The manager then communicates the key points in those discussions. Afterward, the employee prepares a career plan and reviews it with his or her manager (Byham, 2000).

Demographic Needs Assessment

The objective of a demographic needs assessment is to determine the training needs of specific populations of workers. Demographic needs assessment is also helpful in determining the specific needs of a particular group, such as workers over 40, women, or managers at different levels. Demographic needs assessment can also be used to assess whether all employees are given equal access to growth experiences and developmental challenges, which are known to be useful on-the-job methods for promoting skill development. For example, one large study of managers compared the developmental career experiences of men and women. In general, men were more likely to have been assigned to jobs that presented difficult task-related challenges (e.g., operation start-ups and "fix-it" assignments). Women were more likely to have been assigned to jobs that presented challenges caused by obstacles to performance (e.g., a difficult boss or a lack of support from top management) (Olson & Sexton, 1996, p. 59; Baugh, Lankau, & Terri, 1996; Ohlott, Ruderman, & McCauley, 1994). If an organization finds demographic differences such as these, it might conclude that an intervention is needed to ensure men and women equal access to valuable developmental challenges—and equal exposure to debilitating obstacles. These demographic differences may also suggest the need for diversity training.

At Delta Airlines, an assessment of the demographic characteristics of its pilots led to a decision to focus training efforts on women and members of ethnic minority groups. At the time, only 1% of Delta's pilots and flight engineers were minorities and only 5% were women. At the same time, Delta and other airlines found it increasingly difficult to recruit pilots, due in part to the smaller pool of military pilots available. To bolster the ranks of minority applicants, Delta awarded a grant worth $1.65 million to Western Michigan University to pay for flight training for women and minorities.[3]

HRD professionals must recognize that assessing the needs for training does not end here. It is important to analyze needs regularly and at all four levels in order to evaluate the results of training and to assess what training is needed in the future. At the organizational level, HRD professionals must be proactive in working with senior executives who set the organization's goals, strategies, performance expectations, and determine and analyze the accompanying training needs. At the job or task level HRD professionals must also be proactive in working with the leaders (or teams) who specify how the organization's goals and strategies are going to be achieved and important HRD needs. At the demographic level, HRD professionals must be proactive in working with others across departments and divisions within the organization. At the employee level HRD professionals must partner with the leaders and employees who do the work to achieve those goals and strategies and analyze important HRD needs, while keeping in mind that performance is a function both of ability (hence, training) and motivation (the desire to perform well).

METHODS OF COLLECTING AND ANALYZING TRAINING AND HRD NEEDS DATA

To evaluate the results of training and to assess what training is needed in the future, needs must be analyzed by utilizing the methods of gathering needs assessment data. HRD professionals can choose from a variety of specific and different methods for conducting the needs assessment. The more common techniques include: advisory committees, assessment centers, attitude surveys, group discussions, employee interviews, exit interviews, management requests, observations of behavior, performance appraisals, performance documents, questionnaires, and skills test. While the organization, job/task, person and demographic needs assessment are all important, as highlighted earlier, focusing on the employee's needs as determined by the organization's strategic agenda is especially important. It is at the employee/or group level at which training is conducted.

There are four ways to determine the employee training or HRD needs:

1. Directly observe employees in their actual or future work settings.
2. Interview employees to see what they have to say about their job, performance problems, opportunities and solutions.
3. Ask supervisors, co-workers, customers about employees' training needs.
4. Examine the problems or opportunities employees have given the organization's strategic agenda.

In essence, any gaps between the expected and actual performance, results and potential opportunities should suggest training and nontraining needs. Active solicitation of suggestions from the people who know the most about the relative importance of practices, competencies, and the KSAOCs important to achieving specific results serves as the best way of determining training needs. As noted in the previous section, employees themselves, co-workers, supervisors, managers, senior executives and HRD oversight committees all can provide valuable information on critical success factors and accompanying training needs.

Regardless of the methods used to collect data during the needs assessment, HRD professionals will want the information to be reliable—or in other words, to reflect the real work situation. Collecting data from multiple sources is one way of increasing the reliability of the information gathered during a needs assessment. HRD professionals should use at a minimum two methods for collecting data.

In deciding upon a data collection method, HRD professionals should consider the following criteria (Robinson & Robinson, 1995):

1. The type of data desired. Do you and your clients want descriptive data that describe the problem or opportunities in narrative terms or quantified data that provide numerical information?
2. The size and location of the groups from whom data will be collected.
3. The resources available for data collection, including how many people are available to collect data.
4. The potential constraints to collecting the data, including reasons for each constraint.
5. The cost and available funds for collecting data.
6. The amount of time available to collect data.

Data collection methods that can be used to collect data include: one-on-one interview (either face to face or on the telephone), focus group interviews, questionnaires or surveys, direct observation, and documentation review (the review of organizational documents). The one-on-one interview, focus group interview, and direct observations are most frequently used to collect descriptive data, such as the information used to describe specific performance problems or opportunities. Questionnaires can be quite useful in collecting data for the following reasons: They are well suited for collecting quantifiable data, they allow easy computer tabulation of quantifiable data, they can reach small or large number of people, they ensure the confidentiality of the respondent, they are familiar to respondents who will tend to respond candidly, they present all questions in a consistent manner to respondents, and they cost less than other data collection methods. HRD professionals should use at a minimum two methods for collecting data.

The following sections discuss in more detail various ways of collecting data and the advantages and disadvantages of each approach.

Reviewing Organizational Documents

Organizational documents like HRM and other types of records can provide clues regarding performance problems, opportunities and HRD issues. Advantages of this method are that records provide objective data to identify trouble spots and document performance problems. Disadvantages of this method are that reviewing records can take a long time and may reveal more about past than present situations. Even when the records do reflect current problems, they very seldom indicate causes or possible solutions. Different types of records to check include the following.

Productivity, Sales, and Cost Records
Low productivity and wasted time or materials may indicate a need for cost-control or specific skills training. Declining sales figures can stem from poor customer service or low product quality. By checking customer complaints training personnel can determine whether the same problems—either with quality control or with customer service—keep coming up. If so, perhaps a refresher or upgrading course is needed for employees in these jobs.

Employee Performance Evaluations and Merit Ratings
Performance evaluations, along with job descriptions, record the KSAOCs required for each job (and class of jobs) and how well current employees are doing given the organizations expected business results. Merit-rating forms also can reveal particular areas where employees slip and might benefit from additional training.

Accident and Safety Reports

Excessive safety problems or accident problems usually result from inadequate training. If problems tend to cluster in certain departments or certain jobs, employees could benefit from a starter or refresher course in safety training.

Employee Attendance Records

High absenteeism and tardiness can occur when employees feel inadequate in their positions and need further training. Or these problems may arise when a department manager needs more training in how to lead or take on a new role as a team leader when he or she has historically been use to supervising individual employees.

Employee Grievance Filings and Turnover Rates

Employee grievances often reflect problems with either the employee, the immediate supervisor, or the work environment. High turnover can result when employees feel that they are unable to successfully perform their jobs because their skills need upgrading. HRD professionals should talk with managers and check trainee turnover with an eye to determining if: new employees leave during their training periods? Do they tend to stay through training, but quit soon after they make the transition to the actual work? If either of these conditions is present, the problem may be solved, for example, through training or nontraining interventions.

Conducting One-on-One Interviews

Interviews regarding HRD needs can be done in person or by phone, formally or informally. Advantages of this method are that interviews can reveal feelings, opinions, and unexpected information or suggestions, including potential solutions to problems and potential opportunities. Disadvantages of using this technique include the time and labor involved in conducting interviews. In addition, good results depend on an unbiased interviewer who listens well and does not judge, interrupt, or distort responses.

Persons to consider interviewing for information on HRD needs include the following individuals.

Affirmative Action Officers

An organization's plans to increase the employment of minorities and women or to improve the promotability of those already employed create possible HRD needs for these targeted groups. In addition, affirmative action plans could generate a demand for diversity training for co-workers or supervisors. Also, plans to downsize the organization create problems and opportunities that may have an impact on these targeted groups.

Employment Recruiters

Recruiters are in a position to offer useful information on the KSAOCs of new employees and the changing expectations of new employees as related to training and development opportunities when compared to competitors. If recruiters are having trouble filling particular jobs because of a scarcity of qualified applicants, on-the-job training of current employees or a remedial course for new hires can remedy the situation. If hiring managers routinely administer pre-employment tests for particular positions, test results could point to common areas of weakness among new hires.

Senior Executives

Because senior executives establish the organization's strategic agenda, they can provide the information needed to meet changing circumstances. HRD professionals should ask, for example, whether future plans call for any expansion or changes in operations that may alter the organization's HRM and HRD needs.

Low- and Midlevel Managers

First-line managers and department heads are directly responsible for operationalizing the organization's strategic agenda and performance in their areas. They know what their employees need to learn to improve their present performance and meet future goals. HRD professionals should hold regular meetings with low and mid-level managers to keep abreast of and help identify solutions to address changes in their needs.

Conducting Focus Group Interviews

Focus group meetings resemble face-to-face interviews in many ways. Unlike individual interviews, however, focus groups involve simultaneously questioning a number of individuals (often from various departments and various levels within the organization) about HRD needs.

The number of focus groups to use depends on the number of different work groups with unique training demands. Focus group sessions are more valuable when participants have similar work processes, work closely with each other, or face common situations, such as working with external customers. Focus group topics should address issues such as the following:

1. What skill/knowledge will our employees need for our organization to stay competitive over the next one, three, five years?

2. What problems does our organization have that can be solved through training?

Advantages of this method are that focus groups tap many sources and supply qualitative information often omitted when using other inclusive data collection methods, like written questionnaires. Focus groups also can build support for training program proposals and develop participant's problem analysis skills for future feedback. Disadvantages include the time needed to conduct focus groups and the possibility that the group leader may sway the direction of the discussion. In addition, good results depend on group members' ability and willingness to attend and participate in meetings.

Conducting Direct Observations

Direct observation is appropriate to use when the population or the random sample is relatively small and it is important to note deviations from required procedures. Direct observations can examine on-the-job performance, simulations of work settings, or written work samples. In a small organization, HRD professionals may be able to pinpoint areas where training is needed simply by watching how jobs are done in various departments. Whatever method is used, HRD professionals must be sure to talk to employees—they know better than anyone what will help them to improve their job performance.

Advantages of this method are that observations provide a reality check and generate fairly accurate data on performance and work flows with minimal disruption. Disadvantages of conducting observations are that this method is labor-intensive, requires a highly skilled observer, and can be seen as spying.

Using Surveys or Questionnaires

As suggested earlier, surveys and questionnaires generally use a standardized format for gathering information. Common survey methods include polling and other forms of questioning, all of which can be administered by mail, phone, or hand. Normally the use of surveys and questionnaires involves developing a list of skills required to perform particular jobs effectively and asking employees to check those skills in which they believe they need training. Table 3.2 shows some typical areas that a needs assessment questionnaire might cover.

Table 3.2. Needs Assessment Questionnaire with Selected Questions

Instructions: Please read the list of training areas carefully before answering. Circle Yes if you believe you need training in that skill, either for use in your current job or for getting ready for promotion to a better position. Circle the question mark if uncertain. Circle No if you feel you do not need training in that area.

1. How to more effectively manage my time
    Yes   ?   No
2. How to handle stress on the job
    Yes   ?   No
3. How to improve my written communication skills
    Yes   ?   No
4. How to improve my oral communication skills?
    Yes   ?   No
5. How to improve my listening skills
    Yes   ?   No
6. How to improve my personal productivity
    Yes   ?   No

Employee attitude surveys can also be used to uncover HRD needs. Usually most organizations bring in an outside party or organization to conduct and analyze employee attitude surveys. Attitude surveys completed by a supervisor's direct reports can provide information on training needs for the supervisor. For example, when one supervisor received low scores regarding her or his fairness in treating direct reports, compared with other supervisors in the organization, the supervisor may need training, in that area (McCall, Lomardo, & Morrison, 1988; McCauley et al., 1994).

Similarly, if the customers of a certain unit seem to be particularly dissatisfied compared with other customers, training may be needed in that unit. Thus, customer surveys can serve a dual role: providing information to management about service and pinpointing employee deficiencies. In particular, a customer survey may indicate areas of training for the organization as a whole, or particular functional units.

Advantages of this technique are that surveys and questionnaires cost little, are easy to administer and tabulate, can reach many people in a short time, ensure confidentiality, and identify the scope of a problem. Disadvantages of using surveys include the time and difficulty of constructing clear and unambiguous questions. In addition, written surveys tend to deter individuals from freely expressing their views, which can sacrifice some of the detail and qualitative information gathered using other methods. Surveys also tend to do a better job of identifying problems than pinpointing causes or possible solutions.

Sampling

Sampling is an abbreviated form of surveying. Instead of polling all employees, sampling surveys a small, selected group of employees. Advantages of sampling are that it is less time-consuming than a regular survey and can target the most important users of training. Disadvantages of sampling are that inappropriate sample selection can bias the results, and the uniqueness of the sample may make it difficult to compare training survey results from year to year.

Administering Group Tests

Testing a group of potential training participants can identify which employees could most benefit from training. It also can highlight weak areas of KSAOCs that the HRD initiative should target.

Advantages of using tests are that testing quantifies knowledge and ability levels and provides useful 'before' data for later use in evaluating the effectiveness of the training. Disadvantages of tests are that many measure only knowledge, not actual job performance, and designing tests that accurately measure the right knowledge or skill can prove difficult.

RECORDING NEEDS ASSESSMENT INFORMATION

Along with particular methods for collecting and analyzing needs assessment information there are a number of tools available to HRD professionals for recording the information. These tools are briefly discussed below.

Chart or Check Sheets

Organizations can use a chart or check sheets to monitor the HRD needs of an individual employee. A suggested chart has seven columns: employee, task, nature of training needed, completion date of training, performance level desired, performance level attained and date of assessment. This chart should keep track of performance weaknesses, HRD efforts undertaken, and the performance improvement targeted and performance level attained as a result of the training undertaken. The information on the chart indicates the managers' assessment of HRD needs and ROI in terms of job performance. The chart can be used for newcomers without KSAOCs needed for a job, employees performing marginally due to skill deficiency and employees whose job has or will significantly change.

Check sheets can use simple hash marks to record how often certain events occur. This type of information often is charted as a frequency graph that shows the relative severity of different problems. To construct a check sheet, HRD professionals should take the following steps: decide exactly what events to record; determine the time period for data collection (hours, days, or possibly months); design a clear and easy-to-use form for recording events; and record events using a consistent format and random observations.

Line Graphs

A line graph visually represents trends in a particular activity over a specified time period. By tracking a particular activity (on-time delivery, productivity), line graphs to help to identify changes as soon as they occur, allowing prompt attention to problems.

Line graphs can display occurrences of a particular activity, as well as average trends over time. Averages are useful for monitoring future activity to determine if a change is significant enough to cause concern. A change of six or more points from the average is usually worth investigation.

Pareto Charts

A Pareto chart is a bar chart that shows the relative importance of different events. The most frequent events are charted on the far left, with other data recorded in descending order to the right. Like a check sheet, a Pareto chart identifies root causes of problems.

TRANSLATING NEEDS ASSESSMENT INFORMATION INTO HRD NEEDS

Once an organization has gathered needs assessment data, the next step is to analyze the information to identify HRD, training and nontraining needs common to the organization, several departments or groups of employees. Typical triggers for training include performance problems, poor communication skills, technological advances, or strategic initiatives, such as a move toward quality management or diversification.

When examining needs assessment information, HRD professionals must be sure to distinguish between actual training needs and isolated problems. Some problems common to several employees may best be addressed through other HRM programs, such as the performance management system or employee disciplinary policy. Consideration should also be given to ways in which a shared problem may require different HRD solutions. For example, a communication problem may exist throughout the organization, but the underlying cause might involve interpersonal or human relations skills training in one department, managerial training in another department, and so on.

Identifying HRD Objectives

After completing the four types of analyses in the needs assessment, the HRD professionals should begin to develop program or learning objectives for the various performance discrepancies. Learning objectives describe the performance you want learners to exhibit. Well-written learning objectives should contain observable actions (e.g., time on target, error rate for things that can be identified, ordered, or chartered), measurable criteria (e.g., percentage correct), and the conditions of performance (e.g., specification as to when the behavior should occur).

Though HRD objectives can be developed without deriving learning objectives, there are several advantages to developing them. First, the process of defining learning objectives helps the HRD professional identify criteria for evaluating the HRD initiative. For example, specifying a learning objective of a 20% reduction in waste reveals that measures of waste may be important indicators of program effectiveness. Second, learning objectives direct HRD professionals to the specific issues and content to focus on. This ensures that the HRD professionals are addressing important topics that have been identified through strategic HRM-HRD planning. Also, learning objectives guide learners by specifying what is expected of them at the end of various HRD initiatives. Finally, specifying objectives makes those responsible for HRD more accountable and more clearly linked to HRM planning and other HRM activities, which may make the initiatives easier to sell to line managers. More will be said about HRD objectives in Chapter 4.

In the end, regardless of the methods used to collect needs assessment information, the success of needs assessment is dependent upon organizational support, and HRD professionals must ensure that such support exists from each level of the organization.

Gaining Support for the Needs Assessment

Flawed needs assessment processes, a lack of organizational support for needs assessments, and inadequate HRD professional expertise are common problems that can undermine the needs assessment and the initiatives built upon its results. Some solutions for countering these problems when conducting a needs assessment are as follows.

First, HRD professionals should make sure that they have developed rigorous and thorough procedures for gathering information on HRD needs. Besides increasing the variety of sources used, the needs assessment process should target specific areas of inquiry. In particular, HRD professionals should ask for the following information: details of optimal performance; details of actual performance; feelings of employees, supervisors, experts, and others; and causes of problems paired with HRD, training and non-training recommendations and solutions.

Next, HRD professionals should seek to create organizational support for the needs assessment process. However, often seeking such support is not necessary if the HRD professionals have effectively partnered with clients who take the lead on getting and maintaining organizational support for the needs assessment. Recommended ways to achieve this objective include the following: Document the needs assessment and how it contributes to the bottom line. (How does the needs assessment contribute to streamlining the HRD initiative? How does it help identify policy changes that diminished the need for HRD? How has it shown that a new management training or development initiative would enhance the transfer of skills back to the job?) Make a case for needs assessment through analogies to other functions in the organization. (Would a manufacturing department introduce a new product without testing it first?) Finally, increase the expertise of those responsible for completing needs assessment projects. HRD professionals should be wary of a needs assessment process that has no expert, as well as one that has indecisive or conflicting experts.

CONCLUSION

In light of the substantial emphasis placed on HRD in recent years, it would seem likely that most organizations would have developed extensive methods to identify HRD needs. Surprisingly, however, too many organizations still conduct HRD in a haphazard manner. And, too often vast amounts of HRD dollars are still spent on the "fad of the year" program. The resources wasted on needless or inappropriate HRD initiatives cannot help but have backfiring effects on organizations. Money squandered on inappropriate HRD initiatives are not available for use in other more needy areas of the organization. Additionally, employees become frustrated attending programs that prove to be of little value in helping them meet the increasing demands placed on them back on the job, and as one would expect they become resistant to future HRD efforts. In order to be effective and worthwhile, HRD initiatives must be driven by an organization's needs. For HRD to be successful it requires that needs assessment be continual, that it interface with other organizational areas, and that it incorporate the use of various analyses.

NOTES

1. Burlington Industries, Inc. b. Ellerth, 118 S. Ct. 2527 (1998); *Faragher v. City of Boca Raton*, 118 S. Ct. 2575 (1998).
2. For more information about diagnosing the learning climate, see Tannenbaum (1977).
3. "Delta Air will Give School Grant to Train Minorities as Pilots," *Wall Street Journal* (January 10, 2001), p. A6.

CHAPTER 4

DESIGNING EFFECTIVE HRD INITIATIVES

INTRODUCTION

Regardless of the method employed or outcomes of a systematic needs assessment HRD initiatives must be designed with the ultimate goal of emphasizing or achieving "pivotal" employee competencies (or knowledge, skills, abilities and other characteristics (KSAOCs)) which should be derived from the organization's strategic goals and objectives. To do this, HRD professionals must simultaneously engage in the following significant actions while at the same time being attentive to other important design issues:

1. Identify the kinds and levels of KSAOCs that employees need to attain high levels of performance and to achieve organizational results.
2. Develop and maintain structures, conditions, and climates that are conducive to learning.
3. Generate and provide the necessary resources to conduct a program design.
4. Identify and provide access to off-the-job as well as on-the-job learning resources.
5. Provide individual assistance and feedback on various dimensions of individual performance.

6. Serve as role models and mentors to trainees and the organization in the pursuit of mastery of "pivotal" KSAOCs.
7. Develop efficient learning processes that take into account individual learning styles, strategies, abilities, and work and life circumstances.

To successfully design, implement and evaluate their HRD initiatives, HRD professionals should not lose sight of these responsibilities when designing new HRD initiatives. This is especially the case when it comes to creating the right conditions and establishing objectives for HRD efforts

This chapter first discusses the importance of creating the right conditions for HRD before moving to a discussion of establishing objectives. Next the chapter focuses on developing HRD program content driven by three types of learning objectives: cognitive knowledge, skill-based, and affective outcomes. The chapter then takes a look at decisions related to identifying the resources important to designing effective HRD activities. The chapter then addresses the issue of designing effective HRD efforts for adults and revisits the topic of learning styles and first introduced in Chapter 2. The chapter then discusses the importance of communicating HRD initiatives to other organizational stakeholders. The chapter concludes with a look at a number of factors important in planning for, designing and implementing HRD programs.

DESIGNING HRD: CREATING THE RIGHT CONDITIONS

A simple framework with five components can be offered as an initial guide HRD professionals should consider in designing HRD initiatives. By attending to these components, HRD professionals and their organizations can ensure that the right conditions are in place. Both the design of the HRD activities and a consideration of how HRD activities are integrated into the HRM system contribute to ensuring that these components are in place (Kraiger, 2001; Sloan, 2000). The five components identified by Personnel Decisions International (PDI), a large HRM consulting firm, are as follows (Maurer, 2001; Colquitt, LePine, & Noe, 2000):

- *Insight:* People need to know what it is they need to learn. Employees gain insight into what they need by participating in person analysis and receiving feedback about their current skills and competencies.
- *Motivation:* People need to be motivated by internal and external means to put in the required effort. Some employees may be eager to learn simply for the sake of learning, but most are likely to be more

motivated when they believe that participation in HRD activities will lead to positive benefits. Thus, motivation to participate can be increased by integrating HRD activities with other facets of the HRM system (e.g., performance management, promotions, incentives, and rewards).

Even when explicit rewards are not directly tied to participation in HRD activities, motivation can be enhanced by clearly communicating that participation is valued by the organization. One way to send the message is by involving everyone—including top-level managers. When everyone has been targeted as needing training, for example, as is often the case with major organizational change efforts, top managers often participate first, and other employee groups are scheduled in hierarchical sequence.

1. *New Skills and Knowledge.* People must be shown how to acquire the needed competencies. The design and content of the HRD activities themselves address this issue.
2. *Real World Practice.* Programs that engage participants in realistic activities improve the likelihood that they will apply their learning. Similarly, when at their jobs, employees should have the opportunity to practice what is learned. The program design can ensure that HRD activities are realistic, but managers and peers share responsibility for encouraging people to practice applying their new competencies while on the job.
3. *Accountability.* Of course, the responsibility for applying new learning is not carried by managers and peers alone. All employees need to feel personally accountable for using what they learned. Here again, other facets of the HRM system become relevant. The most direct approach to holding employees accountable is to include assessment of improvement as part of the performance appraisal process.

ESTABLISHING HRD OBJECTIVES

As introduced in Chapter 3, HRD objectives define what participants will be expected to learn or do as a result of participating in an HRD program and are essential to the success of such endeavors. Unfortunately, far too many training programs, for example, have no objectives. In these situations, "training for training's sake" appears to be the maxim. This philosophy makes it virtually impossible to evaluate the strengths and weaknesses of a training program or HRD intervention.

As a result of conducting strategic (organization), job (task), person and demographic analyses, HRD professionals and managers will have a more complete picture of the organization's HRD learning needs. Next, objectives must be agreed upon and established for meeting those needs.

Establishing objectives is one of the most important steps in any HRD program. For the organization to manage its investment properly, the organization should know in advance (that is, prior to training) what it expects of its employees. For example, consider the implications if employees are producing at a level of 80% of capacity before training and are still producing at a level of 80% after undergoing training designed to boost productivity. An appropriate question that arises is the extent to which the training was effective. It is surprisingly difficult to evaluate the effectiveness of training, however, if the organization had no predetermined objectives or goals. Thus, HRD professionals must look at the current state of affairs, decide what changes are necessary, and then formulate these changes in the form of specific training objectives.

For example, consider the case of an insurance claims office. Assume that claims adjusters are currently processing insurance claims at an average rate of six business days per claim. Responses and feedback from customers suggest that some customers are becoming unhappy because they would like to have their claims processed more quickly. Using this information and other relevant data, the HRD professional—working with operating managers—might decide that an appropriate and reasonable goal is to cut the average processing time from six to four days. Thus, a "four-day processing average" becomes the goal of this particular training endeavor.

As evidenced in our discussion thus far, objectives should state the outcome the program or learning initiative is intended to produce, including the specific performance expected, the conditions under which it will be performed, and the criteria to be used to judge whether the objective has been achieved. Robert Mager, an internationally known training and development expert, emphasizes the importance of instructional objectives by noting that "before you prepare instruction, before you select instructional procedures or subject matter or material, it is important to be able to state clearly just what you intend the results of that instruction to be. A clear statement of instructional objectives will provide a sound basis for choosing learning methods and materials and for selecting the means for assessing whether the instruction will be successful" (Mager, 1990, 1999; Holton & Bailey, 1995). Mager defines an objective as a "description of a performance you want learners to be able to exhibit before you consider them competent" (Mager, 1984, p. 3).

Objectives for any HRD initiative program that do not relate directly to specific job KSAOCs should also be considered. Examples of these kinds of objectives include development and promotion opportunities, self-study, and employee health and safety.

Data collected from needs assessment are useful for defining program objectives because they identify the deficiencies or challenges to be addressed. For example, suppose the needs assessment data from a retail organization determines that its new sales clerks take at least six weeks to be able to explain products in their department where the industry average is two weeks. A training program could be designed that would decrease the amount of time it takes new sales clerks to be able to explain the function of each product in their department. An objective for the new sales clerks training might be to "demonstrate an ability to explain the function of each new product in the department within two weeks." The new sales clerk training would not have been possible without determining training needs which were identified using appropriate analyses, then establishing training objectives and priorities by was of a "gap analysis," which indicated the distance between where the organization was with its employees capabilities and where it needed to be. In this instance, training objectives were set to close the gap.

Mager states that useful objectives include three critical aspects or qualities, that is, they should describe (1) the performance the trainees (learners) should be able to do, (2) the conditions under which they must do it, and (3) the criteria (how well they must do it) used in judging its success (Mager, 1997, p. 3). Program objectives that lack clear statements concerning performance, conditions, and criteria are often ambiguous and can cause those who interpret the objectives differently to feel frustrated and come into conflict with one another. HRD professionals can increase the likelihood that objectives are clear by choosing words carefully and having the objectives reviewed by others (such a potential participants and managers). If a reviewer is confused, the objectives should be revised.

Well-written training objectives will benefit HRD in at least three important ways:

1. HRD objectives help determine which methods are appropriate by focusing on the areas of employee performance that need to change.
2. HRD objectives clarify what is to be expected of both the HRD staff and the participants.
3. HRD objectives provide a basis for evaluating the program after it has been completed.

Writing objectives for behaviors that can be directly observed by others can be easier than writing objectives for behaviors that are unobservable. When dealing with broad or "unobservable" objectives, it is necessary to specify observable behaviors that indicate whether an unobservable outcome has been achieved (Mager, 1997).

In many cases, simply presenting learners with objectives for learning or performance may be enough to elicit the desired behavior (Mager, 1997). That is, sometimes people do not meet performance expectations because they were never clearly told what the expectations were or how they were supposed to meet them. Clear objectives provide this information and represent the organization's expectations, which can play a key role in shaping employee performance.

Writing objectives is an essential and challenging aspect of effective HRD. The following are some questions HRD professionals should answer when writing objectives:

- Is your main intent stated (concerning what you want the learner to do)?
- Have you described all of the conditions that will influence learner performance?
- Have you described how well the learner must perform her or his performance to be considered acceptable?

Experience has shown that well-written learning objectives can past the test of the *SMART* model. In other words, the learning objective is *specific, measurable, attainable, results-oriented, and time-based.* Being specific in wording forces the HRD professionals to "think through" what the HRD activity is supposed to accomplish—to phrase the learning objective in a way that clearly outlines what the HRD activity is trying to address (i.e., employee's performance gap). The only way that one can be certain, for example, that training has accomplished its objective is to be able to compare the *after* with the *before*. This means that the learning objective must indicate how successful training will be measured. Part of thinking through a learning objective is ascertaining the realism of the goal—is it attainable given the proposed training and resources available? The training proposed should have a definitive, positive effect. It should be one that improves either an existing situation, creates a new situation, or removes existing roadblocks to improved employee performance. Finally, the learning objective should indicate an end point—the length of or when training will be completed.

Finally, regardless of the HRD initiative, HRD professionals must ensure that the objectives also state the specific number of people to be trained, for example, the specific KSAOCs on which the training should focus (the desired behavior of the learner at the end of training), and the period within which the training should be completed. These statements explicate what the learner is expected to know and to do after participating in the training program. For example, part of an organization's training could be based on the following objective:

To have forty-four employees complete the training program on total quality management techniques by January 1, 2007. At least 50% of these individuals should be first-level supervisors and middle managers, each of whom should be able to provide total quality management review and coordination for any department within the organization.

DEVELOPING PROGRAM CONTENT

An HRD program must have content congruent with its learning objectives. Three types of learning objectives that the organization may be concerned about are cognitive knowledge, skill-based, and affective outcomes (Sternberg & Gigorenko, 1997; Kraiger, Ford, & Salas, 1993).

Cognitive Knowledge

Cognitive knowledge includes the information people have available to themselves (what they know), the way they organize this information, and their strategies for using this information. Of these, what people know is by far the type of cognitive knowledge that most organizations try to address through HRD systems and activities like the following.

Company policies and practices. Orientation programs are frequently used for building cognitive knowledge. These programs brief new employees on benefit programs and options, advise them of rules and regulations, and explain the policies and practices of the organization.

Basic knowledge and the three Rs. Increasingly, organizations are concerned about cognitive knowledge of a more basic nature: the three Rs (reading, writing, and arithmetic). Training programs designed to correct basic skill deficiencies in grammar, mathematics, safety, reading, listening, and writing are still necessary in today's organizations. The need for training in basic language skills has also continued to grow as U.S. employers hire increasing numbers of recent immigrants.

The big picture. Employees striving for or currently in managerial positions may need knowledge about the organizational structure, the organization's products and services, the organization's business strategies, and changing conditions in the environment. Much of this type of knowledge information is learned through standard job assignments as well as through temporary developmental learning experiences, such as serving on a task force or taking an overseas assignment.

Skills

Whereas cognitive knowledge is essentially inside the head, skills are evident in behaviors. Whereas cognitive learning often involves studying and attending to information, skill-based learning generally involves practicing desired behaviors, such as those that demonstrate technical and motor skills.

Owing to rapid changes in technology and the implementation of automated offices, and industrial and managerial systems, technological updating and skill building continue to be a major focus of HRD programs. Skills in communication, conducting performance appraisals, team building, leadership, and negotiation are also increasingly in demand. The development of interpersonal competencies is essential for lower- and middle-level managers as well as for employees who have direct contact with the public, such as sales associates.

Affective Outcomes

When the desired results of socialization, training, or developmental experiences is a change in motivation, attitudes, or values, or all three, the learning objectives of interest are affective outcomes. The Disney Company's orientation and training programs briefly discussed later in this chapter are clearly intended to influence the affect of cast members. They learn about the key Disney "product"—happiness—and their roles in helping to provide it (Rubis, 1998).

The objectives of building team spirit and socializing employees into the organizational culture aren't the only affective outcomes of an HRD system. In fact, HRD activities often are designed in part to develop employees' feelings of mastery, and self-confidence in their ability to take on new tasks and make decisions that might otherwise seem too risky. Self-confidence enhances task performance. This is a point not lost on athletes, their coaches, or sportscasters—nor, apparently, is it lost on the many organizations now providing wilderness or outdoor training.

HRD programs designed to enhance employees' emotional intelligence are another example of efforts that target affective outcomes. Emotional intelligence involves recognizing and regulating emotions in ourselves and in others. It includes self-awareness, self-management, social awareness, and relationship management. One objective of emotional intelligence training is to teach people techniques to deal with emotions in the workplace. For example, people who work in customer service jobs may benefit from training that teaches them to keep their emotions in check when dealing with customers who are upset and angry. For people in many other jobs that create stress, emotional intelligence training can help lower the experience of stress and may contribute to overall improved health (Laabs, 1999; Goleman, 1998; Cherniss & Goleman, 2001).

DETERMINING THE RESOURCE NEEDS IN DESIGNING HRD ACTIVITIES

What resources are needed? Resources are the material and personnel needed for designing, implementing, and evaluating HRD initiatives (see Chapter 6 for a discussion of resources needed in evaluating HRD). For example, among the training materials that need to be developed and assembled are: program outlines, session plans, participant materials—workbooks, reading, handouts, etc., audio-visual aids—overhead transparencies, videos, flip charts, etc., and evaluation sheets. Some of the other activities that have to be carried out during this phase are: (a) background reading so that one is up-to-date on the subject, (b) reviewing existing materials and altering and replacing them, (c) briefing supervisors and external trainers, and (d) logically sequencing individual training sessions so that it all fits and flows together.

The HRD professionals must determine if there are sufficient resources, such as trainers, equipment, and funding to implement a quality HRD program. If not, they must decide whether or not these resources can be acquired in a reasonable period of time. If the resources needed to accomplish the learning activity are not under the HRD staffs control, they must develop a strategy for obtaining these resources. To a large extent, identifying and acquiring resources are interdependent factors to which the HRD professionals must attend throughout the HRD activity or process.

When and where is the program conducted? This is the phase when the whole learning or HRD process comes together. If the planning and preparation have been thorough, then the chances of success are vastly increased. A key consideration at this point is when and where the HRD program is to be conducted. And, as noted previously, employees learn on and off the job.

On-the-job training is most often used to train new employees for relatively simple jobs. Employees learn by actually performing the work under the guidance of an experienced worker or supervisor. Through advice and suggestions, the more experienced employee teaches the new one effective work methods. Generally, on-the-job training programs are used by organizations because they provide "hands-on" learning experience that facilitates learning transfer and because they can fit into the organization's normal flow of activities. Separate areas for training are thus unnecessary, and employees can begin to make a contribution to the organization while still in training.

Off-the-job training is any form of training performed away from the employee's work area. Some methods involve training employees away from their usual workstations but still within the agency's facilities. Other methods involve training employees in locations outside the agency. In reality, the decision comes down to the following choices: when the training staff and participants can be available, at the job itself, on site but not on the job—for example, in a training room in the agency, and off site, such as in a hotel, conference center, or university or college classroom. More will be said about on- and off-the-job training or HRD in Chapter 5.

The decision to "make or buy" HRD programs is critical to determining the resources needed for designing such efforts. Such a decision also has implications for where programs will be conducted, the use of internal or external HRD professionals to facilitate the programs, and the learning methods that will be used in the programs.

In-House versus Outsourced Programs

A series of decisions must be made regarding the development and delivery of the HRD program after a manager and HRD professionals have identified the program objectives. One of these decisions is whether to design the program internally, purchase it (or portions of it) from an outside vendor, or use some combination of the two (Sims, 1998). Outside vendors or consultants provide a wide variety of services, including:

- Assisting with conducting needs assessment;
- Guiding internal staff to design or implement a program;
- Designing a program specifically for the organization;
- Presenting a previously designed program.
- Conducting a train-the-trainer program to improve the facilitation and instructional skills of internal content experts (Carnevale, Villet, & Holland, 1990).
- Providing supplemental training materials (exercises, workbooks, computer software, videos).

The many services that outside vendors offer impact the initial decision that HRD professionals must make in whether to conduct in-house or outsource their HRD efforts. An in-house training or HRD program is conducted on the premises of the organization primarily by the organization's own employees. Many larger organizations, such as Texas Instruments and Exxon, have large HRD staffs. These HRD staffs consist of individuals who are familiar with the organization, its jobs, and its employees. Moreover, these individuals are also experts in designing and implementing HRD

Designing Effective HRD Initiatives   93

programs. Thus the organization itself assumes the responsibility for training and developing its employees.

There are several obvious advantages to in-house training and HRD. The major advantage is that the organization can be assured that the content of its training and HRD efforts are precisely and specifically tailored to fit the organization's needs. That is, by definition there will be a close working relationship between line managers and the HRD staff as the various HRD programs are planned and conducted for current employees. Another advantage is flexibility, particularly regarding scheduling, because the training and learning programs can be taught at times that are most convenient for the employees. For example, an employee can usually reschedule a training (or other HRD) activity with relatively little difficulty.

The alternative approach of HRD initiatives is to use an outsourcing strategy. An outsourced HRD program involves having people from outside the organization, perform the training for example. This approach might involve sending employees to training or other HRD programs at colleges and universities, a consulting firm's headquarters, or similar locations. The primary advantage of outsourced programs is cost. Because the organization does not have to maintain its own HRD staff, or even its own HRD facilities, the cost is typically lower than would be possible with an in-house HRD program.

Another advantage is quality assurance. Although an organization has reasonable control over its own HRD staff, the individuals who are assigned the responsibility of doing the HRD effort might not be particularly skilled trainers or educators. Thus, the effectiveness of the learning effort might be compromised. Professional trainers, however, are almost always highly trained themselves and are also skilled educators. On the other hand, outsourced programs may be more likely to be a bit general and even generic and thus have less applicability and direct relevance to the organization.

Most small to mid-sized organizations rely strictly on either in-house or outsourced learning initiatives. Most larger organizations, however, are likely to rely on a combination of in-house and outsourced learning efforts. For example, even organizations like Exxon that have a large HRD operation internally are still likely to occasionally use outside trainers and developers to assist in specialized areas. And some organizations are even experimenting with outsourced training provided solely in-house. That is, an independent contractor, usually a consulting firm, may take over an organization's HRD function, but continue to operate and conduct the training inside the organization.

Finally, a special form of outsourced training and development involves partnerships between business and education. Many leading business schools such as Northwestern, University of Michigan, and Harvard run highly regarded management development programs that attract participants from major corporations from around the world. These programs may be generic, customized by industry or firm size, or even created for a single organization. Many other major public and private universities also offer various programs of this type for business. And even regional schools and community colleges are moving into this area by providing basic training and development for first-line supervisors and entry-level technical employees (DeNisi & Griffin, 2001; Sims, 1998; Werner & DeSimone, 2006).

A number of factors should be considered when making a decision to outsource or purchase any HRD programs. For example, suppose a small manufacturer desires to computerize its billing operation. Given the nature of the training needed, it is likely that the organization's management would contract with an outside vendor because as suggested earlier, (1) the organization would probably not have the expertise to design the program in-house, (2) management would not likely have the time to design the program, and (3) it is not likely that the organization has an HRD department or full-time HRD professional. In general, when the number of people needing the HRD intervention is small, it is more likely that the project will be outsourced. That is, those needing the intervention may be sent outside the organization for the program. This could come in the form of the organization providing the resources for professional development or tuition reimbursement at a leading business or regional school or community college as suggested in the previous paragraph (Werner & DeSimone, 2006).

When an organization decides to outsource part or all of an HRD program, a vendor must be chosen. One rational way to do this is to determine the match between the vendor's product or capability with the organization's needs and objectives. The criteria for these decisions vary among organizations, but in general they include:

1. *Cost:* price relative to program content and quality.
2. *Credentials:* including certificates, degrees, and other documentation of the vendor's expertise.
3. *Background:* number of years in business and experience in the particular content area.
4. *Experience:* vendor's prior clients, success with those clients, references.
5. *Philosophy:* comparison of the vendor's philosophy to that of the organization.
6. *Delivery method:* training methods and techniques used.
7. *Content:* topics included in the program or materials.
8. *Actual product:* including appearance, samples, or whether a pilot program is available.

9. *Results:* expected outcomes.
10. *Support:* especially in terms of implementation and follow-up request for proposal (RFP): the match between a vendor's offer and the requirement spelled out in the organization's request for proposal (Carnevale et al.).

Regardless of whether or not HRD professionals and their organizations decide to "make or buy" HRD programs they should first conduct a needs assessment so that they can make an informed decision. Asking the following questions can help narrow the choice: How often and to how many employees will the HRD initiative be offered?

- Will the HRD initiative involve generic KSAOCs or a specific technical need?
- Will participants be lower-level or upper-level managers?
- Will the content of the initiative involve proprietary or competitive information?
- How urgently is the training or development needed?

Selecting Who Will Provide the Training

Once the organization has made a decision to design its own HRD program, or has purchased a program that it will run, trainers must be selected, provided that the instructional format will include one. Selecting trainers can be fairly easy when an organization has a large, multifaceted training staff with the competencies and subject matter expertise to train in high demand areas (Werner & DeSimone, 2006).

If training is to be planned and conducted with optimum effectiveness, trainers must be competent. Training competency involves the knowledge and varied skills needed to design and implement a training program. Effective trainers must be able to communicate their knowledge clearly, use various instructional techniques, have good interpersonal skills, and have the ability to motivate others to learn. Only those best-qualified by education, experience, subject and technical knowledge and skill, and pedagogical knowledge and skill should be selected as trainers. In addition, the selected trainer must have the ability to plan, organize, execute, and evaluate the training program.

Subject matter expertise refers to the mastery of the subject matter which may be either technical knowledge or skill. However, subject-matter expertise alone does not guarantee that an individual will be an effective trainer—many experts make poor trainers. Ideally, then, a subject matter expert (SME) should have the ability to train others. Individuals who lack the ability to design and implement effective training programs may rely too heavily on a single method of training that may be inappropriate to the subject matter (such as using a lecture format only to train employees in CPR and other first-aid techniques), or they may lack the interpersonal skills to effectively interact with or motivate participants (Werner & DeSimone, 2006).

Alternatively, trainers who lack subject matter expertise may rely too heavily on a book or other training materials and not be able to explain important concepts and/or how these are applied to the job. To some extent this dependence on trainer skills can be lessened by providing prepackaged materials or a program designed by training experts. However, most organizations depend on their internal training staff to design the entire program, from needs assessment to evaluation. Hence, trainers must be aware of how people learn, the most appropriate methods for assessing learning needs, how to establish training objectives and integrate them with the diagnosed learning needs, how to bring together the different learning methods to accomplish these objectives, and, perhaps most important, how to communicate effectively. There are a number of alternatives to assist organizations in securing and assisting less qualified trainers in addition to contracting with an outside vendor to include:

1. Teaming with skilled trainers with in-house SMEs form an instructional team (Burke & Day, 1986).
2. Using a training technique that does not require a human trainer, such as online instruction or computer-aided programs.
3. Train-the-trainer programs, which involve identifying in-house content experts who lack training skills and training them to become effective trainers.

University programs, private training consultants, and formal programs established by such organizations as the American Management Association or the American Society for Training and Development—all may help provide competent trainers to team with in-house SMEs, offer online or computer-aided programs or assist in an organization's train-the-trainer programs as part of a process to aid less qualified trainers. Very often, the accomplishment of the HRD mission and the achievement of training objectives hang in the balance of how effective the organization is in selecting its trainers.

For this reason, a carefully selected list of prerequisites for trainer selection must be developed by HRD professionals and their organizations for each HRD initiative. Such a listing will provide a firm basis for identifying potential trainers, interviewing and evaluating a trainers' ability, and making final selection decisions.

Criteria for Selecting a Trainer

Criteria for the selection of a trainer can be identified by HRD professionals by analyzing the training program from two perspectives: training program content or subject-matter, and training strategy or method. The type, level, and difficulty of the program content determine the kind and amount of expertise the trainer must possess. The training strategy determines the professional knowledge and training skills required of trainers. Therefore, the training objectives, the content of the program, and the training strategies are the source of criteria HRD professionals and organizational managers should use for selecting a trainer.

A trainer cannot teach what she or he does not know. For this reason, a first consideration in the identification of potential trainers is to locate individuals who possess the knowledge and skills that are required by the training program.

A second consideration is the experience the trainer has in using the principles of learning and training as they apply to adult learners as discussed in Chapter 2. Knowing and doing are quite different things, particularly in training. There are many identifiable skills and abilities associated with training duties. Among the most important are the skills needed to select and use a variety of pedagogical or training methods, techniques, and aids; the skill to deal with individual differences (for example, learning styles, strategies, and skills) among trainees; the ability to motivate and guide trainees; and the ability to construct, use, and interpret evaluative designs or instruments on the effectiveness of the training program and the trainer.

Another criterion is that the trainer must be a good communicator both orally and in writing. Most of the basic methods used in training (lecture, demonstration, conference), many of the techniques of instruction (illustrating, questioning, and explaining), and many of the learning aids require good communication skills. In addition, effective written communication skills are necessary for such training tasks as writing and preparing lesson plans and writing material on black boards or butcher paper. Further, each and every HRD activity requires some degree of effective communication throughout the organization before, during and after if it is to succeed.

A final criterion in selecting a trainer is the ability to work with people. Effective interpersonal skills are the cornerstone of facilitating, motivating and working with an increasingly diverse group of learners in a training program. However, the selection of trainers can be enhanced by deciding on the specific roles, activities, knowledge, and skill requirements the trainer must successfully perform. Some of these roles might be the following: needs assessment and diagnosis; determine appropriate training approach; program design and development; develop material resources (make); manage internal resources (borrow); manage external resources (buy or monitor their implementation); individual development planning and counseling; job/performance-related training; conduct traditional classroom or online training; group and organization development; training research; manage working relationships with managers, clients, and HRD and HRM staff; manage the HRD area or function; and professional self-development. There should also be an understanding that there are a variety of people (internally and externally) who may be selected to develop, facilitate, and evaluate an HRD program.

HRD activities like training programs can be provided by several people, including:

- supervisors and managers,
- coworkers,
- an internal subject matter, and
- the employee.

Who is selected to teach or facilitate the training program often depends on where the program is held, what skills or competencies are taught, and the training necessary for the trainers. A basic organizational orientation is usually handled by a member of the HRM staff. Literacy and technical competences are usually taught by the immediate job supervisor or a coworker, although technical competencies may also be taught by internal or external SMEs. Interpersonal, conceptual, and integrative competencies for management are often taught by or HRD specialists, university professors, or consultants.

Supervisors and Other Managers

In many organizations, on-the-job training is the only form of training offered. In these circumstances, supervisors almost always are the providers of whatever training employees receive. For development activities that involve mentoring, supervisors and managers are appropriate also, as they are in the best position to assess their employees' career needs. Furthermore, because of their position in the organization, supervisors and managers are accessible to employees and have control over the employees' work assignments, which facilitates their effectiveness (see, e.g., Ragins & Cotton, 1999).

Coworkers

When Disney trains new hires, the company's message is delivered by some of the best "cast" members in the company. Dressed in full costume, they show through example how to create happiness—the most important aspect of their role. After the initial training session, new cast members are paired with experienced employees for 16 to 38 hours of "paired-training," which is essentially one-to-one coaching. As the Disney example illustrates, coworkers, can be very effective trainers. Often, coworkers are more knowledgeable about the work than anyone else.

Coworkers play an important role in management development programs, which commonly bring together employees from different parts of the organization for several days of training. Participants in such programs often report that the most valuable learning occurs through conversations with their colleagues. Furthermore, exposure to the perspectives of colleagues working around the world helps employees develop more sophisticated "mental maps" of how business is conducted in different locations. Exxon's Global Leadership Workshop takes advantage of this phenomenon. Twice a year, about 30 participants from around the world participate in the workshop. IBM uses a similar model for its eight-day global leadership training program (Black & Gregersen, 2000).

Experts

SMEs may not be familiar with procedures in a specific organizational culture. As a result, they may be respected for their expertise but mistrusted because they aren't members of the work group. Still, if no one in the immediate work environment possesses the knowledge needed, or if large numbers of individuals need to be trained, the only option may be to hire experts. Experts who are expressive when delivering training and well organized are especially effective (Towler & Dipboye, 2001).

Employee

Self-paced instruction is also an option. With the growing popularity of computer-based training, self-paced instruction is also becoming more common. Trainees benefit from this method by learning at a speed that maximizes retention. However, if they aren't given incentives to complete the instruction in a specified period of time, they may place it on the back burner.

HRD professionals and other organizational members can also make the trainer selection decision based on the extent to which the trainer will be involved in the training process. This problem-solving process can be broken down into five broad areas (roles) the trainer will perform: analysis, design, development, delivery, and evaluation. With this information, the following should be taken into consideration when selecting a trainer (Wehrenber, 1989; Sims, 1990).

When selecting trainers for the *analyzer* role, look for evidence of:

- *experience in:* observing work, job/task or occupational analysis, interviewing, negotiating with supervisors and other managers, dis-

covery of performance discrepancies, and presenting information (written and oral) to various audiences;
- *knowledge of:* principles and current theories in the behavioral science, motivation theories, adult learning theories, and job design and redesign.

When selecting for the *designer* role, look for evidence of:

- *experience in:* designing training and other learning programs; selecting alternative training or learning methodologies (i.e., using inexpensive non-classroom training when appropriate), and developing clear performance (training/learning) objectives;
- *knowledge of:* a wide-range of performance-enhancing methods, training methods, and the elements of a clear performance (training/learning) objective.

When selecting for the *developer* role, look for evidence of:

- *experience in:* developing lesson plans, training schedules, training aids, and other instructional materials; writing such training materials as instructions, workbooks, and job aids; planning training or other learning events; and using a wide range of training or learning media;
- *knowledge of:* media selection, principles involved in developing written instructional materials, and adult-learning theories.

When selecting trainers for the *delivery* role, look for evidence of:

- *experience in:* speaking before groups, managing or facilitating classroom or learning process, dealing with conflict, giving performance feedback, and using various training media;
- *knowledge of:* training or learning objectives, individual and group behavior, specific techniques of public speaking (such as getting and keeping participants' attention and keeping discussions going), and the use of humor.

When selecting trainers for the *evaluator* role, look for evidence of:

- *experience in:* observing and measuring performance (designing training evaluation programs), presenting (in writing, visually, and orally) results of evaluation, applying statistical techniques to data, and comparing performance to standards;
- *knowledge of:* work measurement techniques, training/learning evaluation design options, statistical measurements analysis, and data collection.

All the selection criteria (competencies) described above should be used by HRD professionals and others in organizations to select trainers. These core competencies can also become categories on which to base evaluation of trainers once they are in the job. Looking for evidence of all the previously described competencies can enhance the selection of a trainer.

Selecting Training Methods and Media

A critical step in the training or HRD process is to select the appropriate training or learning methods. A variety of methods are available to help HRD professionals in their efforts to design successful learning activities. One way of classifying training is by the degree of activity expected or required of learners. On one end, the lecture method and videotapes are generally the least active (or most passive) for training. At the other extreme, highly experiential methods such as role-playing exercises, games, simulations, and outdoor training demand the greatest amount of activity or action from learners. Other approaches such as computer-based instruction or videoconferencing fall somewhere in between (Werner & DeSimone, 2006). And, as noted in our brief discussion of resources earlier, training methods can also be grouped into two broad categories: on-the-job methods, which typically occur in the employee's normal work setting, and off-the-job methods like classroom training, which typically take place away from the job (such as in a lecture hall or conference room). Some training methods, like computer-based training (CBT) can be implemented using a computer at an employee's workstation or desk, in an organization classroom, or even at an employee's home. Many of these methods will be discussed in more detail in Chapter 5.

With such a variety of training or learning methods available, how do HRD professionals choose which approach is most appropriate for maximum learning? Several factors should be considered:

1. The objectives of the program. This factor is paramount. Some approaches are more appropriate for achieving particular objectives than others. For example, if the objective is to improve interpersonal skills, then more active approaches such as role playing, behavior modeling or videotaping would be better choices than the lecture or computer-based training methods.
2. Time and money available in. In an ideal world, HRD professionals would have all the time and money they need to accomplish their goals. Unfortunately, in many organizations, HRD professionals are asked by managers to design and implement programs quickly, while spending little money as possible. Competing needs may also force HRD professionals to select certain approaches because of their low cost.

3. Availability of other resources. Some methods require highly trained trainers and specialized equipment and facilities to be delivered effectively. Again, tradeoffs are likely to be necessary by choosing alternative approaches with less demanding resources.
4. Learner characteristics and preferences. The issue here is both learner readiness and the diversity of the target population. Methods such as CBT require a fairly high level of literacy. If literacy or fluency is a problem, either a less reading- and writing-intensive method (such as videotape) may be used, or literacy training must be done first. Similarly, because individuals have different learning styles, some learning methods may be more appropriate than others. For example, as suggested in our discussion of learning styles in Chapter 2 (and later in this chapter), in designing any program, HRD professionals must pay particular attention to the principles of learning laid out in Chapter 2, and in particular to the learning styles described by David Kolb (Sims, 1998; Werner & DeSimone, 2006).

In any case, the selection of training methods requires that HRD professionals have the knowledge of different HRD techniques, and then use sound judgment in their decision making. HRD professionals should investigate all available methods, and when in doubt, consult experienced colleagues, instructional designers, and consultants.

DESIGNING EFFECTIVE HRD EFFORTS FOR ADULTS

In meeting the HRD accountability requirements HRD professionals must ensure that they design HRD interventions that consider individual learning styles as discussed in Chapter 2. For example, auditory learners learn best by listening to someone else tell them about the HRD content. Tactile learners must "get their hands on" the training and development resources and use them. Visual learners think in pictures and figures and need to see the purpose and process of the training. HRD professionals who address all these styles by using multiple HRD methods can design more effective HRD programs.

Training and developing many different people from diverse backgrounds, poses a challenge in today's work organizations. In addition to considering cultural, gender, and race/ethnicity diversity, HRD design sometimes must address some special issues presented by adult learning. For instance, an organization is training a group of 35 customer service representatives, 15 of whom are under age 25 and highly computer and Internet literate, and the remainder of who are older and not as computer proficient. Certainly, the training design must consider that all the learners are adults, but they come with widely varying learning styles, experiences, and anxieties.

Training older adults in technology may require attention to explaining the need for changes and to building the older learners' confidence in their abilities to learn new technology. In contrast, younger adults are likely willing to try new technology because of their exposure to computers and technology. As a consequence of differences such as these, a variety of HRD designs and delivery considerations must be assessed when developing HRD initiatives for adults of various ages.

The work of Knowles (1984) and others (Kolb, 1984; Sims, 1998) on adult learning discussed in Chapter 2 suggests that adults:

- have the need to know why they are learning something;
- have a need to be self-directed;
- bring more work-related experiences into the learning process;
- enter a learning experience with a problem-centered approach to learning;
- are motivated to learn by both extrinsic and intrinsic factors.

Clearly, adult learners present different issues for HRD based on these principles. For instance, HRD professionals cannot expect to do a "brain dump" of material without giving participants the context of bigger picture of why participants need the HRD information. This concept is referred to as whole learning or Gestalt learning. As applied to job training, this means that instructions should be divided into small elements after employees have had the opportunity to see how all the elements fit together—that HRD professionals should present the big picture first.

Adult learners should be encouraged to bring work-related problems to HRD activities as a way to make the material more relevant to them. Effective HRD should involve participants in learning by actively engaging them in the learning and problem-solving process. Active practice occurs when participants perform job-related tasks and duties during HRD. It is more effective than simply reading or passively listening. For instance, if a person is being trained as a customer service representative, after being given some basic selling instructions and product details, the trainee calls a customer and uses the knowledge received. Active practice can be structured in two ways. The first, *spaced practice*, occurs when several practice sessions are spaced over a period of hours or days. The second, *massed practice* occurs when a person performs all the practice at once. Spaced practice works better for some types of skill or physical learning that requires muscle memory, whereas for other kinds of learning, such as memorizing tasks, massed practice is usually more effective. Imagine the difficulty of trying to memorize the lists of options for 20 dishwasher models, one model a day for 20 days. By the time an appliance distribution salesperson learned the last option, the person likely would have forgotten the first one.

HRD Benefits and Use of Differences in Learning Styles

The greater the variety of learning and assessment activities HRD professionals provide in their learning initiatives, the better suited the HRD designs will be to the diversity of learning styles presented by learners, and the more likely it will be that more learners will learn to a higher degree. Clearly, there are benefits of learning style awareness and accommodation in HRD initiatives to include:

- More learners will have their needs met and have successful learning experiences.
- If HRD professionals understand how learners learn, they can design more effective learning experiences.
- If learners understand how they learn best, they can learn more effectively.
- Being aware of one's preferences and biases will help make HRD professionals better as they try not to emphasize those at the detriment of other strategies.
- As the diversity in organizations and HRD initiatives increase (learners of different generations, learners from different cultures) there will be more diverse needs that must be taken into account if HRD professionals hope to enhance learners and their organization's learning.
- When learners know HRD professionals care about their learning needs, the rapport between learner and HRD professionals is enhanced. The better the rapport, the greater the learning.

Of course the analysis and subsequent discussion of learning styles can be the most useful part of the design and implementation of the HRD or learning process, rather than the acquisition of a particular label. Most learners do not fall entirely into one category. Therefore, while "talking shorthand" about the use of styles as part of HRD design, it should be recognized that a better understanding of the components of the basic approaches to learning possessed by learners is important to HRD, rather than arbitrary, black-and-white definitions.

The style classification discussed in Chapter 2 can be used in the following way:

1. It can help learners to understand their own likely approach to HRD opportunities, and perhaps how to use that basic approach better. It

may be important to note on this point that the author takes the view that increased self-knowledge is enabling rather than disabling.
2. With less certainty, it may help learners increase their range of learning: a desirable goal will be that each learner will have a fully integrated range of styles as suggested by Kolb's (1998) learning model discussed in Chapter 2. However, in reality, by the time learners actually get to an HRD program, for example, it may be too late to aim realistically at this point.
3. It certainly should help HRD professionals, supervisors or mentors to suggest HRD opportunities that are congruent with learning style instead of antagonistic to it.
4. HRD professionals should be able to construct learning groups more effectively in the sense of more consciously choosing which learners to put with which other learners in learning groups or on a real-time job or work-related activity. The questions that are opened up here are clearer than the answers, if for example one is using different learning style classifications. Do you put Convergers and Divergers together? Do you put Visuals and Tactiles together?
5. Perhaps part of the answer to the last question is derived from the view that HRD professionals can design HRD efforts which help learners understand what they might learn about each other. It may be that with a group that has devoted some attention to analyzing learning styles and their differences, learners within the group, and perhaps the whole group, will be better able to make use of the skills available in it. For example, instead of seeing the Assimilator as a noncontributory, that person may be someone capable of contributing in a particular way. Perhaps more important, because more frequently, individuals should be able to assess better potential relationships of style between a manager or HRD professional and a learner. It is easy to see that an Assimilator will have significant differences in learning from a Diverger. Again reality obtrudes; it is likely that the learning styles reflect basic learning and communication patterns, and the discomfort is likely to arise in many areas other than learning.
6. HRD professionals can design learning initiatives that allow learners to refine and improve their understanding of learning skills or strategies. Examples of learning skills are:
    - The ability to establish effectiveness criteria for yourself.
    - The ability to measure your effectiveness in different situations.
    - The ability to identify your own learning needs.
    - The ability to plan personal learning agendas.
    - The ability to take advantage of learning opportunities.

- The ability to review your learning processes.
- The ability to listen to others.
- The capacity to accept help.
- The ability to face unwelcome information.
- The ability to take risks and tolerate anxieties.
- The ability to analyze what other successful performers do.
- The ability to know yourself.
- The ability to share information with others.
- The ability to review what has been learned.

Clearly HRD professionals should design learning initiatives which help learners improve their skills or strategies and should be capable of relating skills to particular learning styles and to particular learning or HRD opportunities. Learning-style information can be crucial to an HRD professional's credibility and ability to place a learner in relevant learning experiences. In order to best meet the accountability demands of HRD initiatives, HRD professionals must continually find a response to the question: How do learning, learning styles, and the associated learning skills or strategies relate to HRD opportunities we design?

COMMUNICATING HRD INITIATIVES

Communicating HRD initiatives can be compared to marketing a new product. Consider the fact that approximately 90% of all new consumer products fail. In some cases, the failure is due to a poor product that does not fill a current need. In other cases, however, the product fails because of a breakdown in the marketing system. The product may have been inadequately researched, the salespeople may not have been properly trained, the distribution system may have been poor, or the overall marketing strategy may have been misguided. Unfortunately, many well-designed HRD initiatives also fail because they are not properly "marketed." In the case of HRD initiatives, the customers are the employees and the price is often employee commitment, motivation and cooperation.

Communication is much more than talking, speaking, and reading. True communication takes place when an understanding has been transferred from one party or source to another. Therefore, communication can be defined as the transfer of information that is meaningful to those involved.

In this light, each and every HRD activity requires some degree of effective communication to succeed. For example, think of the important role communication plays in employee orientation, management development and career planning. In all too many instances, HRD professionals spend tremendous amounts of time designing or developing very good initiatives, only to subsequently do a poor job of communicating to others about them or their value to the organization. The end result is often great initiatives that go largely unused.

An HRD professional's first step in becoming an effective communicator is to develop an appreciation for the importance of communication. The problem is not that HRD professionals tend to belittle the importance of communication; rather, they often fail to think consciously about it.

Guidelines for Communicating HRD Initiatives

As just discussed, it is helpful for HRD professionals to develop a marketing approach when implementing their programs. Even when this is successfully done, there are numerous other communication-related guidelines to follow. Some of these are discussed next.[1]

Avoid communicating in profession-specific, peer group or "privileged-class" language. The level of communication should be determined by the receiving audience and not by the instigator of the communication. The key is to consciously remember for whom the communication is intended.

Don't ignore the cultural aspects of communication. Be careful with words, symbols, and expressions. Today's workforce is much more culturally sensitive than it was one or two decades ago. Avoid any expressions that can easily be taken out of context and offend someone in your intended audience.

Back up communications with management action. The old saying "People watch what you do and not what you say" is certainly true with employee/organization communications. Promises made either orally or in writing must be backed up by actions if they are to succeed.

Periodically reinforce communications. This is especially true with many HRD-related communications. It is a good idea, for example, to periodically remind organizational members of the value of the HRD-initiatives they are involved in.

Transmit information not just data. Data can be defined as "the raw material from which information is developed; it is composed of acts that describe people, places, things, or events that have not been interpreted." Data that have been interpreted and that meet a need of one or more individuals (i.e., employees or managers) are called information. Employees receive piles of data from numerous sources, but until the data have been interpreted, they are of little value. HRD professionals need to guard against transmitting numbers, statistics, and other data that have little meaning without an accompanying interpretation.

Don't ignore the perceptual and behavioral aspects of communication. Try to anticipate employee and manager reactions to communications and act accordingly. For example, it might be a good strategy to informally separate older employees from younger employees when introducing a new career development program through employee meetings. It would only be natural for these different groups to have different questions and levels of interest.

The preceding suggestions largely involve good common sense. It is not that HRD professionals are not practical; rather, they often do not take the time to think through a communication. One good approach is to ask, "How could this message be misinterpreted?" The answer to this question should then be taken into account when structuring communication.

HRD professionals should view communicating about HRD initiatives as an important part of the HRD-design process. Communication should be a process that begins with the needs assessment and is ongoing during the design, delivery, and evaluation of HRD activities. Communicating related HRD initiatives is an important part of the HRD professional's efforts to plan for and address their organization's HRD needs.

SOME FACTORS IMPORTANT IN PLANNING AND DESIGNING HRD ACTIVITIES

Planning is probably the most important activity in designing HRD activities. An HRD department that has carefully planned has made efforts to do the following:

1. Understand the nature of the current HRD situation;
2. Clarified the goals and objectives that the HRD department would like to achieve;
3. Understand the key outcomes at stake in their HRD efforts, and are able to identify which ones are most important to whom, what each one would like to achieve, and what will be minimally acceptable;
4. Understand the fundamental predictability of various HRD processes, so that they can strategically plan how to achieve HRD goals and objectives; and
5. Understand how organization, department, and employee's HRD needs and previous HRD experiences are likely to affect HRD strategy.
6. If an HRD department is able to consider and evaluate each of these factors, it most likely has a clear sense of direction on how to proceed. This sense of direction and the confidence derived from it will be the single most important factor in affecting the outcomes of HRD efforts.

Designing Effective HRD Initiatives   109

The following factors are important in planning for, designing and implementing HRD programs:

A. *HRD Program*

1. What kind of HRD program is this going to be (i.e., does it appear possible for all parties—participants, participants' sponsors, HRD department—to achieve their goals)?
2. What has been the nature of the HRD department's relationship with similar HRD efforts in the past, and how will that affect the proposed or HRD efforts?

B. *HRD Objectives*

1. What are the primary (those things which are on the formal agenda) objectives in the HRD program?
2. What are the secondary (how the HRD program will be evaluated) objectives in the HRD program?
3. Which primary objectives are most important?
4. Which secondary objectives are most important?
5. What is the relative importance of the secondary objectives to the primary objectives?
6. Given what is known about the organization and learners, what are the major primary and secondary issues likely to be?

C. *HRD Issues*

1. Given the HRD objectives, assumptions, and information about the organization and learners, what would be the best the HRD department could expect from the HRD program?
2. What would be an "effective or successful" HRD program?
3. What will be the major resources needed for this HRD program?
4. Does the HRD department have all the information they need on each of the HRD issues? If not, where can they get it?
5. Which issues have higher priority for the HRD department? Organization? Their sponsors? Learners? Which have lower priority?
6. Which issues are linked together and therefore easy to address?

D. *Analysis of Program Participants*

1. What are the HRD program participant's major characteristics?
2. What are the HRD program participant's perceived training and development needs?

110 *Human Resource Development: Today and Tomorrow*

    3. Is there anything more the HRD department needs to learn about the participants (i.e., learning styles) to make this HRD program successful?

E. *Analysis of the HRD Program*

    1. What are the strengths of the HRD program?
    2. What are the weaknesses of the HRD program?
    3. At this point, does the HRD department or other key stakeholders want to modify the HRD program?

F. *The HRD Program Process*

    1. What kind of a strategy does the HRD department (or managers) want to use in this HRD program? (Primarily, what kind of tone or climate do we want to set?)
    2. What does the HRD department have to do to get the organization and participants (their sponsors) to make this strategy work?
    3. If the HRD department's strategy or plan does not work, what are the fallback options?
    4. What are the most important items for setting the agenda for the HRD program, e.g., time limits, which items and how they will be discussed (such as participants' KSAs) and exercises to be used (such as experiential learning situations or cases)?
    5. What are the best learning or training methods to use in this program? Why?

In the end, the HRD professionals would do well to check back over these questions to review the overall HRD plan and needs assessment.

CONCLUSION

This chapter described several important activities critical to the effective design of training and other HRD initiatives. HRD professionals must pay particular attention to the learning objectives derived from the needs assessment, while also creating the right conditions in designing and developing HRD efforts. Additional attention must be given to determining the resource needs in designing HRD activities and while paying particular attention to the needs of the adult learners who will participate in the various HRD activities. HRD professionals must also spend quality time communicating to other organizational members about the HRD activities. In the end, HRD professionals will be more effective in designing HRD initiatives that meet the organization's needs if they keep in mind some of the factors important in planning, and designing HRD activities.

NOTE

1. For a more in depth discussion of marketing HRM efforts see Banik (1985) and Pasqueletto (1989).

CHAPTER 5

TRAINING METHODS

Implementing HRD Initiatives

INTRODUCTION

New methods available to those in the HRD profession appear every year. While some are well founded in learning theory or models of behavior change (e.g., behavior modeling), others result more from technological than theoretical developments (e.g., videotapes, computer-based business games). In either case, HRD professionals have a wide variety of methods, materials, and media from which to choose in designing and delivering training initiatives. Which HRD techniques best suit a particular initiative, depends on the learning objectives and cost considerations. Most HRD initiatives use multiple methods and training aids.

This chapter considers the choice of methods for employee training and development. With assessment and objectives agreed upon, program content created, and learning principles in mind, HRD professionals must choose appropriate training or HRD methods. The program objectives greatly influence the design and delivery, as well as the selection of training methods used to conduct or implement training. In recent years there has been an increased use of technology in program implementation. This had come in the form of technology replacing the traditional classroom delivery method (e.g., on-line initiatives), or when technology is blended in or used alone with other classroom techniques.

TYPES OF TRAINING METHODS

Despite the importance of needs assessment, determining program objectives and learning principles, and the like, choices regarding training methods are where "the rubber meets the road" in implementing an HRD program. A major consideration in choosing among various training methods is determining which ones are appropriate for the program objectives or the knowledge, skills and abilities (KSAs) to be learned. For example, if the material is mostly factual, methods such as lecture, classroom, or programmed instruction may be fine. However, if the training involves a large behavioral component, other methods such as on-the-job training, simulation, or computer-based training might work better (Fowler, 1995).

Clearly, training is intended to increase the expertise of trainees in particular areas. When thinking about what training method (or methods) to use, it is useful to consider the current level of expertise that trainees possess. Yin's learning pyramid offers a means for HRD professionals to think about the current level of expertise or KSAs of trainees.[1] At the bottom are learning prerequisites, that is, the basic knowledge or skills the learner needs to get started (Gagne, 1985). The novice learner may easily get confused or anxious, and therefore novice trainees generally require more guided or instruction-centered training methods. In contrast, as learners' existing level of expertise increases, they become more creative and confident. Thus, the desired or ideal training methods are also likely to shift more toward exploratory experiential methods. Midway through Yin's pyramid individual trainees are ready to shift from more guided to more exploratory learning approaches.[2]

Because experiential methods generally require more time to complete than instruction-centered approaches, they are not as commonly used to teach a large number of individuals. To be successful, a training or HRD program should first identify where trainees are in terms of Yin's pyramid, and then provide assistance for all learners to "move up" toward and expert level of performance. In many situations, both guided and experiential approaches will be used, for example, when organizations combine the use of various training methods. A combined approach is especially valuable when learners have different learning styles and preferences.

Although no single training method is by nature superior to any other, the goals of a particular HRD effort may be better served by one method than another or one combination of methods versus another combination. Methods of training delivery are described in the following sections. A critical first point that must be understood by HRD professionals is that the choice of training method should be guided by both the program objectives, as well as an explicit consideration of the current level of learner expertise (e.g., knowledge, skills and abilities).

Many different formats can be used for training and HRD activities. Three general categories of methods are on-the-job, on-site, but not on the job, and off-site. Choices about methods may be constrained by the type of learning that's to occur—cognitive, skill based, or affective—as well as by cost and time considerations. Table 5.1 summarizes the advantages and disadvantages of several HRD formats.

e-Learning

Note that the three major categories of training and HRD methods do not depend on using a specific type of technology. Before the computer, film, and communications industries began to merge, the technology used was often what most clearly distinguished one training method from another. Today, however, technology makes it possible to combine many methods and deliver them as an integrated learning system that combines, for example, computer-based quizzes, video, interactive simulations, and so on. When such technologies are used for HRD, they often are referred to as e-learning. More specifically, e-learning is the use of the Internet or an organizational intranet to conduct training on-line. An intranet is similar to the Internet, but it is a private organizational network behind "firewall" software that restricts access to authorized uses, including employees participating in e-learning. The major advantage of e-learning systems is their potential for speeding up communications within large corporations. A popular example of this is video teleconferencing. Here employees in separate locations can see and talk to each other. A cost study conducted by Kodak estimates that a new product training program beamed by satellite to three cities costs $20,000. Kodak estimated that it would cost five to six times that amount to send engineers and managers on the road to do the same training. More important, six weeks of training time is saved, which is invaluable in a competitive industry (Vicere, 2000; Lorek, 1998; Stevens, 1998). These are among the reasons GM gave for creating an alliance with Unext.com, an e-learning company, and encouraging its 88,000 salaried employees to take courses in marketing, finance, and e-business.[3]

Table 5.1. Advantages and Disadvantages of Several HRD Methods

Type of Program	Advantages	Disadvantages
On the Job		
e-learning and video teleconferencing	• Brings employees together from many locations • Speeds up communications • May reduce costs	• Start-up and equipment costs are high • Requires adaptation to a new learning format • May be done on or off the job
Job rotation	• Gives exposure to many jobs • Allows real learning	• Involves no sense of full responsibility • Provides too short a stay in a job
Internships and assistantships	• Facilitate transfer of learning • Give exposure to real job	• Are not really full jobs • Provide vicarious learning
Apprenticeship training	• Does not interfere with real job performance • Provides excessive training	• Takes a long time • Is expensive • May not be related to job
Supervisory assistance and mentoring	• Is often informal • Is integrated into job • Is expensive	• Means effectiveness rests with the supervisor • May not be done by all supervisors
On-Site, but Not on the Job		
Corporate universities	• Tailored to organization needs • Supports organization vision and culture	• Can be costly • Requires skilled management
Programmed instruction on an intranet or Internet	• Reduces travel costs • Can be just-in-time • Provides for individualized learning and feedback • Provides for fast learning	• Not appropriate for some skills • Is time-consuming to develop • Is cost-effective only for large groups • Often no support to assist when trainee faces learning problems
Interactive videos	• Convey consistent information to employees in diverse locations	• Costly to develop • Do not provide for individual feedback
Off the Job		
Formal courses	• Are inexpensive for many • Do not interfere with job	• Require verbal skills • Inhibit transfer of learning
Simulation	• Helps transfer of learning • Creates lifelike situations	• Cannot always duplicate real situations exactly • Costly to develop
Assessment center and board games	• Provide a realistic job preview • Create lifelike situations	• Costly to develop • Take time to administer
Role-playing	• Is good for interpersonal skills • Gives insights into others	• Cannot create real situations exactly; is still playing
Sensitivity training	• Is good for self-awareness • Gives insights into others	• May not transfer to job • May not relate to job
Wilderness trips	• Can build teams • Can build self-esteem	• Costly to administer • Physically challenging

Rather than being adopted just for its efficiency, e-learning should meet strategic training and HRD needs. Certain criteria to consider before adopting e-learning include the following:

- Sufficient top management support and funding are committed to developing and implementing e-learning.
- Managers and HRD professionals must be "retrained" to accept the idea that training is being decentralized and individualized?
- Current HRD methods (compared to e-learning) are not adequately meeting organizational HRD needs.
- Potential learners are adequately computer literate and have ready access to computers and the Internet.
- Trainees attending prescheduled training programs are geographically separated, and travel time and costs are concerns.
- Sufficient numbers of trainees exist, and many trainees are self-motivated enough to direct their own learning.

Taking existing HRD materials, putting them on the Internet, and cutting the HRD budget is not the way to success in e-learning. An important question is: Can this material be learned just as well on-line as through conventional methods? To create a traditional eight-hour course for use in the classroom requires about 25% of the time required to create the same course for use on-line. Savings come from reducing learner costs (travel, time, hotel, etc.) and spreading the cost of developing the e-course over many trainees. Making e-learning pay often may require ensuring that many people participate as learners (Diekman, 2001).

Some people (especially those with reading problems) do not learn as well on-line. Organizations have found that making some kind of on-line "lab" where employees can go to get away from their desks to study works best. Simulations, including those incorporating virtual classrooms and marketing the training inside the organization, also increase the success of e-learning (Dolezalek, 2003; Webb, 2003).

On-the-Job

On-the-job training (OJT) is hardly a new idea. In fact, it has been around so long that it has become a catch-all-term for everything an employee learns outside a formal classroom or group training environment. OJT means having a person learn a job by actually doing it. Every employee, from mailroom clerk to company president, gets on-the-job training when she or he joins an organization. In many organizations, OJT is the only training available (Wexley & Latham, 2002, pp. 78–79).

More often than not, OJT has the advantage of providing hands-on experience under normal working conditions and an opportunity for the trainer—a manager or senior employee—to build good relationship with new employees. As time becomes a critical resource—and "just-in-time training" is needed most—OJT is viewed by some to be potentially the most effective means of facilitating learning in the workplace (Fowler, 1995). The experienced employee's major role is that of watching over the individual to provide guidance during practice or learning. For example, sales employees use coaching calls where a senior sales employee coaches a new sales employee. Five steps are utilized: (1) Observation of the new employee; (2) Feedback obtained by the new employees; (3) Consensus (i.e., the coach and the new employee arrived at an agreement as to the positives and negatives for the sales call); (4) Rehearsal of a new sales call; and (5) Review of the employee's performance.

Another advantage of OJT is that transfer of training is high. That is, because trainees learn job skills in the environment in which they will actually work, they readily apply these skills on the job. However, on-site training is appropriate only when a small number of individuals need to be trained and when the consequence of error is low. Also, the quality of the training hinges on the skill of the manager or lead employee conducting it (Facteau et al., 1995; Bass & Vaughn, 1966, p. 88).

Although it is used by all types of organizations, OJT is often one of the most poorly implemented training methods. Three common drawbacks include (1) the lack of a well-structured training environment, (2) poor training skills of managers or lead employee conducting the training as noted in the previous paragraph, and (3) the absence of well-defined job performance criteria. To overcome these problems, HRD experts (Chase, 1997, p. 84; Phipps, 1996, p. 33; Olsen & Sexton, 1996) suggest the following:

1. Develop realistic goals and/or measures for each OJT area.
2. Plan a specific training schedule for each trainee, including set periods for evaluation and feedback.
3. Help managers to establish a nonthreatening atmosphere conducive to learning.
4. Conduct periodic evaluations, after training is completed, to prevent regression.

Here are some more specific steps to help ensure OJT success.

A. Determining the training objectives and preparing the training area:

1. Decide what the trainee must be taught to do the job efficiently, safely, economically, and intelligently.
2. Provide the right tools, equipment, supplies, and material.

3. Have the workplace properly arranged just as the trainee will be expected to keep it.

B. Presenting the instruction:

Step 1: Prepare the Learner

1. Put the learner at ease-relieve the tension.
2. Explain why he or she is being taught.
3. Create interest, encourage questions, find out what the learner already knows about this or other jobs.
4. Explain the whole job and relate it to some job the worker already knows.
5. Place the learner as close to the normal working position as possible.
6. Familiarize the worker with equipment, materials, tools, and trade terms.

Step 2: Present the Operation

1. Explain quantity and quality requirements.
2. Go through the job at a slow pace several times, explaining each step. Between operations, explain the difficult parts, or those in which errors are likely to be made.
3. Again go through the job at a slow pace several times; explain the key points.
4. Have the learner explain the steps as you go through the job at a slow pace.

Step 3: Do a Tryout

1. Have the learner go through the job several times, slowly explaining each step to you. Correct mistakes and, if necessary, do some of the complicated steps the first few times.
2. Run the job at the normal pace.
3. Have the learner do the job, gradually building up skill and speed.
4. As soon as the learner demonstrates ability to do the job, let the work begin, but don't abandon her or him.

Step 4: Follow Up

1. Designate to whom the learner should go for help.
2. Gradually decrease supervision, checking work from time to time against quality and quantity standards.

3. Correct faulty work patterns before they become a habit. Show why the learned method is superior.
4. Compliment good work; encourage the worker until he or she is able to meet the quality and quantity standards (see Berliner & McLarney, 1974, pp. 442–443; Sullivan & Miklas, 1985; Behrenberg, 1987).

Many forms of OJT training focus on exposure to developmental experiences. Job enrichment, job rotation and apprenticeships are such forms. Job enrichment, for example, gradually builds new duties or more challenging responsibilities into an employee's current position, allowing the person to acquire new skills while on the job.

Job rotation allows employees to gain experience at different kinds of narrowly defined jobs in the organizations. It is often used to give employees and future managers a broad background. One main advantage of job rotation is that it makes flexibility possible in the department. For example, when one member of a work unit is absent, another can perform that job. Usually, job rotation programs rotate employees through jobs at a similar level of difficulty. The extent of training and long-run benefits may be limited, however, because employees aren't in a job long enough to learn very much and may not be motivated to work hard because they know they will move on in the near future.

The philosophy of having employees learn while doing also underlie the use of developmental job assignments. However, with developmental assignments, employees are placed in a new job that presents significantly more difficult challenges. The assumption is that the process of learning to deal with the challenges will result in the employee developing new competencies. Components of a developmental job include:

- Unfamiliar responsibilities.
- Responsibility for creating change (e.g., to start something new, fix a problem, deal with problem employees).
- High levels of responsibility (e.g., high-stakes and high-visibility assignments; job involving many stakeholders, products, or units).
- Boundary-spanning requirements (e.g., working with important stakeholders outside the organization).
- Dealing with diversity (working with people from multiple cultures or demographic backgrounds) (McCauley, 1999).

Developmental assignments are also frequently used in management development efforts as described in Chapter 9.

Often the most informal program of training is supervisor assistance or mentoring. Supervisory assistance is a regular part of the supervisor's job. It includes day-to-day coaching, counseling, and monitoring employees on how to do the job and how to get along in the organization. The effectiveness of these techniques depends in part on whether the supervisor creates feelings and mutual confidence, provides opportunities for growth, and effectively delegates tasks.

Mentoring, in which an established employee guides the development of a less-experienced worker, or protégé, can increase employees' competencies, achievement, and understanding of the organization (Willis & Dubin, 1990; Schneer & Reitman, 1990; Greenhaus, Parasuraman, & Wormley, 1990; Murrell, Crosby, & Ely, 1999; Higgins & Kram, 2001). At AT&T for example, protégés are usually chosen from among high-potential employees in middle or entry-level management. Protégés are usually counseled by executives on how to advance and network in the organization, and they sometimes offer personal advice.

In recent years, more and more organizations and individuals have turned to coaches to discuss difficult situations as they arise and work through alternative scenarios for dealing with those situations. Coaching is typically used for employees and high-level executives who hold visible and somewhat unique jobs when traditional forms of on-the-job training are impractical. An effective coaching program helps managers change themselves and, in the process, change their organizations.

OJT training can save money, since it requires no special training equipment and makes a new hire at least partly productive right away. For mentoring, coaching, and buddy systems, however, these savings must be weighed against the lost productivity of the skilled person assigned to the trainee. For job enrichment and job rotation, the company must anticipate lowered productivity in whatever position the trainee holds. Quality of training can suffer unless an organization trains and develops the right employees and managers to serve as coaches and mentors, and selects the right experiences and skills to include in a job rotation or enrichment program.

Apprenticeship Training

An extension of OJT is apprenticeship training. With this method, individuals entering into an industry, particularly in the skilled trades such as machinist, laboratory technician, or electrician, are given thorough instruction and experience. Apprenticeship training is mandatory for admission to many skilled trades. It traditionally involves having the learner/apprentice study under the tutelage of a master craftsperson.[4] These programs are formally defined by the U.S. Department of Labor's Office of Apprenticeship Training, Employer and Labor Services (OATELS) and involve a written agreement. The bureau has established the following minimum standards for apprenticeship programs:

1. Full and fair opportunity to apply for an apprenticeship.
2. A schedule of work processes in which an apprentice is to receive training and experience on the job.
3. Organized instruction designed to provide apprentices with knowledge in technical subjects related to their trade (e.g., a minimum of 144 hours per year is normally considered necessary).
4. A progressively increasing schedule of wages.
5. Proper supervision of on-the-job training, with adequate facilities to train apprentices.
6. Periodic evaluation of the apprentice's progress, both in job performances and related instruction, with appropriate records maintained.
7. No discrimination in any phase of selection, employment, or training.

In the United States today, nearly 35,000 organizations have registered their programs with the U.S. Department of Labor's Bureau of Apprenticeship and Training. And the number of apprentices, including minorities, women, youth, and dislocated workers totals more than 350,000. (Approximately 66% of these are in construction and manufacturing industries.)

Although employee wages are typically less while the trainees are completing their apprenticeships, the method does provide compensation while individuals learn their trade. Registered apprenticeship programs range from one to six or more years in length. For the apprentice, this translates into an "industry scholarship" worth $40,000 to $150,000.

Somewhat less formalized and extensive are internship and assistantship programs. Internships are often part of an agreement between schools and colleges, and local organizations. As with apprenticeship training, individuals in these programs earn while they learn, but at a lower rate than that paid to full-time employees or master crafts workers. Internships are a source not only of training but also of realistic exposure to jobs and organizational conditions. Hewlett-Packard's internship program enables the company to evaluate college students and prepare them for future jobs.[5]

Assistantships involve full-time employment and expose an individual to a wide range of jobs. However, because the individual only assists other workers, the learning experience is often vicarious. This disadvantage is eliminated by HRD programs that combine job or position rotation with active mentoring and career management.

Electronic Performance Support Systems (EPSS)

People don't believe everything they learn. The same applies to training. Dell, for example, introduces about 80 new products per year, so it's unrealistic to expect Dell's technical support people to know everything about every product. Dell's training therefore focuses on providing its employees with the skills they need every day, such as Dell's rules, culture and values, and systems and work processes. Computer-based support systems then deliver the rest of what they need to know, when they need it. For example, when a customer calls about a specific technical problem, a computerized job aid helps walk the customer rep through the solution, question by question (Tyler, 2000). More will be said about this later.

Organizations have long used job aids of one sort or another. A job aid is a set of instructions, diagrams, or similar methods available at the job site to guide the worker (Blanchard & Thacker, 2002, p. 247). Job aids work particularly well on complex jobs that require multiple steps, or where it's dangerous to forget a step. Airline pilots use job aids (such as a checklist of things to do prior to takeoff). The General Motors Electromotive Division in Chicago gives workers job aids in the form of diagrams; these show, for example, where the locomotive wiring runs and which color wires go where.

Electronic performance systems (EPSS) are today's job aids. They are sets of computerized tools and displays that automate training, documentation, and phone support, integrate this automation into applications, and provide support that's faster, cheaper, and more effective than the traditional methods.[6]

When you call a Dell service representative about a problem with your new computer, she or he is probably asking questions that are prompted by an EPSS; it takes you both, step-by-step, through an analytical sequence. Without the EPSS, Dell would have to train its service reps to memorize an unrealistically large number of solutions.

Similarly, without EPSS, a new travel agent might require months of training, rather than days. At Apollo Travel Services, in Chicago, an EPSS guides travel agents' questions, and makes it harder to make mistakes. For example, when agents start to schedule an option that goes against a customer's established travel policies—such as booking managers to fly first class instead of coach—a dialogue box reminds the agent of the policy. It also asks him or her to choose from a list of appropriate reasons, if overriding the policy.[7]

On-Site, but Not on the Job

Training at the work site but not on the job is appropriate for required after-hours programs and for programs in which contact needs to be maintained with work units but OJT would be too distracting, or harmful. It's also appropriate for voluntary after-hours programs and for programs that update employees' competencies while allowing them to attend to their regular duties.

For example, when a Northwest grocery store chain switched to computerized scanners, it faced the problem of training thousands of checkers spread out across three states. The cost of training them off-site was prohibitive. Yet management also was fearful about training employees on the job, lest their ineptitude offend customers. To solve the problem, the grocery chain developed a mobile training van that included a vestibule model of the latest scanning equipment. Checkers were trained on-site but off the job in the mobile unit. Once the basic skill of scanning was mastered, employees returned to the store, and the trainer remained on-site as a resource person. According to one store manager, the program was effective because employees could be trained rapidly and efficiently, yet no customers were lost owing to checker error or slowness.

A growing trend in the United States is the development of corporate universities that offer programs tailored to the needs of the organization. Corporate universities focus on the education of employees and sometimes customers. McDonald's Hamburger University, begun in 1961, is among the oldest corporate universities. General Electric, an advocate of training and HRD for years, has an up-to-date facility in Croton-on-Hudson, New York, that it uses for divisional and group training. Today, many corporate colleges offer degrees, and hundreds of corporations offer courses leading to degrees. While not always the case, the executive programs at organizations may be under the direction of the chief learning officer (CLO) (Byrnes, 2000; Ward, 1996, p. 12; Raimy, 1997). More will be said about corporate universities and CLOs in Chapter 9.

Computer-Based Training

The rise of computers at work has not only increased the need for computer skills training, but also created new training formats. Computer-based training (CBT) or computer-assisted instruction is interactive, self-paced instruction using software teaching tools. In this situation a trainee sits at a personal computer and operates special training software.

CBT can take a variety of forms: Some employers have formed software libraries containing copies of different tutorial programs that trainees can check out to work on at home. Other companies have staffed computer labs where employees can drop by to practice, with personal assistance available if needed. Still other organizations conduct on-line training, installing learning software on workstation computers, which allows employees to switch back and forth between job applications and training programs as their workload demands.

CBT programs have real advantages. Interactive technologies (wherein trainees receive quick feedback) reduce learning time by an average of 50% (Miller, 1994, pp. 26, 30). They can also be cost-effective once designed and produced. Other advantages include instructional consistency (computers, unlike human trainers, don't have good days and bad days), mastery of learning (if the trainee doesn't learn it, she or he generally can't move to the next step), increased retention, and increased trainee motivation (resulting from responsive feedback).

CBT is increasingly interactive and realistic. For example, interactive multimedia training "integrates the use of text, video, graphics, photos, animation, and sound to produce a complex training environment with which the trainee interacts (Blanchard & Thacker, 2002, p. 248). In training a physician, for instance, an interactive multimedia training system lets a medical student take a hypothetical patient's medical history, conduct an examination, analyze lab tests, and then (by clicking the "examine chest" button) choose a type of chest examination and even hear the sounds of the person's heart. The medical student can then interpret the sounds and draw conclusions upon which to base a diagnosis. Virtual reality takes this realm a step further. Virtual reality "puts the trainee in an artificial three-dimensional environment that simulates events and situations that might be experienced on the job" (p. 248). Sensory devices transmit how the trainee is responding to the computer, and the trainee sees and feels and hears what is going on, assisted by special goggles and auditory and sensory devices (p. 249).

Programmed or Self-Instruction. Programmed instruction is an old on-site training method that has recently become the foundation for many computer-based training programs. Here, the instructional material is broken down into "frames." Each frame represents a small component of the entire subject to be learned, and each frame must be learned successfully before the next one can be tackled.

Self-instruction lets learners learn at their own-pace. Topics can range from the simple (vocabulary building) to the complex (strategic planning). Programmed instruction (PI) can be carried out by the use of computers or booklets, depending on the need. The method is to present a small amount of information, followed by a simple question that requires an answer on the part of the learner. There is immediate feedback for each response as the learner finds the answer on the next page or elsewhere. The learner knows whether he or she is right or wrong immediately. Since the program is designed to have a low error rate, the learner is motivated further. The main advantage to such an individualized problem is that it is self-pacing. For remedial instructions, enrichment material, or short segments, this method works well.

Relative to other training methods, self-instruction offers high mobility and flexibility: it can take place with or without instructors, in a wide variety of learning environments: learning centers, workstations, homes. It can use formats ranging from print texts, to instructional tapes to computers and interactive videodiscs. This flexibility minimizes the disruption to work schedules that training programs can often create. While trainers take a back seat to learners in self-instruction, such programs should have someone monitoring and tracking participants' progress.

Although the development of several authoring systems has eased the burden of developing programmed modules, instruction still must be carefully planned. It's estimated that 1 hour of programmed instruction requires 50 hours of development work. Consequently, this approach is effective only if canned programs (e.g., work processing and database tutorials) are used or if large numbers of employees are to be trained so that development costs for an original program can be justified. The use of intranets for delivering training makes widespread use of programmed instruction much more practical today than it was when it was first introduced several years ago (Bernstein, 2001; Industry Report, 1998).

Off the Job

When the consequences of error are high, it's usually more appropriate to conduct raining off the job. Most airline passengers would readily agree that it's preferable to train pilots in flight simulators rather than have them apprentice in the cockpit of a plane. Similarly, it's usually useful to have a bus driver practice on an obstacle course before taking to the roads with a load of school children.

Off-the-job training is also appropriate when complex competencies need to be mastered or when employees need to focus on specific interpersonal competencies that might not be apparent in the normal work environment. The costs of off-the-job training are high. One cause for concern is that knowledge learned off the job may not transfer to the workplace.

Classroom Training Approaches

Classroom training approaches are conducted outside of the normal work setting. In this sense, a classroom can be any training space set away from the work site, such as the organization cafeteria or meeting room. Although many organizations capitalize on whatever usable space they have available to conduct training sessions, larger organizations like Motorola, Pillsbury and McDonald's maintain facilities that serve as freestanding training centers (e.g., often referred to as corporate universities).

Conducting training away from the work setting has several advantages over on-the-job training. First, classroom settings permit the use of a training technique, such as video/DVD lecture, discussion, role-playing, and simulation. Second, the environment can be designed or controlled to minimize distractions and create a climate conducive to learning. Third, classroom settings can accommodate larger numbers of learners than the typical on-the-job setting, allowing for more efficient delivery of training. On the other hand, two potential disadvantages of classroom methods, as a group, include increased costs (such as travel and the rental or purchase and maintenance of rooms and equipment) and dissimilarity to the job setting, making transfer of training more difficult. Research has shown that the more dissimilar the training environment is to the actual work environment, the less likely trainees will be to apply what they learn to their jobs. For example, the transfer-of-knowledge problem is minimal when trainees work with machines that are comparable to the ones in their actual work environment. However, it may be difficult to apply teamwork competencies learned during a wilderness survival program to a management job in a large service organization (Burke & Baldwin, 1999).

Classroom Lectures. Classroom lectures are used in many organizations to impart information to trainees. Classroom lectures are oral presentations covering particular topics and concepts. Lectures can last an entire class period and are ideal for presenting large amounts of information to groups. Lecturettes are short lectures lasting less than 15 minutes. Lectures have several advantages. It is a quick and simple way to provide knowledge to large groups of trainees, as when the sales force needs to learn the special features of a new product. The HRD professional could use written materials instead, but they may require considerably more production expense and won't encourage the give-and-take questioning that lectures do.

The lecture method has been widely criticized, particularly because it emphasizes one-way communication. It has been suggested that the lecture method perpetuates the traditional authority structure of organizations, thus promoting negative behavior (such as passivity and boredom), and it is poorly suited for facilitating transfer of training and individualized training (Korman, 1971; Middendorf & Kalish, cited in Werner & DeSimone, 2006). Similarly, although a skilled lecturer may effectively communicate conceptual knowledge to trainees who are prepared to receive it, the lecture has little value in facilitating attitudinal and behavioral changes (Bass & Vaughn, 1966). Trainees must be motivated to learn because, when it is used alone, the lecture method does not elicit audience responses.

A related disadvantage of the lecture method is the lack of sharing of ideas among the trainees. Without dialogue, the trainees may not be able to put things into a common perspective that makes sense to them. Also, many people claim to dislike the lecture method.

Further research is needed to identify conditions under which the lecture method is effective as well as ways to improve its effectiveness. At present, two points are clear. First, interesting lectures promote greater learning than dull lectures. HRD professionals should make every effort to make their lectures as interesting as possible. Some experienced trainers have argued that younger workers (i.e., those under thirty) are especially likely to tune out lectures that they perceive to be uninteresting or irrelevant (Zemke, Raines, & Filipczak, 1999). Second, there are advantages to supplementing the lecture with other methods (including question-and-answer sessions, discussions, video, and role playing), particularly when abstract or procedural material is to be presented. For example, a video could complement the discussion by providing realistic examples of the lecture material. These combinations can increase two-way communication and facilitate greater interaction with the material. In the end, while some view lectures as boring and ineffective training methods, studies suggest that they can in fact be quite effective (Winfred et al., 2003).

Discussion Method. The discussion method involves more interchange (i.e., two-way communication) and less structure than other oral instructional methods. Discussions encourage participants and trainers to freely exchange knowledge, ideas, and opinions on a particular subject. Given this dynamic, the discussion method can overcome some of the limitations of the straight lecture approach. A common maxim for discussion facilitators is, "Never do for the group what it is doing for itself" (Werner & DeSimone, 2006, p. 202). However, the success of this method is dependent upon the ability of the trainer to initiate and manage class discussion by asking one or more of the following questions:

- Direct questions can be used to illustrate or produce a very narrow response (e.g., Who are the key players in this case?)
- Reflective questions can be used to mirror what someone else has said to make sure the message was received as intended (e.g., So are you saying that you think this manager failed to connect her actions to the goals and strategies of the organization?).
- Open-ended questions can be used to challenge the trainees to increase their understanding of a specific topic (e.g., But if what this manager did was effective, why are there so many problems, as described at the end of the case?).

Management discussion goes beyond questioning participants. The HRD professional must ensure that trainees are reinforced for their responses. The HRD professional must also act as a gatekeeper, giving everyone an opportunity to express their point of view and not letting the discussion be dominated by a few vocal participants. Managing discussion in large training classes can be difficult. Not only are the opportunities for an individual to participate reduced in a large group, some participants feel intimidated and be reluctant to get involved. Dividing the class into smaller groups, which can then share their ideas with other groups, can increase the opportunity for discussion. Discussions work well when the information presented can be applied in different ways. Discussions also give trainers feedback on how employees are using the knowledge or skills they have learned.

There are several limitations of the discussion method. First, a skilled facilitator is needed to manage the discussion process. Skill in facilitating a discussion is not something that one acquires quickly; skilled facilitators have generally practiced extensively and prepared thoroughly before leading a discussion. Second, sufficient time must be available for meaningful discussion to take place. Third, trainees need to have a common reference point for meaningful discussion to occur. Assigning reading material before the discussion session can help overcome this obstacle.

Adequate time, motivation, and resources must be available for this method to work effectively, which is true of all training methods. In the end, a well-done discussion is more interesting and energizing than a traditional lecture.

Case Study Method

The case study method helps trainees learn analytical and problem-solving skills by presenting a story (called a case) about people in an organization who are facing a problem or decision. Case studies use factual, real-life or fictional events to illustrate organizational problems and issues. Case studies can be presented through lecture, film, or video, but most case studies are written and handed out as course materials. Participants read the case study and use what they have learned in the program to analyze the situation.

A case study can involve guided analysis, with formal questions prepared by the instructor for individuals or groups to answer. More challenging case studies use a less structured format and exercise two types of problem-solving skills: (1) Diagnostic analyses ask trainees to identify the underlying cause of a particular problem. Prescriptive analyses require learners to figure out solutions to a particular problem. (2) Case studies tie course concepts and skills into practical situations. This link, along with the chance to exchange ideas and practice problem-solving, enhances trainees' interest and involvement in the program. HRD professionals can use this technique for either individual or small-group instruction. However, case studies often are complicated and work best when trainees have good analytical reasoning abilities. When presented in a written format, case studies also require that trainees possess well-developed verbal communication and reading comprehension skills.

Although cases vary in complexity and detail, trainees should be given enough information to analyze the situation and recommend their own solutions. In solving problems, trainees are generally required to use a rational problem-solving process that includes:

- restating important facts;
- drawing inferences from the facts;
- stating the problem or problems;
- developing alternative solutions and then stating the consequences of each;
- determining and supporting a course of action.

Proponents of the case study method argue that this form of problem solving within a management setting offers illustrations of the concepts learners are expected to learn and use, improves communication skills, and facilitates the linkage between theory and practice (Osigweh, 1986–1987). Proponents also claim that cases allow learners to discuss, share, and debate the merits of different inferences, problems, and alternative courses of action. Such insight can help learners to develop better analytical skills and improve their ability to integrate new information (Barnes, Christensen, & Hansen, 1994; Naumes & Naumes, 1999; Wasserman, 1994).

The case study method also has vigorous critics who argue that it can cause groupthink, focuses too much on the past, limits the teaching role of the trainer, reduces the learner's ability to draw generalizations, reinforce passivity on the part of the learner, and promotes the quantity of interaction among students at the expense of the quality of interaction (Osigweh, 1986–1987). Other critics claim that cases often lack realistic complexity and a sense of immediacy, and inhibit development of the ability to collect and distill information (Andrews & Noel, 1986). In addition, trainees may get caught up in the details of the situation, at the expense of focusing on the larger issues and concepts they are trying to learn.

To overcome these limitations, the trainer should make expectations clear and provide guidance when needed. In addition, the HRD professional must effectively guide the discussion portion of the case study to ensure trainees have an opportunity to explore differing assumptions and positions they have taken and the rationale for what constitutes effective responses to the case. The point in discussing cases is not necessarily to find the "right" solutions, but to be able to provide a reasoned and logical rationale for developing a course of action. Variations in the case method have also been proposed (Argyris, 1986). One such variation, called a living case, has trainees analyze a problem they and their organization are current facing (Andrews & Noel, 1986).

Osigweh (1986–1987) encourages potential users of the case study method to match factors such as:

- Specific instructional objectives.
- Objectives of the case approach.
- Attributes of the particular incident or case (i.e., its content).
- Characteristics of the learner.
- Instructional timing.
- General prevailing environment (class size, course level, etc.)
- The teacher's own personal and instructional characteristics (p. 131).

Business Games and Simulations

Like the case method, business games are intended to develop or refine problem-solving and decision-making skills. Games are one of the most creative and enjoyable training methods. Most training games have competition (either individual or group), "playing rules," and a designated finish time or final score. These games simulate competition engaged in by departments or other organizations. At least two teams, each of which represents an organization, make decisions concerning, their company's operation. Decisions can be made about production, marketing, finance, human resource utilization, and other challenges. Decisions are based on a set of specified economic theories, presented as a model of the economy.

Some simple management games are not based on analyzing complex problems. Instead, emphasis is placed on making good judgments in a minimum amount of time, based on specific problems and limited rules. In simple games, effective strategies can be reached without making too many decisions and without having to use large amounts of managerial know-how. These management games may oversimplify business relationships and give the impression that running a company can be easy—when, in fact, even the simplest management decisions require the consideration of many factors. When the model is fairly simple, a referee can be responsible for calculating outcomes.

When the model is complex, a computer may be used. The game can be continuous: Teams receive all or part of the results of their decisions on which they make new decisions, thus continuing the game. As learning activities, games offer a number of advantages. They add variety and zest to training programs, and get learners actively involved. They allow trainees to acquire knowledge, practice and apply skills, review materials, and ultimately, achieve course objectives. They are versatile and easily incorporated into different types of training, whether an instructor-led classroom course or a computer-based instructional program.

While games can enhance training by making learning fun, they will only waste time unless HRD professionals relate these exercises to course objectives. After the game has ended, an HRD professional should review what happened during the game, have participants say what they learned, and ask trainees how they can apply this learning to their jobs.

Particularly effective in training are simulations. Simulations are training tools that attempt to replicate the actual job duties and/or working environment. They vary from simple and inexpensive to highly complex and costly designs. Organizations often use simulations when the information to be mastered is complex, the equipment used on the job is expensive, and/or the cost of a wrong decision is quite high.

The airline industry has long used simulators to train pilots. Flight simulations often include motion in addition to visual and auditory realism. This aspect substantially increases the cost of the simulation but makes the training even more realistic. Another type of simulation confronts trainee doctors with an accident victim arriving at the emergency. The trainees choose from a menu of options, with the patient dying if the decision is delayed too long or is incorrect.

Traditionally, simulators have been considered separate from CBT with recent advances in multimedia technology, however, the distinctions between these two methods have blurred considerably. In fact, as the technology develops, simulators are becoming more affordable, and hence accessible, for a wider range of organizations.

In-baskets, one of the least expensive simulations, consist of nothing more than the incoming materials, all demanding action, that might get deposited daily on a manager's or secretary's desk. The goal of this technique is to assess the learner's ability to establish priorities, plan, gather relevant information, and make decisions. The sequence of events involved in an in-basket exercise typically includes the following:

1. The learners are told that they have been promoted to a management position that was suddenly vacated. They are given background information about the organization including personnel, relationships, policies, and union contracts.
2. The learners then receive the contents of the manager's in-basket. This material includes documents such as telephone messages, notes, memos, letters, and reports.
3. The learners are then asked to read, organize, prioritize, and make decisions regarding the issues presented by the in-basket material.

4. At the end of the decision period, the learners' decisions are then evaluated by trained scorers.

The object of this technique is to force learners to make decisions in the allotted time period. Because there is usually insufficient time to read each document and respond, the learners must make quick and accurate decisions. The learners are evaluated not only on the quality of their decisions but also on their ability to prioritize and to deal effectively with all the critical documents.

A common simulation technique for nonmanagers is the vestibule method briefly referred to earlier, which simulates the environment of the individual's actual job. Because the environment isn't real, it's generally less hectic and safer than the actual environment; as a consequence, learners may have trouble adjusting from the learning environment to the actual environment. Vestibule training, on the other hand, involves setting up a classroom that reproduces the equipment and work environment, whether an assembly line, switchboard, or city block, found on the job. For certain positions, such as nuclear power plant operator or airline pilot, where the consequences of mistakes could destroy costly machinery or endanger lives, learners use "simulators" that imitate the functions performed by actual equipment.

With the exception of OJT, simulations are the most realistic and relevant training technique. Unlike on-the-job training, however, simulations allow learners time to practice skills, receive feedback, and engage in trial-and-error learning—without the embarrassment, cost, time pressures, or other negative consequences of making mistakes while performing a job. Not all organizations, even in the same industry, accept these arguments. Some banks, for example, train their tellers on the job, whereas others train them in a simulated bank environment.

Demonstrations, Behavior Modeling and Role Plays

Demonstrations are visual instructional techniques: The instructor performs the behavior or skills to be learned, and the trainees learn by watching. Modeling takes demonstrations one step further by having trainees learn by doing, not just by watching. First, the trainer demonstrates the desired performance, and then participants model the skill or behavior. The trainer provides feedback to trainees, with additional modeling and practice as needed. Behavior modeling is widely used for interpersonal skill training and is a common component of many management training programs.

Research has shown behavior modeling to be an effective training technique. It is described in greater detail in our discussion of management development in Chapter 9.

Role-plays are the most sophisticated of these three instructional methods. Role-playing generally focuses on understanding and managing relationships rather than facts. Trainees are presented with an organizational situation, assigned a role or character in the situation, and asked to act out the role with one or more other trainees. The role-play should offer trainees an opportunity for self-discovery and learning. In many organizations, the role episode is videotaped, as discussed earlier, which allows for better feedback and self-observation.

Although self-discovery and opportunity to practice interpersonal skills are outcomes of role-playing, this method does have some limitations. First, some learners may feel intimidated by having to act out a character (and possibly be videotaped doing so). HRD professionals should take sufficient time in introducing the exercise, explaining the process in detail, and most of all, emphasizing how participation will help each trainee to better understand and apply different interpersonal skills.

All three techniques can be used in either one-on-one or group instruction. Each method can enhance training by illustrating how to apply instruction in practice. Demonstrations are ideal for basic skills training, while role-playing works well for building complex behaviors, such as interpersonal or management skills. Of the three tools, demonstrations are the least threatening to trainees, since they are not called upon to perform themselves. Modeling and role-plays, on the other hand, allow HRD professionals to assess participants' skill levels and to make sure that learners can apply what they have seen.

Wilderness Trips and Outdoor Training

To increase employees' feelings about the here and now and raise their self-esteem, organizations sometimes use programs that involve physical feats of strength, endurance, and cooperation. Frequently, such programs include either low ropes or high ropes elements. A low ropes course typically has limited physical risks, whereas high ropes courses typically have higher perceived risks. Low ropes courses can also be conducted indoors. These programs can also be implemented on wilderness trips to the woods or mountains or water. Siemens, for example, dropped 60 managers from around the world onto the shores of Lake Starnberger, south of Munich, and gave them the task of building rafts using only logs, steel drums, pontoons, and rope. Among the rules for the exercise: No talking. The objective? To teach managers the importance of knowledge sharing. Back on the job, managers can earn bonuses for contributing their knowledge to Share-Net—the company's knowledge management software (Schinzler, 2001).

Whereas many organizations use some variation of outdoor experiences in their management training many other question the degree of transfer to the job that these experiences offer. Organizations using outdoor experiences recognize this concern and thus articulate the link between the competencies developed in the experiences and the competencies needed by the employees on the job. They also are sensitive to employee differences in order to ensure that these experiences can be accommodated to an increasingly diverse workforce (Brown, 1998; Pereira, 1997; Lawson, 1997; McEvoy & Buller, 1997; Patton, 1998). Given the current popularity of outdoor education, HRD professionals should ensure that proper assessment and evaluation are included in any such program that is offered.

SELECTING AND COMBINING METHODS

To choose the HRDmethod (or combination of methods) that best fits a given situation, HRD professionals should first define carefully what they wish to teach. That is the purpose of the needs assessment phase. Only then can those responsible for training choose a method that best fits these requirements. To be useful, the method should meet the minimal conditions needed for effective learning to take place; that is, the training method(s) should: motivate the trainee to improve his or her performance; clearly illustrate desired KSAOCs; allow the trainee to participate actively; provide an opportunity for practice; provide timely feedback on the trainee's performance; provide some means for reinforcement while the trainee learns; be structured from simple to complex tasks; be adaptable to specific problems; and encourage positive transfer from the training to the job.

As evidenced from the discussion to this point there are a wide variety of HRD methods, materials, and media from which to choose in designing and delivering training. Which HRD techniques best suit a particular program depends on course content and cost considerations. Most HRD initiatives can use multiple instructional methods and training aids.

Each of the methods described have certain advantages and disadvantages. As a result of the advantages and disadvantages of the various methods, HRD professionals can handle the tradeoffs in at least two ways. They can perform a systematic tradeoff analysis and choose the most appropriate HRD methodology. They can also combine HRD methods. It is apparent from the discussion of the HRD methods earlier that with a careful analysis, trainers should be able to combine different methods and come up with a more complete and efficient HRD system. This is in fact what many of those responsible for training are currently doing. In many cases HRD professionals will use several different techniques. For example, teaching supervisors how to give performance feedback may first begin with a lecture or overview of the performance appraisal process, followed by small-group discussions or videotapes depicting effective coaching, and then role-plays to have supervisors practice their feedback skills.

The decision of which HRD methods to use in HRD initiatives takes on a new dimension when framed by experiential learning theory and learning styles. For HRD professionals, the question of which HRD methods are best can be better answered when learning, the learning process, and individual learning styles are examined, as discussed in Chapter 2. Kolb's model of experiential learning provides a good theoretical basis for understanding this process and for developing and managing decisions on HRD methods (especially those that are experientially oriented). Clearly, cases, games, and simulations offer learners a rich and more robust view of the workplace environment than, for example, the traditional lecture, or programmed or computer-related methods. But it is also clear that even these methods have a place in the learning cycle. Today more than ever, HRD professionals must be willing to experiment with new technologies and new experiential methods in an effort to prepare organizational learners for an ever-changing workplace. Still, if our Internet, case, and simulation methods, for example, speak only to certain learners, all other learners will not benefit, but if the training and other HRD methods created move learners around the learning cycle, then all learners in a training or HRD initiative will find value in the effort.

It is clear that there is still much to learn about the effectiveness of training methods. Whether HRD professionals use one or a combination of training or HRD methods, a basic understanding of the learning process may be as important as an understanding of the needs assessment that drives training or any other HRD initiative.

When designing training or any other HRD initiative in the future, HRD professionals must work under a new "learning paradigm," where the design of learning initiatives is learner centered and controlled, and essentially experiential, while continuing to replace the "old learning paradigm" where learning, for example in training, are trainer and content centered. HRD professionals must make the important changes in thinking and behavior affecting the design of HRD and the methods they use to enhance learning, the roles both they and learners fulfill, and their expectations regarding learning outcomes. In conclusion, HRD professionals must realize the importance of emphasizing a "designing to learn" focus in all their future HRD efforts.

CONCLUSION

This chapter described a number of training and HRD methods available to HRD professionals in implementing HRD initiatives. There are advantages and disadvantages to all of the methods. Each method has a number of techniques appropriate for particular situations. HRD professionals need to select the best combination of methods that will maximize trainee learning. Technology will continue to have a major impact on the delivery of training and an increase in more state-of-the-art methods available to HRD professionals. However, having state-of-the-art instructional technology should not be the guiding force in choosing a training or HRD method. The specific training method(s) used should be based on the HRD objective.

NOTES

1. L. R. Yin, "Learning Pyramid," as cited in J. M. Werner and R. L. DeSimone, *Human Resource Development* (4th ed.), (Mason,, OH: Thompson/Southwester, 2006).
2. Yin, "Learning Pyramid"
3. M. Schneider, "GM Gives on-line Learning a Boost," Businessweek Online, http://www.businessweek.com/bwdaily/dnflash/apr2001/.
4. "German Training Imported," *BNA Bulletin to Management*, (December 19, 1996), p. 408.
5. "Internships Provide Workplace Snapshot: Policy Guide," *Bulletin to Management*, 48(21), (May 22, 1997), pp. 168; "Personnel Shop Talk," *Bulletin to Management*, 48(21), (May 22, 1997), pp. 162.
6. C. Marion, "What Is the EPSS Movement and What Does It Mean to Information Designers?" http:www.checo.com/~cmarion/pcd/epssimplications.html.
7. http://www.epss.com/lb/casestud/casestud.htm.

CHAPTER 6

EVALUATING HRD INITIATIVES

INTRODUCTION

More and more organizations are investing millions of dollars in training and HRD programs to gain a competitive advantage. As a result of their investments in developing and administering their training and HRD initiatives, organizations are increasingly interested in also evaluating their efforts. That is, organizations are most interested in documenting the impact of training and HRD interventions on the strategic direction of organizations. Examining the outcomes of a training program or HRD intervention helps in evaluating its effectiveness. These outcomes should be related to the program and broader organizational objectives.

Why should training and HRD programs be evaluated?

1. To identify the program's strengths and weaknesses. This includes determining whether the program is meeting the learning objectives, the quality of the learning environment, and whether transfer of training to the job is occurring.
2. To assess whether the content, organization, and administration of the program (including the schedule, accommodations, trainers, and materials) contribute to learning and the use of HRD content on the job.
3. To identify which trainees benefitted most or least from the program.

4. To gather marketing data by asking participants whether they would recommend the program to others, why they attended the program, and their level of satisfaction with the program.
5. To determine the financial benefits and costs of the program.
6. To compare the costs and benefits, for example, of training to non-training investments (such as work redesign or better employee selection).
7. To compare the costs and benefits of different HRD programs to choose the best program.

Walgreens is a good example of an organization that has recognized the importance of their training and HRD efforts based on evaluation data. A Walgreens training course for new technicians was developed to replace on-the-job training they received from the pharmacists who hired them. The course involved 20 hours of classroom training and 20 hours of supervision on the job. Because the company has seven thousand stores, large amounts of money and time were invested in the training, so the company decided to evaluate the program.

The evaluation consisted of comparing technicians who had completed the program with some who had not. Surveys about new employees' performance were sent to the pharmacists who supervised the technicians. Some questions related to speed of entering patient and drug data into the store computer and how often the technician offered customers generic drug substitutes. The results showed that formally trained technicians were more efficient and wasted less of the pharmacist's time than those who received traditional on-the-job training. Sales in pharmacies with formally trained technicians exceeded sales in pharmacies with on-the-job-trained technicians by an average of $9,500 each year (Gerber, 1995).

This chapter takes a look at the various forms of evaluating HRD initiatives. The chapter discusses barriers to evaluating HRD initiatives as well as the objectives and benefits of undertaking HRD initiatives. Next, the chapter focuses on the implications of the availability of resources and constraints for completing evaluations of HRD efforts. The discussion then turns to various evaluation design options available to HRD professionals before discussing Kilpatrick's four-level evaluation model, Phillips' expansion of the Kilpatrick model, a model for designing HRD initiatives with an accompanying evaluation component, and other considerations important to HRD evaluation efforts. A more detailed discussion of how to evaluate HRD initiatives using the Kilpatrick four-level model is provided prior to concluding the chapter with the introduction of an HRD evaluation checklist for HRD professionals to use in completing their HRD evaluations.

CHANGING EVALUATION EMPHASES

It has been suggested that efforts at training evaluation have moved through the following four stages since the 1960s:

1. Stage One focuses on anecdotal reactions from trainers and program participants. Judging from the survey results cited earlier, it appears that many organizations still operate at this level (Saari et al., 1988).
2. Stage Two involves experimental methodology from academic (including time, resources, and the inability to randomly select participants or use control groups that receive no training) make application of these designs difficult, thus discouraging evaluation efforts.
3. Stage Three creatively matches the appropriate research methodology to existing organizational constraints, thus making program evaluation more practical and feasible.
4. Stage Four recognizes that the entire training and HRD process affects the organization, and shifts the focus of evaluation from postprogram results to the entire HRD process (Goldstein, 1980).

Finding ways to perform effective evaluation serves all parties: the organization, the trainer or HRD professional, and the trainees. However, there still continues to be resistance to undertaking evaluations of learning initiatives.

BARRIERS TO EVALUATING LEARNING INITIATIVES

It is difficult to understand why the rigorous evaluation of HRD interventions are not automatically incorporated at their inception. There are a number of reasons including: (see, Sims, 1998; Dionne, 1996; Grove & Ostroff, 1990).

1. *Evaluation of HRD initiatives means different things to different people.* There does not seem to be a consistent definition of what HRD evaluation is among HRD professionals.
2. *Top management does not usually require evaluation.* Frequently top management seems ready to take on faith that certain HRD initiatives are valuable. Moreover, top leaders reward their HRD professional staff for merely staying current with the latest learning fads. When funding is good, top leadership appears to have no problem embracing the value of most learning efforts. Further, when a needs assessment implies that training in certain areas is "good to do," it

appears to be especially easy for top management to rest assured that things are being done properly by HRD professionals and others responsible for HRD.

3. *There is no perceived need by those responsible for HRD.* It is easy for HRD professionals to believe that they have spent so much time and effort in design, usability studies, etc., that it is clear that the learning effort works. They simply don't feel that evaluation needs to be done—a common and easy trap. Part of the problem is that it isn't necessarily an explicit belief of which a person is aware. It is implicit, and only manifested by a variety of excuses, such as it would just be a waste of time and money, "I would only find out what I already know," and so forth.

4. *Most senior-HRD executives (and other staff) do not know how to go about evaluating learning initiatives.* Evaluation of learning is a complex procedure. Most people simply do not know how to evaluate learning efforts properly.

5. *Senior-level HRD managers and staff do not know what to evaluate.* Many people are not clear on what questions should be answered by an evaluation. Should they focus on the number of key people who want to attend the program? The costs per trainee? The degree of enjoyment expressed by trainees? Changes back on the job? A major contributor to this problem is a lack of clear learning objectives.

6. *The serious evaluation of training and HRD in organizations is a difficult task that is perceived as costly and risky.* There are two forces acting on HRD professionals that work against evaluation: cost and risk taking. Many HRD professionals would rather spend their limited funds on developing new and highly visible learning offerings that hopefully will be seen favorably by top management rather than spending scarce dollars on evaluation. The risk with evaluation is that the results may show that an HRD program that top management and others like is not attaining the objectives for which it was designed.

7. *HRD professionals don't have the resources (time, money, personnel, etc.).* This may be because they failed to include this item in the budget, budgets were cut, there were unforseen expenses, time ran short, or any other number of reasons.

8. *HRD professionals (or clients) perceive that they don't have the resources.* For example, HRD professionals may move onto other "critical" projects that have a higher priority than evaluation of the project just completed. They could make the time, but they perceive that relative to other needs, they don't have the time (or money).

9. *HRD professionals don't want to know.* HRD professionals who champion a learning initiative may feel threatened by the prospect of an

objective evaluation of the initiative's effectiveness. Sometimes, unconsciously, HRD professionals simply don't want to know the results of a final evaluation. This is most often the case when they are consciously or unconsciously aware of the fact that they have had to make compromises; they haven't had the resources or time to do the evaluation the way they would have liked. This reason for not performing evaluation is almost always implicit, outside of our awareness.

10. *Attention to evaluation in the design of learning initiatives.* The design, development, and implementation of learning efforts have not always followed logical steps, leaving efforts to evaluate results futile and inconclusive.
11. *Lack of standards.* There is a lack of standards for judging the success of learning efforts. Unfortunately, generally accepted evaluation standards have not been developed for the field of HRM in general and HRD in particular.
12. *A learning effort changes hands.* The learning design team delivers the initiative to an outside vendor (i.e., a company or academic institution). The HRD professionals are done with it, and it is now in the hands of another party. It becomes a question of ownership, and responsibility. Who is responsible for determining the effectiveness of the learning initiative (i.e., does it add value and help achieve the organization's strategic objectives?)? Often it is the client or outside vendor who receives the learning program, who is implicitly responsible for doing the evaluation. But generally they don't feel that they should, they don't know how, or they don't have the time.

The following actions can be used by HRD professionals to counteract barriers to HRD evaluation (see, Sims, 1998; Wexley & Latham, 1991b):

1. Make sure HRD efforts are connected to a specific project, initiative or result. It's often best to link HRD to a specific project and as close to roll-out as possible. Do just-in-time and results-based HRD.
2. To be effective, evaluation should be planned as one or more steps in program design. These steps should focus on planning the evaluation scheme, collecting data, analyzing data, interpreting the results, and communicating them to appropriate stakeholder audiences.
3. Top-level executives need to be educated on the importance of rigorous evaluation and the dangers of taking on faith that a certain learning strategy is worthwhile.
4. HRD managers and their staffs need to be taught the "how to's" of HRD evaluation. They need to be given hands-on HRD where they

are shown how to design questionnaires, use the correct experimental design, statistically analyze data, and calculate utility.
5. HRD managers and top-level leadership need to discuss and determine what exactly needs to be evaluated and why. Learning efforts need to be incorporated into the organization's strategic agenda. It is important that the organization's overall HRM and HRD strategies are aligned.
6. If top management really wants to reinforce rigorous evaluation, it needs to make it clear to the HRD professionals that a certain proportion of the training and HRD budget should be targeted to evaluation.
7. The risk-taking component of evaluation needs to be minimized by rethinking the purpose of evaluation. Rather than thinking of evaluation as a live or die decision for a learning initiative, evaluation needs to be thought of as a way of finding out if there's anything wrong with the program and, if there is, correcting it.
8. Examine the cost of evaluation when compared to the perceived value derived from the process. In some cases, an evaluation may not be worth the added cost.
9. Develop and adopt acceptable performance measures, standards, and indices for training and HRD and report the results publicly or through benchmarking projects.

A critical ingredient that should not be missing in any HRD area is a focus on continuous improvement—*kaizen*, as the Japanese refer to it. Past performance is no benchmark for the future, and HRD professionals must see the evaluation of learning efforts as a continuous improvement tool. However, as noted earlier in many instances HRD professionals may be too focused, for example, on the content of training, fixed training goals and standards and tend to be more concerned with their performance compared with the past than their ability to evaluate their current training and HRD activities.

HRD professionals make a fatal error if they persist in not taking a proactive approach in evaluating *all* of their HRD efforts. That is, those activities that fall under the umbrella of HRD should be perceived as moving targets that continuously stretch the HRD area to do better. The challenge to these HRD professionals in organizations is to be sure that they are continuously updating their HRD efforts and performance. This keeps the emphasis on continuous improvement in HRD through evaluation where it should be. The next section discusses the objectives and benefits of HRD evaluation.

HRD EVALUATION OBJECTIVES AND BENEFITS

The primary and overriding objectives of the evaluation of learning initiatives should be to collect data that will serve as a valid basis for improving the learning system and maintaining quality control over its components. It must be emphasized that *all* components of the system and their interaction are the objects of scrutiny and that HRD professionals should ensure that learning initiatives are designed with *a priori* consideration given to evaluation. That is, HRD professionals should be committed to evaluating the effectiveness of their initiatives. Several potential benefits result from evaluating learning efforts are:

1. Improved accountability and cost effectiveness for learning initiatives which might result in an increase in resources.
2. Improved effectiveness (Are initiatives producing the results which they were intended?).
3. Improved efficiency (Are the initiatives producing the results for which they were intended with a minimum waste of resources?).
4. Greater credibility for the HRD professionals to include information on how to do a better job now or in future initiatives or to redesign current or future initiatives;
5. Stronger commitment to and understanding of HRD by key executives and managers so they can make up for deficiencies and confirm/disconfirm subjective feelings about the quality of organizational HRD.
6. Formal corrective feedback system for developing strengths and weaknesses of learning participants. Learners that understand the experience more fully and are more committed to the initiative.
7. Leaders better able to determine whether to send potential recruits to future learning initiatives.
8. Quantifiable data for organizational researchers and HRD initiative developers interested in learning research.
9. Increased visibility and influence for learning initiative sponsors.
10. Increased knowledge and expertise in the development and implementation of learning initiatives that produce the results for which they were intended.

This is not an exhaustive list of the objectives and benefits of evaluating HRD initiatives, however, HRD professionals must continually ask themselves what are the objectives of evaluation, and what do they want to gain by conducting an evaluation.

A priori consideration of evaluation gives the HRD professional at least five important advantages:

1. The ability to identify relevant audiences, interested in training and HRD evaluation, early in the process to ensure that evaluation feedback addresses their interests and information needs.
2. The development of an evaluation process that complements the learning initiative. Evaluative methods can be carefully incorporated to minimize any disruptive effects on the learning initiative.
3. The ability to construct a research design that allows for valid conclusions about the initiative's effectiveness. This includes finding appropriate pre-measures, selecting appropriate groups or individuals to train and develop, identifying comparison groups, and isolating extraneous variables prior to beginning HRD efforts.
4. The ability to delineate material, data, and HRM and HRD requirements for evaluation and incorporating these as part of the learning initiative, not simply as an appendix to the learning initiative.
5. The ability to modify the learning initiative based on feedback gained through ongoing evaluation. Corrective feedback is crucial when modifying or upgrading subsequent stages of the learning initiative. Thus, HRD professionals committed to evaluation can enjoy benefits and advantages that have long been sacrificed in HRD designs without evaluation.

HRD EVALUATION RESOURCES AND CONSTRAINTS

Another important key to the success of evaluations of HRD interventions depends on the extent to which the HRD professionals can overcome problems through a methodologically sound design and implementation scheme. The evaluation plan should be developed through selection of alternatives assessed against the objectives of the evaluation and existing constraints and resources. A familiarity with available resources, imposing constraints, and methodological alternatives will allow accurate, useful, and practical learning program evaluations.

As noted in our discussion in Chapter 4 on designing HRD initiatives, HRD professionals must also pay particular attention to the availability of resources and constraints for such learning initiative evaluation endeavors. Resources are needed to evaluate learning initiatives. Constraints can limit evaluation effectiveness. Both are considerations in selecting evaluation methods and procedures. For example, time is a constraint for most training evaluations and is often perceived as one of the major barriers to conducting training evaluations. The time available for collecting, analyzing, and reporting evaluation results is limited. This influences not only procedures for data collection and analysis, but also the type of data collected. Time may not permit development of tailored survey instruments for collecting reaction data and HRD professionals may turn to alternatives such as off-the-shelf questionnaires. Such a decision may reduce evaluation time, however, the evaluator may be constrained to measure what the instrument purports to measure, rather than variables of interest. Some resources/constraints issues are:

1. *Funding.* This refers to the dollars allotted to cover HRD evaluation planning and implementation.
2. *Time.* Evaluation can take place immediately or at periodic intervals after learners return to the job. A sequence of "milestones" can be used. This includes completion of pretest and post-test data collection, data analysis, and dissemination of results to appropriate audiences.
3. *Human resources.* Trained personnel such as statisticians, computer specialists, research methodologists, and other HRD professionals, can be resources in evaluation.
4. *Organizational climate.* Evaluation is facilitated or hampered by the level of trust and openness of executives, managers, employees, or participants. Do people seek, and are they receptive to, evaluative feedback?
5. *Availability of data.* Evaluation is improved by the availability and quality of organizational information. Examples are records of individual, group, department and organization performance, reports, and personnel HRD records. Data can be obtained from surveys, interviews, and observations of employees.
6. *Details of the learning evaluation action plan.* A good evaluation plan contains objectives, timetables, procedures, participants, locations, and possible use of strategies.
7. *Audiences.* The success of evaluation depends partly upon the information needs and interests of the key participants in the HRD process.
8. *Technical ability.* Evaluation requires the availability of standardized instruments, computerized analyses, stored data, logistics in collecting and disseminating results, and the abilities of persons involved.
9. *Ethical concerns.* Evaluations must recognize issues of privacy, employee and organizational confidentiality, obtrusiveness, and other harmful or illegal aspects of data collection and reporting.

To a large extent, these are interdependent factors to which the HRD professionals must attend during the training program and HRD intervention planning analysis.

HRD EVALUATION DESIGN OPTIONS

Upon identifying important learning outcome criteria, the organization's HRD professionals must select an experimental design to measure changes in these variables. The HRD professionals have to make choices about how to design the evaluation of learning to achieve valid results. For example, the key result is how to design the evaluation to show whether HRD did in fact produce the observed results. This is called *internal validity*; the secondary question of whether HRD would work similarly in other situations is referred to as *external validity*.

Designing a good evaluation effort involves knowing when to collect evaluation measures and which groups to collect them from. Together, these factors determine the experimental design used to assess the impact of learning initiatives. More specifically, the HRD evaluation design refers to the steps taken to ensure: (a) that a change occurred (e.g., employee productivity increased, accidents declined, etc.); (b) the change can be attributed to the training effort, for example; and (c) that a similar change could be expected if the training, for example, were done again with other employees.

Of course, the ability to make such statements will depend on the experimental rigor incorporated in the learning evaluation process. Conclusive statements about the effectiveness of a training program can be made only when the trainer strictly adheres to experimental principles such as manipulation of variables, random assignment, control of extraneous and/or confounding variables, and equivalence of groups. Unfortunately, conducting experimentation in the field has proven to be a difficult, almost overwhelming, task. Many organizations generally demand that all employees in a department be trained, not only those randomly selected. It is also difficult for HRD professionals to control the many variables that can affect a worker's job behavior at a given time (e.g., interaction with co-workers, supervisor, personal relationships, promotions, etc.). However, previous HRD program evaluations have been able to overcome these difficulties by using several highly effective designs for evaluating learning interventions.

Different evaluation designs can provide relatively weak or strong evidence about the effects of HRD activities. The three major categories of evaluation designs are nonexperimental, quasi-experimental, and experimental.

Experiments

The most rigorous evaluation designs are experimental designs. In a true experiment, employees split into two groups: the "treatment" group participates in the training or HRD activity being evaluated, and the "control" group does not participate. Employees in both groups are assessed at Time 1—for example, they are given a knowledge test or their levels of job performance are measured. Employees in the treatment group then experience the training and HRD activity (X). At Time 2, employees in both groups are assessed again. By comparing the responses of employees in the treatment and control groups at Time 1 and Time 2, the following questions can be answered with a high degree of certainty:

- Did a change take place from Time 1 to Time 2—for example, did employee productivity increase?
- Was the change caused by the training and HRD activity (x)? If the change occurred in both groups, then it cannot be explained by the training and HRD activity.

Quasi Experiments

As briefly alluded to earlier, organizations generally want all employees in a section trained, not just a few who are randomly selected. Consequently, they're more likely to use quasi-experimental designs, which do not involve randomly assigning employees to the treatment and control groups. Two quasi-experimental designs are: time series design and nonequivalent control group design. In the time-series design, several measures are taken before the treatment and several after. This design is easy to use and may require very little extra effort. For example, in many organizations job performance is regularly assessed. So, it is easy to compare the performance of employees before and after the training and HRD activity. The problem is that you cannot be certain that the training and HRD activity accounts for the change. A new reward system, seasonal changes, new equipment, and a variety of other changes may have occurred at about the same time as the training and HRD, and they may have caused the change in performance.

The nonequivalent control group design is similar to the experimental design, with one big difference. In this design employees are not randomly assigned to the treatment and control groups. Instead, employees in one location may be given training and then compared with employees at a different location. Or, if the training is voluntary, employees who chose to receive the training may be compared to those who did not. This is a practical design that allows for a comparison between those who did and did not receive training. But if a difference is found, you cannot be completely confident that the training caused it. For example, there may be many other differences between those who volunteered for the training and those who did not, and these differences may account for the change. Despite this drawback, the practicality of the nonequivalent control group design makes it a good choice.[1]

Nonexperiments

Unfortunately, in most organizations, experiments and quasi experiments are never conducted to evaluate training and HRD activities. Despite the huge investments made in these activities, most organizations do not know whether their investments really pay off. When evaluations are conducted, often they rely on the weakest design—namely nonexperiments. The two nonexperimental designs (one-shot case study design and one-group pretest-posttest design) are much simpler, far less costly, and far less time consuming than the other designs. But with ease and low cost come less accuracy and confidence in measuring change that may have been the result of a training program—or any other HRD program to produce change.

There is no one appropriate evaluation design (see, Carnevale & Schultz, 1990; Sackett & Mullen, 1993; Tannenbaum & Woods, 1992; Avery, Maxwell & Salas, 1992). Several factors need to be considered in choosing one:

- Size of the training program.
- Purpose of training.
- Implications if a training program does not work.
- Company norms regarding evaluation.
- Costs of designs and conducting an evaluation.
- Need for speed in obtaining program effectiveness information.

For example, if an HRD professional is interested in determining how much employees' communication skills have changed as a result of a behavior-modeling training program, a pretest/posttest comparison group design is necessary. Trainees should be randomly assigned to training and no-training conditions. These evaluation design features give the HRD professional a high degree of confidence that any communication skill change is the result of participating in the training program (Grove & Ostroff, 1991).

Evaluation designs without pretesting or comparison groups are most appropriate if the HRD professional is interested in identifying whether a specific level of performance has been achieved (for example, can employees who participated in behavior-modeling training adequately communicate their ideas?). In this situation the HRD professional is not interested in determining how much change has occurred.

Regardless of the design selected, HRD professionals must adhere to certain basic experimental principles. First, when possible, both pre and posttest data should be collected on relevant criteria. Second, selection of participants should be randomized when possible. If it is not possible, solid quasi-experimentation should be employed. Third, reliability of data collected should be monitored throughout the evaluation. Fourth, when statistical analyses are performed, characteristics of the sample and data should conform to the assumptions of tests used. Finally, the evaluation process (i.e., training, data collection and implementation) should be conducted in a manner to allow valid inferences about the effectiveness of training and HRD.

EVALUATION MODELS AND FRAMEWORKS

A model of evaluation outlines the criteria for and focus of the evaluation. Because an HRD initiative can be examined from a number of perspectives, it is important to specify which perspectives will be considered. Many different frameworks of HRD evaluation have been suggested (Werner & DeSimone, 2006). Two of the most widely used models to evaluate learning programs are Kirkpatrick's four-level model of program evaluation and Phillips work on measuring ROI. We will discuss Kirkpatrick's model first.

Kilpartick's Four-Level Evaluation Model

Kirkpatrick's four-level model is the most popular and influential framework for training evaluation. Kirkpatrick first advanced his four-step model of program evaluation in the late 1950s. It has since become common to refer to the steps as "levels." Kirkpatrick argues that training efforts can be evaluated according to four criteria: reaction, learning, job behavior, and results.

1. Participant reaction (Level 1)—measuring participants' satisfaction with the program as well as their stated intentions to take future action based on what they have learned. The critical question asked at this level is: Did the trainees like the program and feel it was valuable? At this level, the focus in on the trainees' perceptions about the program and its effectiveness. This is useful information. Positive reactions to a training program may make it easier to encourage employees to attend future programs. But if trainees did not like the program or think they didn't learn anything (even if they did), they may discourage others from attending and may be reluctant to use

the skills or knowledge obtained in the program. The main limitation of evaluating HRD programs at the reaction level is that this information cannot indicate whether the program met its objectives beyond ensuring participant satisfaction.

2. Participant learning (Level 2)—measuring participants' changes in skills, knowledge, or attitudes. The critical question asked at this level is: Did the trainees learn what the HRD objectives said they should learn? This is an important criterion that an effective HRD program should satisfy. Measuring whether someone has learned something in training may involve a quiz or test—clearly a different method from assessing the participants' reaction to the program.

3. Application of participants' learning on the job (Level 3)—measuring changes in participants' behavior or application of practices transferred from the program back to the job setting. The critical questions asked at this level is: Does the trainee use what was learned in training back on the job? In addition to focusing on training transfer this is also a critical measure of training success. There are many examples of trainees who have learned how to do something but choose not to. If learning does not transfer to the job, the training effort cannot have an impact on employee or organizational effectiveness. Measuring whether training has transferred to the job requires observation of the trainee's on-the-job behavior or viewing organizational records (e.g., reduced customer complaints, a reduction in scrap rate).

4. Results (Level 4)—measuring the impact of changes resulting from learning in the program in terms of specific organizational results. The critical questions asked at this level are: Has the training or HRD effort improved the organization's effectiveness? Is the organization more efficient, more profitable, or better able to serve its clients or customers as a result of the training program? Meeting this criterion is considered the "bottom line" as far as most managers are concerned. It is also the most challenging level to assess, given that many things beyond employee performance can affect organizational performance. Typically at this level, economic and operating data (such as sales or waste) are collected and analyzed.

Kirkpatrick's framework has several advantages that support its popularity with HRD professionals. First, the framework is straightforward and easy to understand. Second, it highlights the limitations of program evaluations that are completed by participants immediately at the close of a program (often cynically referred to by HRD professionals as "smile sheets") for assessing the results of a training event. Third, Kirkpatrick opens up thinking about what really constitutes learning and about facilitating learning transfer as an important aspect of the trainer's role. Fourth, the framework highlights learning as a potential drive of performance. In addition to its widespread acceptance by HRD professionals, Kirkpatrick's model has stimulated research in the field of industrial and organizational psychology (Alliger & Janak, 1989). Kirkpatrick's model also provides the foundations for Phillips (1997) extensive work on return-on-investment in training and development.

Criticism of the Kirkpatrick Model

Despite its popularity Kirkpatrick's model has received intense criticism (see, Alliger et al., 1997; Alliger & Janak, 1989; Holton, 1996a; Swanson & Holton, 1999; Bushnell, 1990). The chief criticisms are as follows:

- Not supported by research—Research has consistently shown that the levels within the framework are not related, or only correlated at a low level.
- After training focus—Evaluates only what happens after training, as opposed to the entire training process.
- Emphasis on reaction measures—Research has shown that reaction measures have nearly a zero correlation with learning or performance outcome measures.
- Failure to update the model—The model has remained the same for the last forty years with little effort to update or revise it.
- Not used—The model is not widely used. Despite decades of urging people to use it, most do not find it a useful approach.
- Can lead to incorrect decisions—The model leaves out so many important variables that four-level data alone are insufficient to make correct and informed decisions about training program effectiveness.

Despite the criticisms, Kirkpatrick's framework provides a useful way of looking at the possible consequences of training and reminds us that HRD efforts often have multiple objectives.

Expansion of the Kirkpatrick Evaluation Model

Efforts have been undertaken to expand Kirkpatrick's four-level approach. These include:
- expanding the reaction level to include assessing the participants' reaction to the training methods and efficiency (Kaufman & Keller, 1994);

- distinguishing between cognitive and affective reactions to training (Tan, Hall, & Boyce, 2003);
- splitting the reaction level to include assessing participants' perceptions of enjoyment, usefulness (utility), and the difficulty of the program (Warr & Bunce, 2003);
- adding a fifth level (beyond results) to specifically address the organization's return on investment (ROI) (Phillips, 1996b);
- adding a fifth level (beyond results) to address the societal contribution and outcomes created by an HRD program (Kaufman & Keller, 1994).

Others have distinguished between impact evaluation, which can include improvement in financial results as well as other measures such as behavior changes, reduced turnover, improved job satisfaction indexes and the like, and cost effectiveness evaluation (Rossi, Freeman, & Lipsey, 1999). Recent work on return on investment (ROI), pioneered by Jack Phillips (1997), is familiar to HRD professionals as it represents a significant development in HRD evaluation. Phillips positions ROI as a fifth level, building on the previous four levels of the Kirkpatrick framework, that examines results in relationship to investment the same way that earnings-on-capital invested is assessed.

In Phillips' formulation, ROI is calculated as net program benefits divided by program costs × 100. As a formula:

$$ROI(\%) = \text{Net Program Benefits}/\text{Program Costs} \times 100$$

The ROI calculation builds on the definitions of results expected on Level 4 of the Kirkpatrick framework.

Conducting an ROI is not a simple process. However, thinking in terms of demonstrating a credible ROI analysis can lead to better rigor in evaluation practices, even if computing ROI does not prove feasible in particular circumstances.

There are a number of issues that need to be resolved in order to conduct an ROI analysis of a training program or HRD intervention (Phillips, 1997). Some issues, such as isolating the impact of the learning event from other contextual factors that influence results measures are common to Level 4 assessment. Other issues are specific to the ROI analysis; determining program costs and converting results data into monetary benefits. In resolving these ROI issues the best rule of thumb is to always use the most credible and conservative data sources. Also, it is critical to involve management in developing the ROI process since management's judgment about the analysis will determine its credibility. HRD professionals embarking on an ROI analysis should view it as a process of organizational learning about the ROI the organization is making to execute its strategy, rather than as a campaign for justifying the HRD budget. If the ROI analysis is assessing initiatives that are making a meaningful contribution, the budget argument will be strengthened. However, HRD professionals should always keep in mind that the ROI analysis must be viewed in the context of total contributions to performance. More will be said about ROI analysis later in this chapter.

After introducing a model that focuses on designing training initiatives with an accompanying emphasis on HRD evaluation the remainder of this chapter will revisit the purpose and specific types of HRD evaluation criteria. Particular attention will be given to the when, what, and how of HRD evaluation. Additionally, discussion returns to a more detailed discussion of collecting four types of data based on Kirkpatrick's model. Further, discussion will provide a more in-depth look at return on investment (ROI) as an evaluation tool. The chapter will end with a brief look at an HRD evaluation checklist that HRD professionals can use as a guide to conducting evaluations of their HRD efforts.

FURTHER CONSIDERATIONS FOR THE ORGANIZATION AND DESIGN OF HRD EVALUATION

The considerations for developing evaluations of HRD initiatives must include a formal diagnosis of an organization's strategic agenda, HRD needs and the learning efforts. This diagnosis should specify HRD evaluation objectives, evaluation criteria, and resources and constraints that will be encountered in planning and implementing the evaluation process. Wherever evaluation is called for, the HRD professionals must ensure that objectives are made in terms of clear statements that provide some amount of measurability. Criteria are those specific measures that establish whether or not objectives are met. As discussed earlier in this chapter resources and constraints include not only money, personnel, equipment, time and space, but also, attitudes, norms and values of the organization toward HRD interventions. From the possible HRD evaluation techniques, techniques are selected that will most likely achieve initiative objectives within given constraints and existing resources. This is a "systems analysis" approach applied to developing a training or HRD evaluation plan. The result is an action plan indicating roughly the objectives and procedures for evaluating HRD interventions.

For example, for HRD evaluations that involve multiple components, specification of evaluation procedures for later sessions will most likely initially be vague; these are developed into more detail by the organization's HRD professionals as their time of implementation draws closer. The important point is that thought is given by the HRD professionals as to how the learning initiatives tie together to meet the overall objectives of the HRD effort(s). The pyramiding of objectives enables the HRD professionals to test assumptions concerning the ability of procedures at lower levels to meet objectives at higher levels.

There is a need for more carefully designed HRD evaluations and HRD professionals should be concerned with developing two major components of a learning initiative. First, the learning content or activities to be included in the initiative should be identified. Second, an outline or program for HRD evaluation should be developed. Simply put, the HRD evaluation plan is created by (1) defining the organization's HRD needs, (2) deciding what has to be evaluated, (3) developing the learning initiative with objectives and criteria clearly laid out to enable evaluation, and (4) developing an evaluation plan based on the objectives, criteria, and activities of the learning initiative. Figure 6.1 presents a model for designing HRD initiatives with an accompanying evaluation component. The left side of the model illustrates the *HRD design process* and presents the steps for developing the learning initiative content. The right side of the model, labeled *evaluation design process*, presents steps necessary for designing the

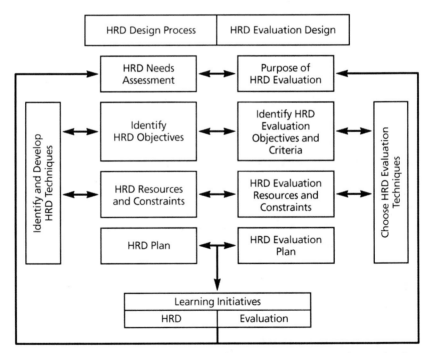

Figure 6.1. Model for designing HRD programs with accompanying evaluation plans.

evaluation plan. Since the focus of this chapter is HRD evaluation, the right side of the model is of immediate concern.

HRD EVALUATION PURPOSE AND CRITERIA

The first step in planning HRD evaluation is determining the purpose for evaluating the initiative; for example, what do you want to know about the HRD initiative? Each kind of question necessitates consideration of how the evaluation initiative should be designed to provide answers. Stufflebeam et al. (1971) suggests three purposes for evaluation relevant to HRD evaluation that are in line with our earlier discussion on evaluation design options. First, evaluation can be used to identify differences in behavior. Individuals or groups may be compared to other individuals or groups, to ideals or standards (as in performance appraisal), or with themselves at different moments in time (a time-series study). As noted earlier, this is a *comparative* evaluation. Evaluation can also investigate causes of behavior. The variables, within a learning initiative, responsible for changes within individuals or groups can be identified through experimental manipulation. This is *explanatory* evaluation. Finally, a *predictive* analysis can evaluate how well HRD performance data correlate with other variables such as changes in individual job performance and/or system performance. The purpose for HRD evaluation will impact each step in developing both the content and evaluation components of the learning initiative.

In order to ensure that a training or HRD activity attains the objectives for which it was designed, HRD effectiveness must be measured by the organization's HRD professionals and non-HRD staff. Providing valid and reliable measures of the HRD initiative concerns several issues: when to conduct evaluations, what to measure, and how to measure.

WHEN TO CONDUCT EVALUATIONS

The evaluation process actually begins before any employee receives training, for example. By identifying areas for improvement, the needs assessment conducted prior to the design of HRD initiatives serves as the first stage of evaluation, known as *formative evaluation*. Surveys or tests conducted to identify learning needs can later serve as pre-HRD measures to evaluate how much learning took place. The design of learning objectives likewise should reflect the need to establish measurable, achievable criteria that can be used to evaluate the impact of the learning initiative. The final part of a formative evaluation involves examining the HRD initiative design to make sure it will have the desired impact.

In contrast to formative evaluation, a *summative evaluation* takes place after initial implementation of a learning initiative. This evaluation looks at whether the learning initiative is fulfilling its purpose and turning out employees who have achieved the desired learning objectives. Besides evaluating the success or failure of a completed training or other learning effort, summative evaluations are useful for identifying ways to improve an ongoing learning initiative.

The following sections look at each type of evaluation in greater detail.

Formative Evaluation

Formative evaluation measures the potential effect of an HRD initiative. Conducted during initiative design and development, a formative evaluation, for example, defines and refines learning materials to maximize learning and achieve particular results. The purpose is to create a learning initiative that has the greatest impact possible.

Ideally, the formative evaluation should involve people who have not participated in designing the initiative. This outside involvement allows the learning initiative to be viewed in the same way that initiative participants will see it. Outside input can come from the following: one-to-one assessment, small group evaluation, and pilot testing. Each of these types of formative evaluation is discussed in more detail below.

One-to-one Evaluation

One-to-one evaluations involve an HRD professional and one person who is willing to participate in the learning process. Conducting several one-to-one evaluations are important to obtain a range of perspectives. The following types of people can provide the most assistance during this process: *subject matter experts* (SME) can make sure the content of the training initiative is technically correct; *HRD or other colleagues* can edit the initiative and comment on the positioning, set-up, or debriefing of activities or exercises, and *members of management and the target audience* can review learning techniques and materials for appropriateness, clarity of language, instructions and effect.

A formative evaluation can be as simple as asking someone for a few minutes of help working through a link, or calling an SME to see if two steps can be lumped together or if they must be performed separately. Including individuals who will provide the most trustworthy feedback provides the most useful data for the one-to-one evaluation by identifying and addressing problems for the course to be ready for the pre-pilot test.

Pre-Pilot Test

A pre-pilot test measures the learning initiative's impact on multiple participants. This type of test is especially useful for group exercises or activities like games, simulations, and role-plays. The test session gives the HRD professionals a chance to try out instructions, learning techniques, and to assess group dynamics and synergy.

Ideally, members of the employee population who will participate in the learning activity should be involved in the pre-pilot test. The pre-pilot test should be performed after problems identified during the one-to-one evaluations have been addressed, but HRD professionals should not wait to test the course until everything is perfect.

To conduct a pre-pilot test, the learning initiative design should have progressed far enough that the HRD professionals have developed the following parts: materials needed to conduct learning exercises and activities; written instructions for all activities and exercises, including guidelines for trainers and individual directions for different roles in group exercises; learning objectives for the activities; and a checklist to track time, errors, omissions, mechanical problems, or logistic difficulties.

Using the information from the pre-pilot test checklist, HRD professionals should get a picture of the type and degree of changes that need to be made for the initiative to operate smoothly. The HRD professionals should try to make all improvements identified through the pre-pilot test before conducting a final pilot test.

Pilot Test

The pilot test has many different names: alpha or beta test, field test, dry run, and pretest. Whatever the name, the purpose is the same: to obtain feedback from a large sample of the planned training audience. Properly conducted, the pilot test answers several questions about the learning initiative's design. Does the initiative's content reflect the work environment? What improvements can be added? Has enough time been scheduled for each module or component? Does the initiative hold together? That is, do the transitions and themes work? And, are the practice items appropriate for the instructional content and job context?

In every way possible, the pilot test should resemble the actual learning initiative. The only difference between the pilot test and the actual initiative is that an evaluator should hold feedback sessions with small focus groups of pilot test participants.

Pilot Test Evaluation

A pilot test evaluation is one of the most important parts of a formative evaluation. It is usually recommended that the person conducting the focus feedback sessions should be any member of the HRD area except the individuals, who will be busy running the course. The evaluator serves as both an impartial observer and a repository for participants' comments during the pilot test. At the end of the pilot test, evaluators record and report their own observations as well as conclusions offered by the test participants.

HRD professionals should take note of the following items when observing the pilot test: the need for additional directions for activities; emotions and feelings shown by participants during activities or exercises; and participants' level of involvement during various parts of the initiative, including any point at which participants seem to tune out.

Besides getting specific information wanted by the HRD professionals, evaluators should ask the following questions when debriefing pilot test participants:

- How did the learning activities fulfill the module's objectives?
- Did the presentation and activities have a logical, coherent, and easy-to-follow sequence?
- Did each session cover a reasonable amount of information in the time available?
- Did presentations include enough well-chosen examples to clarify concepts?
- Did presentations use audiovisuals that clarified and supported the oral presentation?
- Did the learning methods stimulate adequate practice, activity, and thinking?
- Did ideas interrelate clearly and flow smoothly from one activity to another and from one module to another?
- At the end of a lesson, could both the HRD professional and the participants identify what objectives had been achieved and where further explanation and practice were needed?

When evaluating trainers, for example, during the pilot test, a combination of methods gives the most comprehensive and useful evaluation. Trainer performance appraisals provide a manager's view of a trainer's performance and are the most common measurement criteria. Many organizations look at participants' evaluations of the trainer during the pilot test and post-training learner performance ratings to determine how many participants successfully transfer course material to their jobs. An increasingly popular method of evaluating trainers is peer review, in which other trainers complete their own questionnaires to identify a trainer's strengths and areas that need improvement.

At a minimum three groups should receive a final report summarizing the findings of the pilot test evaluation. The first group is the learning initiative's design and development team—the HRD professional, subject matter experts, and so on. This group will want minute details on how the participants and instructor(s) reacted to the learning initiative. The second group needing evaluation results are the initiative trainers, who will want feedback on their work. Finally, customers (line managers and more recently senior leaders) of potential participants will want to know how the initiative was received. An evaluator may need to report the data differently for each group's evaluation report.

This written feedback marks the transition between formative evaluation and implementation of the actual learning initiative. It also begins the summative evaluation process since the evaluation forms used to pilot-test participants can be revised to collect feedback throughout the learning initiative's life span.

In order to ensure that a learning initiative attains the objectives for which it was designed, HRD effectiveness should be measured by the organization's HRD professionals. Providing valid and reliable measures of the HRD effort concerns the what, when and how of HRD evaluation.

WHAT TO MEASURE: SUMMATIVE EVALUATION

Summative evaluation assesses whether a new learning initiative has met its objectives. It also helps to ensure the continued success of an ongoing learning initiative. Summative evaluation, for example, measures the impact of HRD interventions on participants and on the organization; it answers the question, "Did the initiative do what it was supposed to do so that the organization can meet its business goals?"

Ideally, the variables measured in HRD evaluation should incorporate the key features of the learning initiative as well as its expected results. In addition, the measurement of both the learning initiative effort and its outcome variables are necessary for in-progress and learning-outcomes evaluation feedback. The HRD professionals should avoid the tendency to measure only learning-outcomes variables while neglecting learning initiative variables altogether.

The successful implementation of HRD evaluations generally takes considerable time and learning. It must be empirically determined that training, for example, has been implemented appropriately; it cannot simply be assumed. In-HRD training evaluation feedback serves this purpose, guiding the implementation process and helping to interpret outcome data. Outcome measures are ambiguous without knowledge of how well the HRD initiative has been implemented. Measurement of the HRD initiative levels variables helps to determine the correct interpretation of outcome measures.

Points to cover in a summative evaluation of HRD include the following:

- *Tasks.* Are tasks sequenced properly for effective, efficient learning? Does the initiative include learning activities that are not boringly easy or overwhelmingly difficult?
- *Topics.* Does the initiative omit essential information? Is any information misleading or wrong?
- *Training methods.* Do participants feel they get enough feedback and practice? Do they and their supervisors consider the course useful? Do participants and HRD professionals consider learning activities and materials to be worth the time and effort invested in them?
- *Tests.* Do tests demand that participants demonstrate—rather than describe—what they have learned? Do learners consider the tests fair? Do participants and their supervisors consider the tests reasonable indicators of ability to perform on the job?
- *Productivity.* Has productivity—as measured by absenteeism, turnover, rework rates, or quality tests—improved for individuals or groups after training, for example?

Summative evaluation takes place after a learning intervention like training has ended. The evaluation techniques used should cause as little disruption as possible. For example, HRD professionals should hand out forms to trainees during the last session and allow time at the end of class for filling out the forms. HRD professionals should also complete an evaluation form once the initiative has concluded.

While HRD professionals and participants can complete their feedback forms immediately after a learning initiative, measuring the impact of training, for example, on performance will take longer. Supervisors observing trained employees' performance can provide some qualitative information about the effectiveness of training within a few weeks of an initiative's conclusion. Obtaining hard data—such as changes in absenteeism, output, errors, and so on—involves tracking specific criteria over longer periods of time.

HOW TO MEASURE

Measurement of any HRD intervention and its outcome variables involves operationalizing the variables so that appropriate data can be collected. This includes providing operational definitions of the variables that specify empirical information needed and how it will be collected. Operational definitions are extremely important in measurement because they provide precise guides about what characteristics of the learning initiative are to be observed and how they are to be observed. They tell those responsible for evaluation exactly how to measure learning and outcomes variables. For example, two key dimensions of good measures of surveys used in HRD evaluation are validity and reliability. Validity refers to whether a particular measure actually does measure what it purports to. Reliability refers to whether the measure is stable over time or situations (Nunally, 1978). Evaluation instruments that are valid and reliable can be useful for HRD needs assessment, for guiding the implementation of HRD, and for evaluating the immediate and long-term learning outcomes.

The criteria used in evaluating an HRD initiative will depend on its purposes. Whatever the purposes of the evaluation, HRD professionals can make use of five general categories, adapted from Suchman (1967):

1. Evaluation of *effort* assesses input, regardless of output. The questions "What did you do?" and "How well did you do it?" are addressed.
2. Evaluation of *performance* focuses on the results of the initiative. This requires clear statements of objectives; it asks "Did any change occur?" and "Were objectives achieved?"
3. Evaluation of *adequacy* determines how effective the initiative was. For example, participants in an initiative may exhibit considerable practical application change, but the number of participants may be inadequate in determining the benefits of the initiative for the organization.
4. Evaluation of *efficiency* is concerned with alternate ways of achieving the same ends that are more efficient in terms of time, money, human resources, materials, and convenience.
5. Evaluation of *process* focuses on the operation of an HRD initiative, with emphasis on how and why it works or does not work.

While several criteria have been tested through the years Kirkpatrick's four-levels of training evaluation (reaction, learning, job behavior, and results) and the addition of the a fifth level (return on investment) by Phillips, both briefly discussed earlier in this chapter, provide the foundational framework for any training or HRD assessment process. Each one of these areas are discussed in more detail in the following sections.

Assessing Employee Reactions

Employee reactions to training, for example, are evaluated by conducting interviews or administering questionnaires to participants. Here, the HRD professionals are interested in whether participants liked the initiative, whether they thought the instruction was clear and helpful, and/or whether they believe that they learned the material. Measuring employee reaction from training is absolutely essential. Gaining direct feedback from a customer (that is, initiative participants) is important to measure satisfaction with the different parts of the initiative. In addition, this feedback provides needed input on the strengths and weaknesses of the training process including issues such as initiative content, duration, handout materials, videos, experiential exercises, simulations, games, and even the learning climate. Phillips notes that this level of evaluation is important with new initiatives, for which initial feedback enables initiative sponsors to make adjustments (Phillips, 1997).

HRD professionals should include input on specific action items generated from the initiative when collecting data on participants' reactions. This can be accomplished through a series of questions that determine how participants plan to implement what they have learned, step by step. This action planning approach requires initiative participants to think about specific areas where the material can be applied and assists in the transfer of the learning to their work environment.

To effectively measure participants' reactions HRD professionals should conduct surveys of trainees through the life span of the learning initiative. HRD professionals should compare survey results over time to detect shifts in participants' views of the initiative. These shifts may signal a need to update the content, replace the trainer, or make other adjustments to the initiative.

HRD professionals should develop a standard series of questions for gathering participants' reactions. Standardizing these questions allows tracing participants' responses to an initiative across time. It also provides a way to compare one learning initiative to another or to a different type of intervention. While the exact number and types of questions to ask will depend on the course objectives, all feedback forms should ask learners about the following points: demographics, activities, learning materials, trainer qualifications, job relevance, initiative characteristics, and initiative objectives.

Initiative participants should complete evaluation forms before the final session ends. Data collected from the evaluation forms should be tabulated, analyzed, and reported on a regular basis using a schedule that reflects the type of initiative and its key initiative sponsors (i.e., line managers). For example, a learning initiative for launching a new product or service will have a different reporting schedule than an established management training or development initiative.

The summary report should indicate how participants felt about the initiative. It should summarize participants' perceptions of the HRD professionals, training media and materials, training methods, and HRD activities. No feedback report, however, can make conclusions about whether employees acquired the knowledge, skills, abilities and other characteristics (KSAOCs) intended. That information comes only after the second level of evaluation: measuring learning or the amount of KSAOCs changes.

While positive employee reactions are necessary for HRD to be successful, positive employee reactions do not necessarily mean that HRD will lead to changes in knowledge or performance (Alliger & Janak, 1989). In fact, trainee reactions constitute the lowest level of training evaluation (Birnbauer, 1987) and often can be misleading. Many studies have confirmed a lack of correlation between overall participant satisfaction and actual learning and subsequent application of the initiative material (Phillips, 1997). While feedback is essential to judge satisfaction with initiative participants, it is ineffective as an overall evaluation of the initiative in terms of learning application and results. Level 1 reaction information can be useful for fine-tuning some aspects of the HRD initiative such as scheduling and mode of teaching. However, additional levels of evaluation are needed on learning changes, transfer of learning, and results.

Assessing Employee Learning

For most HRD initiatives, participants are expected to learn something. Learning objectives usually focus on changes in KSAOCs. With increased emphasis on building learning organizations, the issue of measuring learning in HRD programs is especially important. Tests on the training material are commonly used for evaluating learning and can be given both before and after training, for example, to compare scores. Of course, learning enough to pass a test does not guarantee that the participant can *do* anything with what was learned. However, learning tests should be considered since they are objective, reliable, and easy-to-administer tools for evaluating HRD effectiveness.

HRD professionals can choose from several options for measuring whether participants have learned what they should have from the course. While objectives testing is important, organizations have devised a variety of measures to assess KSAOCs acquisition. Other methods include a variety of assessments, such as self-assessments, team assessments, facilitator assessment, performance testing, simulations, case studies, skill practices, role-plays, and experiential learning exercises. Which option to use depends on the nature of the learning intervention and the types of KSAOCs the intervention was designed to instill. The discussion below outlines objective testing, simulation, and trainer observation options in more detail.

Objective Testing

Administering a test after training can help tell whether participants have learned relevant skills or knowledge. But unless employees took the same test before training, a good test score could simply reflect prior learning and not any benefit related to the initiative. As noted earlier in the chapter, an alternative is to compare trained employees' test scores to those of an untrained control group of employees, but few organizations are large enough to conduct this type of assessment. A good test score also does not guarantee transfer of learned knowledge and skills to the job. The greater the predictive validity of the test used, however, the more likely that transfer of learning will take place for high scorers.

Simulations

As noted in Chapter 5, simulations evaluate a participant's ability to perform a specific task or a series of tasks, or to apply knowledge to a task. Simulations are best suited, for example, for training that involves equipment (such as computers) for discrete operations (such as parts assembly). For management training and development, simulations might involve in-basket or critical-incident exercises. Unlike objective testing, simulations measure application of knowledge to a task and more closely predict transfer of training to the job. Like tests, however, a high score on a simulation exercise does not necessarily reflect learning gained through training, unless pretesting or a control group is used.

HRD Professional Observations

Ideally, an HRD professional is a skilled observer of performance. Once training has ended, most HRD professionals find it difficult to recall details about each person's performance. However, an HRD professional usually can provide feedback about the group as a whole. After completing a major portion of an HRD initiative, HRD professionals should fill out a feedback sheet rating participant's mastery of the module's objectives and suggesting revisions that might improve the initiative. Helpful questions include the following:

- What learning activities, lecturettes, discussions, and so on went well?
- What learning activities, lecturettes, discussions, and so on need modification? How should they be modified?
- Did the module(s) move too quickly or too slowly for the HRD professional or the participants? Specify which module(s) had poor pacing.
- Did participants seem to find the information easy or difficult to understand? Specify the types of information where this happened.
- Did participants understand course notes, participant activities, and instructions? Specify parts which participants seemed to find confusing.

Phillips suggests that a certain percentage of learning initiatives should be targeted for learning measurement (Phillips, 1997; Sims, 1998). Therefore, HRD professionals must develop specific criteria to select those initiatives which learning will be measured. Measuring learning is critical when the organization has determined it is important for participants to have prescribed KSAOCs that are necessary and essential for job success. In situations where competency building, major change, and transformation are underway, high levels of learning assessment would be required. In areas where a large body of technical knowledge must be accumulated, as in knowledge of information technology, knowledge assessment becomes critical.

Although measuring participants' learning is important because it provides some assurance that participants possess the desired KSAOCs, there is still no assurance of application on the job. Consequently, Level 3 evaluation is needed to determine the specific application of knowledge, skills and attitudes.

Assessing Job Behavior (Application or Transfer of Learning)

Perhaps the most critical issue of any learning intervention is the transfer of acquired KSAOCs to actual on-the-job application. Transfer of learning, or Level 3 evaluation, concerns whether behavioral or performance changes taught in training, for example, are expressed on the job. Can participants now do things they could not before (e.g., negotiate, conduct an appraisal interview)? Do they demonstrate new behaviors on the job? Has their performance improved? A follow-up evaluation takes time, adds cost to the training process, and is often disruptive. According to Phillips, these three issues alone have kept many organizations from appropriately using Level 3 (Phillips, 1997).

There are many ways transfer of acquired KSAOCs can be assessed. The most common ways to collect data for Level 3 are: follow up surveys; follow-up questionnaires; observation on the job; interviews with participants and their co-workers, mangers, and key customers; follow-up focus groups; initiative assignments; action planning; performance contracting; and learning intervention follow-up sessions. The challenge for HRD professionals is to select methods that fit the organization's culture, budget, and time constraints.

Positive transfer of learning is perhaps the most critical goal of training. Since training, for example, represents a step toward improving job performance and/or organizational effectiveness, a lack of transfer in KSAOCs to the job may indicate a poor training effort.

A quality learning initiative can ensure participants acquire and demonstrate certain KSAOCs within the intervention's controlled learning environment. But once participants leave this controlled setting, the HRD function alone cannot guarantee participants will apply their newly learned

KSAOCs on the job. Transfer of learning is a partnership among the interested parties. Without this partnership, transfer of learning becomes more difficult to track, and the odds of any transfer taking place drop.

For many HRD interventions, a check of KSAOC application is sufficient for the evaluation process. For others, however, a connection with actual business performance is desired, since it is possible to obtain positive application of knowledge and skills yet have no impact on an organization performance measure. For example, if the needs assessment is inadequate or improper, KSAOCs acquired in the HRD intervention will not necessarily improve the desired organization performance measures. When evidence of an impact on organizational objectives is needed, the next level of evaluation is necessary to determine performance improvement.

Assessing Results or Bottom Line Measures

Transfer of learning to the job should produce measurable improvement in the trained employee's performance, for example, as well as the supervisor's evaluation of the employee. The ultimate goal of improving job performance is to contribute to the organization's bottom line. Organizational leaders (and HRD professionals) are interested in finding answers to questions such as: "Did the organization actually save money following the HRD intervention?" or "How well were the HRD dollars invested?"

As noted earlier, today's leaders are interested in knowing how HRD actually improved the business in terms that they really understand. Leaders now require bottom line performance from major HRD initiatives. The difficulty in making this connection stems from the origin of most HRD efforts. Sometimes it is difficult to understand the relationship between organization problems, challenges and opportunities and a specific learning need. Some needs assessment processes do not link KSAOC deficiencies to organization performance problems or opportunities. Thus, a more complete needs analysis process may be needed to include measures of organization results. When this is the case, it is possible to link HRD efforts to their impact on organization results.

Particularly in tight budgetary times, the HRD function must show senior leadership how training and other learning efforts affect overall productivity and profits. Results are evaluated by measuring the effect of the HRD intervention on the achievement of organizational objectives. For example, recognizing there are many factors that can influence a particular organization performance measure in an organization, the HRD evaluation strategy also must include a method to isolate the effects of the learning initiative from other influences. There are a variety of methods available to accomplish this task: use of a control group arrangement, trend line analysis of performance data, use of forecasting methods of performance data, participant's estimate of HRD's impact (percentage), supervisor's estimate of HRD's impact (percent), management estimate of HRD's impact (percentage), use of previous studies, direct reports of other factors; calculating or estimating the impact of other factors, and use of customer impact.

This step often is overlooked in HRD evaluation, largely because some HRD professionals believe the analysis would prove overwhelming. But much of the data used to evaluate the organizational impact of HRD already is compiled regularly for department reports and other purposes. All HRD professionals have to do is analyze this data for before and after-learning interventions. Sources of information to examine for post-HRD effects include the following:

Productivity Reports

Look at hard production data, such as production turnover, sales reports, task completion times, error rates, or manufacturing totals. Comparing figures before and after HRD interventions can help leaders and HRD professionals determine whether any HRD-related performance improvements have taken place that affect the organization's bottom line.

HRM Reports

Information gathered for HRM purposes may show learning outcomes that affect organizational goals. Safety reports, for example, may show reductions in workplace accidents or equipment damage after employees received training for example. HRD professionals should also examine other records for reductions in absenteeism, grievance filings, turnover, customer complaints, and so on.

Cost Analysis

HRD professionals should use the costs of trainers' fees, materials, facilities, travel, training time, and the number of trainees to determine the hourly cost of training for each participant.

The specific sources of data and approaches to measuring organization impact vary. Monitoring organization performance is the most common and credible approach (Sims, 1998; Phillips, 1997). Specific performance measures are monitored for improvement after an HRD intervention is conducted. Other techniques that have proven useful in recent years to measure impact include action planning, performance contracts, and the use of follow-up questionnaires.

It is critical for organizational leaders and HRD professionals to define specific criteria to determine which initiatives should be evaluated at Level 4. Criteria include such items as the importance of the HRD initiative in meeting organizational goals, the size of the target audience, and the cost of the initiative.

Though the Level 4 results or bottom-line evaluation is extremely important and pushes HRD evaluation to the next level desired in many organizations, it still falls short of what is considered to be an ideal evaluation. It is possible for an HRD initiative to have a positive impact on the bottom line or important business results yet represent a negative return on investment (ROI). In this situation, the cost of the HRD initiative has exceeded monetary benefits. Because of this situation, the ultimate level—the ROI—must be calculated for some select HRD efforts.

Measuring and Calculating Return on Investment

ROI has been used to evaluate performance of business endeavors for many years. The purchase of equipment, acquisition of another company, or the development of a new product line or service are subjected to an ROI methodology, in which the payoff of the investment is captured. Today, more organizations are demanding the same evaluation of HRD for major HRD expenditures. The process requires two additional steps: The Level 4 organization results must be converted to monetary benefits, and the actual cost of the initiative must be captured.

Converting organization measures to monetary values is a very difficult task for some measures, such as market share and customer satisfaction. Fortunately, several techniques are available to make this conversion with reasonable accuracy. The process is applied methodically with the credibility and accuracy desired by many organizations: converting output to contribution, converting the cost of quality and employees' time, using historical costs, using internal and external experts, using data from external databases, using participants', supervisors', senior leaders' and staff estimates.

When conducting an ROI impact, HRD intervention costs should include all direct and indirect costs. For example, typical training program costs that HRD professionals should include are development costs, initiative materials, trainer costs, facility costs, travel/lodging/meals, participant salaries and benefits, and administrative/overhead costs.

HRD professionals can select from a number of different methods for determining HRD's (ROI). A traditional ROI formula involves the following steps:

- *Calculate the HRD return.* The HRD evaluation should have produced some payoff measure, such as increased sales, the value of higher productivity, the cost savings of less equipment damage, and so on.
- *Figure the HRD investment.* This figure reflects the total costs of conducting HRD initiatives.

Add together the following expenses:

- *Initiative expenses.* Include expenses for participants' and HRD professional travel, lodging, and food, as well as trainers, salaries, and facility rental.
- *Materials and equipment expenses.* Factor in costs for materials, supplies, and equipment operations.

To figure total HRD investment, deduct any offsetting factors from total expenses:

- *Initiative revenues.* Paybacks from HRD might come from program participants' accumulation of frequent flyer coupons, or from resale or rental of HRD materials.
- *Equipment revenues.* Resale, rental, or reuse of HRD equipment for other purposes can offset the cost of purchasing the devices.
- *Subtract the HRD investment from the HRD return.* This calculation yields net (after expenses) HRD return.
- *Calculate ROI by dividing the net HRD return by the HRD investment.* This final calculation should yield a figure greater than one. If not, the organization has actually lost money by training and developing employees.

In short, the ROI formula is the net program benefit as assessed in the analysis of changes in critical financial indices, divided by the program cost. As noted earlier, a simple way of expressing this formula is:

$$\text{ROI (percentage)} = \frac{\text{Benefits} - \text{Costs}}{\text{Costs}} \times 100$$

In reality only a small number of HRD initiatives should receive Level 5 evaluation (Phillips, 1997). Because so few HRD initiatives should receive this level of evaluation the criteria needed to select the initiatives are extremely important. HRD professionals must ensure that the criteria and the initiatives identified for evaluation at this level are developed and ultimately approved by senior management. The importance of senior leadership involvement at this level cannot be underestimated since HRD initiatives selected for evaluation at this level are critical to the organization's success, represent major investments, involve large audiences, or have high visibility in the organization or to external customers.

As mentioned previously, the levels of evaluation described above should be viewed, not as an individual approach, but as a cascading process of increased sophistication. Each level provides useful and important information. An overall process that makes use of techniques from each level is more likely to generate useful data that verifies the impact of HRD on the organization and its members.

Benchmarking

As HRD efforts are increasingly viewed from a strategic standpoint, there is increased interest in benchmarking developmental services and practices against those of recognized leaders in industry. Benchmarking is a logical process involving systematic steps or phases. When implemented successfully the benchmarking process should be an integral part of an organization's evaluation of HRD interventions like training. Benchmarking HRD analyzes critical areas for improvement and is based on collecting data from organizations that have been identified as having the best practices in HRD. This ultimately leads to action necessary to make improvements to move toward using the best practices in HRD. Benchmarking HRD provides the organization with information on key variables that are important to measuring and improving their learning initiatives.

While no single model for exact benchmarking exists, the simplest models are based on the late W. Edwards Deming's classic four-step process. The four-step process would require that HRD professionals:

1. *Plan.* Conduct a self-audit to define internal processes and measurements;
2. *Do.* Collect data through surveys, interviews, site visits, and/or historical records.
3. *Check.* Analyze data to discover performance gaps and communicate findings and suggested improvements to management.
4. *Act.* Establish goals, implement specific changes, monitor progress, and redefine benchmarks as a continuous improvement process.

To use benchmarking successfully, HRD professionals must clearly define the measures of competency and performance and must objectively assess the current situations and identify areas for improvement. To this end, experts in this area are attempting to work out ways of measuring what HRD departments or functions do. Three broad areas that most HRD professionals consider essential to measure are:

1. Training or learning activity: How much training or learning is occurring?
2. Training or HRD results: Do training and HRD achieve their goals?
3. Training or HRD efficiency: Are resources utilized in the pursuit of this mission?

The American Society for Training and Development (ASTD) and its Benchmarking Service has comparison data that allows organizations to measure and benchmark training and development activities against each other. The service has training-related data (i.e., on training costs, staffing, administration, design, development, and delivery of training programs) from more than 1,000 participating employers who complete detailed questionnaires annually. Training also can be benchmarked against data from the American Productivity & Quality Center and the Saratoga Institute (Mathis & Jackson, 2006). Initiatives such as these not only help organizations evaluate their training programs but the process serves as a feedback loop to reinitiate needs assessment and design for future training (Bohlander, Snell, & Sherman, 2001; Bassi et al., 1998; Day, 1995).

HRD EVALUATION CHECKLIST

Improvements in employee performance and achievement of organizational results are the goal of the evaluation of HRD outcomes. A checklist of such a process that HRD professionals can use to evaluate the results of HRD interventions might include:

1. Does the evaluation design fit the objectives of the HRD initiative?
2. Does the design address important issues such as initiative participant' needs and expectations? These include both process and content issues.
3. Does the evaluation method reflect standards incorporated by those responsible for developing the HRD initiative and required by the organization?
4. Does the evaluation structure provide a framework where emergent issues can be addressed? Can the design be modified to address participants' changing needs if the organization's strategic agenda changes without sacrificing objectives?
5. Can the design be carried out in the time allotted?
6. Does the design provide a mix of experiential learning exercises and other activities that appeal to diverse participants (i.e., different learning styles such as listening, discussing, and performing)?
7. Is the material logically and psychologically sequenced?
8. Is there appropriate redundancy in information and application practice presented in training?
9. Does the evaluation design allow for ongoing development of a learning climate?

Several possibilities exist for developing an evaluation system for HRD interventions, and many designs can be combined to form other alternate designs. The question of which design to use depends on several factors. The nature of the HRD initiative and the practical considerations of the organization's work environment may dictate the appropriate design. The more complex the design, the more costly the evaluation effort. The availability of control groups and the ease of randomization are other factors that enter into the decision. The effects of factors outside the immediate environment must also be considered. If a design is less than optimum, the HRD professionals must also be considered, and the HRD professionals should be prepared to defend its action in terms of tradeoffs.

CONCLUSION

Today's HRD professionals must develop evaluations of their learning efforts that consider a range of options given the available resources and overcome resource shortages and organizational constraints when they do occur. In any learning effort HRD professionals should work to document that HRD does have some beneficial effects in leadership's view. Effective HRD evaluation requires that HRD professionals pay attention to the following points:

1. Integrate the plan of HRD evaluation into the overall design of learning efforts. HRD evaluation should never be treated as a last minute "add on."
2. An HRD evaluation design: (a) without pre and post-HRD measurements cannot measure behavior change *and* (b) without a control group cannot allow for valid evidence that any behavior change is due to the HRD effort. So both (a) and (b) are essential for significant evaluation of results.
3. HRD professionals *must* work closely with employees, supervisors, managers and executives on specific results to be expected at the end of HRD interventions and the means of assessing those results.
4. A committee of various stakeholders should be responsible for evaluating *all* HRD initiatives.
5. To the extent practical, HRD evaluation should be conducted on as many levels as possible (i.e., Level 1 to Level 5).
6. HRD evaluation should be related to on-the-job performance and directly tied to achievement of business results.
7. As noted earlier, organizational stakeholders must recognize that not all deficiencies can be corrected by training or other HRD interventions (e.g., selection, poor equipment, ineffective management, etc., may be the problem) and should be willing to use HRD alternatives when and where appropriate.

8. Senior executives, managers and HRD professionals should not confuse attitudes with behavior, e.g., while they may want to train for proper attitudes toward delegation by supervisors or safety by employees, the real payoff is in changes in employee's *behavior.*
9. HRD customers and HRD professionals should assess criteria for program participant selection and procedures. There is nothing to gain or little point, for example, in training the wrong people.
10. HRD professionals should not be overlooked in the evaluation of HRD initiatives. This is a continuous, rather than a one-time operation and extends to program content, outlines, nature of instruction, methods, learning aids, facilities, climate (atmosphere), etc.
11. Where appropriate, outside resources should be used for a professional evaluation job: HRD consultants, statisticians, educators, etc.

Not every HRD effort needs to be evaluated to the same extent. New initiatives and those with high visibility and expense should be evaluated more thoroughly than proven programs and those that are offered less frequently. The key is to have a well-planned evaluation strategy that sets the stage for how and to what extent each HRD initiative will be evaluated. While those with little evaluation experience may see this task as daunting and burdensome, it remains an essential aspect of HRD.

In the end, the final success of HRD evaluation depends on the extent to which HRD professionals can overcome problems through a methodologically sound design and implementation scheme. The evaluation strategy should be developed through selection of alternatives assessed against the objectives of the evaluation and existing constraints and resources. A familiarity with available resources, imposing constraints, and methodological alternatives will allow accurate, useful, and practical HRD effort evaluations. HRD professionals cannot afford to lose sight of the fact that the challenges now faced by organizations, and the importance of HRD in meeting those challenges, demand serious and sustained evaluation efforts—and results (Haccoun & Saks, 1998).

NOTE

1. For a good example of this design, see Klein and Weaver (2000).

CHAPTER 7

EMPLOYEE SOCIALIZATION AND ORIENTATION

INTRODUCTION

The ability of an organization (or group) to control its members' behaviors depends on the extent to which newcomers learn the organizations (or group's) roles, rules, and norms. Newcomers do not initially know what is expected of them and what they can and cannot do (Jones, 1983). A newcomer to a group of secretaries, for example, does not know whether it is all right to take a long lunch one day and make up the time the next day or whether it is acceptable to work from 8:30 to 4:30 instead of from 9:00 to 5:00. Newcomers are outsiders, and only when they have learned the group's roles, rules, and norms do existing group members accept them as insiders. The process by which newcomers learn the roles, rules, and norms of a group or organization is socialization.

Socialization is the process by which organizations bring new employees into the culture. In terms of culture, socialization involves a transmittal of values, assumptions, and attitudes from the older to the newer employees. Socialization attempts to make the "fit" between the new employee and the organization's culture more comfortable for the employee and the organization.

This chapter first discusses several environmental changes that HRD professionals should be aware of and the implications for socialization efforts. Next, the chapter describes the socialization as a learning and change process. The stages of socialization are then described, followed by the characteristics of an effective socialization. A more specific form of

Human Resource Development: Today and Tomorrow, pages 177–203
Copyright © 2006 by Information Age Publishing
All rights of reproduction in any form reserved.

socialization, new employee orientation, is then discussed before discussing the implications of socializing an increasingly diverse workforce. The last section of the chapter takes a brief look at socialization as an integration strategy.

ENVIRONMENTAL CHANGES THAT ARE IMPACTING EMPLOYEE SOCIALIZATION EFFORTS

Over the years, HRM and HRD professionals have accepted that the first contact employees have with an organization after being hired is crucial for their success in the workplace (Buchanan, 1974; Feldman, 1976a). The initial socialization process that a firm undertakes has been found to affect long-term consequences for various outcomes, including employee job satisfaction and turnover (Ashforth & Saks, 1996; Buckley et al., 1998, 2002; Wanous, 1980a). While a variety of approaches have been examined regarding the most effective socialization processes, the one common finding among researchers in this area is that environment does indeed have a potent impact on the effectiveness of socialization (Allen & Meyer, 1990; Cooper-Thomas & Anderson, 2002). As HRM and HRD professionals seek to insure the augmentation of human capital in their organizations on a long-term basis, it is clear that the impact of environment on socialization cannot be ignored by an organization.

As stated, environmental changes are continuing to have a dramatic effect on the business processes of organizations. The three changes, which have specifically influenced development of effective socialization processes, include: (1) the knowledge economy, knowledge management and knowledge workers, (2) the increase in market velocity, and (3) the ever changing psychological contract between the organization and its employees. In the following section, we explain each of these changes in further detail and discuss their implications for socialization processes. Next, we will present a review of some relevant research in the area of employee socialization. Then, we will conclude by discussing a recently-developed socialization procedure, which addresses the challenges faced in today's changing environment.

The Knowledge Economy, Knowledge Management and Knowledge Workers

For much of history, competitive advantage among organizations was measured in terms of physical capital. However, as the information age has evolved, "intelligence" became the raw material that many organizations make and sell through their "knowledge workers." Knowledge has increasingly become the most valuable economic resources, as illustrated by the declining percentage of employees performing unskilled labor in the United States—a decline from 90% at the start of the 20th century to approximately 20% today (Spira, 2000). Conversely, the growth of "knowledge work" reflects a changing economy, in which information acquisition, assimilation and dissemination have become a part of the core business processes, even in industries that seem to revolve around tangible goods. Knowledge management is the way an organization identifies and leverages knowledge in order to be competitive. It is the art of creating value by using organizational intellectual capital, which is what the organization (or, more exactly, the people in the organization) knows, and it includes intellectual properties such as patents and copyrights (Lewison, 2001).

The key characteristics of today' knowledge economy is a "greater reliance on intellectual capabilities than on physical inputs or natural resources" (Powell & Snellman, 2004). The main implication for HRM and HRD professionals is that recruiting, orienting, and socializing employees who contribute to the key intellectual capabilities of the organization have become much more important for organizational success in the new knowledge economy (Novicevic & Buckley, 2001).

The rise of knowledge economy also drives an increase in the number of employees that can be considered "knowledge workers." Although the conceptualization of the knowledge worker is nearly fifty years old (Drucker, 1967), businesses are just now grappling with how to effectively manage knowledge workers when they make the majority in the workforce. The knowledge workers differ from manual laborers in that their main outputs are not tangible goods, but intangible ideas, insights and information. In the same way the industrial revolution created the impetus for management researchers, such as Frederick Taylor, to discover new ways how to increase the productivity of manual laborers when these make products; the technological revolution is creating an impetus for contemporary researchers and managers alike to better understand how to increase the productivity of the knowledge worker when these deliver services. This presents a unique challenge, not only because the outputs generated by a knowledge worker are much more difficult to measure than those of a manual worker, but also because the socialization process is much more complicated in terms of role communication (Van Maanen & Schein, 1979). In the case of a knowledge worker many of the details of that employee's role in an organization may be very difficult to communicate, because of their tacit nature. If the organization is not able to easily describe the most crucial aspects of the knowledge worker's job, then role communication is ineffective.

The shift toward a knowledge economy has, thus created a dual challenge for HRM and HRD professionals. While the advancement of the knowledge economy has made the management of human resources more crucial to an organization's success, it has also turned the management of human resources into a more difficult task. Human productivity that is becoming more important is also becoming more difficult to precisely quantify. Therefore, the socialization, which is becoming more crucial for the firm, is also becoming more challenging to accomplish. Managers must thus make significant adaptations in their past practices to increase the effectiveness of employee socialization in this new knowledge-rich environment.

The Increase in Market Velocity

The popular business press and academic researchers alike have recognized the increased speed to which business transactions are conducted today, as well as the unique challenges that this velocity presents to the organizational strategy (Browning & Reiss, 1999; Kotha & Kotha, 2001). To stay in tune with the warp speed of market change, organizations need to develop dynamic capabilities to give them the agility required to face the competitive challenge of a continually changing environment (Helfat, 1997). This means that firms must establish processes internally that allow for quick change and rapid response to changes in the marketplace and actions of key competitors. The execution of these processes creates new challenges for the organizations in many functional areas, including in HRM.

For an organization to recognize the flexibility needed to cope with the increasing market velocity, it needs flexible employees. Unfortunately, in juxtaposition this is too much of the work in HRM, which emphasizes clear role definition as a method of improving performance (Tubre & Collins, 2000). This research has long indicated that decreasing the role ambiguity that an employee perceives will increase the job performance of employees (Jackson & Shuler, 1985). A problem arises, because it becomes difficult to clearly define and communicate a role to an employee, when the role is continually changing due to the accelerating nature of the macro-environment and to the dynamic nature of the organizations' strategies. This forces HRM and HRD professionals and researchers who examine the HRM and HRD functions to begin to look for other ways to accomplish the benefits of role definition in an environment where role definition itself can be very challenging.

Specifically, as organizations face the challenge of socialization under conditions of high market velocity, they can experience difficulty in completing one of the core pieces of this process. Role communication has been long been considered one of the basic elements of socialization (Van Mannen, 1976). Some researchers and practitioners propose that if an organization effectively communicates both the potentially good and bad aspects of an employee's role in the socialization process, the firm could reap the benefits with higher levels of job satisfaction and lower levels of turnover (Wanous, 1980b). The empirical evidence supports this balanced approach to role communication as well (Buckley et al., 1998, 2002). However, in the current hypercompetitive market environment with an increasing need for strategic agility and the subsequent increasing uncertainty about what an employee's job may entail in the future, it can become difficult to effectively communicate a stable set of tasks for the role that an employee is to perform in the ever-changing workplace. This issue may become particularly problematic when an employer presents what is represented as a "realistic" representation of the role that an employee will perform, but organizational needs later change and make that representation inaccurate. This situation could potentially be hazardous to the employee's perception of the organization and is likely to ultimately lower his or her commitment to the organization, thus bringing about the negative outcomes that the organization was attempting to prevent with the "realistic" representation—low job satisfaction and increased turnover.

In effect, the increased market velocity and the subsequent need for employee flexibility complicate some of the traditional human resource processes, particularly socialization. The challenge for HRD professionals is to develop pre-socialization and socialization techniques that could accomplish the desired organizational benefits while not requiring the job details that managers could not provide. More will be said about possible pre-socialization and socialization techniques later in this chapter.

The Ever Changing Psychological Contract

In addition to the challenges brought about by the new knowledge economy and the increased market velocity, managers and HRD professionals are also facing difficulties in implementing socialization programs because of the changing nature of psychological contracts. A psychological contract is the implicit understanding of the exchange agreement between an employee and the organization for which the employee works (Rousseau, 1995). While the typical psychological contract for the organizations of the industrial economy included an expectation that if an individual 'worked hard' they could expect to have a job at the same organization until retirement, corporate downsizing and new "leaner" organizations have changed this expectation for organizations of the knowledge economy (Sullivan,

1999). The psychological contract about the employment relationship has changed because the employer can no more implicitly promise a long-term employment while an employee can no more promise a long-term loyalty. Therefore, the psychological contract of today is more about what the employee and employer offer each other for the short-term. Sullivan (1999, p. 471) summarizes this situation succinctly, "Under the old contract, workers exchanged loyalty for job security. Under the new contract, workers exchange performance for continuous learning and marketability."

This decline of loyalty under the "new" psychological contract has engendered employee retention as a major issue for organizations dependent on knowledge workers (Capelli, 2000; Kostman & Scheiman, 2005; Stroh & Reilly, 1997). As the dysfunctional turnover of talent has become very costly for a business, comprehensive efforts have been made to develop new strategies how to retain quality employees (Frank, Finnegan, & Taylor, 2004; Marshall, 2000). In the past, managers could assume that an employee would stay with the organization until retirement, but today's managers can no longer make this assumption, as turnover is inevitable under the broken psychological contract. Therefore, a major responsibility of today's HRD professional is the reduction of dysfunctional turnover and a minimization of the costs associated with such turnover.

Accompanying the decrease in loyalty due to the changed psychological contract are inflated expectations of younger employees about personal fulfillment from their jobs (Kranhold, 2004; Sullivan, 1999). These 21st-century employees are no longer satisfied with working only for a paycheck; they expect a higher level of personal gratification and fulfillment from their job. As in many cases the employer may be unfortunately incapable of meeting the employee's expectation, this perceived violation may further deteriorate the psychological contract between the organization and its employees. Research has shown that such violations produce significant negative consequences, including increased turnover, stress, and decreased loyalty to the organization (Turnley & Feldman, 1999). The bright side of this issue for HRD professionals is that recent research has shown that specific preparation for socialization of newcomers may help prevent perceptions of psychological contract violations (Robinson & Morrison, 2000). This means that appropriate pre-socialization processes have the potential of preventing some of the undesired consequences that arise from these violations.

While the eroding psychological contract presents significant challenges for the global organizations of the 21st century, the current research efforts on finding a solution to the complex problems are encouraging. Reducing turnover has become an issue of the scope that was not faced by previous generations; however, ore-socialization processes can be now addressed by powerful tools in facilitating the "joining-up" process for both individual and organization. Appropriate organizational entry preceding the socialization phase appears to be a way for today's employers to face the turnover challenges and reduce the negative consequences associated with the broken psychological contract between employees and the organization. More will be said about the psychological contract later in this chapter.

SOCIALIZATION AS A LEARNING AND CHANGE PROCESS

Organizational socialization is a process of learning and of change. It is a learning process because newcomers try to make sense of the organization's physical workplace, social dynamics, and strategic/cultural environment. Researchers have identified various content dimensions of organizational socialization (Holton, 1996b; Chao et al., 1994). Newcomers must learn a wide variety of information and behaviors to be accepted as an insider. Newcomers need to learn about the organization's performance expectations, power dynamics, corporate culture, company history, and jargon. They also need to form successful and satisfying relationships with other people from whom they can learn the ropes (Mignerey, Rubin, & Gorden, 1995). The content of socialization has also been divided into the following categories of learning:

1. Preliminary learning—including the discovery that learning will be necessary, what to learn, and whom to learn from.
2. Learning about the organization—including the goals, values, and policies of the organization.
3. Learning to function in the work group—including the values, norms, roles, and friendships within the group.
4. Learning how to perform the job—including the necessary skills and knowledge for a particular job.
5. Personal learning—learning from experience with the job and organization, including self-identify, expectations, self-image, and motivation (Fisher, 1986).

Intel includes many of these content elements in its employee socialization process. A complete package of materials about the company are sent to hew hires before they begin their first day. On day one, recruits learn about Intel's corporate strategy and get a clear message about performance expectations. A month later, they spend an entire day learning about Intel's corporate culture. At the six-month mark, employees experience a two-hour review of how much they have learned about Intel (Mieszkowski, 1998). The idea is to transmit knowledge in a way that enables new recruits to form a cognitive map of the physical, social, and strategic/cultural dynamics of the organization without information overload.

Clearly, newcomers often face a difficult challenge when entering an organization. Organizations should use multiple approaches to facilitate the learning that must occur during successful socialization.

Organizational socialization is also a process of change, because individuals need to adapt to their new work environment (Ashforth & Saks, 1996; Fisher, 1984). Newcomers who learn in the content areas noted in the last section should undergo attitude and behavioral changes. Feldman proposed that socialization learning includes acquiring a set of appropriate role behaviors, developing work habits and abilities, and adjusting to the work group's norms and values (Feldman, 1981). That is, they develop new work roles, adopt new team norms, and practice new behaviors. To varying degrees, newcomers also acquire the values and assumptions of the organization's dominant culture as well as the local subcultures. Some people quickly internalize the organization's culture; a few others rebel against these attempts to change their mental models and values. Ideally, newcomers adopt a level of creative individualism in which they accept the essential elements of the organization's culture and team norms, yet maintain a healthy individualism that challenges the allegedly dysfunctional elements of organizational life.

Socialization is a continuous process, beginning long before the first day of employment and continuing throughout one's career within the organization. However, it is most intense when people move across organizational boundaries, such as when they first join an organization, move to a new department or regional branch office, get transferred to (or back from) an international assignment, or get promoted to a higher level in the organization. For each of these transitions, employees need to adjust to an entirely new work context as well as learn role-specific behaviors (Pinder & Schroeder, 1987; Adler, 1991).

SOCIALIZATION STAGES

The stages of socialization coincide generally with the stages of a career. Although researchers have proposed various descriptions of the stages of socialization (Feldman, 1976b, 1981), three stages sufficiently describe it: (1) anticipatory socialization, (2) accommodation, and (3) role management (Ogbonna & Harris, 1998). Each stage involves specific activities that, if undertaken properly, increase the individual's chances of having an effective career. Moreover, these stages occur continuously and often simultaneously.

Anticipatory Socialization

The first stage involves all those activities the individual undertakes prior to entering the organization or to taking a different job in the same organization. In this stage, the individual forms an impression about what membership in an organization is like. Information about organizations is available from a variety of sources, such as rumors, anecdotes, advertisements, the media, employment recruiters, and increasingly through the Internet.

People are vitally interested in two kinds of information prior to entering a new job or organization. First, they want to know as much as they can about what working for the organization is really like. This form of learning about the organization is actually attempting to assess the organization's culture. Second, they want to know whether they are suited to the jobs available in the organization. Individuals seek out this information with considerable effort when they are faced with the decision to take a job, whether it is their first one or one that comes along by way of transfer or promotion. At these times, the information is specific to the job or the organization.

We also form impressions about jobs and organizations in less formal ways. For example, our friends and relatives talk of their experiences. Parents impart both positive and negative information to their offspring regarding the world of work. Although we continually receive information about this or that job or organization, we are more receptive to such information when faced with the necessity to make a decision.

These impressions influence expectations that may in turn affect an individual's behavior. For example, people's expectations when looking for jobs may attract them to one organization, reject another organization from their consideration, and affect their decision to remain at an organization where they initially choose to work. It is desirable that the information transmitted and received during the anticipatory stage accurately and clearly depicts the organization and the job.

Managers and HRD professionals must provide accurate information and help correct inaccurate expectations to avoid the potential negative consequences for performance, satisfaction, and tenure. We know that individuals differ considerably in the way they decode and receive information. Yet if the fit between the individual and the organization is to be optimal, two conditions are necessary. The first condition is realism; both the individual and the organization must portray themselves realistically. The second condition is congruence. This condition is present when the individual's skills, talents, and abilities are fully utilized by the job. Either their overutilization or underutilization results in incongruence and, consequently poor performance (Gershon et al., 2004). The extent to which individuals believe there is a lack of fit in either of these conditions it will affect their behavior, both in terms of whether they will attempt to join the organization and how they may interact with organization members.

Organizations like the Calvert Group, Nordstrom's, Citicorp, and Hewlett-Packard have worked extremely hard to attract and retain employees who have values congruent with the organizations unique cultures. For example, Nordstrom has built so strong a culture around serving the customer (letting go any employee who fails to become socialized) that the entire employee manual is a 5 × 8-inch card with one rule on it: "Use your good judgment in all situations" (Jones, 1983).

Conflicts When Exchanging Information

Recruits and organizations need an open exchange of accurate information during the anticipatory stage to ensure that they form the same psychological contract. Unfortunately, various conflicts make it difficult for both parties to send or receive accurate information (Porter, Lawler, & Hackman, 1975, Ch. 5).

One conflict occurs between the organization's need to attract qualified recruits and the recruit's need for complete information to make accurate employment decisions. Many organizations use a "flypaper" approach by describing only positive aspects of the job and organization and neglecting to mention the undesirable elements in the hope that the best recruits will get "stuck" on the organization. This approach may lead recruits to accept job offers on the basis of incomplete or false expectations (Cable et al., 2000).

The second type of conflict occurs between the recruit's need to look attractive to employers and the organization's need for complete information to make accurate selection decisions. The problem is that recruits sometimes emphasize favorable employment experiences and leave out less favorable events in their careers. This tactic provides organizations with inaccurate data, thereby distorting their expectations of the job candidate and weakening the quality of organizational selection decisions.

The third type of conflict occurs when recruits refrain from asking important career decision questions to avoid conveying an unfavorable image. For instance, recruits usually don't like to ask about starting salaries and promotion opportunities. Yet, unless the organization presents this information, recruits might fill in the missing information with false assumptions that produce an inaccurate psychological contract.

Finally, conflict occurs when organizations avoid asking certain questions or using potentially valuable selection devices because doing so might put the organization in a bad light. For instance, some organizations refuse to use aptitude or ability tests, because they don't want to give the impression that the organization treats employees like mice running through a maze. Unfortunately, without the additional information, organizations may form a less accurate opinion of the recruit's potential as an employee.

In spite of these conflicts, recruits do manage to discover some information about the organization. They learn from casual acquaintances with current and former employees. They receive some information from brochures, public news about the organization, and initial recruitment visits. Recruits also learn from their visits to the organization.

Accommodation

The second stage of socialization occurs after the individual becomes a member of the organization, after he or she takes the job. During this stage, the individual sees the organization and the job for what they actually are. Through a variety of activities, the individual attempts to become an active participant in the organization and a competent performer on the job. This breaking-in period is ordinarily stressful for the individual because of anxiety created by the uncertainties inherent in any new and different situation. Apparently, individuals who experienced realism and congruence during the anticipatory stage have a less stressful accommodation stage. Nevertheless, the demands on the individual do indeed create situations that induce stress.

Four major activities constitute the accommodation stage: All individuals, to a degree, must engage in (1) establishing a new interpersonal relationship with both co-workers and supervisors, (2) learning the tasks required to perform the job, (3) clarifying their role in the organization and in the formal and informal groups relevant to that role, and (4) evaluating the progress they are making toward satisfying the demands of the job and the role.

If all goes well in this state, the individual feels a sense of acceptance by co-workers and supervisors and experiences competence in performing job tasks. The breaking-in period, if successful, also results in role definition and congruence of evaluation. These four outcomes of the accommodation stage (acceptance, competence, role definition, and congruence evaluation) are experienced by all new employees to a greater or lesser extent. However, the relative value of each of these outcomes varies from person to person (Van Maanen, 1978). Acceptance by the group may be a less valued outcome for an individual whose social needs are satisfied off the job, for example. Regardless of these differences due to individual preferences, each of us experiences the accommodation stage of socialization and ordinarily moves onto the third stage.

Role Management

During the role management stage in the socialization process, employees settle in as they make the transition from newcomers to insiders. They strengthen relationships with co-workers and supervisors, practice new role behaviors, and adopt attitudes and values consistent with their new position and organization. However, in contrast to the accommodation stage, which requires the individual to adjust to demands and expectations of the immediate work group, the role management stage takes on a broader set of issues and problems. Specifically, during the third stage, conflicts arise.

One conflict is between the individual's work and home lives. For example, the individual must divide time and energy between the job and her or his role in the family. Because the amount of time and energy is fixed and the demands of work and family are seemingly insatiable, conflict is inevitable. Employees must redistribute their time and energy between work and family, reschedule recreational activities, and deal with changing perceptions and values in the context of other life roles. They must address any discrepancies between their existing values and those emphasized by the organizational culture. Employees unable to resolve these conflicts are often forced to leave the organization or to perform at an ineffective level. In either case, the individual and the organization are not well served by unresolved conflict between work and family.

The second source of conflict during the role management stage is between the individual's work group and other work groups in the organization. This source of conflict can be more apparent for some employees than for others. For example, as an individual moves up the organization's hierarchy, he or she is required to interact with various groups both inside and outside the organization. Each group can and often does place different demands on the individual, and to the extent that the demands are beyond the individual's ability to meet them, stress results. Tolerance for the level of stress induced by these conflicting and irreconcilable demands vary among individuals. HRD professionals should keep in mind that generally, the existence of unmanaged stress works to the disadvantage of the individual and the organization.

CHARACTERISTICS OF EFFECTIVE SOCIALIZATION PROCESSES

Organizational socialization processes vary in form and content form organization to organization. Even with the same organization, various individuals experience different socialization processes. For example, the accommodation stage for a university-trained management recruit is quite different from that of a person in the lowest-paid occupation in the organization. As Van Maanen has pointed out, socialization processes are not only extremely important in shaping the individuals who enter an organization, but they are also remarkably different from situation to situation (Van Maanen, 1978). Either explanation permits the suggestion that, while uniqueness is apparent, some general principles can be implemented in the socialization process (Boice, 2000).

Effective Anticipatory Socialization

The organization's primary activities during the first stage of socialization are recruitment and selection and placement programs. If these programs are effective, new recruits in an organization should experience the feeling of realism and congruence. In turn, accurate expectations about the job results from realism and congruence.

Recruitment programs are directed toward new employees, those not now in the organization. As noted earlier, many organizations use a flypaper approach to recruiting. In reality, this strategy of exaggerating positive features and ignoring negative aspects of the jobs tends to produce a distorted psychological contract that eventually leads to lower trust and higher turnover (Morrison & Robinson, 1997). A better approach is to give recruits a realistic job preview (RJP), that is, a balance of positive and negative information about the job and work context (Breaugh, 1992, Ch. 7; Wanous, 1992, Ch. 3).

For example, one public transit company shows recruits a video depicting angry riders, knife attacks, and other abuses that bus drivers must endure on their routes. Applicants then meet with a union representative who explains, among other things, that new drivers are typically assigned night shifts and the poorest routes. Finally, applicants are given the opportunity to drive a bus.

Although RJPs scare away some applicants, they tend to reduce turnover and increase job performance (Truby, 2001). RJPs help recruits develop more accurate preemployment expectations that, in turn, minimize reality shock. RJPs prepare employees for the more challenging and troublesome aspects of work life. Moreover, applicants engage in self-selection when given realistic information. There is also some evidence that RJPs increase organizational loyalty. A possible explanation is that organizations providing candid information are easier to trust. They also show respect for the psychological contract and concern for employee welfare (Wanous & Collela, 1989).

Although the RJP occurs during the recruitment process, it can also be considered an HRD intervention in that it shares many of the same goals and techniques as other HRD approaches. The socialization process really begins before an employee formally joins the organization and the RJP addresses its initial step (i.e., anticipatory socialization) by attempting to adjust unrealistic impressions and reinforce accurate expectations (Werner & DeSimone, 2006).

It is desirable to give prospective employees information not only about the job but also about those aspects of the organization that affect the individual. It is nearly always easier for the recruiter to stress job-related information to the exclusion of organization-related information. Job-related information is usually specific and objective, whereas organization-related information is usually general and subjective. Nevertheless, the recruiter should, to the extent possible, convey factual information about such matters as pay and promotion policies and practices, objective characteristics of the work group the recruit is likely to join, and other information that reflects the recruiter's concerns.

Selection and placement practices, in the context of anticipatory socialization, are important conveyers of information to employees already in the organization. Of prime importance is the manner in which individuals view career paths in organizations. The stereotypical career path is one that involves advancement up the managerial hierarchy. This concept, however, does not take into account the differences among individuals toward such moves. Greater flexibility in career paths would require the organization to consider lateral or downward transfers (Recardo & Jolly, 1997).

Effective Accommodation Socialization

Effective accommodation socialization comprises five different activities: (1) designing orientation programs, (2) structuring training programs, (3) providing performance evaluation information, (4) assigning challenging work, and (5) assigning demanding bosses.

Orientation programs are seldom given the attention they deserve. The first few days on the new job can have very strong negative or positive impacts on the new employee. Taking a new job involves not only new job tasks but also new interpersonal relationships. The new person comes into an ongoing social system that has evolved a unique set of values, ideals, frictions, conflicts, friendships, coalitions, and all the other characteristics of work groups. If left alone, the new employee must cope with the new environment in ignorance, but if given some help and guidance, she or he can cope more effectively (Thomas & Anderson, 2002).

Thus, organizations should design orientation programs that enable new employees to meet the rest of the employees as soon as possible. Moreover, specific individuals should be assigned the task of orientation. These individuals should be selected for their social skills and be given time off from their own work to spend with the new people. The degree to which the orientation program is formalized can vary, but in any case, the program should not be left to chance. (A detailed discussion of orientation programs will be provided later in this chapter.)

Training programs are invaluable in the breaking-in stage. Without question, training programs are necessary to instruct new employees in proper techniques and to help them develop requisite skills. Moreover, effective training programs provide frequent feedback about progress in acquiring the necessary skills. What is not so obvious is the necessity of integrating formal training with the orientation program.

Performance evaluation, in the context of socialization, provides important feedback about how well the individual is getting along in the organization. Inaccurate or ambiguous information regarding this important circumstance can only lead to performance problems. To avoid these problems, it is imperative that performance evaluation sessions take place in face-to-face meetings between the individual and manager and that in the context of the job the performance criteria must be as objective as possible. Management by objectives and behaviorally anchored rating scales are particularly applicable in these settings.

Assigning challenging work to new employees is a principal feature of effective socialization programs. The first jobs of new employees often demand far less of them than they are able to deliver. Consequently, they are unable to demonstrate their full capabilities, and in a sense they are being stifled. This is especially damaging if the recruiter was overtly enthusiastic in "selling" the organization when they were recruited.

Assigning demanding bosses is a practice that seems to have considerable promise for increasing the retention rate of new employees. In this context, "demanding" should not be interpreted as "autocratic." Rather, the boss most likely to get new hires off in the right direction is one who has high but achievable expectations for their performance. Such a boss instills the understanding that high performance is expected and rewarded; equally important, the boss is always ready to assist through coaching and counseling.

Socialization programs and practices intended to retain and develop employees can be used separately or in combination. HRD professionals are well advised to ensure that their organizations establish policies most likely to retain those recent hires who have the highest potential to perform effectively. This likelihood is improved if the policies include realistic orientation and training programs, accurate performance evaluation feedback, and challenging initial assignments supervised by supportive, performance-oriented managers.

192   Human Resource Development: Today and Tomorrow

Effective Role Management Socialization

Organizations that effectively deal with the conflicts associated with the role management stage recognize the impact of such conflicts on job satisfaction and turnover. Even though motivation and high performance may not be associated with socialization activities, satisfaction and turnover are, and organizations can ill afford to lose capable employees.

Retention of employees beset by off-job conflicts is enhanced in organizations that provide professional counseling and that schedule and adjust work assignments for those with particularly difficult conflicts at work and home. Of course, these practices do not guarantee that employees can resolve or even cope with the conflict. The important point, however, is for the organization to show good faith and make a sincere effort to adapt to the problems of its employees. Figure 7.1 summarizes what HRD professionals and their organizations can do to encourage effective socialization.

New Employee Orientation

Orientation is the introduction of new employees to the organization, their work units, and their jobs. As suggested earlier, employees receive orientation from their coworkers and from the organization. The orientation from coworkers is usually unplanned and unofficial, and it often provides the new employee with misleading and inaccurate information. This is one of the reasons the official orientation provided by the organization is so important. An effective orientation program has an immediate and lasting impact on the new employee and can make the difference between her or his success or failure. On the other hand, poor orientation can result in disenchantment, dissatisfaction, anxiety, turnover, and other employee problems.

Socialization Stage	Practices
Anticipatory socialization	1. Recruitment using realistic job previews 2. Selection and placement using realistic career paths
Accommodation socialization	1. Tailor-made and individualized orientation 2. Social as well as technical skills training 3. Supportive and accurate feedback 4. Challenging work assignments 5. Demanding but fair supervisors
Role management socialization	1. Provision of professional counseling 2. Adaptive and flexible work assignments 3. Sincere person-oriented managers

Figure 7.1.   A checklist of effective socialization practices.

Goals of Orientation

An orientation program generally has a clear and specific set of goals intended to provide clear messages and accurate information about the organizational culture, job, and expectations. Unfortunately, what is clear to one person may be muddled to another. One important goal is to reduce anxiety and uncertainty for new employees. When newly hired individuals come to work for the first time, they are likely to experience considerable anxiety and uncertainty. For example, they may be unfamiliar with such basic issues as how often they get paid, where the HRM department office is, where the company cafeteria is, where they are supposed to park, normal work hours, who will provide their job-related training, and so forth. An effective orientation program provides answers to these questions efficiently and effectively for new employees. In many organizations new employees are also briefed on their benefit options and choices and enroll in various benefit programs during orientation.

A related goal of orientation is to ease the burden that socializing newcomers place on supervisors and coworkers. In the absence of orientation, an organizational newcomer would have little choice but to direct his or her questions to a supervisor or coworkers, and those individuals would thus spend considerable time answering questions and providing information to new employees. Some informal indoctrination is inevitable, of course, and may serve the beneficial purposes of helping new people get better acquainted and integrated into their work group. But if informal indoctrination is the only vehicle for orientation, supervisors and coworkers would have to spend a disproportionate amount of time answering questions. Moreover, newcomers might not always get complete or accurate answers to their questions, simply because other employees are not likely to be completely up-to-date on every detail of the employment relationship with the organization.

Another goal of orientation is to provide favorable initial job experiences for new employees. As noted earlier, realistic job previews are important as a way to avoid problems of disenchantment and disappointment when people encounter jobs that are different from what they expected. In similar fashion an effective orientation program can complement and reinforce this process by making sure that a new employee's initial job experiences are positive and effective. The orientation program, for example, will help newcomers feel like part of a team; allow them to quickly meet their coworkers, their supervisors, and other new employees; and in a variety of other ways ease the transition from being an outsider to being an insider.

Basic Issues in Orientation

A variety of basic issues must be dealt with in planning an orientation for new employees. These issues include the content of the orientation, the length of the orientation, and the decision of whom will actually conduct the orientation. The content of the orientation is of obvious importance. Most organizations try to provide their employees with a set of basic understanding of organizational policies and procedures that are relevant to that particular employee. For example, hourly workers who are expected to punch a time clock or sign a time card must be educated in the mechanics of where these things are located, how they are handled, how to fill them out, and so forth.

Similarly, the orientation should provide information about issues such as hours of work, compensation, and schedules and direct the individuals to the appropriate offices and managers to answer various questions. For example, an orientation program might tell new employees to direct any questions or concerns regarding potential discrimination to the organization's EEOC officer.

Some organizations also find it appropriate to include as a part of their orientation a general overview and introduction to the business itself. This introduction would include such things as information about the organization's history, its evolution, its successes, and perhaps even some of its failures. Organizations that have a strong organizational culture are especially likely to include this type of information as a part of the orientation process. This approach enables newly hired employees top to understand that culture and to know how to function within it. At Southwest Airlines, for example, newcomers watch a video featuring the organization's CEO Herb Kelleher, welcoming them to the team and explaining the organization's approach to doing business. But the real message is perhaps best conveyed by the format of the video—Kelleher delivers his "speech" in the form of rap music, backed by a team of other Southwest employees!

In many cases the duration or length of an orientation program is a function of what the organization intends to impart during that orientation. Obviously, the more material that it wants to convey to new employees, the longer the orientation will need to last. In some cases an organization may attempt to handle orientation in only an hour or two. More typically, however, orientation is likely to take a half-day or perhaps even a full day. And occasionally, organizations may provide an initial orientation and then have a brief follow-up session a few days or weeks later to answer questions or deal with issues that have arisen after employees have had a brief opportunity to experience life in the organization.

Finally, the organization must decide who will actually conduct the orientation session. In many situations a number of individuals are a part of the orientation process. For example, one or more HRD professionals are likely to be involved in new-employee orientation. In some cases operating managers are also actively involved. Union officials occasionally involve themselves in orientation when an organization's workers are represented by a strong labor union. Sometimes organizations use current operating employees to facilitate the orientation program as well.

An interesting trend that some organizations are experimenting with involves having retired employees perform the orientation. For example, Hewlett-Packard invites retired employees to coordinate and run the orientation process in a number of its manufacturing plants around the United States. The company has found this strategy to be particularly effective because it helps convey the idea to new employees that the organization must clearly be a good place to work if retirees are willing to come back and help orient newcomers.

The primary role of HRD professionals in new employee orientation is to design and oversee the orientation program. Specifically, this may include producing or obtaining materials (such as workbooks and seminar leader guides), conducting training sessions, designing and conducting the evaluation study, and in some cases conducting parts of the orientation program itself (focusing on such things as available services, employee rights, benefits, and workplace rules).

HRD professionals can also play an important role in encouraging all levels of management to become involved in the orientation program and support it. Establishing a steering committee and finding ways for key managers to stay involved in the process (e.g., meeting with newcomers, conducting orientation sessions) are two ways this can be accomplished. Furthermore, HRD professionals should take steps (such as interviewing and surveying newcomers and supervisors) to ensure that the orientation program is being carried out as planned and that the program is current and effective.

Problems with Orientation Programs

Many problems or criticisms of orientation programs have been identified:

- An overemphasis on paperwork.
- A sketchy overview of the basics.
- Suffocation or information overload (giving newcomers too much information too quickly).
- Mickey Mouse assignments where the new employee's first tasks are insignificant duties, supposedly intended to teach the job "from the ground up."

- Scare tactics (heavy emphasis on failure rates or the negative aspects of the job).
- Too much selling of the organization.
- Emphasis on formal, one-way communication (using lectures and videos without giving newcomers a chance to discuss issues of interest or ask questions).
- One-shot mentality (e.g., limiting the orientation program to only the first day at work.
- No diagnosis or evaluation of the program.
- Lack of follow-up (St. John, 1980; Feldman, 1988).

Information overload is a particularly common problem as many orientation programs cram a large amount of information into a short period. This is done for convenience and practicality purposes. However, a person can absorb only so much information in a given time period before learning efficiency drops and stress increases (remember the maxim: The mind can only absorb what the seat can endure!") HRD professionals should be sensitive to the issue and try to prevent information overload by:

- Including only essential information during the initial phase of orientation.
- Providing written materials that trainees can take with them and review later (or look up online), especially for complex benefits plans and important topics such as the organization mission and work rules.
- Conducting the program in phases to space out presentation of the material (e.g., Southwest Airlines holds its orientation once a week, rather than for one week straight) (Tyler, 1998).
- Following up with the newcomers to make sure they understand major issues and to answer any additional questions they may have.

Designing and Implementing an Employee Orientation Program

Instead of a quick and information-overload orientation program, a more systematic and guided procedure is appropriate. Following are a few guidelines for such a program:

1. Orientation should begin with the most relevant and immediate kinds of information and then proceed to more general policies of the organization. It should occur at a pace that the new employee is comfortable with.

2. The most significant part of orientation is the human side; giving new employees knowledge of what supervisors and coworkers are like, telling them how long it should take to reach standards of effective work, and encouraging them to seek help and advice when needed.
3. New employees should be "sponsored" or directed in the immediate environment by an experienced worker or supervisor who can respond to questions and keep in close touch during the early induction period.
4. New employees should be gradually introduced to the people with whom they will work, rather than given a superficial introduction to all of them on the first day. The object should be to help them know their coworkers and supervisors.
5. New employees should be allowed sufficient time to get their feet on the ground before job demands on them are increased.

The problems cited above can be avoided and the guidelines can be included in orientation programs by paying attention to the basic principles that should guide any HRD intervention: needs assessment, design, implementation, and evaluation (Werner & DeSimone, 2006). As suggested earlier, many issues must be considered when designing an orientation program (Sims, 2002; Cohen, 2003). Corning provides a good model for developing an orientation program (McGarrell, 1984). Corning, like many other firms, faced a difficult problem: new people were getting the red-carpet treatment while being recruited, but once they started work, it was often a different story—a letdown. Often their first day on the job was disorganized and confusing, and sometimes this continued for weeks. One new employee said, "You're planting the seeds of turnover right at the beginning."

Managers at Corning realized that they needed a better way to help new employees make the transition to their new company and community. Corning needed a better way to help these new people get off on the right foot-to learn the how-tos, the wheres, and the whys, and to learn about the company's culture and its philosophies. And the company had to ensure the same support for newly hired secretaries in a district office, sales representatives working out of their homes, or engineers in a plant. Corning followed ten steps in designing its program:

1. Set objectives. Corning's objectives included:
   - Reduce turnover in the first three years of employment by 17%.
   - Reduce time to learn the job by 17%.
   - Provide newcomers with a uniform understanding of the company.
   - Build a positive attitude toward the company and communities.

2. Form a steering committee.
3. Research orientation as a concept.
4. Interview recently hired employees, supervisors, and corporate officers.
5. Survey the orientation practices of top companies (the program at Texas Instruments proved particularly helpful).
6. Survey existing company orientation programs and materials.
7. Select content and delivery method.
8. Pilot and revise materials.
9. Produce and package and print and audiovisual materials.
10. Train supervisors and install the system.

Three features distinguish the Corning approach from others: (1) It is an orientation process, not a program. (2) It is based on guided self-learning. New people have responsibility for their own learning. (3) It is long-term (15 to 18 months), and it is in-depth. An evaluation study revealed that this program met or exceeded all of its objectives, including reducing voluntary turnover by 69%.

Some organizations are combining orientation programs with computer-based training to create multimedia capabilities. Using computer-based training (CBT), Lazarus Department Stores was able to cut orientation-training time in half, orienting 2,500 new employees in six weeks. Duracell International has developed an orientation program that lets employees around the world view video clips from company executives. IBM Global Services' orientation programs have eliminated paper in the classroom by giving students instruction on the web and facilitating their discussion of the materials (via Lotus Notes). This is in keeping with IBM's commitment to use the days and weeks of orientation to teach new hires the technology it sells to its customers. Of course, these types of programs supplement—but do not replace—the value of face-to-face orientation (Haskell, 1998; Bennett, Lehman, & Forst, 1999; Gist & Stevens, 1998).

Orientation Kit

Each new employee should receive an orientation kit, or packet of information, to supplement the verbal orientation program. The kit, which is normally prepared by the HRD professionals, can provide a wide variety of materials. Care should be taken in the design not only to ensure that it offers essential information, but also as noted earlier does not give too much information. Some materials that might be included in an orientation kit include these:

- Company organization chart.
- Map of the company's facilities.
- Copy of policy and procedures handbook.
- List of holidays and fringe benefits.
- Copies of performance appraisal forms, dates, and procedures.
- Copies of other required forms (e.g., expense reimbursement form).
- Emergency and accident prevention procedures.
- Sample of company newsletter or magazine.
- Telephone numbers and locations of key company personnel (e.g., security personnel).
- Copies of insurance plans.

Many organizations require employees to sign a form indicating they have received and read the orientation kit. This is commonly required in unionized organizations to protect the company if a grievance arises and the employee alleges he or she was not aware of certain company policies and procedures. On the other hand, it is equally important that a form be signed in nonunionized organizations, particularly in light of an increase in wrongful discharge litigation. Whether signing a document actually encourages new employees to read the orientation kit is questionable.

Orientation Follow-Up

The worst mistake an organization can make is to ignore the new employee after orientation. Almost as bad is an informal open-door policy: "Come see me sometime if you have any questions." Many new employees are simply not assertive enough to seek out the supervisor or HRD representative—more than likely, they fear looking "dumb." National Semiconductor uses focus groups of randomly selected new employees to find out what they like and don't like (Starcke, 1996). It found that many of the topics covered during orientation need to be explained briefly again—once the employee has had the opportunity to experience them firsthand. This is natural and understandable in view of the blizzard of information that often is communicated during orientation. In completing the orientation follow-up, HRD professionals should review a checklist of items covered with each new employee or small group of employees to ensure that all items were in fact covered. They should then make sure that the completed checklist is signed by the supervisor, the HRD representative, and the new employee.

Evaluation of the Orientation Program

At least once a year, HRD professionals should review the orientation program to determine if it is meeting its objectives and to identify future improvements. To improve orientation, HRD professionals need candid, comprehensive feedback from everyone involved in the program. There are several ways to provide this kind of feedback: through roundtable discussions with new employees after their first year on the job, through in-depth interviews with randomly selected employees and supervisors, and through questionnaires fro mass coverage of all recent hires.

Finally, organizations should realize that new employees will receive an orientation that has an impact on their performance—either from coworkers or from the organization. It is certainly in the best interest of the organization to have a well-planned, well-executed orientation program.

All HRD professionals need to understand the important role that orientation plays in helping newcomers to an organization learn the ropes and get off to a good start. In addition, HRD professionals should know the relevant goals of orientation for their particular organization and be willing and able to make appropriate contributions to the orientation process, especially as it affects new employees in their own area. In the end, effective orientation should achieve several purposes:

- Establish a favorable employee impression of the organization and the job.
- Provide organization and job information.
- Enhance interpersonal acceptance by co-workers.
- Accelerates socialization and integration of the new employee into the organization.
- Ensure that employee performance and productivity begin more quickly.

In the end, effective orientation efforts contribute to both short-term and long-term success for employees. The following considerations are important for HRD professionals to keep in mind as they design and implement the process of orienting new employees. They apply to any type of organization, large or small, and to any function or level of a job (Starcke, 1996; Johnson, 2004):

1. The impressions formed by new employees within their first 60 to 90 days on a job are lasting.
2. Day 1 is crucial—new employees remember it for years. It must be managed well.
3. New employees are interested in learning about the total organization—and how they and their unit fill into the "big picture." This is

just as important as is specific information about the new employee's own job and department. For example, new employees at Corning go through an intranet scavenger hunt that requires them to use information learned during orientation and to demonstrate that they are comfortable with using the company's intranet system.
4. Give new employees responsibility for their own orientation, through guided self-learning, gut with direction and support. For example, one organization has its orientation program on CD-ROM so that employees can self-pace their learning (Finney, 1996).
5. Provide information in reasonable amounts so as to avoid information overload.
6. Recognize that community, social, and family adjustment is a critical aspect of orientation for new employees.
7. Make the immediate supervisor ultimately responsible for the success of the orientation process.
8. Thorough orientation is a "must" for productivity improvement. It is a vital part of the total management system—and therefore the foundation of any effort to improve employee productivity.

These lessons are exciting and provocative. They suggest that HRD professionals should be at least concerned with preparing the new employee for the social context of his or her job and for coping with the insecurities and frustrations of a new learning situation as with the development of the technical skills necessary for job performance.

SOCIALIZING A CULTURALLY DIVERSE WORKFORCE

Due to the changing demographics in the United States, differences in the employee pool are going to continue to increase over the next few decades. HRD professionals will have to study socialization much more closely and help their organizations intervene so that the maximum benefits result from hiring an increasingly diverse workforce. Studying the ethnic background and national cultures of these workers will have to be taken seriously. The HRD and managerial challenge will be to identify ways to integrate the increasing number and mix of people from diverse national cultures into the workplace. Some obvious issues for HRD professionals and their organizations with ethnically diverse workforces to consider include these:
- Coping with employees' unfamiliarity with the English language.
- Increased training for service jobs that require verbal skills.
- Cultural (national) awareness training for the current workforce.

- Learning which rewards are valued by different ethnic groups.
- Developing career development programs that fit the skills, needs, and values of the ethnic group.
- Rewarding managers for effectively recruiting, hiring, and integrating a diverse workforce.
- Do not focus only on ethnic diversity but also learn more about age, gender, and workers with disability diversities.

Socializing involving an ethnically diverse workforce is a two-way proposition. Not only must the HRD professionals ensure that managers and other organizational members learn about the employees' cultural background, but the employee must also learn about the rituals, customs, and values of the organization or the work unit (Jameison & O'Mara, 1991, pp. 84–89). For example, Merck has an educational program to raise its employees' awareness and attitudes about women and minorities (Eagly et al., 2003). The program emphasizes how policies and systems can be tailored to meet changes in the demographics of the workplace. Procter & Gamble has stressed the value of diversity. The organization uses multicultural advisory teams, minority and women's networking conferences, and "onboarding" programs to help new women and minority employees become acclaimed and productive as quickly as possible. Ortho Pharmaceutical initiated a program to "manage diversity" that is designed to foster a process of cultural transition within the organization. Northeastern Products Company established an outside English as A Second Language (ESL) program to meet the needs of Hispanic and Asian employees. A buddy system has been established at Ore-Ida. A buddy (English speaker) is assigned to a new employee (whose first language is not English) to assist him or her with communication problems.

SOCIALIZATION AS AN INTEGRATION STRATEGY

It is possible to view socialization as a form of organizational integration, because individuals need to adapt to their new work environment (Ashforth & Saks, 1996; Fisher, 1984). Specifically, socialization from the change process or integration perspective is a strategy for achieving congruence of organizational and individual goals. Thus, socialization is an important and powerful process for transmitting the organizational culture as suggested in the beginning of this chapter in our discussion of socialization as a change process.

Organizational integration is achieved primarily by aligning and integrating the goals of individuals with the objectives of organizations. The greater the congruity between individual goals and organization objectives, the greater the integration. The socialization process achieves organization integration by, in effect, undoing the individual's previously held goals and creating new ones that come closer to those valued by the organization. In its most extreme form, this undoing process involves debasement techniques such as those experienced by U.S. Marine Corps recruits, military academy plebes, and fraternity and sorority pledges.

Integration of organizational and individual interests can also involve ethical issues. These ethical issues are most evident when the two parties do not share the same information or hold the same legitimate power. Ethics involves moral issues and making choices. It is not realistic to assume that the organization and an individual will always make the same ethically based decision. Individuals are challenged to make moral decisions that are fair and the right thing to do. By examining an organization's code of ethics an individual can acquire some knowledge about how ethical issues are typically handled.

Rensis Likert is a spokesperson for the use of leader and peer socialization. While presenting his ideas on leadership theory, Likert stresses the importance of the leader who maintains high performance standards and group-centered leadership techniques. The leader sets high standards for his or her own behavior and performance, and through group-centered leadership, encourages the group to follow the example. If successful, the leader creates a group of high performance that is apparent to a new employee assigned to the group (Gibson et al., 2006).

The common thread recommended to organizational leaders in any country is the active role played by the leader and the group members in integrating goals and objectives. Effective socialization, particularly during the accommodation and role management stages, requires joint and supportive efforts of leaders and direct reports alike.

CONCLUSION

In closing, it should be clear to HRD professionals that newcomers face a significant challenge when joining an organization and it benefits both the individual and the organization to facilitate the socialization process. Socialization continues throughout an employee's career. HRD professionals should recognize the implications of environmental changes on the socialization process and cannot afford to ignore other training and career development activities that facilitate this ongoing socialization process. New employees need support and timely performance reviews and challenging assignments, and all employees can benefit from assistance in developing their careers.

CHAPTER 8

HRD AND CAREER MANAGEMENT AND DEVELOPMENT

INTRODUCTION

Understanding and finding ways to influence the careers of employees in an organization is a critical part of HRD. Career development provides a future orientation to HRD activities. More than ever before employees and the organizations they work for must be able to adapt and change if they are to be successful and develop and maintain a competitive advantage. Given the turbulent environment of the past decade and every indication that the future environment will be one of rapid change, globalization, increased competition, continued changes in the employment relationship, and flatter, less hierarchical structures, contemporary organizations will need employees who are able to grow and change correspondingly regardless of the type of work. To the extent organizations can assist employees in being better prepared for new responsibilities within the organization, enhance the employability of the employees over the long haul, and understand how employees make decisions about future work, organizations, managers and their HRD personnel can do a better job of planning to meet their human resource needs.

This chapter first discusses the basics of career management to include the necessity of career development and defines career success. Next, the chapter focuses on general career progression and adult life cycle stages. The roles the organization, managers, employees and HRD professionals must play in career development are discussed before identifying several career-related myths. The chapter then explains how people choose careers before identifying several career development tools and activities that can be used by HRD professionals in implementing career development efforts. Before concluding the chapter with a look at implementing and evaluating career development systems the chapter discusses special career issues.

CAREER MANAGEMENT: UNDERSTANDING THE BASICS

Traditionally, career development efforts targeted managerial personnel to help them look beyond their current jobs and to prepare them for a variety of future jobs in the organization. But development for all employees, not just managers, is necessary for organizations to have the needed human resource capabilities for future growth and change.

Mergers, acquisitions, restructurings, and layoffs all have influenced the way people and organizations look at careers and development. In the "new career," the individual—not the organization—manages his or her own development. Such self-development consists of personal educational experiences, training, organizational experiences, projects, and even changes in occupational fields.[1] Under this system the individual defines career success, and the result may or may not coincide with the organizational view of success.

Organizations promote this "self-reliance" in career development by telling employees they should focus on creating employability for themselves in the uncertain future. However, employability must also be defined in such a way that it provides value for the employing organization. It is a dilemma of sorts that if employers give employees unrestricted access to development opportunities, employers may not be able to retain talent in the highly competitive labor markets of today.

Careers, Career Planning and Career Development

In everyday parlance, the word career is used in a number of different ways. People speak of "pursuing a career"; "career planning" workshops are common; college and universities hold "career days" during which they publicize jobs in different fields and assist individuals in "career counseling." A person may be characterized as a "career" woman or man who shops in a store that specializes in "career clothing." Likewise, a person may be characterized as a "career military officer." We may overhear a person say, "That movie 'made' his career" (i.e., it enhanced his reputation) or in a derogatory tone, after a direct report has insulted the CEO, "He can kiss his career good-bye" (i.e., he has tarnished her reputation). Finally, an angry supervisor may remark to her dawdling direct report, "Williams, are you going to make a career out of changing that light bulb?"

As these examples illustrate, the word career can be viewed from a number of different perspectives. From one perspective a career is a sequence of positions occupied by a person during the course of a lifetime. This is the objective career. From another perspective, though, a career consists of a sense of where a person is going in her or his work life. This is the subjective career, and it is held together by a self concept that consists of (1) perceived talents and abilities, (2) basic values, and (3) career motives and needs (Schein, 1996). Both of these perspectives, objective and subjective, focus on the individual. Both assume that people have some degree of control over their destinies and that they can manipulate opportunities in order to maximize the success and satisfaction derived from their careers (Greenhaus, 1987). They assume further that HRM and HRD activities should recognize career stages and assist employees with the development tasks they face at each stage. Career planning is important because the consequences of career success or failure are linked closely to each individual's self-concept, identity, and satisfaction with career and life.

Organizations have a significant impact on employees' careers, through their effects on the HRM process. Recruiting, selecting, placing, training, developing, appraising, promoting, and separating the employee all affect the person's career, and therefore career satisfaction and success. Some organizations institute relatively formal career management processes, while other organizations do relatively little. We can define career management as a process for enabling employees to better understand and develop their career skills and interests, and to use these skills and interests effectively both within the organization and after they leave the organization.

Career development is the lifelong series of activities (such as workshops) that contribute to a person's career exploration, establishment, success, and fulfillment. For the organization, career development is an ongoing, formalized effort by an organization that focuses on developing and enriching the organization's human resources in light of both the employees' and the organization's needs. Career planning is the deliberate process through which someone becomes aware of personal skills, interests, knowledge, motivations, and other characteristics; acquires information about opportunities and choices; identifies career-related goals; and establishes action plans to attain specific goals. Career development and career planning should reinforce each other. Career development looks at individual careers from the viewpoint of the organization, whereas career planning looks at careers through the eyes of individual employees.

The Necessity of Career Development

If an organization assists employees in developing career plans, these plans are likely to be closely tied to the organization; therefore, employees are less likely to quit. Taking an interest in employees' careers can also improve morale, boost productivity, and help the organization become more efficient. The fact that an organization shows interest in an employee's career development has a positive effect on that employee. Under these circumstances, employees believe the company regards them as part of an overall plan and not just numbers. An emphasis on career development can also have a positive impact on the ways employees view their jobs and their employers.

From the organization's viewpoint, career development has three major objectives:

1. To meet the immediate and future human resource needs of the organization on a timely basis.
2. To better inform the organization and the individual about potential career paths within the organization.
3. To utilize existing human resource programs to the fullest by integrating the activities that select, assign, develop, and manage individual careers with the organization's plans (Winterscheid, 1980).

Today's careers are boundaryless and tend to be characterized by features such as the following (see, Sullivan, 1999; Arthur & Rousseau, 1996):

- Portable knowledge, skills, and abilities across multiple organizations.
- Personal identification with meaningful work.
- On-the-job action learning.
- Development of multiple networks of associates and peer-learning relationships.
- Responsibility for managing your own career.

The concept of a boundaryless career raises an interesting question, namely, what is the meaning of "career success?"

Definition of "Career Success"

The tradition-oriented "organization man" of the 1950s had a clear definition of success and a stable model for achieving it. However, massive changes in the business environment as introduced at various points in this book have forced employees at all levels to explore alternative models of career success, and they are confronted with a variety of possibilities (Rousseau &

Wade-Benzoni, 1995). Is it occupational success? Job satisfaction? Growth and development of skills? Successful movement through various life stages? Traditionally, career development and success have been defined in terms of occupational advancement, which is clear and easy to measure. Today, however, it seems appropriate to consider a new model, as more careers tend to be cyclical in nature. That is, they involve periodic cycles of skill apprenticeship, mastery, and reskilling. Lateral, rather than upward, movement often constitutes career development, and cross-functional experience is essential to multiskilling and continued employability. Late careers increasingly are defined in terms of phased retirement (Watson Wyatt Worldwide, 2004; Allen, 2004). In this new world, the ultimate goal is psychological success, the feeling of pride and personal accomplishment that comes from achieving your most important goals in life.

GENERAL CAREER PROGRESSION AND ADULT LIFE CYCLE STAGES

The typical career of many individuals today probably includes different positions, transitions, and organizations—more so than in the past, when employees were less mobile and organizations were more stable as long-term employers. Therefore, it is useful to think about general patterns in people's lives and the effects on their careers.

For years, researchers have attempted to identify the major developmental tasks that employees face during their working lives and to organize these tasks into broader career stages (such as early, middle, and late career) (Levinson, 1985; Sheehy, 1977). Many theorists in adult development describe the first half of life as the young adult's quest for competence and for a way to make a mark in the world. According to this view, a person attains happiness during this time primarily through achievement and the acquisition of capabilities. The second half of life is different. Once the adult starts to measure time from the expected end of life rather than from the beginning, the need for competence and acquisition changes to the need for integrity, values, and well-being. For many people, internal values take precedence over external scorecards or accomplishments such as wealth and job title status. In addition, mature adults already possess certain skills, so their focus may shift to interests other than skills acquisition. Career-ending concerns, such as life after retirement, reflect additional shifts.

Contained within this life pattern is the idea that careers and lives are not predictably linear but cyclical. Individuals experience periods of high stability, followed by transition periods of less stability, and by inevitable discoveries, disappointments, and triumphs. These cycles of structure and transition occur throughout individuals' lives and careers. The cyclical view may be an especially useful perspective for individuals affected by downsizing or early career plateaus in large organizations. Such a perspective argues for the importance of flexibility in an individual's career. It also emphasizes the importance of individuals' continuing to acquire more and diverse knowledge, skills, and abilities.

Although a number of models have been proposed like the one above, very little research has tested their accuracy. Moreover, there is little, if any, agreement about whether career stages are linked to age or not. Most theorists give age ranges for each stage, but these vary widely. Consequently, it may make more sense to think in terms of career stages linked to time. This would allow a "career clock" to begin at different points for different individuals, based on their backgrounds and experience (Milkovich & Anderson, 1982).

Such an approach allows for differences in the number of distinct stages through which individuals may pass, the overlapping tasks and issues they may face at each stage, and the role of transition periods between stages. The lesson for HRD professionals is that all models of adult life-cycle stages should be viewed as broad guidelines rather than as exact representations of reality.

WHO IS RESPONSIBLE FOR CAREER DEVELOPMENT?

What are the roles and responsibilities of the organization and individuals with regard to career development or management? Which has primary responsibility? The answer is that the organization, the manager, and the employee (to include the HRD and career development specialists) all play roles and share responsibilities in planning, guiding, and developing the employee's career. Before providing a more detailed discussion of the various roles and responsibilities in career development efforts the following list provides a brief outline of how one might view the roles and responsibilities of organizations, individual employees and managers (Otte & Hutcheson, 1992, p. 56):

Organization
- Communicate mission, policies, and procedures.
- Provide training and development opportunities.
- Provide career information and career programs.
- Offer a variety of career options.

Manager
- Provide timely feedback.
- Provide development assignments and support.

- Participate in career development discussions.
- Support employee development plans.

Individual
- Accept responsibility for your own career.
- Assess your interests, skills, and values.
- Seek out career information and resources
- Establish goals and career plans.
- Utilize development opportunities.
- Talk with your manager about your career.
- Follow through on realistic career plans.

Organization's Role

The organization has primary responsibility for instigating and ensuring that career development takes place. Specifically, the organization's responsibilities are to develop and communicate career options within the organization to the employee. In reality, an employer's career development responsibilities really depend somewhat on how long the employee has been with the organization. Before hiring, realistic job previews can help prospective employees more accurately gauge whether the job is indeed for them, and particularly whether a job's demands are a good fit with candidates' skills and interests. Especially for recent college graduates, the first job can be crucial for building confidence and a more realistic picture of what he or she can and cannot do: Providing challenging first jobs (rather than relegating new employees to "jobs where they can't do any harm"), and having an experienced mentor who can help the person learn the ropes, are important. Some refer to this as preventing a reality shock, a phenomenon that occurs when a new employee's high expectations and enthusiasm confront the reality of a boring, unchallenging job.

The organization should carefully advise an employee concerning possible career paths to achieve each employee's career goals. The organization should supply information about its mission, policies, and plans and for providing support for employee self-assessment, training, and development. More specifically, after a person has been on the job for a while, an employer can take steps to contribute in a positive way to the employee's career. Career-oriented appraisals—in which the manager is trained not just to appraise the employee but also to match the person's strengths and weaknesses with a feasible career path and required development work—is one important step. Similarly, providing periodic, planned job rotation can help the person develop a more realistic picture of what he or she is (and is not) good at, and thus the sort of future career moves that might be best.

Significant career growth can occur when individual initiative combines with organizational opportunity. Career development programs benefit managers by giving them increased skill in managing their own careers, greater retention of valued employees, increased understanding of the organization, and enhanced reputations as people-developers. As with other HRM or HRD programs, the inauguration of a career development program should be based on the organization's needs as well.

Assessment of needs should take a variety of approaches (surveys, informal group discussions, interviews, etc.) and should involve personnel from different groups, such as new employees, managers, plateaued employees, minority and women employees, and technical and professional employees. Identifying the needs and problems of these groups provides the starting point for the organization's career development efforts (More will be said about these various approaches and groups later in this chapter). Organizational needs should be linked with individual career needs in a way that joins personal effectiveness and satisfaction of employees with the achievement of the organization's strategic objectives. Organizations can best meet their responsibilities in career development efforts by promoting the conditions and creating the environment that will facilitate the development of individual career plans by the employees.

Promoting the conditions and creating the environment that will facilitate the development of employee's careers requires that the organization be a proactive force in the career development process. To do so, organizations must think and plan in terms of shorter employment relationships. This can be done, as is often the case in professional sports, through fixed-term employment contracts with options for renegotiation and extension.

Additionally, organizations must invest adequate time and energy in job design and equipment. Given the mobility among workers is expected to increase, careful attention to these elements will make it easier to make replacements fully productive as soon as possible. Perhaps the most persuasive reason for helping employees manage their own careers is the need to remain competitive. Although it might seem like a contradiction, such efforts can enhance an organization's stability by developing more purposeful, self-assured employees. Organizations that recognize the need to provide employees with satisfying opportunities will have the decided advantage of a loyal and industrious workforce.

The Manager's Role

It has been said that "the critical battleground in career development is inside the mind of the person's charged with supervisory responsibility (Randolph, 1981). Although not expected to be a professional counselor, the manager can and should play a role in facilitating the development of a direct report's career. First, and foremost, the manager should serve as a catalyst and sounding board.

Managers should encourage employees to take responsibility for their own careers, offering continuing assistance in the form of feedback on individual performance and making available information about the organization, about the job, and about career opportunities that might be of interest. The manager should show an employee how to go about the process and then help the employee evaluate the conclusions.

Managers or supervisors are provided with a number of opportunities to be actively involved in developing employee's careers. For example, during career-oriented appraisals described in the last section, managers (or supervisors) can serve as a source of information about an employee's strengths and weaknesses through the performance evaluation process. Manages can also provide accurate information about career paths and opportunities within the organization, support the employee's career plans (e.g., nominate the employee for training and development opportunities), and serve as a key source of feedback to the employee on career progress.

The involvement of one's immediate supervisor or manager in career development programs has been identified as one of the critical components to the success of such efforts (Leibowitz, Farren, & Kaye, 1986; Leibowitz, Feldman, & Moseley, 1992). Several roles a manager might perform to assist direct reports in developing their careers are (Liebowitz & Schlossberg, 1981): communicator, counselor, appraiser, coach, mentor, advisor, broker, referral agent, and advocate. Based on an analysis of critical incidents gathered from employees, there are four roles that managers and supervisors should be trained to perform in order to fulfill their responsibility as career developers (Liebowitz & Schlossberg, 1981). These roles include:

1. Coach—one who listens, clarifies, probes, and defines employee career concerns.
2. Appraiser—one who gives feedback, clarifies performance standards and job responsibilities.
3. Adviser—one who generates options, helps set goals, makes recommendations, and gives advice.
4. Referral Agent—one who consults with the employee on action plans and links the employee to available organizational people and resources.

Corning Inc. defines the roles of manager's in the career development process as (Leibowitz et al., 1990): (1) appraising performance; (2) coaching and supporting; (3) guiding and counseling; (4) providing feedback;

(5) supplying information; and (6) maintaining integrity of system. Successful career development at organizations like Corning, Inc. results from a joint effort by the organization, the immediate manager, and the individual; the organization provides the resources and structure, the immediate manager provides the guidelines and encouragement, and the individual makes the necessary decisions and does the planning.

The Employee's Role

While our discussion thus far demonstrates that there is more than enough work for the organization and manager to do in developing employees' careers when it comes to developing an individual's career, the reality is that each employee should accept the primary responsibility for his or her own career success. This is one task that no employee should ever leave to a manager or employer.

In today's dynamic work environment, individuals are increasingly responsible for initiating and managing their own career planning. While many employees in the past felt they had the luxury of turning over responsibility for their career progress to their employers, the changes in the social contract between employers and their employees has necessitated that everyone should recognize and accept personal responsibility. One need only track the number of mergers, acquisitions, restructurings and the demise of organizational loyalty to see that today's employees should continue to change their attitudes toward career management, from passive and complacent to proactive.

Career planning is not something one individual can do for another; it has to come from the individual. Only the individual knows what she or he really wants out of a career, and certainly these desires vary appreciably from person to person. For the individual employee, the career planning process means matching individual strengths and weakness with occupational opportunities and threats. The person wants to pursue occupations, jobs, and a career that capitalize on her or his interests, aptitudes, values, and skills. She or he wants to choose occupations, jobs, and a career that make sense in terms of projected future demand for various types of occupations.

Career planning requires a conscious effort on the part of the employee; it is hard work, and it does not happen automatically. Each employee must identify his or her own knowledge, skills, abilities, interests, and values and seek out information about career options in order to set goals and develop career plans.

Before employees can engage in meaningful career planning, they must not only have an awareness of the organization's philosophy, but they must also have a good understanding of the organization's more immediate goals. Otherwise, they may plan for personal change and growth without knowing if or how their own goals match those of the organization. For example, if the technology of a business is changing and new skills are needed, will the organization retrain to meet this need or hire new talent? Is there growth, stability, or decline in the number of employees needed? How will turnover affect the need? Clearly, an organizational plan that answers these kinds of questions is essential to support individual career planning.

Although an individual may be convinced that developing a sound career plan would be in his or her best interest, finding the time to develop such a plan is often another matter. The organization can help by providing trained specialists to encourage and guide the employee. This can best be accomplished by allotting a few hours of organization time each quarter to this type of planning. Individuals and organizations must constantly recognize that individuals like their organizations change over time, their needs and interests change. Thus, it would be unrealistic to expect individuals to establish their career goals with perfect understanding of where they are going or—for that matter—where the organization is going. So while goal setting is critical, building in some flexibility is a good idea.

Of course, career planning only gets one so far. During 2000–2003, many people who had previously worked hard to train as computer systems analysts were devastated to find that the dot-com collapse had dramatically reduced the need for systems analysts. However, uncertainties like these only underscore the need for keeping one's finger on the pulse of the job market, so as to be better positioned to move when a career change is required.

Many people make the mistake of changing occupations (or of remaining unhappily in their present jobs) when they could be happier without making a big career change. For some people a little fine-tuning will often suffice. The employee, if dissatisfied at work, has to figure out where the problem lies. Some people may like their occupations and the employers for whom they work, but not how their specific jobs are structured. Others may find their employers' ways of doing things are the problem. In any case, it's not always the occupation that's the problem. Why decide to switch from being a lawyer to teacher, when it's not the profession but that law firms' 80 hour-week's that's the problem?

HRD's Role

HRD and Career Development (CD) professionals are generally responsible for ensuring that career-related information is kept current as new jobs are created and old ones are phased out. Working closely with both employees and their managers, HRD and CD specialists should see that accurate information is conveyed and that interrelationships among different career paths are understood. Thus, rather than bearing the primary responsibility for preparing individual careers plans, HRD and CD personnel work to see that the organization promotes the conditions and create the environment that will facilitate the development of individual career plans by the employees.

Like any other HRM activity, if career development is to succeed, it must receive the complete support of top management. Ideally, senior line managers and HRD and CD personnel will work together to design and implement a career development system. The system should reflect the goals and culture of the organization, and the HRD philosophy should be woven throughout. An HRD philosophy can provide employees with a clear set of expectations and directions for their own career development. For a program to be effective, managerial personnel at all levels must be trained in the fundamentals of job design, performance or career-oriented appraisal, career planning, and counseling.

In many ways, an HRD professional's role is the same in career development initiatives as it is in any other HRD activity: to ensure that the organization has programs and activities that will help the organization and its employees to achieve their goals. This role involves all of the foundations in needs assessment, design, implementation, and evaluation.

In addition, in light of changes in the career landscape, Hall (1996) offers the following suggestions for career development and HRD professionals to help individuals become "masters of their own careers":

- Start with the recognition that each individual "owns" her or his career.
- Create information and support for the individual's own efforts at development.
- Recognize that career development is a relational process in which the career practitioner plays a broad role.
- Become an expert on career information and assessment technologies.
- Become a professional communicator about your services and the new career contract.
- Promote work planning that benefits the organization as a whole, over career planning that is unrelated to organizational goals and future directions.
- Promote learning through relationships at work.
- Be an organizational interventionist, that is, someone willing and able to intervene where there are roadblocks to successful career management.

- Promote mobility and the idea of the lifelong learner identity.
- Develop the mind-set of using natural (existing) resources for development.

HRD professionals also must examine the employment practices used by their organization, and determine the extent to which these practices promote or work against the kinds of career management behavior they want employees to engage in (Arthur, Claman, & DeFillippi, 1995).

Successful career development results from a joint effort by the organization, the immediate manager, the individual, and the HRD or CD professionals. The organization provides the resources and structure, the individual does the planning, the immediate manager provides guidance and encouragement, and the HRD professionals ensure that the organization has programs and activities that help employees develop their careers.

CAREER-RELATED MYTHS

Individuals in organizations hold many myths related career development and advancement. Frequently, such myths are misleading and can inhibit career development and growth. The following discussion explores these myths and provides evidence disproving them.

Myths Held by Employees[2]

Myth 1: Career Development and Planning Are Functions of Human Resource Development Personnel. The ultimate responsibility for career development and planning belongs to the individual, not to HRD professionals or the individual's manager. HRD professionals should assist the individual and answer certain questions, but they cannot take sole responsibility for developing a career plan for him or her. The individual must take a proactive role in making career-related decisions.

Myth 2: Rapid Advancement along a Career Path Is Largely a Function of the Kind of Manager One Has. A manager can affect a direct report's rate of advancement. However, those who adhere to this myth often accept a defensive role and ignore the importance of their own actions. Belief in this myth provides a ready-made excuse for failure. It is easy and convenient to blame failures on one's manager.

Myth 3: There Is Always Room for One More Person at the Top. This myth contradicts the fact that the structures of the overwhelming majority of today's organizations have fewer positions available as one progresses up the organization. Adherence to this myth fosters unrealistic aspirations and generates self-perpetuating frustrations. There is nothing wrong with wanting to become president of the organization; however, an individual must also be aware that the odds of attaining such a position are slim. It is important that individuals recognize that they should pick career paths that are realistic and attainable.

Myth 4: Good Direct Reports Make Good Managers. This myth is based on the belief that those employees who are the best performers in their current jobs should be the ones who are promoted. This is not to imply that good performance should not be rewarded, for it should. However, when an individual is being promoted, those making the decision should look carefully at the requirements of the new job in addition to the individual's present job performance. How many times has a star salesperson or engineer been promoted into a managerial role, only to fail miserably! Similarly, outstanding athletes are frequently made head coaches, and everybody seems surprised when the former star fails in that job. Playing a sport and coaching require different talents and abilities. Because someone excels at one job does not mean he or she will excel at all jobs.

Myth 5: The Key to Success Is Being in the Right Place at the Right Time. Like all the career-related myths, this one has just enough truth to make it believable. One can always find a highly successful person who attributes all of her or his success to being in the right place at the right time. People who adhere to this myth are rejecting the basic philosophy of planning: that a person, through careful design, can affect rather than merely accept the future. Adherence to myth 5 is dangerous because it can lead to complacency and a defeatist attitude.

Myth 6: All Good Things Come to Those Who Work Long, Hard Hours. People guided by this myth often spend 10 to 12 hours a day trying to impress their managers and move ahead rapidly in the organization. However, the results of those extra hours on the job often have little or no relationship to what the manager considers important, to the person's effectiveness on the job, or (most important in this context) to the individual's long-range career growth. Unfortunately, many managers reinforce this myth by designing activities "to keep everyone busy."

Myth 7: Always Do Your Best, Regardless of the Task. This myth stems from the puritan work ethic. The problem is that believers ignore the fact that different tasks have different priorities. Because there is only a limited amount of time, a person should spend that time according to priorities. Those tasks and jobs that rank high in importance in achieving one's career goals should receive the individual's best effort. The idea is to give something less than one's best effort to unimportant tasks in order to have time to give one's best effort to the important ones.

Myth 8: The Way to Get Ahead Is to Determine Your Weaknesses and Then Work Hard to Correct Them. Successful salespeople do not emphasize the weak points of their products; rather, they emphasize the strong points. The same should be true in career development and planning. Individuals who achieve their career objectives do so by stressing those things they do uncommonly well. The secret is to first capitalize on one's strengths and then try to improve deficiencies in other areas.

Myth 9: The Grass Is Always Greener on the Other Side of the Fence. Regardless of the career path the individual follows, another one always seems a little more attractive. However, utopia does not exist. More than likely, the job Jane Doe holds involves many of the same problems every working person might face. As the individual assumes more and more personal responsibilities, the price of taking that "attractive" job becomes higher in terms of possibly having to relocate, develop a new social life, and learn new duties. This is not to say that job and related changes should not be made; however, one should avoid making such changes hastily.

Myth 10: It Is Wise to Keep Home and Work Life Separated. An individual cannot make wise career decisions without the full knowledge and support of her or his spouse. Working husbands and wives should share their inner feelings concerning their jobs so that their spouses will understand the basic factors that weigh in any career decisions.

A healthy person usually has interests other than a job. Career strategy should be designed to recognize and support, not contradict, these other interests. Career objectives should be a subset of one's life objectives. Too often, however, career objectives conflict with, rather than support, life objectives.

Myths Held by Managers[3]

Myth 1: Career Development Will Raise Expectations. Many managers fear that an emphasis on career development will raise employee expectations to unrealistically high levels. Career development should do just the opposite: It should bring employees' aspirations into the open and match their skills, interests, and goals with opportunities that are realistically available.

Myth 2: We Will Be Overwhelmed with Requests. This myth is based on the fear that employees will deluge their managers for information about jobs in other parts of the organization and that employees will expect the organization to provide them with a multitude of career opportunities. While this fear is very realistic in the minds of many managers, it is basically unfounded.

Myth 3: We Do Not Have the Necessary Systems in Place. This myth is based on the belief that before the organization can introduce career development, it must first put in place a whole series of other human resource planning mechanisms, such as job posting and succession planning. In reality, many organizations have implemented successful career development programs with few formal mechanisms beyond the basic requirement of providing employees with effective career planning tools.

Myth 4: Managers Will Not Be Able to Cope. Management often becomes concerned that introducing career development and planning will place managers in a counseling role for which they are ill prepared. While coaching and counseling should be an important part of any manager's job, the key to career development and planning is to place the responsibility primarily on the employee.

HOW PEOPLE CHOOSE CAREERS

There are four general individual characteristics that affect how people make career choices. They are as follows:

- *Interests:* People tend to pursue careers that they believe match their interests. Both over time, interests change for many people, and career decisions eventually are made based on special skills, abilities, and career paths that are realistic for them.
- *Self-image:* A career is an extension of a person's self-image, as well as a molder of it. People follow careers they can "see" themselves in and avoid those that do not fit with their perceptions of their talents, motives, and values.
- *Personality:* An employee's personality includes his or her personal orientation (for example, inclination to be realistic, enterprising, or artistic) and personal needs (including affiliation, power, and achievement needs). Individuals with certain personality types gravitate to different clusters of occupations.
- *Social backgrounds:* Socioeconomic status and the educational levels and occupations of a person's parents are included in that person's social background. Children of a physician or a welder know from a parent what that job is like and may either seek or reject it based on how they view the parent's job.

Less is known about how and why people choose specific organizations than about why they choose specific careers. One obvious factor is timing—the availability of a job when the person is looking for work. The amount of information available about alternatives is an important factor as well. Beyond these issues, people seem to pick an organization on the basis of a "fit" between the climate of the organization as they view it and their own personal characteristics, interests, and needs.

IMPLEMENTING CAREER DEVELOPMENT

Organizations have a wide range of possible career development tools and activities from which to choose in implementing their career development efforts. For our purposes, successful implementation of a career development initiative involves four basic steps at the individual level: (1) the individual's assessment of his or her abilities, interests, and career goals; (2) organization's assessment of the individual's abilities and potentials; (3) communication of career options and opportunities within the organization; and (4) career counseling to set realistic goals and plans for their accomplishment (Stone, 1981, p. 324).

Self-Assessment

Many individuals never stop to analyze their abilities, interests, and career goals. It isn't that these individuals don't want to analyze these factors; rather, they simply never take the time. While this is not something an organization can do for the individual, the organization can provide the impetus and structure.

An individual's self-assessment should not necessarily be limited by current resources and abilities; career plans today increasingly require that the individual acquire additional training and skills. However, this assessment should be based on reality. For the individual, this involves identifying personal strengths—not only the individual's developed abilities but also the financial resources available.

A variety of self-assessment materials are available commercially; and some organizations have developed tailor-made forms and training programs for the use of their employees. Self-assessment activities, such as self-study workbooks or career planning workshops, focus on providing employees with a systematic way to identify capabilities and career preferences. Self-assessment is best used as a first step in the process (i.e., at the stage of self-exploration—which involves gathering information about one's self and the environment) rather than as the only activity in a career management program (Gutteridge, 1986). Self-assessment activities can be done by an individual alone, in groups, or in some combination of the two. Effective self-assessment should (1) set the stage for the self-assessment experience and (2) help an individual explore her or his values, interests, skills, feelings, personal resources, and goals for decision-making styles (Smith, 1988). This information can help answer questions such as "Who am I?" "What do I want out of my life and my career?" and "How can I best achieve my career goals?"

Self-assessment workbooks provide information and a series of exercises to help an individual discover his or her values, abilities, and preferences. These workbooks can be purchased from a third party or designed specifically for an organization. The advantages of self-assessment exercises developed by third-party sources are that they are readily available and have been designed by career development experts. However, they are not designed to fit within an organization's specific HRD and career development strategy. HRD staff that use such self-assessment workbooks may need to make modifications, or develop supplementary materials to fill these gaps.

Self-assessment workbooks designed to complement an organization's overall HRD strategy may do better at making employees aware of resources and opportunities within the organization. Such workbooks can include a statement of the organization's career development policy and associated procedures; information on the organization's structure, career paths, and job specifications; information about related training, education, and development programs; and instructions on how employees can obtain further information, such as names, addresses, and phone numbers of resource persons within the organization (Burack & Mathys, 1980).

Like other self-assessment approaches, career planning workshops provide a structured experience in which participants develop, share, and discuss personal information about their strengths, weaknesses, goals, and values (Gutteridge, 1986). Workshops can be made up of one or more sessions that focus on what career planning and management is all about, self-discovery, reality testing of insights gained during self-discovery through discussions with the facilitator and other participants, identification of possible career directions and opportunities, and career goal setting (Leibowitz, Farren, & Kaye, 1986).

The advantages of career planning workshops include the ability to reach many people at once, opportunities to gain support from peers and to develop networks, and exposure to other people's ideas and reactions. In addition, feedback from the facilitator and other group members may help the individual recognize any self-deception or self-ignorance that might go undetected if a self-assessment workbook were used alone. Potential disadvantages include scheduling problems, difficulty in designing an experience that suits all the participants' needs (especially if they come from different organizational levels), and the possibility that some people may be intimidated by the group setting (Liebowitz et al., 1986).

If performed effectively, self-assessment activities can provide an individual with a sound basis on which to develop realistic career goals and strategies. Self-assessments and evaluation of the environment are important first steps in establishing effective career goals and strategies (Greenhaus, Callen, & Godshalk, 2000).

Assessing Employee Potential

Organizations have a vested interest in ensuring that they have individuals available who are ready to fill key positions when those positions become vacant. This means that organizations, managers and HRD professionals must establish clear understanding of the talent base they have at their disposal. To this end, many organizations evaluate the potential, or promotability, of technical, professional and managerial employees. Those identified as high-potential employees can then be "groomed" for these positions. Several ways that assessing employee potential can be done are through potential ratings, assessment centers, and by succession planning. Assessing employees potential typically begins with the use of potential ratings and moves into the more sophisticated methods like assessment centers.

Employee potential ratings (EPS) are similar to employee performance appraisals or evaluations. An employee's manager or supervisor typically performs them. They measure multiple dimensions, and include a summary or overall rating of the employee's potential for advancement. The main difference between EPS and performance ratings is that EPSs focus on the future rather than the past or present. This method requires the rater to judge whether an employee is likely to be successful in jobs requiring he or she may not currently use. Also, the results of potential evaluations are unlikely to be made known to the employee. Ratings of potential are subject to the same problems as performance evaluations (i.e., rating errors and biases). Raters should be trained in the proper way to conduct such an evaluation.

Identifying and developing talent in individuals is a role that all managers or supervisors should take seriously. As they conduct formal appraisals, they should be concerned with their direct reports' potential for managerial or advanced technical jobs and encourage their growth in that direction. In addition to immediate managers or supervisors others in the organization who have the power to evaluate, nominate, and sponsor employees with promise should be actively involved in assessing employee potential.

Assessment centers, which can be used as part of the employee selection process, can also be used to assess potential for advancement (Boehm, 1988). The assessment center can be an excellent source of information as it allows the organization to evaluate individuals as they participate in a series of situations that resemble what they might be called upon to handle on the job. In an assessment center, small groups of employees perform a variety of exercises, while being evaluated by a group of trained assessors. The exercises can include simulations, role-plays, group discussions, tests, and interviews. The exercises should measure relevant skills and aptitudes for a given position. The assessors are typically managers who are one or two organizational levels above those being evaluated (assessees). Assessors should be specifically trained for this task. The assessors write a detailed report on each assessee and usually make an overall judgment about the assessee's promotability. When used for developmental purposes, the intensive assessment feedback is provided to the employee to increase self-awareness. The feedback from a developmental assessment center can be used by the employee to develop career goals and a plan for future development. While career development assessment centers can be expensive to use, they provide a rich source of data. Care should be taken in designing assessment center procedures to include assessment of skills that can be developed in a reasonable amount of time and to include exercises that permit multiple opportunities to observe participants in each dimension (Thornton, 1992).

The assessment center method offers great flexibility of form and content, the use of multiple assessment techniques, standardized methods of interpreting behavior, and pooled assessor judgments which all help to account for the successful track record of this approach over the past five decades. It has consistently (a) demonstrated high validity; (b) assessment center ratings also predict long-term career success; and (c) both minorities and nonminorities and men and women acknowledge that the method provides them a fair opportunity to demonstrate what they are capable of doing in a management job (Cascio, 2006).

Despite its advantages, the method is not without potential problems, including the following (see, Lievens, 2002; Gaugler & Thornton, 1989; Reilly, Henry, & Smither, 1990):

- Adoption of the assessment center method without carefully analyzing the need for it and without adequate preparations to use it wisely.
- Blind acceptance of assessment data without considering other information on candidates, such as past and current performance.
- The tendency to rate only general "exercise effectiveness," rather than performance relative to individual behavior dimensions (e.g., by using a behavioral checklist), as the number of dimensions exceeds the ability of assessors to evaluate each dimension individually.
- Lack of control over the information generated during assessment: for example, "leaking" assessment ratings to operating managers.
- Failure to evaluate the utility of the program in terms of dollar benefits relative to costs.
- Inadequate feedback to participants.

Each of these problems can be overcome. Doing so will allow even more accurate prediction of each candidate's likely potential.

Succession planning is a third way of conducting potential evaluations (Karaveli & Hall, 2003). This process is most often done for upper-level management positions. It requires senior managers to identify employees who should be developed to replace them. Information generated during succession planning may not be communicated to the employee. If potential evaluations are made known to the employee and her or his superiors, this information can be used to create a self-fulfilling prophecy. That is, if managers believe the employee has a high potential for advancement, they may be more likely to evaluate the person favorably and promote her or him more quickly than actual performance warrants. If succession plans are not communicated to the employee, the organization runs the risk of a mismatch between the employee's career plans and its plans for the employee. Making this information available to the employee can ensure that the employee develops realistic career plans and reduces the chances that the person will refuse the position.

Under an optimal succession planning system, individuals are initially identified as candidates to move up after being nominated by management. Then performance evaluation data are reviewed, potential is assessed, developmental programs are formulated, and career paths are mapped out. Sophisticated succession planning helps ensure that qualified internal candidates are not overlooked.

One problem with many succession planning efforts, especially informal plans and those for large organizations, is the "crowned prince" syndrome (McElwain, 1991; "Executive Succession," 2001). This occurs when management considers for advancement only those who have managed to become visible to senior management. Another problem with succession planning is that so much information must be tracked that it is very difficult to do it manually. In situations such as this, the succession plan should be computerized using mostly data that are already available from HR personnel.

Communicating Career Options

To set realistic career goals, employees must know the options and opportunities that are available. The organization can do several things to facilitate such awareness. Posting and advertising job vacancies is one activity that helps employees get a feel for their career options. Clearly identifying possible paths of advancement within the organization is also helpful. This can be done as part of the performance evaluation process. Another good idea is to share HRM planning forecasts with employees.

Job Posting

Job posting is one of the most common career development activities. It involves making open position in the organization known to current employees before advertising them to outsiders. In a typical job posting program, the organization publishes the job description, job requirements, pay range, and an application procedure for vacancies, and it provides a form for employees to submit. The vacancies can be posted in a common area, such as on a bulletin board reserved for that purpose. Increasingly, such postings are done online, using the organization's website or intranet. Interested employees can then apply and be considered for the vacant position. Job posting systems are widely used in both private and public sector organizations.

Career Paths

Career paths represent employees' movements through opportunities over time. While most career paths are thought of as leading upward, good opportunities also exist in cross-functional or horizontal directions (Karr, 2002). Career paths can be defined as a sequence of developmental activities involving informal and formal education, training, and job experiences that help make an individual capable of holding more advanced jobs (Burack & Mathys, 1980, p. 78).

Career paths exist on an informal basis in almost all organizations. However, career paths are much more useful when formally designed and documented. Such formalization results in specific descriptions of sequential work experiences, as well as how the different sequences relate to one another. Career paths should:

- Represent real progression possibilities, whether lateral or upward, without implied "normal" rates of progress or forced specialization in a technical area.
- Be tentative and responsive to changes in job content, work priorities, organizational patterns, and management needs.
- Be flexible, taking into consideration the compensating qualities of a particular employee, managers, direct reports, or others who influence the way that work is performed.
- Specify the skills, knowledge, and other attributes required to perform effectively at each position along the paths and specify how they can be acquired. (If specifications are limited to educational credentials, age, and experience, some capable performers may be excluded from career opportunities.)

An innovative use of career paths called "skill supply chains" allow employees to move to other organizations as they succeed where they are. For example, in Philadelphia, more than 200 employers (fast-food restaurants, banks, supermarkets, retailers, hotels, etc.) participate in a skill supply chain in the form of a "tiered employment" system aimed at underemployed entry-level workers. People enter the paths at tier 1 after receiving four weeks of customer service training, and find themselves flipping burgers or cleaning hotel rooms. They have to be successful for six months, with counselors checking attendance and performance. If they do well, they can apply for tier 2 positions either at their current employers or at another organization in the system. After a year in tier 2, successful employees can apply for tier 3 jobs, which include entry-level store manager jobs. Viewing each job not as a dead end but as a rung on a ladder makes people stay and perform well. This kind of career path system is based on the same drivers as those that operate in a private employer's career path system (Raimy, 2002).

Career Counseling

Individual career counseling involves one-on-one discussions between the employee and an organizational representative (i.e., immediate manager, an HRM specialist (HRD professionals) or a combination of the two). In most cases, it is preferable to have the immediate manager conduct counseling with appropriate input from HRD professionals. The immediate manager generally has the advantage of practical experience, knows the organization, and is in a position to make a realistic appraisal of organizational opportunities. Career counseling sessions can range from brief, informal talks, to the annual performance evaluation discussion, to a series of discussions with a manager or counseling professional (Gutteridge & Otte, 1983).

Career counseling can answer a wide range of questions and can either stand alone or supplement other career development activities. The career counseling process can be viewed in three stages:

1. Opening and Probing—This stage establishes rapport and determines the employee's goals for the counseling session(s).
2. Understanding and Focusing—This includes providing assistance in self-assessment and establishing career goals and strategies.
3. Programming—This stage provides support for implementing the career strategy (Burack & Mathys, 1980).

During this process, the counselor can suggest actions to the employee and provide support and feedback about the ideas and results of actions taken by the employee.

Some managers are reluctant to attempt counseling because they haven't been trained in the area. However, it is not necessary to be a trained psychologist to be a successful counselor (Meckel, 1981). Generally, managers who are skilled in basic human relations are successful as career counselors. Developing a caring attitude toward employees and their careers is of prime importance. Being receptive to employee concerns and problems is another requirement. Following are some specific suggestions for helping managers become better career counselors.

1. *Recognize the limits of career counseling.* Remember that the manager and the organization serve as catalysts in the career development process. The primary responsibility for developing a career plan lies with the individual employee.
2. *Respect confidentiality.* Career counseling is very personal and has basic requirements of ethics, confidentiality, and privacy.
3. *Establish a relationship.* Be honest, open, and sincere with direct reports. Try to be empathetic and see things from the direct report's point of view.
4. *Listen effectively.* Learn to be a sincere listener. A natural human tendency is to want to do most of the talking. It often takes a conscious effort to be a good listener.
5. *Consider alternatives.* An important goal in career counseling is to help direct reports realize that a number of choices are usually available. Help direct reports expand their thinking and avoid being limited by past experience.
6. *See and share information.* Be sure the employee and the organization have completed their respective assessments of the employee's abilities, interests, and desires. Make sure the organization's assessment has been clearly communicated to the employee and that the employee is aware of potential job openings within the organization.
7. *Assist with goal definition and planning.* Remember that the employee must make the final decisions. Managers should serve as "sounding boards" and help ensure that the individual's plans are valid (Meckel, 1981).

In addition to the suggestions above it is important that the manager's role in the career development process is clarified. Additionally, they must have the opportunity to discuss their own career development concerns. Finally, the role of the counselor or developer should be incorporated into the organizational reward system (e.g., included in managers' performance evaluation) (Gutteridge, 1986).

It is usually a good idea for an organization not to depend on any one source of information but to use as many as are readily available. Such an approach provides a natural system of checks and balances.

Job Rotation and Mentoring

Providing periodic, planned job rotation can help an individual develop a more realistic picture of what he or she is (and is not) good at, and thus the sort of future career moves that might be best. Job rotation involves assigning an employee to a series of jobs in different functional areas of the organization. These assignments are typically lateral rather vertical moves, and can involve serving on task forces or moving from line to staff positions. Job rotation is a good way to introduce variety into an employee's career. In addition, it provides the employee with a chance to learn and use new skills and to better understand different organizational functions. It can also serve to help the employee build networks within the organization, and be better prepared for future promotion opportunities, when they become available.

The success of many individuals in their careers can often be tied back to others who influenced them. These individuals frequently mention immediate managers who were especially helpful as career developers. Many of these individuals also mention others at higher levels in the organization who provided guidance and support to them in the development of their careers. These executives and managers who coach, advise, and encourage employees of lesser rank are called mentors.

Generally, the mentor initiates the relationship, but sometimes an employee will approach a potential mentor for advice. Most mentoring relationships develop over time on an informal basis. However, in proactive organizations there is an emphasis on formal mentoring plans that call for the assignment of a mentor to those employees considered for upward movement in the organization. Under a good mentor, learning focuses on goals, opportunities, expectations, standards, and assistance in fulfilling one's potential.

Mentoring functions can be divided into two broad categories: career functions and psychosocial functions:

- Career functions. Career functions are those aspects of the relationship that enhance career advancement. They include sponsorship, exposure and visibility, coaching, protection, challenging assignments.
- Psychosocial functions. Psychosocial functions are those aspects that enhance the protégé's sense of competence, identity, and effectiveness in a professional role. They include role modeling, acceptance

and confirmation, counseling, and friendship. Both functions are viewed as critical to management development.

Not surprisingly, mentoring is also being done over the Internet. Known as *e-mentoring*, the process is mediated via web sites that bring experienced business professionals together with individuals needing counseling. Even though participants in e-mentoring typically never meet in person, many form long-lasting e-mail connections that tend to be very beneficial. Still, most participants see these connections as supplements to—rather than substitutes for—in-organization mentors.

SPECIAL CAREER ISSUES

There are a number of career issues that can be problematic for organizations and individuals although for different reasons. Those are career plateaus (or the lack of the opportunity to move up), dealing with technical professionals who do not want to go into management, dual-career couples, and issues related a diverse workforce (women, people of color, and older workers).

Career Plateaus

The pyramidal structure of many organizations together with a shrinking number of management positions typically means that a time will come in an individual's career when she or he will not longer be able to "move up" in the organization. In addition, career progress is not likely to be a continuous upward journey, but rather one that includes periods of movement and periods of stability. These factors contribute to what has been termed a career plateau. A career plateau has been defined as "the point in a career where the likelihood of additional hierarchical promotion is very low (Ferrence, Stoner, & Warren, 1997, p. 602). Career plateauing takes place when an employee reaches a position from which he or she is not likely to be promoted further (Applebaum & Firestone, 1994). Virtually all people reach a plateau in their careers; however, some individuals reach their plateaus earlier than others. Plateaued employees are those who "reach their promotional ceiling long before they retire (Kaye, 1989, p. 57; Bandwick, 1986).

Plateaued employees present a particular challenge for employers. They can affect morale if they become negative, but they may also represent valuable resources that are not being well used. HRD professionals should (1) assess whether employees are plateaued by determining employees' perceptions of the extent to which their careers are stalled and attempt to identify the reasons for the plateau, and (2) tailor the action used to resolve an employee's problems according to the cause of the plateau.

HRD professionals and organizations can help employees cope with plateaus by providing opportunities for lateral growth where opportunities for advancement do not exist. Other actions that can aid in managing the plateau process are: (1) prevent plateauees from becoming ineffective (prevent a problem from occurring); (2) integrate relevant career-related information systems (improve monitoring so that emerging problems can be detected and treated early); and (3) manage ineffective plateauees and frustrated employees more effectively (cure the problem once it has arisen). (The first action basically involves helping plateauees adjust to the solid-citizen category and realize they have not necessarily failed. Available avenues for personal development and growth should be pointed out. The second suggestion can largely be implemented through a thorough performance appraisal system. Such a system should encourage open communication between the managers and the person being appraised.

Because plateaued employees often include a significant number of employees who are worth rehabilitating it would pay for most organizations to address this issue seriously. At least five possibilities exist:

- Provide alternative means of recognition. Some possibilities include assigning the employee to a task force or giving other special assignments, participation in brainstorming sessions, representation of the organization to others, and training of new employees.
- Develop new ways to make their current jobs more satisfying. Some possibilities here include relating employees' performance to total organizational goals and creating competition in the job.
- Effect revitalization through reassignment. The idea here is to implement systematic job switching to positions at the same level that require many similar, though not exactly the same, skills and experiences as the present job.
- Utilize reality-based self-development programs. Instead of assigning plateauees to developmental programs designed to help them move into future jobs (which a majority of development programs do), assign them to development programs that can help them perform better in their present jobs.

Change managerial attitudes toward plateaued employees. It is not unusual for managers (and supervisors) to give up on and neglect plateaued employees. Such actions are quickly picked up by the affected employees and only compound the problem (Payne, 1984).

Technical and Professional Workers

Technical and professional workers, such as IT systems experts, engineers, scientists, and physical therapists, present a special challenge for organizations (Orndoff, 2002). Many of these individuals want to stay in their technical areas rather than enter management; yet advancement in many organizations frequently requires a move into management. Most of these people like the idea of the responsibility and opportunity associated with advancement, but they do not want to leave the professional and technical puzzles and problems at which they excel.

The dual-career ladder is an attempt to solve this problem. A dual-career ladder is a system that allows a person to advance up either a management ladder or a corresponding ladder on the technical/professional side of a career. Dual-career ladders are now used at IBM and many other organizations. They are most common in technology-driven industries such as pharmaceuticals, chemicals, electronics, and computers. For instance, a telecommunications organization created a dual-career ladder in its data processing department to reward talented technical people who do not want to move into management. Different tracks, each with attractive job titles and pay opportunities, are provided.

Unfortunately, the technical/professional ladder is sometimes viewed as "second class citizenship" within the organization. For a second or third career track to be taken seriously, the standards applied to technical/professional promotions must be just as rigorous as those applied to management promotions.

Dual-Career Couples

As the number of women in the workforce, particularly in professional careers continues to increase, so does the number of dual-career couples. The U.S. Bureau of Labor Statistics estimates that 81% of all couples are dual-career couples. Marriages in which both mates are managers, professionals, or technicians doubled over the past two decades. Problem areas for dual-career couples include family issues and job transfers causing relocations (Kuperbusch, Levenson, & Ebling, 2003; Moen, 2001). In these dual-career partnerships both members follow their own careers and actively support each other's career development.

As with most lifestyles, the dual-career arrangement has its positive and negative side. For example, for dual-career couples with children, family issues may conflict with career progression and have difficulties related to the need for quality childcare, the time demands, and the emotional stress. A significant number of organizations are concerned with the problems facing dual-career couples and offer assistance to them. Flexible working schedules are the most frequent organizational accommodation to these couples. Other arrangements include leave policies where either parent may stay home with a newborn, policies that allow work to be performed at home, day care on organization premises, and job sharing.

Probably the main problem these couples face is the threat of relocation. Thus, in job transfer situations, one partner's flexibility may depend on what is "best" for the family. Special difficulties exist when the transfer is overseas (Cook, 2002a,b). For example, a spouse who wants to work may not be able to get a work permit, may find that local residents have priority in the job market, or may find incompatible certification/licensing. Many large organizations now offer one kind of job-finding assistance for spouses of employees who are relocated, including payment of fees charged by employment agencies, job counseling firms, and executive search firms. Organizations are also developing networking relationships with other employers to find jobs for the spouses of their relocating employees. These networks can provide a way to "share the wealth and talent" in a community while simultaneously assisting in the recruitment efforts of the participating organizations (Fraze, 1999).

Career Development for Today's Diverse Workforce

Women and people of color tend to experience relatively less career progress in organizations, and bias and more subtle barriers are often the cause. To meet the career development needs of today's diverse workforce organizations need to break down the barriers women and people of color face in achieving advancement. The first major study of the glass ceiling by the Glass Ceiling Commission in 1991 revealed that women and minorities are held back not only from top executive positions but also from lower-level management positions and directorships. The Department of Labor defines the glass ceiling as "Those artificial barriers based on attitudinal or organizational bias that prevent qualified individuals from advancing upward in their organizations into management level positions" (U.S. Department of Labor, 2001).

According to the Glass Ceiling Commission's initial report, the three most common practices that contribute to the creation of a glass ceiling are (1) word-of-mouth recruiting (or using executive search firms without stating an interest in a diverse array of candidates), (2) inadequate access to developmental opportunities for women and minorities, and (3) a lack of responsibility among senior management for equal employment opportunity efforts.[4]

Amendments to the Age Discrimination in Employment Act removing ceilings on retirement make it even more important that organizations pay attention to the long-term career development of all employees, including the older worker. There are at least four myths about older workers that tend to make them vulnerable to discrimination in training and advancement opportunities.

One myth is that older workers are less motivated, less efficient, and less productive than younger workers. A second myth is that older workers are resistant to change and less flexible than younger workers. A third myth is that older workers tend to have poor attendance records. A fourth myth is that older workers have more accidents. Despite the fact that research has dispelled all of these myths, subtle discrimination stemming from such myths can, of course, affect the self-confidence and risk taking of older workers, and might discourage them from pursuing training opportunities (Mitchell, 1988). With people living longer and thus staying in the workforce longer organizations must recognize the importance of ensuring that their career management system addresses the challenges presented by the older worker.

Regardless of whether the organization is confronted with a more diverse workforce that is dominated by more women, minorities, older workers or the disabled today's HRD professionals and their organizations would do well to keep in mind the following suggestions for toppling job-advancement barriers formulated by the Glass Ceiling Commission, which closed in 1995:

- Demonstrate commitment. Top management should communicate its dedication to diversity and enact policies that promote it.
- Hold line managers accountable for progress by including diversity in all strategic business plans. Performance appraisals, compensation incentives, and other evaluation measures should reflect this priority.
- Use affirmative action as a tool to ensure that all qualified individuals compete based on ability and merit.
- Expand your pool of candidates. Look for prospects from noncustomary sources who may have nontraditional backgrounds and experiences.
- Educate all employees about the strengths and challenges of gender, racial, ethnic, and cultural differences.
- Initiate family-friendly programs that help women and men balance their work and family responsibilities.[5]

In the end, HRD professionals must accept the fact that there are problems, and work on eliminating barriers to job-advancement or career barriers. HRD professionals have a responsibility to ensure that their organizations create a culture that evaluates, hires, and promotes on the basis of merit.

IMPLEMENTING AND EVALUATING EFFECTIVE CAREER DEVELOPMENT SYSTEMS

Career development and planning initiatives have the best chance of succeeding when HRD personnel use a systematic approach to creating and implementing an effective career development system that mirrors the following (see, Leibowitz, 1986; Gutteridge et al., 1993):

A. *Identify Needs*
   1. Link career development to business strategy.
   2. Align employee and organization needs.

B. *Build a Vision for Change*
   3. Build systems and link them to other management and HR systems (e.g., quality initiatives, orientation, performance evaluation, compensation).
   4. Use a variety of tools and approaches.

C. *Develop a Plan for Action*
   5. Create a corporate infrastructure, but implement career development systems in individual business units or divisions.
   6. Ensure line manager participation, starting with system development.

D. *Implement for Impact and Longevity*
   7. Hold line managers accountable and give them the skills they will need to fulfill their responsibilities.
   8. Follow up initial implementation with a series of activities that keep career development salient (e.g., information sharing, career action teams).

E. *Evaluate and Maintain Results*
   9. Evaluate.
   10. Continuously improve the career development effort.
   11. Maintain high visibility and ongoing communication of career development.

Like any other HRD initiatives it is important that senior management supports the career development program.

Given the ever changing or turbulent environment which organizations are confronted with it is critically important that career development efforts are directly tied to an organization's strategic plan. This means that needs assessment data should include organization-level data on goals, strengths, weaknesses, resource availability, organizational climate, and on the organization's strategic HRM plan. Like all HRD activities, career development should fit into the overall HRM strategy. Employee recruiting, selection, compensation, benefits, and HRD activities have an impact on career development, and all can be used to successfully facilitate the process.

It is also critical that an organization's career development efforts are benchmarked by HRD professionals against effective approaches used by other organizations. Such benchmarking can be achieved by discussions with HRD professionals in other organizations and actual site visits to those organizations considered leaders in career development programs.

The attitude held by many people that career development is primarily an individual's responsibility, and therefore this is not a beneficial area for organizational activity is an attitude that HRD professionals must confront "head-on" during their efforts to develop and implement career development efforts. Remember our earlier reference to this attitude in career development Myth 1. HRD professionals and their organizations must avoid taking this notion to an unhealthy extreme that could encourage their organizations to abdicate any involvement in the career development process. This attitude must be overcome if a career management system is to gain wide acceptance. One way to overcome this attitude and benefit both the organization and the individual is to make clear from the start what purpose the career development programs will serve. Are these programs intended to ensure that the organization has the necessary talent to remain effective? Enhance employee growth and decision-making? Address the EEO and affirmative action pressures? Improve the organization's reputation or image? Regardless of the purposes, they should be clearly stated. Achievement of these goals should then be evaluated once the program is in operation. The use of a top-management sponsored steering committee, together with the input from a variety of employees as to the planning, design, and testing of these programs, can further build support, understanding, and commitment.

HRD professionals and their organizations are also realizing that career management works best when activities are coordinated within an integrated career development system (Baruch, 2003). Organizations like Boeing, 3M, and Bechtel effectively use integrated career development systems that have the following four elements in common: (1) involvement of senior management early to gain visible, up-front support; (2) establishment of guiding principles from the beginning; (3) development of the systems from the line upward, involving employees from all levels and areas of the organization; and (4) flexibility so that organizational units can tailor the system to fit their needs.

To enhance the effectiveness of their organizations career development efforts, HRD professionals should keep in mind the following recommendations concerning how to enhance organizational career development initiatives:

1. Integrate individual developmental planning with organizational strategic planning.
2. Strengthen the linkages between career development and other HRM systems.
3. Move career development systems toward greater openness.
4. Enhance the role of managers in career development through both skill building and accountability.
5. Develop and expand peer learning and other team-based developmental approaches.
6. Stress on-the-job development; de-emphasize traditional training programs that are isolated, one-shot events.
7. Emphasize enrichment and lateral movement.
8. Identify and develop transferable competencies.
9. Include values and lifestyle assessments in career development activities.
10. Implement a variety of career development approaches to accommodate different learning styles and the needs of a diverse workforce.
11. Tie career development directly too organizational quality initiatives.
12. Expand career development measurement and evaluation.
13. Continue to study best practices and organizational career development in a global context (Gutteridge et al., 1993).

Evaluating Career Development and Planning Activities

Career development programs are much more difficult to evaluate than other HRM or HRD programs. One of the primary difficulties involves establishing specific objectives. General objectives, such as to create better employees, provide little guidance for evaluation purposes. Even when good objectives are established, it is difficult to design a career development program that can fulfill all of them. Career development tends to be an ongoing process, which compounds the difficulties of evaluation.

One systematic approach to evaluating programs consists of five steps:

1. Determine the history and rational of the program.
2. Determine the degree to which the program places primary emphasis on its most important goals.
3. Analyze change occurring in employees and the organization, that is, program effectiveness, comparing the outcomes of the program with its stated objectives.

4. Examine the general adaptability of the program.
5. Introduce modifications as required.

Feedback from employees and their managers about the usefulness of specific elements of a career development program is one of the most critical elements of the evaluation process.

CONCLUSION

Today, organizations and individuals need to take a more active, systematic approach to career management and development. A career development program is a dynamic process that should integrate individual employee needs with those of the organization. The individual employee, the manager, and the employer (especially HRM and HRD professionals) all have roles in the individual's career development.

It is the responsibility of the employee to identify her or his own KSAs as well as interests and values and to seek out information about career options. The organization should provide information about its mission, policies, and plans and what it will provide in the way of training and development for the employee.

Organizations must keep a steady watch on their human resource needs and requirements. This ongoing analysis involves an analysis of the competences or KSAs required for jobs, the progression among related jobs, and the supply of ready (and potential) talent available to fill those jobs. Employees must take responsibility for analyzing their KSAs, interests, and career goals. Organizations must also identify the career opportunities and requirements for the organization and establish a clear understanding of the talent base they have at their disposal. Organizations often rely on various mechanisms to communicate career options to include posting and advertising job vacancies and sharing HRM planning forecasts with employees.

Career counseling programs are very important to an organization interested in career development for its employees. Such programs usually address a wide variety of career-related issues and are readily accessible to people in the organization. Dual-career and meeting the challenges for today's increasingly diverse workforce require that organizations work to break down the barriers such employees face in achieving advancement.

In an environment of increasing competition, continuous change, increased globalization, and new organizational structures have resulted in changes in career patterns for individual employees. Organizations and many employees have recognized that the traditional career paths are no longer feasible and are increasingly relying on creative career planning to meet the demands of the new world of work.

Unlike other HRM and HRD activities career management, development and planning are much harder to evaluate. Therefore, career management and development activities can be judged only by individuals at that point in their lives where they feel they have or have not realized their potential.

NOTES

1. "The Top 25 Managers," *Business Week*, January 14, 2003, pp. 65–68.
2. For more detailed information on myths held by non-management employees see Staats (1977) and Soverwine (1977). Also see Byars and Rue (2006, pp. 208–209).
3. For a more detailed discussion of myths held by managers see Moses (1987). Also see Byars and Rue (2006, pp. 208–209).
4. "The Glass Ceiling," *HR Magazine*, October 1991, pp. 91–92.
5. "Dismantling the Glass Ceiling," *HR Focus*, May 1996, p. 12.

CHAPTER 9

MANAGEMENT DEVELOPMENT

INTRODUCTION

The increasing rate of change in the external environment of organizations, and the many new challenges facing managers at all levels in organizations suggest that organizations must have high-quality, flexible, adaptive, skilled and competent managers if it is to survive and thrive. Many organizations have and will continue to undergo wrenching transformations during the twenty-first century in order to compete effectively on a global scale. With customer value, sustainable revenue growth, and shareholder value the key criteria for business success, organizations must continue to seek lower costs and increase efficiency by restructuring (e.g., with flatter hierarchies, and fewer permanent employees) and empowering employees to be more a part of organizational decision making.

Management development is an important element as organizations attempt to gain a competitive advantage. Management development is one major way for organizations to increase the chances that managers will be effective in helping their organizations gain a competitive advantage. While many have believed that the ability to manage (like the ability to lead) was primarily an inborn capability, the current prevailing view is that the knowledge skills, abilities and other characteristics (KSAOCs) required to be an effective manager can be learned or enhanced (Campbell et al., 1970). It is clear that developing management talent throughout the organization is a necessity in order to compete. Organizations must be willing to make the investment in management development in coming years.

Human Resource Development: Today and Tomorrow, pages 241–273
Copyright © 2006 by Information Age Publishing
All rights of reproduction in any form reserved.

Management development is a very popular HRD activity. Although management development has been defined in many ways, the following definition captures the essence of management development as it can and should be practiced in organizations: Management development is concerned with providing current and future managers with opportunities to learn, grow, change, experience, and develop attitudes, knowledge, and skills necessary to function effectively in the organization.

This chapter discusses management development and its contemporary reality in today's changing organizations. After discussing the management development process the chapter will describe the leadership competency model before providing a brief discussion of the role of management development in organizations. Next, the chapter discusses different approaches to management development and problems with management development efforts. The chapter then focuses on the globally competent manager and describes one organization's experience with global leadership competencies. The chapter will then discuss individual management development plans (IMDPs) as a tried and tested tool for improving management development initiatives. Before concluding the chapter with a brief look at how to evaluate management development activities the chapter describes the relationship between globalization and leadership development plans.

THE CONTEMPORARY REALITY OF MANAGEMENT DEVELOPMENT

Increasingly, organizations and HRD professionals use management development efforts to spur organizational change. For instance, a management development effort might be designed to transform a traditional organizational culture into one that emphasizes continuous improvement, organizational learning and total quality management. Clearly, management development is an important element in organizational efforts to improve their competitiveness and achieve their strategic agendas. Leaving development to chance greatly reduces the likelihood that the organization will achieve the kinds of changes it needs and desires.

The contemporary view of management development is one that enhances an organization's effectiveness while simultaneously maintaining a competitive advantage. Second, it is increasingly global in outlook and builds on an organizational structure that minimizes functional, unit, and international boundaries. Third, it is building organizational effectiveness through the continuous alignment of organizational members, business process and structures with vision, values, strategies, and learning. Fourth, management development programs are increasingly customized and systematical relative to individual needs.

Underlying the contemporary view of management development is the assimilation of management development efforts with strategic planning along with efforts to teach the more intangible aspects of leadership, market/client thinking (which is often cross-cultural), adaptability, implementation strategies, and change management. Strategically linked management development activities that include specific assignments along with education and training are intended to go a long way toward accomplishing these kinds of learning. The goal is to obtain the fullest use of human resource capabilities by developing managers to assume positions of greater responsibility.

A prevalent theme of contemporary management development involves the integration of management development activities with strategic goals focused on performance improvement and effectiveness to attain a competitive advantage. Recurring management development objectives for performance improvement and effectiveness include: management of organizational change and adaptation to unique situations; reducing cycle time for virtually every major process and activity; promoting continuous learning and improvement; introducing and extending quality management principles and practices; managing cultural diversity and also cross cultural communications; and building leadership and relational skills.

Human knowledge and competencies have strategic importance in that they are the counterparts to the core competencies of their particular organization. This recognition then becomes a logical point-of-entry to the effective learning organization as management development plays a key role in its accomplishment. Additionally, long-term competitiveness depends on fully developing and using all of the expertise and talent in the organization. Also, today's knowledge-based organizations must have "know-how" as their main asset and continuous development as a way of organizational life.

Today, high-performing, leading organizations are increasingly distinguished by a number of features of their management development approaches. Their sustained profitability and general management effectiveness provide benchmarks which HRD professionals should be aware of for virtually all organizations regardless of size and geographic scope of operations (Sims, 1998). These features are as follows (see, Sims, 1998).

Contemporary management development is clearly linked to business plans and strategies. General competency development is still a necessary condition but not a sufficient one. The fast pace of change demands a faster cycle time for development, application and change. Increasingly, today's management development designs are initiated by business priorities and imperatives while continuing the individual's progress. The key point is the importance of linking management development to an organization's overall strategic direction (i.e., management development efforts are clearly driven by the extent to which the process flows logically from a company's strategic agenda). The focus of the process is to identify and develop the talents and perspectives that the organization needs to achieve its long-term strategic objectives. Specific initiatives are built around a market-oriented focus, coupled with a strong element of competitive analysis, to help managers at *all* levels understand the strength and weaknesses of the organization and what it will take to build competitive advantage. This understanding is related to the organization itself—the systems, structures, processes, goals, and relationships necessary for success in a highly competitive world.

Contemporary management development emphasizes integrating overall organizational strategy, marketing, technology, and so on. Historically, the emphasis in management development in organizations has been on the management of technology—that is, on teaching managers how best to manage the research and development function in order to produce technologically driven or enhanced products and services. Contemporary management development aims to provide the KSAOCs that make it possible for managers to conceptualize and manage at the intersection of strategy, marketing, technology, and so on. The object is not to convert managers into technologists, but rather to provide managers with the insights and understanding they need in order to use technology to create a unique competitive advantage based on customer needs.

Globalization and cross-cultural orientation. Contemporary management development activities are internationally focused on successfully meeting challenging communication issues. The vast majority of management development efforts recognize the broad implications of internationalization to all aspects of business life, from working on multifunctional-multiregional product design teams, to the running of transnational organizations that have shareholders, employees, customers, suppliers, and creditors all over the world. Even though the organization may be small or domestically oriented in terms of product or service, economic, competitive, and sourcing considerations dictate their global outlook as they acknowledge that global issues impact all levels and dimensions of the organization. The importance of this reality is highlighted by Bolt's research which suggests that competition resulting from an increase in internationalization was the factor most likely to affect future management development strategies (Bolt, 1989). Consequently, globalization of management development often means conducting real or virtual classes in different parts of the world, sometimes in more than one language, for a geographically heterogeneous group of participants, with an international faculty whose members have a diverse set of teaching, research, and consulting experiences.

Boundaryless. Organizations until recently developed managerial layers as they grew to help the organization with coordination, control, reporting, and succession issues. Today's contemporary organizations are increasingly recognizing the adverse effects of excessive layers. Simply reducing layers without leadership training would not necessarily lead to success. Management development programs that focus on leadership will only succeed if they instill a sense of confidence in the employee. Deep-seated changes in individual attitudes and mindsets often represent one of the greatest challenges in developing management development efforts. Like any HRD initiative in an organization, a sincere commitment from top management to fully support management development initiatives and roles are critical to the success of contemporary management development efforts.

Contemporary management development provides the organization with "glue" to integrate subsidiaries and other units that need their own autonomy. The contemporary role of management development is a tool for organizational development that helps drive flexibility, commitment, and competitiveness of the entire organization. HRD professionals have increasingly recognized that this view has changed from a long-standing focus on "getting the right people into the right places at the right times" through recruitment, succession planning, training, and other forms of development.

Contemporary management development has an increased focus on leadership. Vicere and Fulmer (1998) have recently noted that in today's changing business environments, traditional processes for developing leadership talent are in such a state of flux that a new vocabulary is emerging. There is little interest in the old mainstay term *management development.* Managers today are often viewed as bureaucrats whose function is to create complexity and preserve the status quo. *Executive education* is a more desirable term, but in today's flatter, more networked organizations, there is less demand for "executives," often viewed as aloof and removed from the realities of the competitive marketplace. And the word education connotes the esoteric contemplation of academic issues, a process at odds with today's fast-paced business environment. Vicere and Fulmer (1998) point out that there does seem to be great interest in the term *leadership development,* which characterizes processes for identifying and developing exceptional people capable of moving an organization into the twenty-first century. People who can broaden the horizons of participants so that they can see and understand different realities or alternative courses of action.

Contemporary management development focuses on growing and developing entrepreneurial leaders. This demand has arisen as an outgrowth of downsizing, decentralization, and cost reduction, coupled with a renewed emphasis on growing the top line profitably. Small has become beautiful, as long as it is combined with flexibility, responsiveness, and ingenuity to meet customer needs in a profitable way. Given the complexity of business in today's highly competitive international marketplace, significant advantage can be attained by combining small size with the economies of scale, purchasing power, and sophisticated systems infrastructures of large corporations. Management development initiatives are expected to grow and develop people who have the KSAOCs that enable them to successfully think and act like entrepreneurs.

In contemporary management development individual learning is focused within the context of organizational learning. Experiential learning, continuous learning and adaptation are program hallmarks (Senge, 1990). Approaches thoughtfully combine on-the-job experiences and formal programmed learning in both individual and group situations. Individual, group and unit learning are coordinated.

Contemporary management development has a career development focus. This builds individual trust and commitment. Central authority and command are de-emphasized and trust and partnership are emphasized. Systematic needs assessments are tailored to the individual and are oblivious to race and gender issues. Age and maturity factors are viewed in the framework of individual work, career, and life cycles.

Benchmarking for program improvement is a cornerstone of contemporary management development. Searching out and examining highly effective management development practices by experienced benchmarkers to adopt the best and adapt them to their own organizations is an ongoing occurrence for HRD professionals. It provides direction and clear targets, and it allows the organization to determine both what is being done (compared to similar organizations and programs) and where progress is needed to improve overall performance. Benchmarking is used by HRD professionals (and their organizations) to advance performance through careful implementation and continuous refinement of management development efforts. HRD professionals should ensure that several critical success factors to the benchmarking process are in place. These factors are: a well-designed performance measurement and benchmark system, senior leadership support, customer responsiveness, benchmarking training for the management development team, and resources, especially in the form of time, funding, and personnel which enable the benchmarking of management development to be effective. Benchmarking is also used to ensure that management development initiatives set and meet strategic expectations or targets.

Contemporary management development contributes to the bottom line. Management development no longer relies on its intrinsic value to demonstrate its real worth to the organization. Increasingly, it has been transformed along with the changes affecting the organization. With this transformation management development is subjected to increased accountability and a requirement to show a measurable contribution to the organization.

HRD professionals are adapting measurement processes and in some cases management development efforts are increasingly profit centers. In this respect, management development is just one of many organizational functions that were traditionally taken for granted as necessary, unmeasurable, and was forced to respond to pressures to show their contribution in measurable terms.

The contemporary management development features presented above can serve as the basis for benchmarking management development in any organization. The contemporary view of management development has been evolving between HRD professionals and their organizations and their current management development focus provides a clear view of the future of management development that responds to customer needs. This simply means delivering management development initiatives that are better, cheaper, and faster. Better means providing insights, KSAOCs, tools, and perspectives that enable managers to effectively address current and projected organizational needs and challenges. Cheaper means management development experiences that provide a higher learning yield for every corporate dollar expended. And faster means quicker design and delivery of management development programs, as well as shorter-duration learning experiences, faster response times, and more program evaluations. It is in other words, becoming increasingly apparent that management development must have the same fundamental characteristics as most products and services.

THE MANAGEMENT DEVELOPMENT PROCESS

Management development is concerned with providing current and future managers with opportunities to learn, grow, change, experience, and develop attitudes, knowledge, and skills necessary to function effectively in the organization. Management development programs need to be constructed the way any sound HRD program is: though needs assessment, design, implementation, and evaluation. The management development process model identified in Figure 9.1 should be applied to management education and development efforts as well. The following recommendations should be kept in mind by HRD professionals during the management development process identified in Figure 9.1:

1. Management development must be tied to the organization's strategic plan to be responsive to the needs of the organization and those of the individuals being developed.

2. A thorough needs assessment, including investigating what managers in the organization do and the KSAOCs they need to perform effectively, is essential.
3. Specific objectives, both for the overall program and for each of its components (e.g., on-the-job experiences, classroom training, and so on) should be established.
4. Involvement in and commitment of senior management in all phases of the process, from needs assessment to evaluation, is critical. Simply stated, it is management's responsibility to ensure that the organization has a high quality management team.
5. A variety of developmental opportunities, both formal and on-the-job, should be used. Further, as emphasized by action learning advocates, there must be a linkage between what is learned in the classroom and what people are actually doing in their jobs.
6. The program should be designed to ensure that the individuals to be developed are motivated to participate in such activities. The day-to-day demands placed on managers at all levels make it easy to put development issues on the back burner.
7. Action should be taken to evaluate the program regularly and modify and update as needs change.

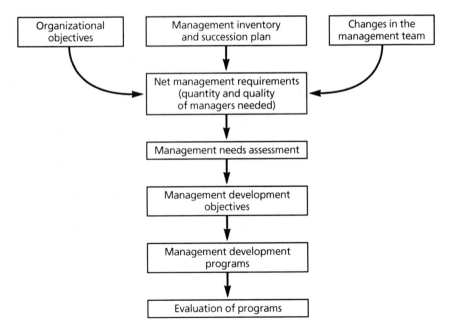

Figure 9.1. The management development process.

Unfortunately, many management development programs do not conform to these basic expectations. Effective management development program efforts will continue to be critical for managers to successfully take on a more proactive role in their organizations and society. The competitive climate of the twenty-first century dictates that organizations take a more proactive posture regarding management education and development in order to be competitive (Longnecker & Ariss, 2002).

Management Needs Assessment

Every organization has physical, financial, and human resource needs. Needs relate to what the organization must have to achieve its objectives. A fundamental need of any organization is the need for an effective leaders or managers. One method of meeting this need is the use of a well-organized management development process. However, before management development activities are undertaken, the specific development needs of the managers in the organization must be determined. Thus, management needs assessment is a systematic analysis of specific management development activities the organization requires to achieve its objectives. The management development needs of an organization are a direct result of the overall needs of the organization and the development needs of individual managers. Several methods exist to determine management development needs: a management needs survey, competency studies, task analysis, and performance analysis. A management needs survey focuses on the knowledge, skills, abilities and other characteristics (KSAOCs) required in performing the job. Competency studies examine the competencies required in performing managerial jobs. Task analysis is concerned with what tasks are required in performing the managerial job. Performance analysis deals with job performance requirements in performing the managerial job.

Some organizations are doing a good job of needs assessment for management development and as a result have a clearer idea of the competencies and issues their development programs should address. For example, the Blanchard Valley Health Association, a healthcare system in Findlay, Ohio, used needs assessment to formulate its Leaders for Tomorrow program. This year-long program includes classroom learning, small-group discussion, computer learning modules, and an "action learning" component, where managers work on job-related projects (Salopek, 2004). Second, the State of Idaho completed an intensive needs assessment before implementing its Certified Public Managers (CPM) program for state managers (Patton & Pratt, 2002). Third, Aeroquip-Vickers had top manages identify the top twenty-five competencies that managers needed for future success. This was then used to form a managerial success profile that

250 *Human Resource Development: Today and Tomorrow*

guided subsequent management development efforts in this organization (LaHote, Simonetti, & Longnecker, 1999).

Establishing Management Development Objectives

After the management development needs of the organization have been determined, objectives for the overall management development program and for individual programs must be established to meet those needs. Both types of objectives should be expressed in writing and should be measurable. HRD professionals can categorize these objectives within three broad categories: instructional, organizational and departmental, and individual performance and growth. This categorization scheme can also be used for management development objectives.

Instructional objectives might incorporate targets relating to the number of trainees to be taught, hours of training, cost per trainee, and time required for trainees to reach a standard level of knowledge. Furthermore, objectives are needed for principles, facts, and concepts to be learned in the management development programs.

Organizational and departmental objectives concern the impact the programs will have on organizational and departmental outcomes, such as absenteeism, turnover, safety, and number of grievance. Individual and personal growth objectives concern the impact on the behavioral and attitudinal outcomes of the individual. They may also involve the impact on the personal growth of the individuals participating in the programs.

After the overall management development objectives have been established, individual program objectives specifying the knowledge, skills, abilities, concepts, or attitudes that should result must be identified. After these objectives are developed course content and method of instruction can be specified.

LEADERSHIP COMPETENCY MODELING

Leadership competency modeling (LCM) refers to the procedure for systematically understanding the leadership (management) work that gets done in an organization. The basic goal of the procedure is to understand what leaders do, how they do it, and what skills they need to do the work well. LCM is one approach to job analysis. This section describes the LCM approach and its importance to helping HRD professionals in developing an organization's managers and leaders.

The strategic importance of LCM is grounded first and foremost in its usefulness as a systematic procedure that provides a rational foundation on which to build a coherent approach to developing leaders. The role of LCM is especially important given the increasing demands on HRD professionals and their organizations to develop current and future leaders as part of the organizations efforts to change (e.g., as restructuring the organization around key processes) and remain competitive while globalizing.

As noted earlier, LCM is considered to be a specific approach to conducting a job analysis. What distinguishes the LCM approach is that it places much more emphasis on specifying the characteristics that are associated with effective leadership performance in a job. That is, the primary objective of LCM is to describe the knowledge, skills, abilities, values, interests, and personality of successful leaders.

Analyzing Needed Leadership Competencies

Leadership competencies are the knowledge, skills, abilities and other characteristics (KSAOCs) that someone needs to perform a leadership job effectively. Information about required competencies is essential if leadership job analysis results are going to be used by HRD professionals to develop procedures for selecting people to perform leadership jobs and designing HRD programs. Competency information can be obtained using either a standardized or a customized approach.

Standardized approach. A well-known standardized approach to assess ability requirements is the Ability Requirements Approach (Fleishman & Mumford, 1988). Using 50 different ability dimensions, it can be used to assess the level of ability needed in a job. Usually, job incumbents are trained to understand what each ability involves, and then they use a rating scale to report the level of ability required to do the work.

Many HRD professionals and consulting organizations that perform job analysis collect competency information using fairly standardized procedures that they have developed for their own use. For example, Personnel Decisions Inc. developed a taxonomy of managerial competencies that includes the following basic domains:

- Thinking, which includes analytical agility, creativity, planning, strategy development, and business-specific knowledge;
- Communications, which includes verbal, written, listening, and public speaking;
- Inter/Intrapersonal, which includes teamwork, influencing, and adaptability, and dependability;
- Leadership, which includes supervision, motivation, decisiveness, and work commitment;

- General Operations Management, which includes materials management, facilities and security, information management, and international operations; and
- Functional Business Knowledge, which includes economics, accounting and finance, marketing and sales, and managing human resources (Schippman, 1999).

When organizations hire this firm to conduct job analysis for managerial jobs, the HRD consultants use a fairly standardized process to assess the required levels of competencies for the focal jobs.

Customized approach. This procedure involves asking subject matter experts (SMEs) (usually incumbents and supervisors) to identify all the KSAOCs that they think may be necessary to perform the work. A group interview meeting may be held to create the list of possible competencies to examine. Based on the results of the group interview meeting, a competency-rating questionnaire is created and distributed to SMEs. Respondents rate the competencies along a number of dimensions: whether the competency is used at all in the position, importance, whether a new incumbent needs the competency upon entry to the job, and the extent to which the competency distinguishes a superior incumbent from an adequate one.

Based on the results for the competency items the HRD professionals along with other organizational leaders make a determination on exactly what KSAOCs are needed, for example, to be a successful leader. To maximize leadership performance, the organization may want to offer additional HRD initiatives.

MANAGEMENT DEVELOPMENT'S ROLE IN THE ORGANIZATION

For management development to have its intended organizational and individual impact under the new paradigm the commitment of the organization is absolutely critical. Those responsible for current and future management development cannot afford to take the organization's commitment for granted. The real test of the organization's commitment can ultimately only be found in funding, senior leadership participation, attendance, ongoing program evaluation, and the extent to which management development is an equal partner in the organization's overall strategic plan.

Like any commitment on behalf of senior leadership there is no one-way to ensure their commitment to management development. However, one way to determine whether there is commitment to management development is in a documented vision or policy which specifically makes clear the role and purpose of management development. The existence of such a vision or policy should help establish and give meaning to management development in the organization. This means that management development exists to support the organization's overall goals or strategic agenda.

In any case, mere organizational statements without true senior executive or top leadership support are meaningless. Senior leadership must be willing to document how specific examples of management development will contribute to accomplishing agreed upon goals. It is just as important to have all levels of the organization's leadership accountable for attainment of these objectives, starting with top leadership that must lead by example. Accountability implies the need to have measurable ways to check on the progress.

Like any other initiative undertaken in the organization, once top leadership is committed to the role of management development in achieving organizational results a thorough needs analysis must be conducted to determine what the specific goals and objectives are for management development in support of the organizational vision and expected results. Senior leadership is the best source of information on what needs to be done. However, the broader customer base (i.e., current and future leaders and other organizational members) should be consulted for their input. Including others input in the design of management development efforts early on goes a long way toward ensuring ownership of the efforts and a greater stake in the outcome. It is very important for those responsible for management development efforts to avoid being the sole owner of management development initiatives in the organization. Again, management development must be viewed as a key element in the achievement of the organization's visions and achievement of expected results. The role of management development is to make this connection as a part of the organization's commitment to its vision and thus to management development. This point cannot be overstated and HRD professionals should always be attentive to ensuring that management development is part of the overall organizational strategy and vision.

HRD professionals responsible for management development efforts should conduct one-on-one interviews, regularly participate in departmental meetings, leadership roundtables, and use a survey to gather information necessary to determine what should be done. Again, as many of these opportunities as practical should be used to collect pertinent information.

By building customer demands early into the design, delivery and evaluation of management development efforts will ensure that it has an ongoing customer-driven focus. Customer input should be the modus operandi during each cycle of the management development process. This point is especially important when determining how to measure the effectiveness of management development efforts. Including customers in deciding on results which can reinforce management development's support of the overall organizational strategy will go a long way in keeping management development a part of the organization's main agenda.

Ultimately the goal of senior leadership support throughout the management development process is to ensure that managers are provided with effective learning experiences and environments—ones in which they are challenged to resolve both old and new problems using appropriate tools and KSAOCs; where they learn from their experiences and share knowledge and experiences with colleagues; and where they have opportunities to grow intellectually and emotionally as leaders.

There is no question that many organizations emphasize short-term results and impose these expectations on management development. While those responsible for management development in organizations need to ensure that participants are furnished with the KSAOCs they need to perform better in their current and future jobs, the real payoff of management development frequently comes much further down the road. Successful management development initiatives will allow neither themselves nor their organizations to lose of sight of this.

One of the most important decisions to make is how to deliver the management development initiatives. The considerations are many and the implications equally numerous. For example, using internal versus external sources to deliver the management development initiatives presents a number of decisions that must be made by HRD professionals and others involved in the process. Fortunately, as noted in the next section, the options on how to deliver the management development initiatives are plentiful and the decision must be made not solely on the basis of getting the job done but as part of the overall organizational plan.

MANAGEMENT DEVELOPMENT APPROACHES

After the organization's needs have been assessed and its objectives stated, management development programs can be implemented. This section examines some of the more frequently used methods of management development. At this point, recall the list of conditions for effective learning discussed in Chapter 3. These principles of learning also apply to management development programs. There are numerous approaches and types of management development. HRD professionals usually incorporate more than one of the following approaches in their management development efforts.

Company Universities

More and more organizations have their own "universities" or "academies" for management development. It is estimated that more than 2,000 organizations have their own corporate universities (Allen, 2002; Corporate Universities, 2000). Company schools like those at IBM, Motorola, GE McDonald's, Intel, and Xerox educate both current and potential managers in the corporate culture, leadership philosophy and KSAOCs, and methods of doing business. McDonald's, for example, teaches managers its approach to ensuring quality, service and cleanliness at Hamburger University in Oak Brook, Illinois. The courses at Hamburger University include operational procedures that reinforce the organization's philosophy. Hamburger University uses a wide range of training methods, including discussion and lecture, audiovisuals, and hands-on experiences with equipment (Byans and Rue, 2006; Eurich, 1990; Odiorne & Rummler, 1988).

University-Based Programs

Managers in an organization often face difficult jobs due to changing and unknown circumstances. "Churning" at the top of organizations and the stresses of increasingly responsible management jobs contribute to increased turnover in these positions. In an effort to decrease turnover, some organizations are experimenting with a relatively recent phenomenon: special education for its most senior managers. This type of HRD includes education traditionally offered by university business schools.

These programs can be grouped into several broad categories, with a host of subcategories. Three broad market segments are: general management programs; shorter open-enrollment programs; and customized programs. Many business schools offer these types of programs designed specifically for managers. Programs at schools like Harvard, Cornell, Darden, Stanford and Michigan rely heavily on the case study method, in which students do in-depth analyses of real-life companies. General management programs typically address each of the major management disciplines and place them in the contexts of strategic thinking and, increasingly, of change management. Shorter, open-enrollment development programs include programs that are two weeks or less in length and focus on one management function or theme, or on a highly delimited set of these. Customized, company-specific programs are designed to meet a predetermined set of company-specific needs.

Coaching and Mentoring Programs

Coaching and mentoring programs establish an on-the-job relationship between an experienced leader and a less experienced individual in the same career track. Historically, both programs are ones where high-potential employees and less-advantaged female and minority employees learn about organizational operations and are groomed for more responsibility. Acting as a coach or mentor also can enrich the jobs of plateaued mid-level employees.

Coaching. In recent years individual coaching has become popular as another type of developmental intervention for leaders in organizations. Coaching, that is carried out by experienced managers, emphasizes the responsibility of all managers for developing employees. Coaching combines observation with suggestions. Under this method of management development, experienced managers advise and guide trainees in solving managerial problems. The idea behind coaching should be to allow the trainees to develop their own approaches to management with the counsel of a more experienced manager.

One advantage to coaching is that trainees get practical experience and see the results of their decisions. However, there is a danger that the coach will neglect training responsibilities or pass on inappropriate management practices. The coach's expertise and experience are critical with this method.

Like modeling, coaching complements the natural way humans learn. A brief outline of good coaching pointers often includes the following:

1. explaining appropriate behavior;
2. making clear why actions were taken;
3. accurately stating observations;
4. providing possible alternatives/suggestions;
5. following up and reinforcing behaviors used.

In the context of management development, coaching involves a relationship between two managers for a period of time as they perform their jobs. Effective coaching requires patience and good communication skills.

Management mentoring. A method called management mentoring is a relationship in which experienced managers aid individuals in the earlier stages of their careers. Such a relationship provides an environment for conveying technical, interpersonal, and organizational skills from the more-experienced person to a designated least-experienced person. Not only does the inexperienced employee benefit, but the mentor may enjoy the challenge of sharing his or her wisdom (Tyler, 2003).

However, mentoring is not without its problems. Young minority managers frequently report difficulty in finding mentors. Also, men generally show less willingness than women to be mentors. Further, mentors who are dissatisfied with their jobs and those who teach a narrow or distorted view of events may not help a young manager's development. Fortunately, many managers have a series of advisors or mentors during their careers and may find advantages in learning from the different mentors (Billett, 2003). For example, the unique qualities of individual mentors may help less-experienced managers identify key behaviors in management success and failure. Further, those being mentored may find previous mentors to be useful sources for networking (de Janasz et al., 2003).

Many organizations avoid formal coaching and mentoring programs because successful mentoring often involves "chemistry"—something difficult to assign. Instead, some organizations use "sponsor" programs that have experienced leaders show less experienced individuals the ropes without taking formal responsibility for the managers' development.

It is also quite common for organizations to use external mentors and coaches, often consultants or well-known university professors, to provide advice and support senior leaders facing critical issues or challenges. Some organizations like the Levinson Institute in Cambridge, Massachusetts specialize in this activity, as do certain professionals at think tanks like the Center for Creative Leadership.

Experience

Many organizations use development through experience. With this method, individuals are promoted into management jobs and allowed to learn on their own from their daily experiences. The primary advantage of this method is that the individual, in attempting to perform a specific job, may recognize the need for management development and look for a means of satisfying it. However, employees who are allowed to learn management only through experience can create serious problems by making mistakes. Also, it is frustrating to attempt to manage without the necessary background and knowledge. Serious difficulties can be avoided if the experience method is supplemented with other management development techniques.

Management Modeling

A common adage in management development says that managers tend to manage as they were managed. In other words, managers learn by behavior modeling, or copying someone else's behavior. This tendency is not surprising, because a great deal of human behavior is learned by modeling. Children learn by modeling the behaviors of parents and older children. Management development efforts can take advantage of natural human behavior by matching young or developing managers with appropriate models and then reinforcing the desirable behaviors exhibited by learners. The modeling process involves more than straightforward imitation, or copying; it is considerably more complex. For example, one can learn what to do by observing a model who does something wrong. Thus, exposure to both positive and negative models can benefit a new manager. The underlying rationale for behavior modeling is that people can learn by observing other people (models) perform a task provided they are shown clearly what the components of the behavior are, remember what the behavior is, actually perform the behavior, and are motivated to use what they have learned (Decker & Nathan, 1985).

Understudy Assignments

This method is a form of management modeling that assigns a current or future manager to work with another manager for a certain time period. If the organization is grooming the person for a specific management position, the individual may understudy one particular manager. For a broader foundation, understudies may rotate among several managers. Using either method, the individual sees the day-to-day leadership duties, while the manager acts as coach and appraiser.

The advantage of understudy assignments is that the heir realizes the purpose of the training and can learn in a practical and realistic situation without being directly responsible for operating results. On the negative side, the understudy learns the bad as well as the good practices of the incumbent. If an understudy assignment system is used, it should generally be supplemented with one or more of the other management development methods.

Job Rotation

Job rotation is designed to give an individual broad experience through exposure to many different areas of the organization. In job rotation the management trainee goes from one job to another within the organization, generally remaining in each from six months to a year.

One advantage of job rotation is that the management trainees see how management principles can be applied in a cross section of environments.

Also, the training is practical and allows the management trainee to become familiar with the entire operation of the organization. One serious disadvantage of this method is that the management trainee is frequently given mental assignments in each job. Another disadvantage is the tendency to leave the management trainee in each job longer than necessary. Both of these disadvantages can produce negative attitudes.

If the manager coach is reluctant to delegate or finds it hard to share job duties with the understudy, the manager candidate will gain little from the experience. Understudying is most successful when the senior manager's attitudes and work techniques are harmonious with the strategic development objectives of the organization.

Action Learning

Although the above approaches can create a foundation for the creation and transfer of KSAOCs throughout the organization, action learning can help institutionalize the process. Action learning helps make experiential learning intentional and deliberate. Originally, developed as a way to encourage line managers to provide input to modify operating system (Morgan & Ramirez, 1981; Revans, 1982), action learning as it is currently practiced involves having participants select an organizational problem, write a case study describing the problem, and meet with a group of other managers who face similar problems to discuss ways the problem can be dealt with (McGill & Brockbank, 2004). This idea is sort of a "living case" approach, where instead of analyzing situations that have been resolved in the past, participants deal with ongoing problems and issues.

Team-based action learning initiatives can be a very powerful mechanism for linking learning both to the workplace and to the strategic agenda of the organization. Through action learning, an organization can convert individual learning into organizational knowledge through the hands-on resolution of real organization problems. Because the projects are conducted in teams, learning is shared across members, networking is reinforced, new perspectives are encouraged, and leadership skills are practiced. All of this takes place within the context of the organization's strategic imperatives, helping to bring those imperatives to life and give them meaning throughout the organization. In addition, action learning can help resolve business issues related to the pursuit of strategic imperatives, creating an additional return on investment for the organization. Thus, management development is an integral part of strategy implementation and yielding the organization tangible benefits beyond development.

In general, outside courses, seminars, and conferences are practical ways for an organization to develop managers' skills. However, some types of management development are better covered through in-house programs. For example, the corporate controller, marketing vice president, or employee relations' heads can present overviews of problems facing the organization in the financial, sales, or HRM areas. The company's legal counsel likewise can do a better job than an outsider could when explaining how a new law or government regulation affects the organization.

Other Types of Approaches

Whether management development is provided in a company, university business school, or (as is most often the case) a less formal setting, the effort often utilizes special techniques. One such technique is role-playing, in which participants adopt the role of a particular leader placed in a specific situation—for instance, a leader who has to give a negative performance review to an employee. Leadership games are elaborate role-playing exercises in which multiple participants enact a leadership situation.

Programs focusing on organizational culture and values, HRM, financial management, marketing, labor relations, leadership theory, information systems, government requirements, and the like can help expand leaders' horizons. Many organizations offer such courses as part of their in-company management development initiatives. Many other organizations however, find it is easier and less expensive to use outside training resources. For instance, it is not unusual for some organizations to outsource the design, development, and delivery of management development programs, while keeping much of the needs assessment and program evaluation in-house.

Outsourcing of management development efforts centers primarily around issues of expertise and cost. The single most important factor in the outsourcing decision is to acquire content expertise in management issues. However, there has been an increasing trend to furnish in-house management development programs. An important value of having in-house programs lies in the ability to use employees from other functional areas such as HRM, sales, engineering, finance, etc. and top management as facilitators and teachers. Experienced managers often lend enormous credibility to the practical side of what is being taught or implemented. This practice allows the individual, a content expert through hands-on practice, to share company and industry-related experience. On the other hand, having expertise in other areas does not automatically qualify the individual to be an effective facilitator or teacher.

It is important to understand that when designing developmental experiences, organizational managers and HRD professionals should set up a system to analyze and review the management candidate's progress during the trial period. Managers at different levels need feedback for the experience to serve as learning rather than a sink-or-swim situation. This technique requires communication among the participant, their immediate boss, peers, direct reports, higher level managers, and, an HRD professional.

Task force and project assignments. Task force and project assignments provide a valuable source of linking developmental opportunities. Although such assignments are often met with a less-than enthusiastic response by those chosen to participate, they can be very effective developmental experiences.

Also at times, a management vacancy can occur unexpectedly before anyone has been groomed for the job. One option for handling the situation is to appoint the best available prospect as temporary manager. If the manager does well, the placement becomes permanent; if not, then another individual should be appointed as soon as possible. Depending on the position and the individual's progress, the trial period can last anywhere from six weeks to six months.

Task force and project assignments during a regular manager's vacation, absences or assignment to a special project also can serve developmental purposes. By stepping into management positions even for a brief period, individuals gain practical experience that prepares them for the real thing. As a bonus, senior leadership can see how an individual handles a particular management position or situations.

For the experience to prove worthwhile, temporary or acting managers should have full management powers. Some organizations even avoid letting direct reports know that their manager is actually a temporary appointment.

Partial assignment of leadership duties. Some organizations develop their management prospects by assigning them a portion of the position's duties and gradually increasing these responsibilities as the individual becomes proficient. If the individual cannot assume increased responsibilities at the expected rate of progress, the organization may re-evaluate its selection.

This method, when combined with understudying, works particularly well in grooming an individual for particular management positions. Since the individual assumes the position in phases, he or she is better able to do justice to learning each aspect of the job.

Adventure learning. Adventure learning, or experiential-learning programs, use many kinds of challenging outdoor activities, often involving physical risk, to help participants achieve their objectives, which generally fall into two categories.

Group-focused objectives. These objectives include better communication, more creative problem solving, more effective teamwork, and improved leadership. One activity often included in adventure learning is "The Wall," a 12- to 14-foot structure that teams must get over by working together. The wall is viewed as a symbol for any business challenge.

Personal growth objectives. These objectives include improved self-esteem, improved risk-taking skills, increased self-awareness, and better stress management. Rope activities are favorite methods for achieving personal growth objectives. One example of a rope activity is the "electric rope" game. A team has to get every member over a rope strung high up between two trees. Team members must try not to touch the rope, and they cannot use props. The electric rope is viewed as an analogy for a difficult business challenge the team faces at work (Hwang, 2003, p. 562).

PROBLEMS WITH MD EFFORTS

Development efforts are subject to certain common mistakes and problems. Most of the management development problems in the United States have resulted from inadequate HRM planning and a lack of coordination of HRD efforts (Mighty & Ashton, 2003). Common problems include the following: failing to conduct adequate needs assessment, trying out fad programs or training methods, and substituting training for selecting qualified individuals.

Another common management development problem is encapsulated development, which occurs when an individual learns new methods and ideas in a development course and returns to a work unit that is still bound by old attitudes and methods. Therefore, the trainee cannot apply new ways to handle certain situations because of resistance from those having an investment in the status quo. The development was "encapsulated" in the classroom and is essentially not used on the job.

THE GLOBALLY COMPETENT MANAGER

The advent of the global economy has led to recommendations that organizations create management development programs to produce globally competent managers (Bartlett & Ghoshal, 1992; Adler & Bartholomew, 1992; Murray & Murray, 1986). Organizations such as General Electric, ITT, Corning Glass and 3M have incorporated this perspective into their management development programs. Several views exist on the competencies needed to be effective global managers have been conceptualized (see, Bartlett & Ghoshal, 1992; Adler & Bartholomew, 1992; Spreitzer, McCall, & Mahoney, 1997).

Several researchers argue that to succeed in a global environment, organizations need a network of managers who are specialists in global issues, and that organizations do not need to globalize all managers (Bartlett & Ghoshal, 1992). They suggest four categories of managers are needed:

1. Business Managers—This type of manager plays three roles, serving as "the strategist for the organization, the architect of its worldwide asset configuration, and the coordinator of transactions across national borders" (p. 125).
2. Country Managers—This type of manager, who works in the organization's national subsidiaries, also plays three roles, serving as "the sensor and interpreter of local opportunities and threats, the builder of local resources and capabilities, and the contributor to active participation in global strategy" (p. 128).
3. Functional Managers—These managers are functional specialists (e.g., in engineering, marketing, human resources), who "scan for specialized information worldwide, 'cross-pollinate' leading-edge knowledge and best practice, and champion innovations that may offer transnational opportunities and applications" (p. 130).
4. Corporate Managers—These managers serve in corporate headquarters and orchestrate the organization's activities, playing the roles of leader and talent scout (i.e., by identifying potential business, country, and functional managers) and developing promising executives.

Other researchers identify seven transnational skills that they believe are necessary to managing effectively in a global environment: global perspective, local responsiveness, synergistic learning, transition and adaptation, cross-cultural integration, collaboration, and foreign experience (Adler & Bartholomew, 1992). They argue that transnationally competent managers need a broader set of skills than traditional managers. These authors state that an organization's HRM strategies must be modified in order to manage and develop such managers. These authors provide recommendations for how HRM systems can be modified to become more global—for example, developmental activities should prepare managers to work "Anywhere in the world with people from all parts of the world" (p. 59).

Another group of researchers argue that it is important to focus on future challenges that may require different competencies than those required today (Spreitzer et al., 1997). Therefore, they emphasize competencies involved in learning from experience as a part of the set of competencies used to identify international executive potential and develop effective international managers. The authors identified fourteen dimensions that could predict international executive potential. The list includes:

- eight end-state competency dimensions—for example, sensitivity to cultural differences, business knowledge, courage to take a stand, bringing out the best in people, acting with integrity, insight, commitment to success, and risk taking;

- six learning-oriented dimensions—for example, use of feedback, cultural adventurousness, seeking opportunities to learn, openness to criticism, feedback seeking, and flexibility.

Rosen and Digh (2001) organize global competencies into four "literacies": personal, social, business, and cultural literacy. These competencies are interrelated and interdependent and will be expressed differently depending on the national an organizational culture but should be grounded in wisdom from many cultures.

These approaches illustrate how the global environment can impact the approach taken to developing an organization's managers. In addition, they underscore the need to consider an organization's business strategy and environment as foundations for management development efforts.

Clearly, HRD professionals have an opportunity to provide more in-depth, enhanced global management (or leadership) development at all levels of the organization as a key to success. The next section provides a closer look at 3M's efforts to develop global leadership competencies in its managers as part of the organizations' business strategy and changing environment.

Global Leadership Competencies at 3M

At 3M, two forces put pressures on the organization to invest in conducting a customized competency-based job analysis. As was true at many other organizations, the decade of the 1990s saw increased global competition for 3M. The fierce competition, in turn, highlighted the need for highly effective leaders who could steer the company through a period of shrinking margins, pressures on pricing, and the ever-present demand for more innovations. This environment also highlighted the importance of succession planning as an activity that could promote the company's long-term viability. Due to the breadth of businesses and technologies within 3M, it takes years of experience before executives learn to function effectively in the company. Thoughtful succession planning efforts would ensure that the occasional managerial and executive job openings were leveraged as opportunities for leadership development.

The decision to use a customized approach to developing a leadership competency model (LCM) for the company fit well with the company's culture. Innovation is a core competence for 3M, and employees are constantly tinkering with products and systems in order to improve them.

The customized approach also served the objective of involving all key players in the process: HRD professionals worked closely with a team of key executives. Rather than simply hand the executives an off-the-shelf competency model, the HRD professionals held meetings and discussions with the executives to solicit their ideas, craft the language used in describing, the competencies, and so on. After all, the LCM would have important implications for the careers of key talent within the company. Involving executives early in the process would contribute to the validity of the model and also enhance their acceptance of it.

3M is a global company, and its LCM is applied all over the world. Thus, the process of developing the LCM required input from not only the CEO and those reporting directly to him but also representatives of Europe, Asia, Latin America, Canada and the United States.

The dimensions of 3M's global LCM described in Figure 9.2. The competencies listed reflect the corporate values and business strategy. 3M's shared values are these:

1. We satisfy customers with superior quality, value, and service.
2. We provide our investors with a fair rate of return through sustained quality growth.
3. We respect our social and physical environment.
4. We work to make 3M a company employees are proud to be a part of.

The foundation of many HRD practices at 3M is their Global Competency Leadership model, which specifies the following major competencies required for success as a leader in this global corporation.

Fundamental Leadership Competencies
New employees should possess these when hired and refine them through experience in successive managerial assignments.
- Ethics and integrity
- Intellectual capacity
- Maturity and judgment

Essential Leadership Competencies
These competences are developed through experience leading a function or department, and set the stage for more complex executive positions.
- Customer orientation
- Developing people
- Inspiring others
- Business health and results

Visionary Leadership Competencies
These competencies develop as executives take on responsibilities that require them to operate beyond the boundaries of a particular organizational unit and are used extensively in higher-level positions.
- Global perspective
- Vision and strategy
- Nurturing innovation
- Building alliances
- Organizational agility

Figure 9.2. 3M's global leadership competencies.

These values are apparent in the "fundamental" and "essential" categories. The company's corporate strategy is reflected in the "visionary" competencies.

Associated with each of 3M's Global Leadership Competencies are specific behaviors that illustrate exemplary levels of competency. Information about the specific behaviors displayed by top-level executives is used by the CEO during their annual review. Elsewhere in the company, executives and managers refer to the specific behaviors when setting performance expectations, judging performance, and discussing the development needs of their employees. As an example, specific behaviors associated with the competency "global perspective" include the following:

- Respects, values, and leverages other customs, cultures, and values.
- Uses global management team to understand and grow the total business.
- Able to leverage the benefits from working in multicultural environments.
- Optimizes and integrates resources on a global basis, including manufacturing, research, and businesses across countries, and functions to increase 3M's growth and profitability.
- Satisfies global customers and markets from anywhere in the world.
- Actively stays current on world economies, trade issues, international market trends, and opportunities.

The next section discusses the individual management development plans (IMDP) that can be a useful tool in the creation and implementation of successful management development initiatives.

Individual Management Development Plans

Many organizations have implemented the use of employee development plans for all categories of employees. The impetus for the implementation of individual development plans is difficult to pinpoint because they have been used for a variety of purposes. For example, individual development plans have been initiated to support special interest programs to foster upward mobility for minorities, women and disabled workers as well as to identify employees for other types of positions within an organization. Employee development plans should be viewed as yet another tool to facilitate career development and enhance the quality of development.

Organizations can use individual management development plans (IMDPs) to increase both the effectiveness and success of their company's leadership development efforts. IMDPs are driven by an organization's strategic agenda and how it plans to build competitive advantage in the marketplace through its people. The strategic agenda serves as the basis for the establishment of a developmental process for managers (and other employees) as the organization moves toward the future. The benefits of such an approach appear to be many, including:

1. Developing a manager's capabilities is consistent with an organization's HRD policy committed to the ongoing development of individuals to reach their highest potential. Management development is important in the organizational and career-development system.
2. IMDPs enable a manager to acquire the KSAOCs needed for successful performance in the organization. It also eases the transition from an individual's current job to one involving greater career responsibilities.
3. IMDPs assist in management recruitment, retention and morale development. Those organizations which fail to provide such individualized development efforts often lose their most promising managers. Frustrated with the lack of opportunity, achievement-oriented managers will often seek employment with other organizations outside that show more commitment to management development and provide more incentive with individual growth, development and learning for career advancement.
4. IMDP efforts can increase an employee's level of commitment to the organization and improve perceptions that the organization is a good place to work. By developing and promoting managers, organizations create a competent, motivated and satisfied work force.
5. IMDPs provide the employer and employee with a systematic long-term plan for management development. Improvement areas and learning opportunities are outlined in advance with the employee as they relate to increasing the employee's ability to successfully do management work related to achievement of specific business results. Reducing the guessing game by having the employer outline management selection criteria a priori is a critical element to the success of this type of development system.

Organizations, their HRM functions and HRD professionals must be situated to follow a standardized and documented management development process from several aspects:

1. it is tailored and based on an analysis of the actual requirements (competence and KSAOCs) of an actual manager's job given expected business results;
2. it provides management candidates with information about the expectations of the job given the organization's strategic agenda;
3. it provides management candidates with a developmental assessment of their own competence and KSAOCs (i.e., similar to a gap analysis);

4. it serves as a tool where management candidates can compare their expectations with their host organizations expectations and core competence needs for a successful manager in a learning organization; and
5. it documents an individualized management development plan for each manager (and prospective manager) which is in line with the organization's strategic agenda.

To be of real value IMDPs must be part of a systematic process designed to solicit and identify the learning and development needs of managers within the organization. It is a process where a manager and the organization make a commitment toward acquiring the necessary competence and KSAOCs important to the organization's success. And, it is a process where an organization makes a commitment toward providing the manager with a means of identifying and developing his or her current and future learning and development needs.

A key ingredient to the use of IMDPs is the standardization of events. This means that every manager must participate in measurable learning and development activities. Additionally, the overall IMDP process should:

1. Develop an IMDP oversight committee (possibly comprising managers from different organizational levels and an HRD professional to interpret the organization's strategic agenda into management development terms and manage the overall IMDP process (design, implementation, and evaluation).
2. Develop IMDPs for all current and future managers.
3. Develop realistic job previews for all management jobs in the organization and make this information available to all relevant employees.
4. Ensure completion of 360-degree evaluations of all managers based on key performance dimensions linked to the strategic imperatives of the organization. This information is used to formulate an IMDP.
5. Assign each manager an IMDP coach and develop an individualized IMDP plan.
6. Have the IMDP oversight committee review each IMDP plan and make recommendations and suggestions for improvement.
7. Ensure IMDP coaches and managers meet to review the final IMDP plan before implementation.
8. Ensure IMDP implementation begins with specific learning and development activities, completion dates, and meeting dates between IMDP coaches and managers to discuss progress (and the need to revise plans depending on organizational changes—for example, in strategic direction).

9. Ensure the IMDP oversight committee meets to review progress toward achievement of each IMDP's goals (i.e., at least every six months) and assess the overall program based on established evaluation criteria.
10. Generate regular reports for senior leadership by the IMDP oversight committee on the IMDP program to keep them up to date and to identify needed changes in the program.

IMDP Contingencies

As with many other developmental systems, the IMDP process should be time limited. Given the challenging demands on today's organizations, their managers should be expected to work toward achieving their individual and group learning and development goals within a specified time frame. However, the timeframe for a manager's development is most dependent on the current business demands which the manager, her or his supervisor, the IMDP coach and the IMDP oversight committee must not lose sight of.

It should be easy to see that the IMDP process requires ongoing communication to be successful. Because the system is built on providing a manager with continuous feedback and communication on management expectations and on how well they are meeting those expectations everyone must work to ensure that they don't let poor communication hinder the success of the IMDP process.

In conclusion, an effective IMDP process is systematic and aimed at getting the most information about a manager and the learning and development needs and opportunities important to their own and the organization's success to the right people at the right time. The IMDP is not meant to intimidate the manager; rather, the IMDP should provide each manager with the comfort that their organization is committed 100% to providing developmental opportunities for them throughout their tenure in the organization.

Globalization and Leadership Development Plans

At Weyerhaeuser, the HRD plan for creating strategic change emphasized leadership development activities. Leadership development activities also are especially important for organizations whose strategic objectives include adopting a truly transnational organizational structure (Maznevski & DiStefano, 2000; Harvey, Novicevic, & Speier, 2000; Baruch & Peiperl, 2000; Greengard, 2001). As organizations globalize, meeting the leadership challenge is often a top priority. In addition to answering the question of whom will be available for the senior leadership roles, HRD plans should provide a means to ensure that the available people have the competencies required to do the work. Figure 9.3 illustrates some of the different skills needed by international and transnational managers. As Figure 9.3 suggests, managers who competently perform traditional international roles can do so without having developed the skills needed in a transnational organizational.

Because transnational organizations are a relatively recent development, there are few managers in the world with fully developed transnational skills. Even if an organization is prepared to pay any price to hire such manager, it will not be able to find them. They have to be grown by the organization and then retained long enough to reap the rewards of a long-term investment. According to one study of 1,500 executives in 50 different transnational companies, the degree to which the HRD system is transnational lags far behind that of the other systems. For example, on average, these organizations generated 40% of their business from other countries, yet only 8percent of their top 100 executives were from other countries. Furthermore, only one-third of the executives in the study reported having any expatriate experience and less than 20% spoke a second language. Clearly, to begin developing their talent pool of the future,

Skill	International Managers	Transnational Managers
Global perspective	Understand a single foreign country and manage relationships between headquarters and that country.	Understand worldwide business and manage relationships among parts located in dozens of countries.
Synergistic learning	Work with and coach people in each foreign culture separately or sequentially.	Work with and facilitate learning among people from many cultures simultaneously.
Collaboration	Interact within clearly defined hierarchies of structural and cultural dominance.	Interact with all foreigners as equals and facilitate the same behavior in others.
Career perspectives	Expatriation and repatriation occurs primarily to get a specific job done.	Transpatriation experiences are accepted in anticipation of long-term career and organizational development.
Cross-cultural interaction	Use cross-cultural skills primarily on foreign assignments	Use cross-cultural skills on a daily basis throughout one's career.

Figure 9.3. Examples of differing skill levels needed by international and transnational managers.

these organizations must develop new practices to encourage and support the development of transnational leaders (adapted from Davis, 1998).

EVALUATION OF MANAGEMENT DEVELOPMENT ACTIVITIES

Four alternatives based on Kirkpatrick's evaluation model discussed in Chapter 6 can be used for evaluating management development activities (Kirkpatrick, 1994). Each alternative focuses on the following questions:

- Alternative I—Are the trainees happy with the course or program?
- Alternative II—Does the management develop initiative teach the concepts?
- Alternative III—Are the concepts (learning) used on the job?
- Alternative IV—Does the application of the concepts (and learning) positively affect the organization?

For each of the four alternatives, the HRD professionals must determine what might be measured to answer the questions posed by the alternative. Table 9.1 provides a summary of the alternatives and possible measured for evaluation.

Table 9.1. Evaluation Matrix

What We Want to Know	*What Might Be Measured*
I. Are the trainees happy with the course or program? If not, why?	Management trainee reaction during workshop, course, or program
a. Concepts or learning not relevant b. Format of the presentation	Management trainee reaction after workshop, course, or program
II. Do the materials teach the concepts or learning? If not why, not?	Management trainee performance during workshop, course, or program
a. Concepts or learning too complex b. Examples not relevant c. Exercises not relevant d. Format of presentation	Management trainee performance at end of workshop, course, or program
III. Are the concepts and learning used? If not, why not?	Performance improvements
a. Concepts/Learning • Not relevant • Too complex b. Environment not supportive	
IV. Does applications of concepts or learning positively affect the organization? If not, why not?	Performance improvements

HRD professionals remember that for effective management development evaluation, the principal significant questions should be:

- To what extent were the identified management development needs objectives achieved by the program?
- To what extent were the learners' objectives achieved?
- What specifically did the learners learn or be usefully reminded of?
- What commitment have the learners made about the learning they are going to implement on their return to work?

And back at work,

- How successful were the management trainees in implementing their action plans?
- To what extent were they supported in this by their own managers?
- To what extent has the action listed above achieved a Return on Investment (ROI) for the organization, either in terms of identified objectives satisfaction or where possible, a monetary assessment.

HRD professionals and their organizations commonly fail to perform these evaluation processes, especially where:

- The HRD department and professionals, do not have sufficient time to do so, and/or
- The HRD department does not have sufficient resources—people and money—to do so.

Obviously the evaluation cloth must be cut according to available resources (and the culture atmosphere), which tend to vary substantially from one organization to another. The fact remains that good methodical evaluation produces good reliable data; conversely, where little evaluation is performed, little is ever known by HRD professionals and organizations about the effectiveness of their management development initiatives.

CONCLUSION

Management development is one of the most widely offered and important forms of HRD. It should be driven by the organization and tied to the organization's strategic plan. HRD professionals must continue to work with their organizations to develop new management development paradigms that are committed to improving managers and better meeting the organization's strategic agenda. There are a variety of methods of management development and as with other employee HRD initiatives, management development can be achieved both on and off the job.

Given the challenges of increasingly global organizations, many of these organizations have recognized the need to develop globally competent managers and leaders. And to do this they along with HRD professionals have developed leadership competency models build on specific behaviors that illustrate exemplary levels of competency. Organizations are also relying more and more on individual management development plans (IMDPs) to improve the effectiveness and success of their management development efforts. The IMDP process affords employees with information about what successful management and leadership is about in their own and in other organizations, given a specific agenda, be it regional, national or global. The IMDP process highlighted in this chapter can help organizations to ensure that their management development efforts are (1) directed toward helping both organizations and employees meet their needs; (2) undertaken only when they are the most effective way to meet these needs; (3) solidly designed, using the latest state of the art approaches; and (4) carefully administered and thoroughly evaluated.

CHAPTER 10

HRD, ORGANIZATIONAL CHANGE AND DEVELOPMENT

INTRODUCTION

As managers and other organizational members contemplate the future of their organizations as the first decade of the 21st century continues to unfold, they can't escape the inevitability of change. Change is certainly among the most frequently used words on the business, government, and not-for-profit pages of every newspaper throughout the world. Not only have entire countries and empires gone through dramatic and wrenching changes, but so have great organizations such as IBM, Ford, Internal Revenue Service, World Health Organization, and the American Red Cross. Some organizations did not survive: Montgomery Ward no longer exists, and neither does Pan-American Airlines. So it makes a great deal of sense for this book directed at current and future HRD professionals to address the issues associated with managing change and the development of their organizations.

Effective HRD professionals must view managing change as an integral responsibility, rather than as a peripheral one. But we must accept the reality that not all organizations will successfully make the appropriate changes. Those with the best chance for success will demonstrate a commitment to managing change as critical to their surviving and thriving in the 21st century and beyond.

This chapter explores the management of organizational change and development through the application of structural, behavioral, and technological change initiatives and interventions. Our point of view is that the

HRD responsibility for being actively engaged in the management of change can best be undertaken and accomplished with a clear understanding of organizational change and organizational development (OD) processes and interventions. The chapter first offers two models of organizational change. Next, the chapter discusses OD assumptions, values and action research foundations. The discussion then focuses on OD and change interventions available to HRD professionals. The challenge of becoming a learning organization is then introduced before concluding the chapter by discussing the topics of OD and continuous co-evolution, appreciative inquiry and the relationship between HRD and OD.

TWO MODELS FOR MANAGING ORGANIZATIONAL CHANGE

There are a variety of models for managing planned change available to HRD professionals. This section discusses two of those models.

A Model for Managing Change

The process of managing planned change must be approached systematically by HRD professionals and other organizational members. The steps can be portrayed in a logical way as suggested in Figure 10.1. The model consists of specific steps generally acknowledged to be essential to successful change management (Duck, 2001). Organizational members consider each of them, either explicitly or implicitly, to undertake a change program. The prospects of initiating successful change can be enhanced when HRD professionals and others in the organization actively support the effort and demonstrate that support by implementing systematic procedures that give substance to the process.

The model indicates that forces for change continually act on the organization: this assumption reflects the dynamic character of today's world. At the same time, it's the responsibility of HRD professionals and others in the organization to sort out the information that reflects the magnitude of change forces. The information is the basis for recognizing when change is needed; it's equally desirable to recognize when change isn't needed. But once managers and HRD professionals recognize that something is malfunctioning, they must diagnose the problem and identify relevant alternative techniques.

Finally, HRD professionals and other organizational members must implement the change and monitor the change process and change results. The model includes feedback to the implementation step and to the forces-

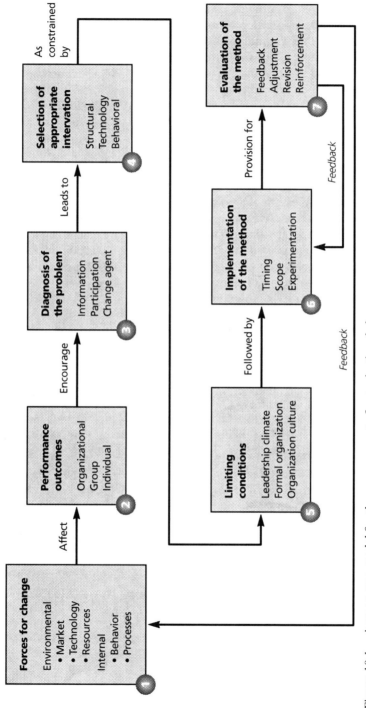

Figure 10.1. A seven-step model for the management of organizational change.

for-change step. These feedback loops suggest that the change process itself must be monitored and evaluated. The mode of implementation may be faulty and may lead to poor results, but responsive action could correct the situation. Moreover, the feedback loop to the initial step recognizes that no change is final. A new situation is created within which problems and issues will emerge; a new setting is created that will itself become subject to change. The model suggests no final solution; rather, it emphasizes that the modern HRD professional and other organizational members operate in a dynamic setting wherein the only certainty is change itself.

Change as a Three-Step Process: The Lewin Model

Change management, that is, the manner by which HRD and other organizational members introduce change, regardless of how ideal their intentions may be—largely determines the success of their efforts. Kurt Lewin, a noted organizational theorist, developed a model of the change process that has stood the test of time and continues to influence the way organizations manage planned change (Lewin, 1947). Lewin's model is based on the idea of force field analysis. Although force-field analysis may sound like something out of a Star Trek movie, it is a technique that can be used to analyze a change and help overcome resistance to it.

Lewin developed a three-stage model of planned change that explained how to initiate, manage, and stabilize the change process. The three stages are unfreezing, changing, and refreezing. Before reviewing each stage, it is important to highlight the assumptions that underlie this model:

1. The change process involves learning something new, as well as discontinuing current attitudes, behaviors, or organizational practices.
2. Change will not occur unless there is motivation to change. This is often the most difficult part of the change process.
3. People are the hub of all organizational changes. Any change, whether in terms of structure, group process, reward systems, or job design, requires individuals to change.
4. Resistance to change is found even when the goals of change are highly desirable.
5. Effective change requires reinforcing new behaviors, attitudes, and organizational practices.

The Lewin model contends that a person's behavior is the product of two opposing forces; one force pushes toward preserving the status quo, and another force pushes for change. When the two opposing forces are approximately equal, current behavior is maintained. For behavioral change to occur, the forces maintaining status quo must be overcome. This can be accomplished by increasing the forces for change, by weakening the forces for status quo, or by a combination of these actions.

For HRD professionals, the first step in conducting a force-field analysis is to develop a list of all the forces promoting change and all those resisting change. Then determine which of the positive and which of the negative forces are the most powerful. The forces can be ranked in order of importance or by rate of strength. To facilitate the change, HRD professionals try to remove or at least minimize some of the forces acting against the change in order to tip the balance so that the forces furthering the change outweigh those hindering the change.

As noted earlier, Lewin's change model suggests that every change require employees to go through three steps. The three steps are:

- Unfreezing-employees recognize the need for change.
- Changing or Moving-employees begin trying to behave differently.
- Refreezing the new behavior becomes part employees' moral behavior and procedures.

In order for change to be fully implemented, the organization must help provide a way for the new behavior to become an established practice.

Unfreezing

In the unfreezing stage, employees must see the status quo as less than ideal. The HRD professionals, managers or other change agents—individual(s) responsible for implementing the change must spell out clearly to affected employees why the change is necessary. Allied Signal's former CEO, Lawrence Bossidy, describes this step colorfully, as the "burning platform theory of change":

> When the roustabouts are standing on the offshore oilrig and the foreman yells, "Jump into the water," not only won't they jump but they also won't feel too kindly toward the foreman. There may be sharks in the water. They'll jump only when they themselves see the flames shooting up from the platform. . . . The leader's job is to help everyone see that the platform is burning, whether the flames are apparent or not. (Tichy & Charan, 1995)

In essence, unfreezing means overcoming fears about the change and other resistance to change. Organizations often accomplish unfreezing by eliminating the rewards for current behavior and showing that current behavior is not valued. Unfreezing on the part of individuals is an acceptance that changes need to occur. In essence, individuals surrender by allowing the boundaries of their status quo to be opened in preparation for change. The organization relies heavily on managers—as management's link to operating employees—to carry out this responsibility, for which they need good communication skills.

According to Ken Blanchard, a behavioral scientist, a major reason many efforts to change fail are that management does not consider the employees' point of view (Blanchard, 1992). Many changes require not only performing new tasks but also adopting new attitudes, such as a willingness to assume decision-making responsibility or a strong commitment to customers. Employees may have difficulty changing their attitudes, especially if they are unsure about management's sincerity.

Changing or Moving

When employees appreciate the need for a change and have received any necessary training, they are ready to begin altering their behavior. It is practical to begin by attempting to make basic changes in employees' behavior, rather than trying to change their values. Values, by their very nature, are more resistant to change. To induce changes in behavior, HRD professionals and other change agents should offer tangible and intangible rewards. As employees' attitudes become more positive, their values may shift as well.

The key to implementing change is to build on success. HRD professionals should determine those aspects of the change over which they have control and then try to carry them out successfully. An HRD professional and other organizational change agents should point out each success the group achieves along the way. For example, a manager who has control over scheduling a change should establish reasonable deadlines. As employees meet each deadline, the manager can praise their achievements. To be more specific, imagine that an accounting department is installing a new computer system. Instead of focusing simply on whether everyone is using the system properly, a manager can establish dates for setting up various pieces of equipment and teaching employees to operate different parts of the system. Then the manager can note that the terminals arrived on time, and that everyone learned how to log on and enter their passwords in a single training session, and so on. This positive reinforcement will help employees to change their behavior and their attitudes.

Refreezing

The change process is complete only when employees make the new behaviors, attitudes, and values part of their routine. In organizations that do not manage change effectively, managers may assume a change effort has succeeded simply because employees merely fulfill the basic requirements of a change without adjusting their routines or their attitudes. In such cases, backsliding is likely. Employees may revert to their old practices when the initial pressure for change eases, because new procedures are less comfortable than the old familiar ones. Changes in the reward structure may be needed to ensure that the organization is not rewarding the old behaviors and merely hoping for new behaviors.

Backsliding is a natural response to change, but it can become a problem unless the HRD professional and other organizational members act to get everyone back on track. For example, a manager should remind employees about what they have achieved so far and what is expected of them in the future. It is important for the organization to continue to reinforce and reward employees for behavior that shows they have made the desired change.

Monsanto's approach to increasing opportunities for women within the company is an illustration of how to use the Lewin model effectively. First, Monsanto emphasized unfreezing by helping employees debunk negative stereotypes about women in business. This also helped overcome resistance to change. Second, Monsanto moved employees' attitudes and behaviors by diversity training in which differences were emphasized as positive, and supervisors learned ways of training and developing female employees. Third, Monsanto changed its reward system so managers were evaluated and paid according to how they coached and promoted women, which helped refreeze the new attitudes and behaviors.

Lewin's model proposes that for change efforts to be successful, the three-stage process must be completed. Failures in efforts to change can be traced back to one of the three stages. Successful change thus requires that old behaviors be discarded, new behaviors be introduced, and these new behaviors be institutionalized and rewarded.

ORGANIZATION DEVELOPMENT

As evident from our discussion to this point "change" is the watchword of the day for many, if not most, organizations. Pressure from increasing technological developments, globalization, competition, workforce changes, and other forces has created an environment that rewards organizations that are capable of identifying trends and issues and responding quickly to them. Organization development (OD) is an element of HRD that can best enable organizations to successfully respond to and manage change. Organizational change is the planned attempt by management to improve the overall effectiveness of individuals, groups, and the organization by altering structure, behavior and processes. If the change is correctly implemented, individuals and groups should move toward more effective performance. Concerted, planned, and evaluated efforts to improve effectiveness have potential for success.

OD is a comprehensive or systematic approach to planned change that is designed to improve the overall effectiveness of organizations. Formally defined, OD is a process by which behavioral science knowledge and practices are used to help organizations achieve greater effectiveness, including improved quality of work life and increased productivity (Cummings & Worley, 2005). It is designed to work on issues of both external adaptation and internal integration.

OD is used to improve performance in organizations of many types, sizes, and settings. It includes a set of tools with which any HRD professional who is concerned about achieving and maintaining high level of productivity will want to be familiar. Because of its comprehensive nature and scientific foundations, OD was frequently implemented with the aid of an external consultant. In today's constantly changing world of work an understanding of OD's basic concepts and techniques are critical for all HRD professionals who are increasingly expected to assist their organizations in taking the necessary steps to improve both the quality of work life and productivity.

Another way of understanding OD is to explain what it is not:

- OD is not a micro approach to change. Management development, for example, is aimed at changing individual behavior, whereas OD is focused on the macro goal of developing an organization-wide improvement in managerial styles.
- OD is more than any single technique. OD uses many different techniques, such as total quality management or job enrichment, and none of them by itself represents the OD discipline.
- OD does not include random or ad hoc changes. OD is based on a systematic appraisal and diagnosis of problems, leading to planned and specific types of change efforts.
- OD is aimed at more than raising morale or attitudes. OD is aimed at overall organizational health and effectiveness. Participant satisfaction may be one aspect of the change effort, but it includes other effectiveness parameters as well.

OD continues to emerge as a discipline concerned with improving the effectiveness of the organization and its members by means of systematic change initiatives. Chester Barnard and Chris Argyris, among other management theorists, have noted that the truly effective organization is one in which both the organization and the individual can grow and develop. An organization with such an environment is a "healthy" organization. The goal of OD is to make organizations healthier and more effective. These concepts apply to organizations of all types, including schools, churches, military forces, businesses, and governments.

Change is a way of life in today's organization, but organizations are also faced with maintaining a stable identity and operations in order to accomplish their primary goals. Consequently, organizations involved in managing change have found that the way they handle change is critical. There is a need for a systematic approach, discriminating between features that are healthy and effective and those that are not. Erratic, short-term, unplanned, or haphazard change that may introduce problems that did not exist before or allow side-effects of the change that may be worse than the original problem. HRD professionals should also be aware that stability or equilibrium can contribute to a health state. Change inevitably involves the disruption of that steady state. Change just for the sake of change is not necessarily effective; in fact, it may be dysfunctional.

OD CHARACTERISTICS, ASSUMPTIONS, VALUES, AND ACTION RESEARCH FOUNDATIONS

A large part of any OD program's success rests with its basic characteristics, assumptions, values, and action research foundations.

Basic Characteristics

Some of the basic characteristics of OD initiatives are:

1. *Change.* OD is a planned strategy to bring about organizational change. Change is planned by organizational members (i.e., managers, HRD and OD professionals) to achieve goals. The change effort aims at specific objectives and is based on a diagnosis of problem areas.
2. *Collaborative Approach.* OD typically involves a collaborative approach to change that includes the involvement and participation of the organizational members most affected by the changes.
3. *Performance Orientation.* OD programs include an emphasis on ways to improve and enhance performance and quality.
4. *Humanistic Orientation.* OD relies on a set of humanistic values about people and organizations that aims at making organizations more effective by opening up new opportunities for increased use of human potential.
5. *Systems Approach.* OD represents a systems approach concerned with the interrelationship of divisions, departments, groups, and individuals as interdependent subsystems of the total organization. A systems approach focuses on the relationship between elements and excellence.

6. *Scientific Method.* OD is based upon scientific approaches to increase organization effectiveness. The scientific approaches supplement practical experience.

In more general terms, OD is based on the notion that for an organization to be effective (i.e., accomplish its goal), it must be more than merely efficient. It must adapt to change.

Underlying Assumptions

The OD foundations for achieving change are rooted in underlying assumptions about individuals, groups and organizations. At the individual level, OD is guided by principles that reflect an underlying respect for people and their capabilities. It assumes that individual needs for growth and development are most likely to be satisfied in a supportive and challenging work environment. It also assumes that most people are capable of taking responsibility for their own actions and of making positive contributions to organizational performance.

At the group level, OD is guided by principles that reflect a belief that groups can be good for both people and organizations. It assumes that groups help their members satisfy important individual needs and can also be helpful in supporting organizational objectives. And it assumes, that effective groups can be created by people working in collaboration to meet individual and organizational needs.

At the organizational level, OD is guided by principles that show a respect for the complexity of an organization as a system of interdependent parts. It assumes that change in one part of the organization will affect other parts as well. And it assumes that organizational structures and jobs can be designed to meet the needs of individuals and groups as well as those of the organization.

OD Values and Principles

OD offers a systematic approach to planned change in organizations that addresses two main goals: outcome goals (namely issues of external adaptation) and process goals (mainly issues of internal integration). Outcome goals include achieving improvements in task performance by improving external adaptation capabilities. In OD, these goals focus on what is actually accomplished through individual and group efforts. Process goals include achieving improvements in such things as communication, interaction, and decision making among an organization's members.

These goals focus on how well people work together, and they stress improving internal integration.

In pursuit of these goals, OD is intended to help organizations and their members by (1) creating an open problem-solving climate throughout an organization, (2) supplanting formal authority with that of knowledge and competence, (3) moving decision-making to points where relevant information is available, (4) building trust and maximizing collaboration between individuals and groups, (5) increasing the sense of organizational "ownership" among members, and (6) allowing people to exercise self-direction and self-control at work (Bennis, 1987). Thus, using OD implicitly involves these values. That is, OD is designed to improve the contributions of individual members in achieving the organizational goals, and it seeks to do so in ways that respect the organization's members as mature adults who need and deserve high-quality experiences in their working lives.

Action-Research Foundations of OD

OD practitioners refer to action research as the process of systematically collecting data on an organization, feeding it back to the members for action planning, and evaluating results by collecting and reflecting on more data after the planned actions have been taken. This is a data-based and collaborative approach to problem solving and organizational assessment. When used in the OD process, action research helps identify action directions that may enhance an organization's effectiveness. In a typical action-research sequence depicted in Figure 10.2, the sequence is initiated when someone senses a performance gap and decides to analyze the situation systematically for the problems and opportunities it represents. The process continues through the following steps: data gathering, data feedback, data analysis, and action planning. It continues to the point at which action is taken and results are evaluated. The evaluation or reassessment stage may or may not generate another performance gap. If it does, the action-research cycle begins anew.

Figure 10.3 identifies one set of frameworks that can assist HRD professionals in accomplishing the required diagnoses. These foundations apply the open systems framework. At the organizational level, the figure indicates that effectiveness must be understood with respect to forces in the external environment and major organizational aspects, such as strategy, technology, structure, culture, and management systems. At the group level, effectiveness is viewed in a context of forces in the internal environment of the organization and major group aspects, such as tasks, membership, norms, cohesiveness, and group processes. At the individual level, effectiveness is considered in relationship to the internal environment of

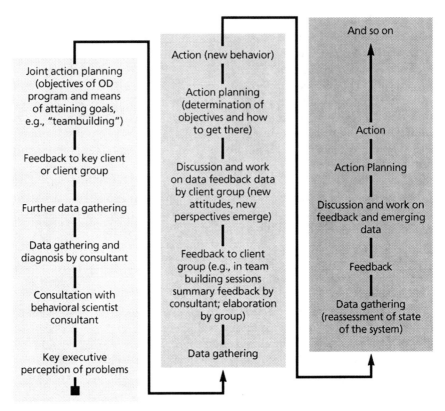

Figure 10.2. An action-research model for organizational development.

the workgroup and individual aspects, such as tasks, goals, and interpersonal relationships.

OD AND CHANGE INTERVENTIONS

The action-research process should engage members of an organization in activities designed to accomplish the required diagnoses and to develop and implement plans for constructive change. Action research, data collection, and the diagnostic foundations should come together through the choice and use of OD "interventions." An intervention is a specific action that HRD professionals and others who are responsible for change take to focus the change process. With less formality, many of these techniques are also now being used by HRD professionals to help them understand and improve their own operations.

Organization-level Foundations

| External environment | → | Strategy
Technology
Structure
Culture
Systems | → | Organizational effectiveness |

Group-level Foundations

| Organizational environment | → | Tasks
Membership
Norms
Cohesiveness
Processes | → | Group effectiveness |

Group-level Foundations

| Work-group environment | → | Tasks
Goals
Needs
Abilities
Relationships | → | Individual effectiveness |

Figure 10.3. Diagnostic foundations of OD and OD techniques: Concerns for individual, group, and organizational effectiveness.

Although intervention has a generally used meaning, it has a specific meaning in the context of OD where it refers to a formal activity. Choice of a particular intervention depends on the nature of the problem that the organization's management and HRD professionals have diagnosed. As change agents HRD professionals along with other organizational members must determine which alternative is most likely to produce the desired outcome, whether it is improvement in skills, attitudes, behavior, or structure.

The literature of OD recognizes that different interventions have different effects on organizations, groups, and individuals. The term depth of intended change refers to the magnitude of the problem to be addressed and the significance of the change required to address the problem.

Depth and Approach of Intended Change

Depth of the intended change refers to the scope and intensity of organizational change efforts (Harrison, 1970; see also, French & Bell, 1984). This idea likens the organization to an iceberg. This analogy draws attention to two important components: the formal and informal aspects of organizations. The formal components of an organization are like that part of an iceberg' that's above water; the informal components lie below the water, unseen, but there nevertheless. The formal components are observable, rational, and oriented to structural factors. On the other hand, the informal components are not observable to all people, affective, and oriented to process and behavioral factors.

Both the formal and informal aspects of organizations can be changed in a methodical, deliberate way. Planned and managed change describes the systematic process of introducing new structures, behaviors, and technologies for accomplishing goals. Organizations can take any of these three approaches:

- *Structural.* This approach focuses on changing or redesigning jobs, workflow, or organizational structure. Organizations can become more organic, virtual, flat, or modular. Jobs and work can be enriched, combined, expanded or converted to a virtual arrangement.
- *Behavioral.* Some refer to this as OD. Team building, diversity training, enhancing or developing leadership skills and attitudes, and modifying employee's knowledge and learning can be included under a behavioral change approach.
- *Technological.* This change could involve computers, intranets, the IT infrastructure, materials, techniques, or automation of work processes.

Identifying Alternative Change Techniques

The particular change techniques chosen in Step 4 in the framework presented in Figure 10.4 depends on the nature of the problem. HRD professionals and other change agents must determine which alternative is most likely to produce the desired outcomes (Arnes, Slack, & Henings, 2004). The three change approaches differ in their focus, namely, to change structure, behavior, or technology.

Structural Change

Logically, organizing follows planning, since the structure is a means for achieving the objectives established through planning. Structural change, in the context of organizational change, refers to managerial attempts to improve performance by altering the formal structure of task and authority relationships. But because structure creates human and social relationships that members of the organization may value highly, efforts to disrupt these relationships may be resisted.

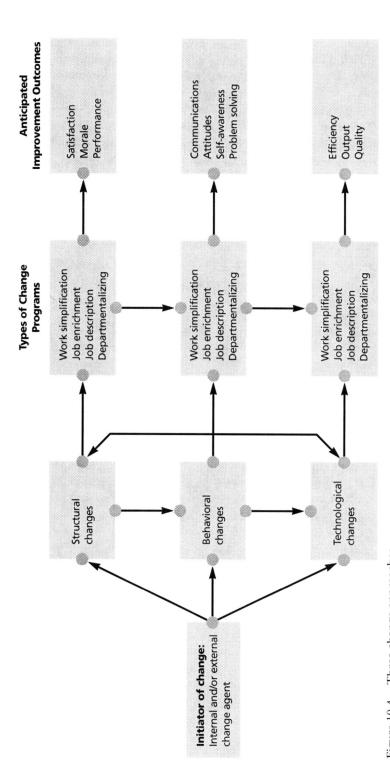

Figure 10.4. Three change approaches.

Structural changes alter some aspects of the formal task and authority system. The design of an organization involves the specification of jobs, the grouping of jobs into departments, the creation of virtual teams and identification of work to be done at remote sites (e.g., in the employee's home), the determination of the size of groups reporting to a single manager, and the distribution of authority, including the provision of staff assistance. Changes in the nature of jobs, bases for departmentalization, locations where work tasks are completed, and line-staff relationships are, therefore, structural changes.

Elements of structural change often include plans, procedures, span of control, and levels of organization. The point that should be taken, however, is not only that any list of structural change approaches is incomplete, but that all structural parts are interrelated. Job changes do not take place in a vacuum; on the contrary, the change affects all surrounding jobs.

Behavioral Change

Behavioral change techniques are efforts to redirect and increase employee motivation, skills, and knowledge bases. The major objective of such techniques is to coordinate performance of assigned tasks. The early efforts to change employee behavior dates back to scientific management work-improvement and employee-training methods. These attempts primarily were directed at improving the skills and knowledge bases of employees. The employee counseling programs that grew out of the early studies (the Hawthorne studies) were (and remain) primarily directed at increasing employee motivation.

Training and development programs for managers have typically emphasized interpersonal relationships and technical skills. These programs attempt to provide managers with basic technical and leadership skills. Since managers are concerned primarily with seeing the work of others, these traditional programs emphasize techniques for dealing with people problems, namely how to handle the malcontent, the loafer, the troublemaker, and the complainer. The programs also include conceptual material dealing with communications, leadership styles, and organizational relationships. The training methods often involve role-playing, discussion groups, lectures, simulations, and organized courses offered by the organization's HRD professionals, universities, consultants, and training organizations.

Training continues to be an important technique for introducing behavioral changes. The vast majority of OD change techniques, like team building, have been directed at changing the behavior of individuals and groups through problem solving, decision making, and communication.

Technological Change

Technological change includes any application of new ways of transforming resources into products or services. In the usual sense of the word, technology means new machines—lathes, presses, computers, and the like. But the concept can be expanded to include all new techniques, whether or not they include new machines.

Technological change involving computers are being implemented by the majority of manufacturing and service organizations (Anderson, 2001). In service organizations, computers now either perform or assist employees in performing a wide variety of tasks such as processing customer banking transactions, airline ticket purchases, life insurance policies, and hospital admissions. Manufacturing processes continue to find new and effective ways to apply computer technology. In many plants, computers now control large parts of the manufacturing process such as materials handling, quality testing, and assembly. Some organizations have created flexible manufacturing systems. These systems produce a part or product entirely by automation. From initial design to delivery, the unit is untouched by human hands (Schilling & Stennsma, 2001).

These technological changes have occurred largely because of the potential of high technology to lower production costs, to boost productivity, and to improve quality. However, although computer and robotics technologies have affected over half of America's jobs, the rate of high-tech implementation in U.S. organizations has fallen far short of projections. The reason: Many high-tech changes haven't delivered expected results.

Many observers believe that the disappointing performance of such technological change is due to HRD professionals and management's neglect of the structural and behavioral changes that must accompany technological change. Specifically, employees' jobs have not been redesigned in a way that both makes the best use of new technology and addresses the employees' social and psychological needs. A mismatch exists between technology, how employees perform their jobs, and how managers supervise employees. Consequently, technology's potential isn't realized (Anderson, 2001).

This neglect is costly because computerizing the workplace requires major structural and behavioral changes for success (Levy & Murnane, 2004). Changes are necessary in a number of areas including the following: employee training, compensation and management style.

Technological innovations can change other aspects of the workplace. The changes can alter working conditions, the social relations among workers, career patterns, and promotion procedures, to name a few. The degree and extent of any changes in behavior and structure depend on the magnitude of the technological change. Essentially, the decision to adopt a technological change must involve consideration of the numerous behavioral and structural impacts that often occur. These impacts must, in turn, be reconciled with the conditions that limit the scope and magnitude of the proposed change.

The three major alternative approaches to change—structural, behavioral, and technological—attempt to improve performance by improving communication, decision making, attitudes, and skills. These approaches are based on the assumption that changes in structure, behavior, and technology can result in improvements for the organization, individuals, and groups. Often changes in one area such as structure are related to changes in the other two areas.

ORGANIZATIONAL, GROUP, AND INDIVIDUAL LEVELS OF OD INTERVENTIONS

The action-research process should engage members of an organization in activities designed to accomplish the required diagnoses and to develop and implement plans for constructive change. Action research, data collection, and the diagnostic foundations should come together through the choice and use of OD interventions. In addition to classifying OD interventions as structural, behavioral or technological major OD interventions can also be categorized with respect to their major impact at the organizational, group, and individual levels of action. And collectively or individually each of these interventions can be included as part of other types of interventions—cultural change, strategic change, and learning organizations.

An effective organization is one that achieves its major performance objectives while maintaining a high quality of work life for its members. OD interventions designed for systemwide application include the following.

Organization-wide Interventions

Survey feedback begins with the collection of data via questionnaire responses from organization members or a representative sample of such responses. The data are then presented, or fed back, to the members. They subsequently engage in a collaborative process to interpret the data and to develop action plans in response.

Confrontation meetings are designed to help determine how an organization may be improved and to take initial actions to better the situation (Beckhard, 1967). The intervention involves a one-day meeting conducted by an OD or HRD facilitator for a representative sample of organizational members, including top management. In a structured format, the HRD professional asks participants to make individual lists of what they feel can be done to improve things. Then, through a series of small-group work sessions and sharing of results, these ideas are refined into a tentative set of actions that top management then endorses for immediate implementation. The major trick here is to get senior managers to propose changing their part of the organization. Confrontation meetings fail if all the proposed changes call for adjustments by direct reports without any alterations by the top managers.

Structural redesign involves realigning the structure of the organization or major subsystems to improve performance. It includes examining the best fit among structure, technology, and environment. In today's highly dynamic environments, in light of the increasing involvement of organizations in international operations and with rapid change in information technology, a structure can easily become out of date. Thus, structural redesign is an important OD intervention that can be used to help maintain the best fit between organizational structures and situational demands.

Collateral organization is designed to make creative problem solving possible by pulling a representative set of members out of the formal organization structure to engage in periodic small-group problem solving sessions (Zand, 1974; Stein & Kanter, 1980). These collateral, or "parallel," structures are temporary and exist only to supplement the activities of the formal structure.

Group and Intergroup Interventions

OD interventions at the group level are designed to improve group effectiveness. The major interventions at this level are team building, process consultation, and intergroup team building.

Team building involves a manager, consultant or HRD professional engaging the members of a group in a series of activities designed to help them examine how the group functions and how it may function better. Like survey feedback at the organizational level, team building involves some form of data collection and feedback. The key elements, however, are a collaborative assessment of the data by all members of the group and the achievement of consensus regarding what may be done to improve group effectiveness. Team building is often done at "retreats" or off-site meetings, where group members spend two to three days working intensely together on this reflection-analysis-planning process.

Process consultation involves structured activities that are facilitated by an OD practitioner or HRD professional and are designed to improve group functioning. Process consultation has a more specific focus than does team building, however: its attention is directed toward the key "processes" through which members of a group work with one another. The process consultant is concerned with helping a group function better on such things as norms, cohesiveness, decision-making methods, communication, conflict, and task and maintenance activities.

Intergroup team building is a special form of team building. It is designed to help two or more groups improve their working relationships with one another and, it is hoped, to experience improved group effectiveness as a result. Here, the OD practitioner or HRD professional engages the groups or their representatives in activities that increase awareness of how each group perceives the other. Given this understanding, collaborative problem solving can improve coordination between the groups and encourage more mutual support of one another as important components in the total organization.

Individual Interventions

Task performance and job satisfaction are important concerns with respect to improving individual effectiveness in the workplace. OD interventions at this level of attention range from those that address personal issues to those that deal more with specific job and career considerations. Individual-level OD interventions include the following.

Role negotiation is a means of clarifying what individuals expect to give and receive of one another in their working relationship. Because roles and personnel change over time, role negotiation can be an important way to maintain task understandings among individuals in an organization. This kind of understanding is quite easily accomplished by helping people who work together clarify what they need from one another to do their jobs well.

Job redesign is the process of creating long-term congruence between individual goals and organizational career opportunities. A good example is the Hackham and Oldham diagnostic approach to job enrichment which involves (1) analyzing the core characteristics of a job or group of jobs, (2) analyzing the needs and capabilities of workers in those jobs, and (3) taking action to adjust the core job characteristics either to enrich or to simplify the jobs to best match individual preferences (Hackman & Oldham, 1980).

Career planning takes the form of structured opportunities for individuals to work with their managers or staff from HRM or HRD on career issues. They may map career goals, assess personal development needs, and actively plan short-term and long-term career moves. Increasingly, career planning is becoming a major part of the support that highly progressive organizations provide for their members.

Cultural Change Interventions

Organizational culture is the basic pattern of shared assumptions, values, and beliefs considered the correct way of thinking about and acting on problems and opportunities facing the organization. Organizational culture defines what is important and unimportant in the organization. Organizational culture is not something that is found in a mission statement or an organizational policy manual. Rather, you might think of it as the organization's DNA—invisible to the naked eye, yet a powerful template that shapes what happens in the workplace (Schein, 1991). Organizational culture is communicated and reinforced through organizational mechanisms like the following:

1. What leaders pay attention to.
2. The way leaders react to crises.
3. Role modeling, coaching and teaching.
4. Criteria for allocating rewards.
5. Criteria for recruiting, selecting, promoting and dismissing employees (Schein, 1985).

Organizational culture change interventions involve more than simply restating values, beliefs, or norms, and communicating them to individuals. Cultural changes involve a complex process of replacing an existing paradigm or way of thinking with another. For example, our earlier discussion of Monsanto's efforts to increase opportunities for women within the company is an illustration of how to make fundamental changes in an organization's culture. Monsanto had to take on a new set of values (as espoused in the vision and mission) to create more opportunities for women within the company.

Strategic Change Interventions

Strategic change interventions focus on efforts to bring about fundamental change in the organizational purpose or mission (i.e., systemwide change). Strategic interventions may be necessary when an organization is faced with external pressures to change and adapt. External pressures come from many sources, including the economic, social, legal, and political arenas (Morhman & Mohrman, 1989). Organizations unable to maintain a "dynamic-fit" between themselves and the demands imposed by their environments will face decline and possible elimination (Lawrence, 1989). Hodgkinson and Wright provide an example of a top management team at a large organization that seemed unable to break out of their "strategic inertia" to face competitive change (Hodgkinson & Wright, 2002).

Becoming a Learning Organization

Because organizations are continually changing, they must learn from the past, competitors, and experts in order to remain competitive. Some organizations have realized that they must be able to develop the capacity to transfer knowledge across the organization by collaborating and sharing expertise and information that is unbounded by status, space, and time. The emphasis on continuous learning, changing, and adapting led to the emergence of an organizational development and change intervention referred to as a learning organization.

Learning is a key ingredient in growing, becoming more effective and socially, responsible and sustaining the organization's value proposition. A learning organization is an organization that has developed the continuous capacity to adapt and change. Just as individuals learn, so too do organizations. "All organizations learn, whether they consciously choose to or not—it is a fundamental requirement for their sustained existence (Kim, 1993). Peter Senge, in his best-selling book the *Fifth Discipline*, described a learning organization as proactively creating, using, and transferring knowledge to change its behavior (Senge, 1990). Sharing knowledge, experience and ideas become a habit in a learning organization.

Basic characteristics of a learning organization are:

1. There exists a shared vision that everyone agrees on.
2. People discard their old ways of thinking and the standard routines they use for solving problems or doing their jobs.
3. Members think of all organizational processes, activities, functions and interactions with the environment as part of a system of interrelationships.
4. People openly communicate with each other (across vertical and horizontal boundaries) without fear of criticism or punishment.
5. People subordinate their personal self-interest and fragmented departmental interests to work together to achieve the organization's shared vision.

Buckman Laboratories of Memphis, Tennessee, is held up as an example of a progressive learning organization. The organization uses forums, training, electronic bulletin boards, virtual conference rooms, and presentations to share information and experiences (www.knowledgenurture.com). By working together and sharing the entire 1,200 person workforce is able to perform feats that previously were impossible. For example, a Buckman sales representative was attempting to close a deal in Indonesia. The plant's decision-making team wanted a proposal within two weeks—an impossible task. The sales rep went to his online forum, explained his predicament, and within 48 hours had volumes of data, information, and facts to prepare the sales proposal. He made the two-week deadline with time to spare and closed the deal.

A number of factors that facilitate organizational learning have been identified as follows (see, Moingeon & Edmondson, 1996, p. 43):

1. *Scanning imperative.* Interest in external happenings and in the nature of one's environment. Valuing the processes of awareness and data generation. Curious about what is "out there" as opposed to "in here."
2. *Performance gap.* Shared perception of a gap between actual and desired state of performance. Disconfirming feedback interrupts a string of successes. Performance shortfalls are seen as opportunities for learning.
3. *Concern for measurement.* Spend considerable effort in defining and measuring key factors when venturing into new areas; strive for specific, quantifiable measures; discourse over metrics is seen as a learning activity.
4. *Experimental mindset.* Support for trying new things; curiosity about how things work; ability to "play" with things. Small failures are encouraged, not punished. See changes in work processes, policies, and structures as a continuous series of grand tryouts.
5. *Climate of openness.* Accessibility of information, relatively open boundaries. Opportunities to observe others; problems/errors are shared, not hidden; debate and conflict are acceptable.
6. *Continuous education.* Ongoing commitment to education at all levels; support for growth and development of members.
7. *Operational variety.* Variety exists in response modes, procedures, systems; significant diversity in personnel. Pluralistic rather than monolithic definition of valued internal capabilities.
8. *Multiple advocates.* Top-down and bottom-up initiatives are possible, multiple advocates and gatekeepers exist.
9. *Involved leadership.* Leadership at significant levels articulates vision and is very actively engaged in its actualization; takes ongoing steps to implement visions; "hands-on" involvement in educational and other implementation steps.
10. *Systems perspective.* Strong focus on how parts of the organization are interdependent; seek optimization of organizational goals at the highest levels; see problems and solutions in terms of systemic relationships.

HRD professionals and other members of the organization can create or contribute to the learning environment. The building and sustaining of a learning organization require a commitment to learning, the generation of creative ideas that are implemented, and the desire to build cohesive teamwork, collaboration, and support. Activities that can be performed to build learning within an organization are (see, Ulrich, Jick, & Von Glinow, 1993; Gibson, Ivancevich, & Donnelly, 2006):

Build a Commitment to Learning

- Make learning a component of the vision and strategic objectives.
- Invest in learning.
- Publicly promote the value of learning.
- Measure, benchmark, and track learning.
- Create rewards and symbols of learning.

Work to Generate Ideas with Impact

- Implement continuous improvement programs.
- Increase employee competence through training, or buy talent from outside the organization.
- Experiment with new ideas, processes, and structural arrangements.
- Go outside the organization to identify world-class ideas and processes.
- Identify mental models of organizational processes.
- Instill systems thinking throughout the organization.

Work to Generalize Ideas with Impact

- Create an infrastructure that moves ideas across organizational boundaries.
- Rotate employees across functional and divisional boundaries.

A major result of an effective learning organization is that knowledge is managed more effectively (Jenkins, Henry & Pinch, 2004). Knowledge management is the sharing of information to achieve innovation, competitive advantage, and productive accomplishments. Although a learning organization leads to knowledge management, it is also true that, by managing knowledge, organizations will learn.

Learning and managing knowledge is not enough in a constantly changing work environment. Pfeffer and Sutton correctly suggest that many organizations have fallen into a knowing-doing gap. What is learned and knowledge gained about change, strategies, and resistance must be converted into action and evaluation. It is easier and more comfortable to talk intellectually about empowerment, converting to more telecommuting, or eliminating layers of management than to actually execute change (Pfeffer & Sutton, 2000). The challenge facing HRD professionals who understand change, learning organizations and knowledge management is to help their organizations to become action oriented and decisive.

Like managers in their organizations, the role of HRD professionals in the learning organization must be that of a designer, teacher, and facilitator who can build shared vision and challenge the traditional model of managing or leading. HRD professionals must help other organizational leaders to view the organization as a system of interrelated parts and communicate how a vision of the future can take on a leadership role in helping other organizational members learn from mistakes and break away from using old patterns of problem solving and decision-making.

Converting a traditional organization to a more learning-oriented institution requires changing the way information and experiences are used. HRD professionals must help managers and other organizational members change the way information is sought, used, stored, and reviewed. Information must be shared, available, and transparent. These requirements are resisted because they are not usually the way information is viewed. HRD professionals who believe in the learning-organization concept actively work to make information, new ideas, and creativity a part of the culture or DNA of their organization.

In summary, what can HRD professionals do to help make their organizations into a continual learner?

Establish a strategy. Management needs to make explicit its commitment to change, innovation, and continuous improvement.

Redesign the organization's structure. The formal structure can be a serious impediment to learning. By flattening the structure, eliminating or combining departments, and increasing the use of cross-functional teams, interdependence is reinforced and boundaries between people are reduced.

Reshape the organization's culture. As noted earlier, learning organizations are characterized by risk taking, openness, and growth. Management sets the tone for the organization's culture both by what it says (strategy) and what it does (behavior). HRD professionals must work with organizational leaders to ensure that they demonstrate by their actions that taking risks and admitting failures are desirable traits. That means rewarding people who take chances and make mistakes. And HRD must help organizational members recognize the importance of encouraging functional conflict. "The key to unlocking real openness at work," says one expert on learning organizations "is to teach people to give up having to be in agreement. We think agreement is so important. Who cares? You have to bring paradoxes, conflicts, and dilemmas out in the open, so collectively we can be more intelligent than we can be individually" (Dumaine, 1994).

OD and Continuous Co-Evolution

Today, a new wave of successful organizations exemplify the use of OD assumptions, values, and techniques without using the term OD. It is not that such organizations as Herman Miller, Cisco, or R&R Partners are trying to force change on their employees. Rather, the managers in these systems take a very practical approach to managing culture. They realize that both external adaptation and internal integration are important for a variety of subcultures within their organizations. They use OD intervention techniques to improve both. They do not dictate values or set common assumptions in isolation but with their fellow employees. They are working with others to help nurture and guide the continual evolution of organizational culture form day to day. Further, they work with their partners in the larger organizational network to disseminate these modern management principle practices. Leading organizations such as Cisco help make the environment for all more hospitable.

Appreciative Inquiry

The bulk of organizational change and development programs start any diagnosis with an emphasis on identifying problems, shortfalls, or deficiencies such as excessive costs or resource limits, and not meeting a previously established performance goal. Participants focus on problems with the existing organizational system and identify ways to correct those problems. Unfortunately, this deficiency model of the world—in which something is wrong that must be fixed—focuses on the negative dynamics of the group or system rather than its positive opportunities.

Appreciative inquiry (AI) is a method of focusing on positive or potential opportunities (Watkins & Mohr, 2001). *Appreciation* means to value, see the best in others, and recognize positive potential. The concept of inquiry refers to the systematic analysis and the openness to discovery. In essence appreciative inquiry involves a method for bringing about positive change. AI proposes that organizations and individuals are creative enough to develop programs, relationships, and behaviors that address success, personal growth, and fulfillment.

It searches for and attempts to bring out the best in people, the organization, and the external environment. AI uses the art and practice of asking probing questions that can strengthen an individual or organization's ability to anticipate, seize, and initiate positive potential (Ludema, Whitney, Griffin, & Mohr, 2003). In a concise form, AI is:

1. A methodology that takes the idea of the social construction of reality by using metaphor and narrative.
2. A positive approach to change that completely lets go of problems based management.
3. An emphasis on individual engagement to bring about creative solutions.

The AI process essentially consists of four steps, often played out in a large-group meeting over a two- or three-day time period, and overseen by a trained change agent. The first step is one of discovery. The idea is to find out what people think are the strengths of the organization. For instance, employees are asked to recount times they felt the organization worked best or when they specifically felt most satisfied with their jobs. The second step is dreaming. The information from the discovery phase is used to speculate on possible futures for the organization. For instance, people are asked to envision the organization in five years and to describe what's different. The third step is design. Based on the dream articulation, participants focus on finding a common vision of how the organization will look and agree on its unique qualities. The fourth stage seeks to define the organization's destiny. In this final step, participants discuss how the organization is going to fulfill its dream. This typically includes the writing of action plans and development of implementation strategies.

AI has proven to be an effective change strategy in organizations as GTE, Avon Mexico, the Cleveland Clinic, and Brazilian food wholesaler Nutrimental Foods. For instance, executives at Nutrimental Foods closed their plants and offices for a day and invited all employees, and a large group of customers and other constituents, to meet in a vacated warehouse. After an hour of instruction by an AI consultant, the 700 participants broke into teams and interviewed each other for half a day. This generated several hundred conclusions about what the company did well. At the end of the day their work was handed off to a group of 150, who were given four days to shape the information into a new and bolder organization vision. The process ended up generating three new strategic business initiatives. And management reports that six months after this AI experience, company sales had increased by several million dollars and profits were up by 300% (Zemke, 1999).

CONCLUSION

HRD has been described as searching for identity while living in the shadow of OD (Grieves & Redman, 1999).

Grieves and Redman suggest that the concept of the knowledge-centered organization that views personal and organizational learning as critical for competitive growth is the driving force behind HRD; the HRD function is "partisan" to the goals and objectives of the organization. In this view, HRD is an organizational strategy for aligning the organizational objectives of knowledge-centered organizations with the competencies and capabilities of their employees.

Clearly, OR and HRD are closely related. Because the intent of most planned interventions is to ultimately bring about changes in individual behavior, it is difficult to introduce change without using HRD programs and processes. While the relationship between OD and HRD is more apparent for individual, group, technological and structural interventions, the need for HRD programs and processes is just as critical in strategic and cultural change interventions.

As organizations and their HRD professionals move further into the 21st century, it is clear that the need for successful organizational development interventions has never been greater. The forces driving organizations toward an increasing bottom-line emphasis are at present stronger than the restraining forces (or at least, those forces seeking to maintain a strong emphasis on employee well being) (Thomas, 1985; Gross, 2005; Grieves, 2003; Werner & DeSimone, 2006). HRD professionals can use OD to play an active role in this situation.

CHAPTER 11

HRD: BRIDGING TODAY AND TOMORROW

INTRODUCTION

Peter Senge popularized the concept of *learning organization* in his book *The Fifth Discipline*. He described them as places "where people continually expand their capacity to create the results they truly desire, where new and expansive patterns of thinking are nurtured, where collective aspiration is set free, and where people are continually learning how to learn together" (Senge, 1990, p. 3). In the coming years, HRD professionals must consistently ask and answer the following questions "Does Senge's description of the learning organization describe their functions or areas within an organization?" and "As a field are we continually expanding our capacity to create the results we (and our organizations) truly desire, where new and expansive patterns of thinking are nurtured, where collective aspiration is set free, and where we are continually learning how to learn?" It is the contention of this book that as long as HRD professionals honestly try to answer these questions, the future will be bright.

In moving forward, HRD professionals and their functions or areas must be proficient in a number of activities: systematic problem solving, experimentation with new approaches, learning from their own experience and history, learning from the experiences and best practices of others, and transferring knowledge quickly and efficiently throughout their functions or areas and the broader organization. In assessing the extent to which HRD professionals are proficient in these areas means that they should be proficient in using the following learning perspective which involves three stages: (1) cognitive—HRD professionals are exposed to new ideas, expand their knowledge, and begin to think differently; (2) behavioral—HRD professionals alter their behavior as needed; and (3) improvement of performance—changes in behavior lead to measurable improvement in results.

HRD professionals dedicated to creating a learning environment should view their own learning and development as a top priority while also recognizing that there will be an automatic carry over to their efforts to create learning organizations. Learning organizations do not simply appear. Learning organizations are fostered by devoting time, energy, and resources onto the learning of organizational members. Taking steps to encourage learning through their own learning and development activities and forums is essential to the improved understanding, performance, and effectiveness of HRD professionals.

To help their organizations learn requires HRD professionals to shed their current roles when necessary and to adapt to the organization constantly changing environment. This means that to be successful in the future HRD must constantly look for ways to learn, change and reinvent itself. The purpose of this final chapter is to offer a concluding look at the future of HRD by discussing the issues above and other related issues that will continue to shape what organizations will expect of their HRD professionals as we move further into the twenty-first century. The chapter will also discuss a number of ways in which HRD professionals might respond to the issues in the coming years. The chapter concludes with a discussion of a process HRD professionals can use to continue to build HRD's strategic value.

THE HRD PROFESSION AND FUNCTION

The HRD profession is much more advanced and sophisticated than it was 30 years ago, when many of us had our initial experiences as practitioners. This continues to be a great era for those in the profession because of our increased capabilities and the expanding opportunities we have to serve our organizations.

Some of us have perceived the dramatic changes in our work environment as threats to the profession. We've faced competition from other providers of HRD services; new developments in HRD technology that are revolutionizing the HRD processes; management philosophies that emphasize increased accountability and a broader role for the HRD function; and a conscious movement away from training for trainings sake to more real-time and cost-effective HRD.

While such developments may have seemed ominous, they continue to prove to be catalysts for positive change. We've been challenged to reassess our roles in today's organizations and to use our capability and potential to help the organization grow, develop and transform itself. When the history of this chapter of HRD is written, I think it will attribute much of this development to the fact that we have embraced quality, continuous improvement, and customer service concepts that have become widely popular in business during this time.

Is there an internal HRD function (or professional) today that is not regularly assessing itself by asking these fundamental questions? Are we focused and aligned without customers? Is our service delivery cost effective and timely? Do we anticipate our customer's needs? Do we provide consistent delivery of value-added benefits? Regularly finding answers to these questions increases the likelihood that HRD professionals will be in a position to proactively respond to the need to change and adapt. Perhaps we understand our ability to reinvent ourselves. Many HRD professionals and functions are continuing to establish the foundation for the future by redefining HRD practices in these terms and are well positioned to move on: but we must continue to be prepared to anticipate the need for further and further change.

We can best anticipate and respond to the need for further change in HRD by remembering that training and HRD historically has been looked at the way a doctor looks at a patient. You do a diagnosis of an individual, find a weakness, and then apply the training or HRD solution so that individual is stronger or better than he or she was before. What HRD must be in today's and tomorrow's organizations is a process consistent with an organization's strategy, so that the strategy is executed better than it would be without the HRD. One strategy is individual, which will have no impact on an organization, and the other is corporate, which will have a mammoth impact.

The important thing for HRD professionals to conceptually understand and practically demonstrate moving forward is that HRD has an impact on the organization rather than on the individual. The point is to make the organization more whole than it was before, and HRD should be a major part of what causes that to happen. However, that will never happen if HRD professionals are doing HRD by picking up people and putting Band-Aids on cuts. It will only do it if there are a vision and strategy, and HRD is an active part of a process of executing the vision and the strategy for everyone.

We must also be attentive to the fact that just applying technology to the HRD systems we have today is not going to solve the kinds of problems and challenges affecting HRD functions and their organizations. Especially if all we do is take a system that doesn't produce the results we want and make it more difficult. That won't do anything but make things worse than some believe they already are.

As HRD professionals we must remember that our HRD initiatives are not just an event. HRD isn't something out of a box. HRD is a continuous process linked to all the ways that people or the organization's human capital is developed, for example, by their job challenges; by their interactions with the people who are in coaching roles with them; by their peers; and by something we call HRD.

And if it is out of a box, now technology can help us. So HRD becomes more continuous. It becomes more online. It can be individualized, but in a strategic context, it can help the organization achieve its goals. Technology has to be seen as a tool inside a much broader context of helping the organization develop its employees to successfully achieve its objectives.

We must also be committed to getting valid, reliable and credible measures of customer satisfaction, employee satisfaction, and the bottom-line impact of HRD efforts. HRD professionals must get these measures into the organization to the right people in a timely way. The problem is that, unlike a lot of financial reporting that is done, satisfaction measures are often one-time events—a single survey done once every 12 to 18 months. They are not systemic, ongoing, continual HRD assessment processes that are plugged in at different levels in the organization.

Finally, at some point we need to spend less time trying to come up with a term or terms (or name) that is all inclusive of what we do in HRD. The real challenge appears to be spending more time making sure we can clearly communicate what we actually do that contributes to achievement of the organization's strategic agenda (i.e., how the HRD activities add value to the organization). The continued emergence of HRD appears to be a move in the right direction.

THE ENVIRONMENT FOR EXCELLENCE: TOWARD THE CONTINUOUS REINVENTION OF HRD

It has been said that doing an excellent job is much more satisfying than doing a mediocre job. As HRD professionals, we need to do everything in our power to provide environments that aren't satisfied with mediocrity—that strive for excellence, not only in HRD, but throughout the organization. And this mandate isn't just the responsibility of HRD; it's for everyone who participates in any HRD initiatives.

Achieving organizational excellence is linked to defining values. When HRD is based on a set of shared values that meshes with the vision, mission and strategy of the organization, a culture that is energized and continually driving toward excellence can prevail. Much of what HRD professionals do supports and validates what the organization has determined to be important by its values. HRD, placed into the context of an organization's values, becomes much more relevant to all involved.

As a profession HRD must continue to strive for excellence and strategically work toward becoming lifelong learners. Clearly, the future of HRD is going to be different from what it is today, and the forces shaping it will continue to put pressure on the profession to regularly change or reinvent itself and its initiatives. For our purposes the use of the word reinvention implies a number of things. First, the reinvention process is a means to an end in transforming the way an organization (and in our case HRD professionals and the HRD function) conducts its key business activities. Second, reinvention can imply starting either over from scratch about the fundamental ways things are done or simply changing the way things are done without having to start over from scratch. HRD professionals and their functions that start over from scratch forget all about how work, for example, was performed in the past and start all over with a clean sheet of paper, thinking about how things can be done best right now given the organization's workforce and HRD needs. When HRD professionals use the latter form of reinvention they also think about how things can be done better through innovation. In either case, reinvention is concerned with both best practices and benchmarking.

The third main focus of reinvention is the customer. Everything that is done starts with the idea of adding value for the customer: improving service, raising quality, lowering costs, and so on. Finally, reinvention suggests a planned process of change in response to changes in the host environment (i.e., organization and HRM function). Achieving such change will in many instances require changes in the HRD professionals and HRD functions, identity, strategy, structure, culture, and the institutionalization of new and better ways of accomplishing their charge.

ATTRIBUTES OF REINVENTED HRD

This section provides a discussion of several attributes of reinvented HRD as we move further into the twenty-first century. The four attributes (strategic orientation, customer orientation, performance orientation, and accountability orientation) are discussed in the following sections.

Strategic Orientation

Reinvented HRD is a catalyst to and a catalyst of improvement in an organization and achievement of the organization's strategic agenda. Thus, reinvented HRD must be inextricably woven into the clarity of the organization's mission, strategic agenda, its HRM systems, and its culture. Like its host organization and HRM function, this means that the HRD function scans the internal environment to stay abreast of changes in strategies and direction of the organization, the HRD needs and characteristics of the workforce, and the needs of senior executives and other managers as they seek to make their organizations and its human resources more productive, flexible, adaptable, and focused.

Combining the internal, organizational characteristics with the external conditions, HRD professionals must help their organizations develop employees who are adaptable, committed, motivated, highly energetic, good performers in diverse groups, good team players, and multi-skilled or reskilled knowledge workers. In short, reinvented HRD is linked to the HRM mission, practices and priorities, and the organization's strategy. It is more macro than micro, supports the organization's strategic directions, and is thus strategic in nature itself.

In helping the organization's achieve their goals, reinvented HRD takes a strategic approach to HRD and looks at the HRD mission and concomitant processes in a radically different light. As highlighted in Chapter 1, a strategic approach to HRD takes place within an overall framework for workforce development that directly contributes to the organization achieving its mission while also revolutionizing its processes. Reinvented HRD eliminates misaligned goals and objectives between HRD initiatives and their host organizations. Reinvented HRD must identify the HRD efforts that are critical if organizations are to accomplish their mission, by identifying (1) what HRD is currently done that is no longer needed, (2) what HRD can be eliminated altogether, (3) how the remaining HRD can be better linked to support and reinforce the organization's strategic agenda, (4) what new HRD initiatives should be offered, and (5) what non-HRD or HRD initiatives should be undertaken. In the end, reinvented HRD must continuously be "rebuilt" based on the basics—the actual HRD efforts required to accomplish the fundamental organizational purpose, versus the processes that have evolved over time.

In summary, reinvented HRD must always provide a clear understanding of the characteristics of and requirements for a strategic approach to HRD that will have a value-added impact on the parent organization. Such a perspective forms connections between HRD missions and practices, HRM missions and practices, and the organization's missions and practices. The premise behind strategic HRD is that HRD decisions that "fit" the organization's current and future conditions positively impact learning, change and performance.

Customer Orientation

Reinvented HRD means encouraging and proactively responding to customer inputs in designing and implementing value-added HRD. Reinvented HRD is always looking for ways to involve customers by asking them what they want, when they want it, and how HRD can better meet their needs. Existing processes for partnering with customers are viewed in a radically different light and efforts are continually in motion to get closer to the customer. Like today's proactive learning organizations, reinvented HRD functions step back and ask the question, How can we get closer to the customer and bring them further into the work, learning, HRD design, implementation and evaluation processes?

In answering this question, reinvented HRD begins by partnering with customers to ensure that *all* HRD is indeed seen by the customer as adding value. Adding value requires that the customers be seen as experts at times and their needs determine the what, when, how, and where of HRD.

Reinvented HRD is driven by a proactive goal of exceeding customer expectations. It requires encouraging the participation of customer groups in identifying necessary employee knowledge, skills, abilities and competencies (KSAOCs) and corresponding HRD needs, and in designing, implementing, and evaluating HRD strategies. By tapping into the considerable expertise of customers, the HRD function further conforms to the organization's strategy. At every level of activity, the HRD function puts the customer first, views customers as experts, regularly communicates with customers to understand their needs, and uses customer input to make HRD more effective.

Performance Improvement Orientation

Reinvented HRD is concerned with the way in which HRD supports employees within the organization to perform at their highest levels so that the entire organization can perform at its highest level. Reinvented HRD must do two things to fulfill this role: (1) support the work done right now in the organization by providing HRD at the place it is needed, at the time it is needed, and in the amount and strength it is needed; and (2) support the work to be done in the future by creating a learning infrastructure that will help employees and the organization learn and grow and change in line with environmental demands.

The dual mission—support the organization now, and help the organization prepare for the future—means that HRD professionals must identify critical workforce KSAOCs and must design HRD initiatives that help employees develop those KSAOCs. For example, today's and tomorrow's organizations need employees that are multi-skilled/reskilled knowledge workers who can effectively work in teams in an increasingly global world. Thus, meeting these new standards requires that HRD professionals recognize the need for a workforce that is more than just technically trained, for example. It requires training and developing people who are capable of analyzing and solving increasingly complex job-related problems, and of being able to "switch gears" and shift from job to job. Reinvented HRD thus is moved to center stage as a means of improving organization performance.

Many organizations will continue to streamline procedures so that fewer employees are needed to get the work done. Such broad-based approaches provide a framework for reinvented HRD aimed at improving employee and organization performance. Reinvented HRD will need to continue to find ways to prepare employees to better work in cross-functional and cross-cultural teams, identify and make recommendations for eliminating low-value work, correct inefficient work processes, and improve product and service quality through cost efficiencies. Reinvented HRD will also need to continue to help employees learn how to examine and evaluate tasks and processes, rather than accepting jobs as they are currently configured. Reinvented HRD will continue to be "best practices" and "benchmarking" oriented in its efforts to respond to customers' needs for quality, variety, customization, convenience, and timeliness.

Accountability Orientation

In today's environment, reinvented HRD must be able to prove that they have quality designs (including a systems rather than a piecemeal approach, and the effective use of the best available technology and alternative HRD methods), timeliness, cost effectiveness, flexibility (including using the most effective providers), and new means for evaluating the impact of their efforts.

Reinvented HRD is committed to increasing its capacity and flexibility for delivering just-in-time and cost-effective HRD that can be easily evaluated by HRD customers and HRD professionals. This means, for example, that HRD continues to move beyond its traditional focus on the creation, for example, of discrete training courses to develop much more flexibility and variety in its HRD programs, to identify more cost-effective and alternative means to bring HRD and learning opportunities into the organization (thus closer to the employee), and, at the same time, to find ways to hold itself accountable (through ongoing and new methods for evaluation of its HRD efforts) for the HRD objectives it seeks to achieve given the organization's broader strategy.

Reinvented HRD is built upon the view that (1) the HRD function no longer has a monopoly to meet the HRD needs of their organization, and (2) competition is the name of the game, as customers will go to those who are best able to meet their HRD needs. So, just as increasing competition and loss of customers fostered the climate of reinventing for many organizations, the increased emergence of these factors on the HRD scene will continue to create a customer accountability environment for the HRD function.

THE EVER CHANGING ROLE OF HRD

A theme throughout this book has been that as the pace and complexity of change in organizations continues HRD must be integrated with the organization's strategic agenda. To do this, HRD professionals will need a much wider exposure to the organization's internal and external environment. They will have to build more bridges with customers, both those in line units and those outside the organization.

HRD professionals will have to help foster an environment for excellence by taking a proactive stance in linking HRD to organizational values and identifying strategic issues where HRD should play a role. This will require increased research on the impact of organization vision and strategy on HRM, HRD and an increased willingness and ability to participate in strategy formulation and implementation.

Indeed, the HRD function needs to take a strategic orientation: from service provider to performance consultant, policy setter, and value purveyor. For example, in response to efforts to decentralize HRM and their HRD efforts, some organizations have pushed centralized HRM and HRD functions into line units. Where this occurs, the HRD function of the future must be prepared for the fact that they may do very little HRD delivery. Rather, it may facilitate creation of the HRD vision, strategy and core values in support of that vision, strategy and core values and then support line units in aligning themselves with all three. A related role for the HRD function will be to foster the development of individual, team, and organizational learning not by teaching but by helping people find ways to build learning strategies into their work.

As suggested in the previous section, organizations will increasingly demand a "strategic," "customer," "performance improvement," and "accountability" orientation, in which they look to HRD to help solve problems, help lead change and performance improvements, and foster a learning environment. These goals call for more work and performance analysis, individual, team and organization development, visioning, and performance consulting services. HRD professionals can add real value to their organizations by meeting such needs.

HRD TOMORROW

To meet the challenges of the future tomorrow's HRD functions must be more sophisticated than their predecessors. Given the expanded role of HRM and HRD must fill, it is essential that HRD professionals be integrally involved in the organization's strategic and policymaking activities.

If tomorrow's HRD professionals are to continue to earn the respect of their colleagues and top management, they must overcome negative impressions and biases sometimes associated with HRM. They can do so in several ways. First, HRD professionals should become well-rounded businesspeople. In addition to having a sound background in the basics of the profession, HRD professionals need to understand business complexities and strategies. The following suggestions can help HRD professionals become more familiar with their businesses:

- Know the organization and business plan.
- Know the industry.
- Support business needs.
- Spend more time with the line people.
- Keep your hand on the pulse of the organization.
- Learn to calculate costs and solutions in hard numbers.

HRD professionals who thoroughly understand their businesses will help overcome the common idea that human resource people are unfamiliar with the operating problems and issues facing the organization. Several pertinent questions that HRD professionals should be able to answer to develop greater understanding of the organization's business strategies are:

1. What are the goals of the organization over the next year, 3 years, 5 years, and 10 years?
2. How would you describe the organization's core business?
3. How does your organization compare with competitors in market share and customer service?
4. Will the organization be growing via merger and acquisition or from internal growth?
5. Will growth be local, national, or global?
6. Will growth be from expansion of current businesses or from an expansion in scope?
7. Instead of growth, will there be downsizing and if so, why?
8. What are the organization's revenue objectives over the short and long terms?

The ability to answer these questions increases the likelihood that the HRD professional of the future will have truly changed from a tactical to a strategic role in the organization.

HRD professionals should also become fully knowledgeable about present and future trends and issues in HRD and other related fields. This will help them guard against becoming enamored with passing fads or ineffective techniques.

Finally, HRD professionals should promote effective human resource utilization within the organization. Rather than taking a moralistic approach when dealing with line mangers, HRD professionals should stress the importance of increasing profits through effectively using the organization's human resources. In this light, HRD professionals should learn to be proactive and seize opportunities to demonstrate how they can positively affect the bottom line, which is critical to gaining and maintaining leadership support for HRD.

THE CONTINUOUS PROCESS OF GAINING AND MAINTAINING LEADERSHIP SUPPORT FOR HRD

Many organizational leaders notice HRD costs but overlook the impact of HRD on organizational learning, change and performance. To gain recognition for its strategic value, HRD professionals will need to work at translating an organization's strategic goals into clear and achievable HRD objectives. To do so, HRD professionals must establish and sustain a foothold in the organization's highest leadership echelon.

HRD professionals should understand what factors favor recognition of HRD's strategic value. Several criteria that demonstrate the inclusion of HRD in strategic planning are: when adequate resources for HRD are proactively allocated; HRD and other HRM issues are given the same weight as other business issues; HRD is used for such things as quality management, team-building, technical skill improvement, and organizational learning; there is ongoing involvement of senior leaders in determining HRD needs and involvement in subsequent HRD efforts; and HRD leaders have ongoing interaction with the organization's most senior leaders and HR leaders.

Sustaining a foothold in the echelons of top leadership will undoubtedly involve ongoing homework for HRD professionals. And this begins by being able to answer the questions presented in the last section. They must learn and understand the organization's strategic challenges so as to propose HRD initiatives that can help address organizational problems, challenges and opportunities. HRD leaders (and other HRD staff) will continue to have a variety of ways for acquiring this business knowledge. They can: acquire and read the organization's strategic plans, department plans, and other documents that describe the goals of each business unit. They can read books and industry journals in order to understand the organization's position in the marketplace. And, they can continue their own education and learning through internal and external courses, etc. to develop the KSAOCs necessary to understand and actively participate in the organization's business.

As HRD professionals increase their understanding and participation in the organization's and strategic challenges, they should actively be involved in developing plans that will highlight the ways in which the HRD initiatives do and will promote and help achieve organizational objectives. By asking questions like the following HRD professionals will be better able to make the link between organization strategy and HRD initiatives: What is the organization's basic business strategy and how does HRD contribute to its eventual success? How is HRD positioned within the organization and the marketplace? How can HRD help prepare employees to achieve the strategic agenda the organization wants to go? What are the most critical HRD initiatives that should be undertaken in the short- and long-term to support the strategic agenda? Who will oversee these initiatives and how will their value be measured? What are the HRD function's most critical assumptions about the organization's HRD needs?

Clearly, there will be an increasingly important role for HRD in helping their organization's achieve their objectives and sustain a competitive advantage. But those in the HRD profession must be willing to continue their recent efforts at reinventing the profession. And an important part of this reinvention must be continued efforts to link HRD to organizational strategy and build HRD's strategic value. The final section of this chapter presents a process for building HRD's strategic value to an organization.

BUILDING HRD'S STRATEGIC VALUE

The following process can help HRD professionals enhance the HRD function's strategic value to the organization. The process is similar to an HRD audit where organization and HRD personnel assess the overall HRD function and not just specific HRD initiatives.

Step 1: Specify goals for the HRD Function

Consider the organization's business conditions and be proactive in identifying specific HRD practices to address these conditions. In developing goals statements, key questions to ask include the following:

HRD: Bridging Today and Tomorrow 315

1. What are the organization's most critical sources of competitive advantage?
2. What organization needs can the HRD function best meet through specific HRD practices:
   - What payoff in time and money does the HRD function contribute to the organization? What would the organization gain or lose by eliminating or subcontracting HRD activities?
   - What benefit do external customers receive from HRD initiatives?
   - What benefit do internal customers receive from HRD initiatives?

Step 2: Assess the Performance of the HRD Function and Its Staff

This step involves auditing current HRD practices and activities. In developing a strategic mission for the HRD function, key issues to address include the following:

1. In which programs, activities, or efforts has HRD played a part? Did these activities have a positive or negative impact? What did HRD contribute to that outcome?
2. Do HRD staff serve as specialists, generalists, partners, or pioneers?
3. What are the HRD function's major strengths and weaknesses?

Step 3: State the Desired Capability of the HRD Function

Consider the responses of steps 1 and 2, and develop a vision for the HRD function by answering the following questions:

1. What does HRD want its customers and employees to think and say about it?
2. Why will HRD be important to the organization—now and in the future?
3. How will HRD work to implement the vision?

Step 4: Prepare an Action Plan for Building Human Capital and Strategic Capability

Look at specific HRD activities and consider what actions HRD needs to take in each area to enhance the organization's overall strategic agenda:

1. *Staffing.* What KSAOCs does HRD need to bring into the function today? Tomorrow? What are the sources of these KSAOCs?
2. *Development.* What KSAOCs does HRD need to develop among its current staff? What actions must HRD take to ensure that its staff acquires these KSAOCs?
3. *Appraisal.* What standards does HRD need to develop? What feedback should it give to HRD professionals? How will HRD measure its success?
4. *Rewards.* What rewards can HRD use to motivate its staff to meet HRD goals?
5. *Function design.* What organization of HRD activities and reporting relationships will best allow the function to meet its strategic goals?
6. *Communication.* What information do which individuals need to help the HRD function achieve its strategic mission?

Step 5: Prepare an Action for Building HRD Professional KSAOCs

This step highlights the personal KSAOCs needed by HRD professionals to serve in a strategic role. Four areas to address in personal action plans include the following:

1. *Activity.* What key activities can each person perform to contribute to the HRD function's capability?
2. *Time.* Where should the individual spend time to build the function's capability?
3. *Information.* What information does each staff member need to receive and/or share to build the function's capability?
4. *First steps.* What are the first steps each individual can take to effect a change?

Once the HRD professionals and their organization have agreed upon and established a strategic approach to HRD they are positioned to ensure a better return on their investment in HRD.

CONCLUSION

The strategic importance of HRD should continue given recent trends in the workforce. Successful HRD in organizations depends on a reinvented HRD that involves a strategic approach to HRD, involves a careful needs assessment, solid HRD program planning, design and evaluation. Reinvented HRD pays attention to designing learning environments that are attentive to characteristics of adult learners and principles of learning. Reinvented HRD recognizes the importance of using a variety of training and learning methods in enhancing employee learning at all levels of the organization. Particular attention is given to changes in technology and its implications for learning and HRD delivery. When focusing on the future training and development of organizational members a reinvented HRD approach is attentive to the changing role of knowledge workers, managers, and leaders and organizational expectations of these employees.

Reinvented HRD recognizes the importance of lifelong learning by HRD professionals and their organizations. Finally, reinvented HRD is committed to proving its value through benchmarking, ongoing evaluation and energy focused on demonstrating the delivery of cost-effective HRD that meets customer objectives and achievement of the organization's strategic agenda.

REFERENCES

Abernathy, D.J. (1999). *Training & Development, 53*(5), 80–84.
Adler, N.J., & Bartholomew, S. (1992). Managing globally competent people. *The Executive, 6*(3), 52–65.
Adler, N.M. (1991). *International dimensions of organizational behavior* (2nd ed.). Belmont, CA: Wadsworth.
Allen, M (2002). *The corporate university handbook: Designing, managing and growing a successful program.* New York: AMA.
Allen, N.J., & Meyer, J.P. (1990). Organizational socialization tactics: A longitudinal analysis of links to newcomers' commitment and role orientation. *Academy of Management Journal, 33,* 847–858.
Allen, S.G. (2004, May). *The value of phased retirement.* NBER working Paper No. W10531. Cambridge, MA: National Bureau of Economic Research.
Alliger, G.M., & Janak, E.A. (1989). Kirkpatrick's levels of training criteria: Thirty years later. *Personnel Psychology, 42,* 331–342.
Alliger, G.M., Tannenbaum, S.L., Bennett, W., Trave, H., & Shotland, A. (1997). A meta-analysis of the relations among training criteria. *Personnel Psychology, 50,* 341–258.
Anderson, T.B. (2001). *Technological change and the evaluation of corporate innovation.* Cheltenham: Edward Elgar.
Andrews, E.S., & Noel, J.L. (1986). Adding life to the case study method. *Training and Development Journal, 40*(2), 28–29.
Appelbaum, S.H., & Firestone, D. (1994). Revisiting career plateauing: Same old problems—avant garde solutions. *Journal of Managerial Psychology, 9*(4), 12–21.
Argyris, C. (1994). The future of workplace learning and performance. *Training & Development, 48*(5), S36–S47.
Argyris, C. (1991, May). Teaching smart people how to learn. *Harvard Business Review,* 5–15.
Argyris, C. (1986). Skilled incompetence. *Harvard Business Review, 64*(5), 74–79.
Argyris, C., & Schon, D.A. (1982). *Theory in practice: Increasing professional effectiveness.* San Francisco: Jossey-Bass.

Arnes, J., Slack, T., & Henings, R. (2004, February). The pace, sequence, and linearity of radical change. *Academy of Management Journal*, 15–39.

Arthur, M.B., Claman, P.H., & DeFillippi, R.J. (1995). Intelligent enterprise, intelligent careers. *The Academy of Management Executive*, 9(4), 7–22.

Arthur, M.B., & Rousseau, D.M. (1996). The boundaryless career as a new employment principle. In M.G. Arthur & D.M. Rousseau (Eds.), *The boundaryless career* (pp. 3–20). New York: Oxford University Press.

Arvey, R.D., Maxwell, S.D., & Salas, E. (1992). The relative power of training evaluation designs under different cost configurations. *Journal of Applied Psychology*, 77, 155–160.

Ashforth, B.E., & Saks, A.M. (1996). Socialization tactics: Longitudinal effects on newcomer adjustment. *Academy of Management Journal*, 39, 149–178.

Bandwick, J.M. (1986). *The plateauing trap* (pp. 1–17). New York: American Management Association.

Banik, J.A. (1985, October), The marketing approach to communicating with employees. *Personnel Journal*, 62–68.

Barnes, L.B., Christensen, C.R., & Hansen, A.J. (1994). *Teaching and the case method: Text, cases, and readings* (3rd ed.). Boston: Harvard Business School Press.

Bartlett, C.A., & Ghoshal, S. (1992). What is a global manager? *Harvard Business Review*, 70(5), 124–132.

Baruch, Y. (2003). Careers systems in transition: A normative model for organizational career practices. *Personnel Review*, 32(1/2), 231–251.

Baruch, Y., & Peiperl, M. (2000, Winter). Career management practices: An empirical survey and implications. *Human Resource Management*, 39(4), 347–366.

Bass, B.M., & Vaughn, J.A. (1966). *Training in industry: The management of learning.* Belmont, CA: Wadsworth.

Bassi, L.J., Benson, G., & Cheney, S. (1996, February). The top ten trends. *Training and Development Journal*, 28–42.

Bassi, L.J., Cheney, S., & McMurrer, D. (1998). A common standard for measuring training results. *Training and Development*, 52(3), 10–11.

Bateson, G. (1972). *Ecology of the mind.* New York: Balentine.

Baugh, S.B., Lankau, M.J., & Terri, A. (1996). An investigation of the effects of protégé gender on responses to mentoring. *Journal of Vocational Behavior*, 49, 309–323.

Beckhard, R. (1967, March/April). The confrontation meeting. *Harvard Business Review*, 45, 149–155.

Belton, R. (1998). Employment law: A review of the 1997 term decisions of the Supreme Court. *Employee Rights and Employment Policy Journal*, 2(2), 267–235.

Bennett, J.B., Lehman, W.E.K., & Forst, J.K. (1999, June). Change, transfer climate, and customer orientation: A contextual model and analysis of change-driving training. *Group & Organization Management*, 24(2), 188–216.

Bennis, W. (1987). Using our knowledge of organizational behavior. in J.W. Lorsch (Ed.), *Handbook of organizational behavior* (pp. 29–49). Englewood Cliffs, NJ: Prentice-Hall.

Berenthal, P.R., Coteryahn, K., Davis, P., Naughton, J., Rothwell, W.J., & Wellins, R. (2004). *Mapping the future: Shaping new workplace learning and performance competencies.* Alexandria, VA: the American Society for Training and Development.

Berliner, W., & McLarney, W. (1974). *Management practice and training.* Burr Ridge, IL: McGraw-Hill.
Bernstein, A. (2001, February 26). Low-skilled jobs: Do they have to move? *Business Week,* 94–95.
Bierema, L.L. (1996). Development of the individual leads to more productive workplaces. In R.W. Rowden (Ed.), *Workplace learning: Debating five critical questions of theory and practice* (pp. 21–28). San Francisco: Jossey-Bass.
Billett, S. (2003). Workplace mentors: Demands and benefits. *Journal of Workplace Learning, 15,* 105–113.
Birnbauer, H. (1987). Evaluation techniques that work. *Training and Development Journal, 41*(1), 53–55.
Black, J.S., & Gregersen, H. (2000, Summer/Fall). High impact training: Forging leaders for the global frontier. *Human Resource Management, 39*(2&3), 173–184.
Blanchard, K. (1992, June). Six concerns in the change process. *Quality Design, 14,* 62.
Boehm, V.R. (1988). Designing developmental assessment centers. In M. London & E.M. Mone (Eds.), *Career growth and human resource strategies: The role of the human resource professional in employee development* (pp. 173–182). New York: Quorum Books.
Bohlander, G.W., Snell, S., & Sherman III, A.W. (2001). *Managing human resources* (12th ed.). Cincinnati, OH: South-Western.
Boice, R. (2000). *Advice for new faculty members.* Boston: Allyn & Bacon.
Bolt, J. (1989). *Executive development: A strategy for corporate competitiveness.* New York: Harper & Row.
Bontis, N. (1996, Summer). There's a price on your head: Managing intellectual capital strategically. *Business Quarterly,* 41–47.
Bowles, J., & Hammond, J. (1996, September 9). Competing on knowledge. *Fortune,* S1–S18.
Breaugh, J.A. (1992). *Recruitment: Science and practice.* Boston: PWSKent.
Brockbank, W. (1999, Winter). If HR were really strategically proactive: Present and future directions in HR's contribution to competitive advantage. *Human Resource Management, 38*(4), 337–350.
Brown, E. (1998, September 28). War games to make you better at business. *Fortune,* 291–296.
Browning, J., & Reiss, S. (1999, April 23). Business on internet time. *The Wall Street Journal,* A14.
Buchanan, B. (1974). Building organizational commitment: The socialization of managers in work organizations. *Administrative Science Quarterly, 19*(4), 533–546.
Buckley, M.R., Fedor, D.B., Veres, J.G., Weise, D.S., & Carraher, S.M. (1998). Investigating newcomer expectations and job-related outcomes. *Journal of Applied Psychology, 83,* 452–461.
Buckley, M.R., Mobbs, T.A., Mendoza, J.L., Novicevic, M.M., Carreher, S.M., & Beu, D. (2002). Implementing realistic job preview and expectation-lowering procedures: A field experiment. *Journal of Vocational Behavior, 61,* 263–278.
Burack, E.H., & Mathys, N.J. (1980). *Career management in organizations: A practical human resource planning approach.* Lake Forest, IL: Brace Park Press.

Burke, L. (1997, Summer). Improving positive transfer: A test of relapse prevention training on transfer outcomes. *Human Resource Development Quarterly, 8*(2), 115–128.

Burke, L., & Baldwin, T.T. (1999, Fall). Workforce training transfer: A study of the effect of relapse prevention training and transfer climate. *Human Resource Management, 38*(3), 227–242.

Burke, M.J., & Day, R.R. (1986). A cumulative study of the effectiveness of managerial training. *Journal of Applied Psychology, 71*, 232–245.

Bushnell, D.S. (1990). Input, process, output: A model for evaluating training. *Training and Development Journal, 44*(3), 41–43.

Byars, L.L., & Rue, L.W. (2006). *Human resource management* (8th ed.). New York: McGraw-Hill/Irwin.

Byham, W. (2000, February). Bench strength. *Across the Board,* 35–41.

Byrnes, N. (2000, November 13). What really happened to the class of GE. *Business Week,* 98–100.

Cable, D.M., Aiman-Smith, L., Mulvey, P.W., & Edwards, J.R. (2000, December). The sources and accuracy of job applicants' beliefs about organizational culture. *Academy of Management Journal, 43,* 1076–85.

Calandra, B. (1999, June 4). Razor sharp. *Human Resource Executive,* 22–25.

Campbell, J.P. (1988). Training design for performance improvement. In J.P. Campbell & R.J. Campbell (Eds.), *Productivity in organizations.* San Francisco: Jossey-Bass.

Campbell, J.P., Dunnette, M.D., Lawler, E.E., & Weick, Jr., K.E. (1970). *Managerial behavior, performance, and effectiveness.* New York: McGraw-Hill.

Capelli, P. (2000). A market-driven approach to retaining talent. *Harvard Business Review, 78,* 103–112.

Carnevale, A.P., & Schulz, E.R. (1990, July). Return on investment: Accounting for training. *Training and Development Journal,* S1–S32.

Carnevale, A.P., Villet, L.J., & Holland, S.L. (1990). *Training partnerships: Linking employers and providers.* Alexandria, VA: American Society for Training and Development.

Cascio, W.F. (2006). *Managing human resources: Productivity, quality of work life, profits* (7th ed.). New York: McGraw-Hill/Irwin.

Caudron, S. (2000). Learners speak out. *Training and Development, 54,* 52–58.

Caudron, S. (1997). Can generation xers be trained?" *Training & Development, 51,* 20–24.

Cell, E. (1984). *Learning to learn from experience.* Albany: State University of New York Press.

Chao, G.T., O'Leary-Kelly, A., Wolf, S., Klein, H.J., & Gardner, P.D. (1994). Organizational socialization: Its content and consequences. *Journal of Applied Psychology, 79,* 450–463.

Chase, N.J. (1997, November). OJT doesn't mean 'sit by Joe.' *Quality, 36*(11), 84.

Chermack, T.J., Lynham, S.A., & Ruona, W.E.A. (2003, August). Critical uncertainties confronting human resource development. *Advances in Developing Human Resources, 5*(3), 257–271.

Cherniss, C., & Goleman, D. (Eds.). (2001). *The emotionally intelligent workplace.* San Francisco: Jossey-Bass.

Clark, C.S., Dobbins, G.H., & Ladd, T.R. (1993). Exploratory field study of training motivation. *Group & Organization Management, 18,* 292–307.

Cohen, C. (2003). Make a good impression. *CA Magazine, 136*(5), 41–42.

Colquitt, J.A., LePine, J., & Noe, R.A. (2000). Toward an integrated theory of training motivation: A meta-analytic path analysis of 20 years of research. *Journal of Applied Psychology, 85*(5), 678–707.

Conner, J., & Smith, C.A. (1988). Developing the next generation of leaders: A new strategy for leadership development at Colgate-Palmolive. In E.M. Mone & M. London (Eds.), *HR to the rescue: Case studies of HR solutions to business challenges.* Houston: Gulf.

Cook, J. (2002a, June 6). The dual-income dilemma. *Human Resource Executive,* 22–26.

Cook, J. (2002b, August). Gender gap. *Human Resource Executive,* 24–29.

Cooper-Thomas, H., & Anderson, N. (2002). Newcomer adjustment: The relationship between organizational socialization tactics, information acquisition and attitudes. *Journal of Occupational and Organizational Psychology, 75,* 423–437.

Corporate universities open their doors. (2000, October 6–8). *Manager Intelligence Report.*

Cummings, T.G., & Worley, C.G. (2005). *Organization development and change* (8th ed.). Cincinnati, OH: South-Western College Publishing.

Cummings, T.G., & Worley, C.G. (1997). *Organization development and change* (6th ed.). Mason, OH: Thomson/South-Western.

Daft, R.L. (1997). *Management* (4th ed.). Mason, OH: Thomson/South-Western.

Darley, W.K., & Smith, R.E. (1995). Gender differences in information processing strategies: An empirical test of the selectivity model in advertising response. *Journal of Advertising, 24,* 41–56.

Davenport, J., & Davenport, J.A. (1985). A chronology and analysis of the andragogy debate. *Adult Education, 35,* 152–159.

Davis, P., Naughton, J., & Rothwell, W. (2004, April). New roles and new competencies for the profession. *Training and Development, 58*(4), 26–36.

Davis, S.L. (1998). Assessment as organizational strategy. In R. Jeanneret & R. Silzer (Eds.), *Individual psychological assessment: Predicting behavior in organizational settings* (pp. 285–329). San Francisco: Jossey-Bass.

Day, L.F.O. (1995). Benchmarking training. *Training and Development, 49*(1), 26–30.

de Janasz, S.C. et al. (2003, November). Mentor *Networks and Career Success. Academy of Management Executive,* 78–89.

Decker, P.J., & Nathan, B.R. (1985). *Behavior modeling training: Principles and applications.* New York: Praeger.

DeNisi, A.S., & Griffin, R.W. (2001). *Human resource management.* Boston: Houghton-Mifflin.

Diekmann, F. (2001, July 23). Everything you wanted to know about e-learning. *Credit Union Journal,* 1–3.

Dilworth, L. (2003, August). Searching for the future of HRD. *Advances in Developing Human Resources, 5*(3), 241–244.

Dionne, P. (1996). The evaluation of training activities: A complex issue involving different stakes. *Human Resource Development Quarterly, 7*(3), 279–286.

Dolezalek, H. (2003, July/August). Pretending to learn. *Training,* 20–26.

Downs, S. (1970). Predicting training potential. *Personnel Management, 2*, 26–28.

Drucker, P.F. (1967). *The effective executive.* New York: Harper & Row.

Duck, J.D. (2001). *The change monster: The human forces that foil corporate transformation and change.* New York: Crown Business.

Dumaine, B. (1994, October 17). Mr. learning organization. *Fortune.*

Dunn, R., & Dunn, K. (1992). *Teaching secondary students through their individual learning styles: Practical approaches for grades 7–12.* Boston: Allyn and Bacon.

Dunn, R., & Ingham, J. (1995, Summer). Effects of matching and mismatching corporate employees' perceptual preferences and instructional strategies on training achievement and attitudes. *Journal of Applied Business Research, 11*(3), 30–37.

Eagly, A.H., Johannsen-Schmidt, C.M., & van Enger, M.K. (2003, July). Transformational, transactional, and laissez-faire leadership styles: A meta-analysis comparing women and men. *Psychological Bulletin,* 569–591.

Eden, D., & Ravid, G. (1982). Pygmalion versus self-expectancy: Effects of instructor and self-expectancy on trainee performance. *Organizational Behavior and Human Performance, 30,* 351–364.

Eurich, N.P. (1990). *The learning industry: Education for adult workers.* Lawrenceville, NJ: Princeton University Press.

Executive succession: A critical governing board responsibility. (2001, October). *Trends On+Line.*

Facteau, J.D., Dobbins, G.H., Russell, J.E.A., Ladd, R.T., & Kudisch, J.D. (1995). The influence of general perceptions of the training environment on pre-training motivation and perceived training transfer. *Journal of Management, 21,* 1–25.

Feldman, D.C. (1988). *Managing careers in organizations.* Glenview, IL: Scott, Foresman.

Feldman, D.C. (1981). The multiple socialization of organization members. *Academy of Management Review, 6,* 309–318.

Feldman, D.C. (1976a). A contingency theory of socialization. *Administrative Science Quarterly, 21,* 433–452.

Feldman, D.C. (1976b, Autumn). A practical program for employee socialization. *Organizational Dynamics,* 64–80.

Ferrence, T.P., Stoner, J.A.E., & Warren, E.K. (1977, October). Managing the career plateau. *Academy of Management Review,* 602–612.

Finney, M.I. (1996). Employee orientation programs can help introduce success. *HR News.*

Fisher, C.D. (1984). Organizational socialization: An integrative review; N. Nicholson, 'A theory of work role transitions.' *Administrative Science Quarterly, 29,* 172–191.

Fisher, C.D. (1986). Organizational socialization: An integrative review. In K. Rowland & G. Ferris (Eds.), *Research in personnel and human resources management* (Vol. 4., pp. 101–145). Greenwich, CT: JAI Press.

Fleishman, E.A., & Mumford, M.D. (1988). Ability requirements scale. In S. Gael (Ed.), *The job analysis handbook for business, industry, and government* (pp. 917–935). (Vol. 2). New York: John Wiley.

Fleming, R. (2001). *VARK: A Guide to learning styles.* Retrieved September 8, 2004, from http://www.vark-learn.com/english/page.asp?p = faq#What%20is20VARK

Ford, J.K., & Noe, R.A. (1987). Self-assessed training needs: The effects of attitudes toward training, managerial level and function. *Personnel Psychology, 40,* 39–53.

Fowler, A. (1995, December 21). How to decide on training methods. *People Management, 1*(25), 36–37.
Frank, F.D., Finnegan, R.P., & Taylor, C.R. (2004). The race for talent: Retaining and engaging workers in the 21st century. *Human Resource Planning, 27*(3), 12–25.
Fraze, (1999, March). Expert help for dual-career spouses. *Workforce,* 18–20.
French, W.L., & Bell Jr., C.H. (1984). *Organizational development: Behavioral science interventions for organizational improvement* Englewood Cliffs, NJ: Prentice-Hall.
Fusaro, R. (1998, June 29). IBM/Lotus to tackle information overload. *Computerworld, 32*(26) 29.
Gagne, R.M. (1985). *The conditions of learning and theory of instruction* (4th ed.). New York: Holt, Rinehart and Winston.
Garavaglia, P. (1995). *Transfer of training: Making training stick,* INFO-LINE, No. 9512. Alexandria, VA: American Society for Training and Development.
Gardner, H. (1993). *Frames of mind: The theory of multiple intelligences* (2nd ed.). New York: Basic Books.
Gaugler, B.B., & Thornton III, C.G. (1989). Number of assessment center dimensions as a determinant of assessor accuracy. *Journal of Applied Psychology, 74,* 611–618.
Gerber, B. (1995, March). Does your training make a difference? Prove it? *Training,* 27–34.
Gershon, R., Stone, P.W., Bakken, S., & Larson, E. (2004, January). Measurement of organizational culture and climate in health care. *Journal of Nursing Administration,* 34–40.
Gibson, J.L., Ivancevich, J.M., Donnelly Jr., J.H., & Konopaske, R. (2006). *Organizations: Behavior, structure, processes* (20th ed.). Boston, MA: McGraw-Hill/Irwin.
Gibson, J.L., Ivancevich, J.M., Donnelly, Jr., J.H., & Konopaske, R. (2006). *Organizations: Behavior, structure, processes* (12th ed.). New York: McGraw-Hill/Irwin.
Gilley, J.W., & Maycunich, A. (2000). *Organizational learning, performance, and change: An introduction to strategic human resource development.* Cambridge, MA: Perseus.
Gilley, J.W., & Mayunich, A. (1998). *Strategically integrated HRD: Partnerships to maximize organizational performance.* Reading, MA: Perseus Books.
Gist, M.E., & Stevens, C.K. (1998, August). Effects of practice conditions and supplemental training method on cognitive learning and interpersonal skill generalization. *Organizational Behavior and Human Decision Processes, 75*(2), 142–169.
Glaser, R. (1984). Education and thinking: The role of knowledge. *American Psychologist, 39,* 93–104.
Goldstein, I.L. (1991). *Training in organizations: Needs assessment, development, and evaluation* (3rd ed.). Pacific Grove, CA: Brooks-Cole.
Goldstein, I.L. (1986). *Training in organizations: Needs assessment, development and evaluation* (2nd ed.). Pacific Grove, CA: Brooks-Cole.
Goldstein, I.L. (1980). Training in work organizations. *Annual Review of Psychology, 31,* 229–272.
Goldstein, I.L., Macey, W.H., & Prien, E.P. (1981). Needs assessment approaching for training and development. In. H. Meltzer & W.R. Nord (Eds.), *Making orga-*

nizations more humane and productive: A handbook for practitioners (pp. 41–52). New York: Wiley-Interscience.

Goldstein, I.L., Macey, W.H., & Prien, E.P. (2001). Needs assessment approaching for training development. In H. Meltzer & W. R. Nord (Eds.), *Making organizations more humane and productive: A handbook for practitioners*. New York: Wiley-Interscience.

Goleman, D. (1998). *Working with emotional intelligence*. New York: Bantam Books.

Gordon, L.V. (1955). Time in training as a criterion of success in radio code. *Journal of Applied Psychology, 39*, 311–313.

Gordon, M.E., & Klieman, L.S. (1976). The predication of trainability using a work sample test and an aptitude test: A direct comparison. *Personnel Psychology, 29*, 243–253.

Gordon, D., & Bull, G. (2003, April, CAL). *Blood from the shoulder of Pallas: Using learning style as a guide when developing learning materials using a virtual learning environment*. Retrieved April 28, 2005, from http://www.comp.dit.ie/dgordon/Publications/publications2.html

Gordon, J., & Zemke, R. (2000, April). The attack on ISD. *Training, 37*(4), 42–53.

Greengard, S. (2001, December). Why succession planning can't wait. *Workforce*, 34–38.

Greenhaus, J.H. (1987). *Career management*. Chicago: Dryden.

Greenhaus, J.H., Callan, G.A., & Godshalk, V.M. (2000). *Career management* (3rd ed.). Fort Worth, TX: Harcourt College Publishers.

Greenhaus, J.H., Parasuraman, S., & Wormley, W.M. (1990). Effects of race on organizational experiences, job performances evaluations and career outcomes. *Academy of Management Journal, 33*, 64–86.

Gremli, J. (1996). Tuned in to learning styles. *Music Educators Journal, 83*, 24–27.

Grieves, J. (2003). *Strategic human resource development*. London: Sage.

Grieves, J., & Redman, T. (1999). Living in the shadow of OD: HRD and the search for identity. *Human Resource Development International, 2*, 81–102.

Gross, (2005). Are profits too high? *Slate-Moneybox*, November 12. Retrieved October 26, 2005, from http//:..slate.msn.com/id/2109617/.

Grove, D.A., & Ostroff, C. (1991). Program evaluation. In K.N. Wexley (Ed.), *Developing human resources* (pp. 185–219). Washington, DC: Bureau of National Affairs.

Grove, D.A., & Ostroff, C. (1990). Training program evaluation. In K. N. Wexley & J. Hinrichs (Eds.), *Developing human resources* (pp. 185–220). Washington, DC: Bureau of National Affairs.

Gupta, K. (1999). *A practical guide to needs assessment*. San Francisco: Jossey-Bass/Pfeiffer.

Gutteridge, T.G. (1986). Organizational career development systems. In D.T. Hall & Associates (Eds.), *Career development in organizations* (pp. 50–94). San Francisco: Jossey-Bass.

Gutteridge, T.G., Leibowitz, Z.B., & Shore, J.E. (1993). *Organizational career development: Benchmarks for building a world-class organization*. San Francisco: Jossey-Bass.

Gutteridge, T.G., & Otte, F.L. (1983). *Organizational career development: State of the practice*. Washington, DC: ASTD Press.

Habermas, J. (1984). *The theory of communicative action*, vol. 1: *Reason and the rationalization of society*; vol. 2: *The life-world and system: A critique of functionalist reason* [T. McCarthy, trans.]. Boston: Beacon.

Haccoun, R.R., & Saks, A.M. (1998). Training in the 21st century: Some lessons from the last one. *Canadian Psychology, 39*(1–2), 33–51.

Hackman, J.R., & Oldham, G.R. (1980). *Work redesign*. Reading, MA: Addison-Wesley.

Hall, D.T. (1996). Implications: The new role of the career practitioner. In D. T. Hall & Associates (Eds.), *The career is dead—Long live the career: A relational approach to careers* (pp. 314–336). San Francisco: Jossey-Bass.

Harewood, W.C. (2005). Using human resource development in managing change. *The Trinidad Guardian*. Retrieved October 19, 2005 from: http://www.guardian.co.tt/archives/2004-09-15/bussguardian16.html

Harrison, R. (1970, April-May). Choosing the depth of organizational intervention. *Journal of Applied Behavioral Science*, 181–202.

Harvey, M., Novicevic, M., & Speier, C. (2000, Winter). An innovative global management staffing system: A competency-based perspective. *Human Resource Management, 39*(4), 381–394.

Haskell, R.E. (1998). *Reengineering corporate training*. New York: Greenwood.

Hays, S. (1999, February). HR strategies help push new razor to number one. *Workforce*, 92–93.

Helfat, C.E. (1997). Know-how and asset complementarity and dynamic capability accumulation: The case of R&D. *Strategic Management Journal, 18*, 339–360.

Heron, J. (1992). *Feeling and personhood: Psychology in another key*. London: Sage.

Hicks, W.D., & Klimoski, R.J. (1987). Entry into training programs and its effects on training outcomes: A field experiment. *Academy of Management Journal, 30*, 542–552.

Higgins, M., & Kram, K.E. (2001). Reconceptualizaing mentoring at work: A developmental network perspective. *Academy of Management Executive, 25*(2), 254–288.

Hilgard, E.R., & Bower, G.H. (1966). *Theories of learning*. New York: Appleton-Century-Crofts.

Hodgetts, R., Luthans, F., & Lee, S.M. (1994, Winter). New paradigm organizations: From total quality to learning to world-class. *Organizational Dynamics, 22*(3), 5–19.

Hodgkinson, G.P., & Wright, G. (2002). Confronting strategic inertia in a top-management team: Learning from failure. *Organization Studies, 23*(6), 949–977.

Holton III, E.F. (1996a). The flawed 4-level evaluation model. *Human Resource Development Quarterly, 7*(1), 5–21.

Holton III, E.F. (1996b, Fall). New employee development: A review and reconceptualization. *Human Resource Development Quarterly, 7*, 233–252.

Holton III, E.F., & Bailey, C. (1995, March). Top-to-bottom curriculum redesign. *Training and Development, 49*(3), 40–44.

Huang, K.T. (1998). Capitalizing in intellectual assets. *IBM Systems Journal, 37*(4), 570–583.

Human Resource Development (HRD) Council. (1997). *Getting results through learning*. Retrieved October 19, 2005 from: http://www.humtech.com/opm/grtl/handbook2/app_d.htm

Hwang, A. (2003). Adventure learning: Competitive (kiasu) attitudes and teamwork. *Journal of Management Education, 22*(7/8), 562–568.

Industry Report 1998. (1998, October). Training by computer: How U.S. organizations use computers in training. *Training,* 71–76.

Ivancevich, J.M. (2001). *Human resource management* (8th ed.). New York: McGraw-Hill/Irwin.

Ivancevich, J.M., & Gilbert, J.A. (2000, Spring). Diversity management: Time for a new approach. *Public Personnel Management, 29*(1), 75–92.

Jackson, S.E., & Schuler, R.S. (2003). *Managing human resources through strategic partnerships* (8th ed.). Mason, OH: South-Western.

Jackson, S.E., & Schuler, R.S. (1985). A meta-analysis and conceptual critique of research on role ambiguity and role conflict in work settings. *Organizational Behavior and Human Decision Processes, 36,* 16–78.

Jameison, D., & O'Mara, J.O. (1991). *Managing workforce 2000.* San Francisco: Jossey-Bass.

James, W.B., & Blank, W.E. (1983). Review and critique of available learning-style instruments for adults. In D. Flannery (Ed.), *Applying cognitive learning styles* (pp. 47–58). San Francisco: Jossey-Bass.

James, W., & Galbraith, M.W. (1985, January). Perceptual learning styles: Implications and techniques for the practitioner. *Lifelong Learning,* 20–23.

Jenkins, M., Henry, N., & Pinch, S. (2004, April). Knowledge, clusters, and competitive advantage. *Academy of Management Review,* 258–271.

Johnson, C. (2004, September 8). Hit the Floor running, start the cart...and other new ways to train new employees. *Employment Management Today,* 6(1), downloaded from www.shrm.org.

Jones, G.R. (1983). Psychological orientation and the process of organizational socialization: An interactionist perspective. *Academy of Management Review, 8,* 464–474.

Karaveli, A., & Hall, D.T. (2003). Growing leaders for turbulent times: Is succession planning up to the challenge? *Organizational Dynamics, 32*(1), 62–79.

Karr, A. (2002, June). Four questions about career pathing. *Customer Interface,* 38–43.

Katz, D., & Kahn, R.R. (1978). *The social psychology of organization.* New York: John Wiley & Sons.

Kaufman, R., & Keller, J.M. (1994). Levels of evaluation: Beyond Kirkpatrick. *Human Resource Development Quarterly, 5,* 371–380.

Kaye, B. (1989, August). Are plateaued performers productive? *Personal Journal,* 57–65.

Keefe, J.W. (1979). Learning style: An overview. In J. W. Keefe (Ed.), *Student learning styles: Diagnosing and prescribing programs* (pp. 1–15). Reston, VA: National Association of Secondary School Principals.

Kiger, P.J. (2001, March). At USA bank, promotions and job satisfaction are up. *Workforce,* 54–55.

Kilpatrick, D.L. (1994). *Evaluating training programs: The four levels.* San Francisco: Berrett-Koehler.

Kim, D.H. (1993, Fall). The link between individual and organizational learning. *Sloan Management Review,* 37–50.

Klein, H., & Weaver, N. (2000). The effectiveness of an organizational-level orientation training program in the socialization of new hires. *Personnel Psychology, 53*, 47–66.

Knowles, M.S. (1990). *The adult learner: A neglected species* (4th ed.). Houston: Gulf.

Knowles, M.S. (1984). *The adult learner: A neglected species* (3rd ed.). Houston: Gulf.

Knowles, M.S. (1980). *The modern practice of adult education: From pedagogy to andragogy* (rev. ed.). New York: Cambridge.

Knowles, M.S. (1973). *The adult learner: A neglected species.* Houston: Gulf.

Knowles, M.S. (1970). *The modern practice of adult education: From pedagogy to andragogy.* New York: Association Press.

Knowles, M.S., & Associates (1984). *Andragogy in action: Applying modern principles of adult learning.* San Francisco: Jossey-Bass.

Kolb, D.A. (1984). *Experiential learning: Experience as the source of learning.* Englewood Cliffs, NJ: Prentice-Hall.

Komaki, J., Heinzemannn, A.T., & Lawson, L. (1980). Effects of training and feedback: Component analysis of a behavioral safety program. *Journal of Applied Psychology, 65*, 261–270.

Korman, A.K. (1971). *Industrial and organizational psychology.* Englewood Cliffs, NJ: Prentice-Hall.

Kostman, J.T., & Scheimann, W.A. (2005). People equity: The hidden driver of quality. *Quality Progress, 38*, 37–42.

Kotha, V.P., & Kotha, S. (2001). Continuous 'morphing': Competing through dynamic capabilities, form, and function. *Academy of Management Journal, 44*, 1263–1280.

Kraiger, K., Ford, J.K., & Salas, E. (1993). Application of cognitive, skill-based, and affective theories of learning outcomes to new methods of training evaluation. *Journal of Applied Psychology, 78*, 311–328.

Kraiger, K. (Ed.). (2001). *Creating, implementing and managing effective training.* San Francisco: Jossey-Bass.

Kranhold, K. (2004, March 29). Your career (A Special Report); Three generations, three perspectives: A conversation about work, loyalty, balance, and retirement. *The Wall Street Journal,* R8.

Kuchinke, K.P. (1999, Summer). Adult development toward what end? A philosophical analysis of the concept as reflected in the research, theory, and practice of human resource development. *Adult Education, Quarterly, 49,* 148–162.

Kupperbusch, C., Levenson, R.W., & Ebling, R. (2003). Predicting husbands' and wives' retirement satisfaction from the emotional qualities of marital interaction. *Journal of Social and Personal Relationships, 20*(3), 335–354.

Laabs, J.L. (1999, July). Emotional intelligence at work. *Workforce,* 68–71.

LaHote, D., Simonetti, J.L., & Longnecker, C.O. Management training and development at Aeroquip-Vickers, Inc: A process model, Part I. *Industrial and Commercial Training, 41*(4), 32–135.

LaHote, D., Simonetti, J.L., & Longnecker, C.O. (1999). Management training and development at Aeroquip-Vickers, Inc: A process model, Part 2. *Industrial and Commercial Training, 31*(6), 213–218.

Lawler III, E.E. (1994). From job-based to competency-based organizations. *Human Resource Management, 15*(1), 3–15.

Lawrence, P.R. (1989). Why organizations change. In A.M. Mohrman, S.A. Mohrman, G.E. Ledford, T.G. Cummings, & E.E. Lawler (Eds.), *Large scale organizational change* (pp. 48–61). San Francisco: Jossey-Bass.

Lawson, C. (1997, July 23). Corporate bonding over a hot stove. *New York Times*, C1, C6.

Leibowitz, Z.B., Farren, C., & Kaye, B.L. (1986). *Designing career development system.* San Francisco: Jossey-Bass.

Leibowitz, Z.B., Feldman, B.H., & Moseley, S.H. (1992). Career development for nonexempt employees: Issues and possibilities. In D.H. Montross & C.J. Shinkman (Eds.), *Career development: Theory and practice* (pp. 324–335). Springfield, IL: Charles C. Thomas.

Leibowitz, Z.B., Feldman, B.H., & Mosley, S.H. (1990, April). Career development works overtime at Corning, Inc. *Personnel*, 38–46.

Leibowitz, Z.B., & Schlossberg, N.K. (1981). Training managers for their role in a career development system. *Training and Development Journal, 35*(7), 72–79.

Levinson, D.J. (1985). *The season's of a man's life.* New York: Knopf.

Levy, F., & Murnane, R.J. (2004). *The new division of labor: How computers are creating the next job market.* Princeton, NJ: Princeton University Press.

Lewin, K. (1951). *Field theory in social science.* New York: Harper Collins.

Lewin, K. (1947, June). Frontiers in group dynamics: Concepts, method and reality in social science. *Human Relations*, 5–41.

Lewison, J. (2001, October). Knowledge management. *SHRM White Paper.* Retrieved from http://www/astd.org, November 14, 2001.

Lievens, F. (2002). Trying to understand the different pieces of the construct validity puzzle of assessment centers: An examination of assessor and assessee effects. *Journal of Applied Psychology, 87*, 675–686.

Littlefield, D., & Welch, J. (1996, April 4). Trainers focus on a more strategic role. *People Management, 2*, 11–12.

Lochanski, J. (1997, October). Competency-based management. *Training and Development, 51*(10), 40–44.

Longnecker, C.O., & Ariss, S.S. (2002). Creating competitive advantage through effective management education. *Journal of Management Development, 27*(3), 640–54.

Lorek, L. (1998, January), Computers, cameras, action. *Human Resource Executive*, 36–38.

Ludema, J.D., Whitney, D., Griffin, T.J., & Mohr, B.J. (2003). *The appreciative inquiry summit: A practitioner's guide for leading large scale change.* San Francisco: Berret-Koehler.

Mager, R.F. (1999). *What every manager should know about training.* Belmont, CA: Lake Publishing.

Mager, R.F. (1997). *Preparing instructional objectives* (3rd ed.). Belmont, CA: Pitman Learning.

Mager, R.F. (1990). *Making instruction work, or skill-bloomers.* London: Kogan Page.

Mager, R.F. (1984). *Preparing instructional objectives* (2nd ed.). Belmont, CA: Pitman Learning.

Mager, R.F., & Pipe, P. (1984). *Analyzing performance problems: Or, you really oughta wanna.* Belmont, CA: Brooks/Cole.

Maier, N.R.F. (1973). *Psychology in industrial organizations* (4th ed.). Boston: Houghton-Mifflin.

Marks-Tarlow, T. (1995). *Creativity inside out: Learning through multiple intelligences.* Reading, MA: Addison-Wesley.

Marquardt, M. (1998). *The global advantage: How world class organizations improve performance through globalization.* Houston, TX: Gulf.

Marquardt, M., & Berger, N.O. (2003, August). The future: Globalization and new roles for HRD. *Advances in Developing Human Resources, 5*(3), 283–295.

Marquardt, M., & Reynolds, A. (1994). *The global organization.* Burr Ridge, IL: Irwin.

Marshall, M (2000). Turnover's terrible toll. *Financial Executive, 16*(6), 11–12.

Martinez, M. (2000). Successful learning: Using learning orientations to mass customize learning. [Online] *International Journal of Educational Technology* (IJET). Retrieved April 28, 2005, from http://smi.curtin.edu.au/ijet/v2n2/martinez/index.html

Martocchio, J.J. (1992). Microcomputer usage as an opportunity: The influence of context in employee training. *Personnel Psychology, 45,* 529–552.

Martocchio, J.J. (1994). Effects of ability on anxiety, self-efficacy, and learning in training. *Journal of Applied Psychology, 79,* 819–825.

Mathieu, J.E., Tannenbaum, S.J., & Salas, E. (1983). The influences of individual and situational characteristics on measures of training effectiveness. *Academy of Management Journal, 35,* 828–847.

Mathis, R.L., & Jackson, J.H. (2006). *Human resource management* (11th ed.). Mason, OH: South-Western/Thompson.

Maurer, T. (2001). Career-relevant learning and development, worker age, and beliefs about self-efficacy for development. *Journal of Management, 27,* 123–140.

Maurier, T.J., & Tarulli, B.A. (1994). Investigation of perceived environment, perceived outcome, and person variables in relationship in voluntary development activity by employees. *Journal of Applied Psychology, 79,* 3–14.

Maznevski, M.L., & DiStefano, J. (2000, Summer/Fall). Global leaders are team players: Developing global leaders through membership on global teams. *Human Resource Management, 39,* 195–208.

McCall, M.W., Lombardo, M.M., & Morrison, A.M. (1988). *The lessons of experience.* Lexington, MA: Lexington Books.

McCauley, C.D. (1999). *The job challenge profile: Participant workbook.* San Francisco: Jossey-Bass.

McCauley, C.D. et al. (1994). Assessing the development components of managerial jobs. *Journal of Applied Psychology, 79,* 544–560.

McElwain, (1991, February). Succession plans designed to manage change. *HR Magazine,* 67–71.

McEvoy, G.M., & Buller, P.F. (1997). The power of outdoor management development. *Journal of Management Development, 16*(3), 208–217.

McGarrell, Jr., E.J. (1984). An orientation system that builds productivity. *Personnel Administrator, 29*(10), 75–85.

McGehee, W., & Thayer, P.W. (2001). *Training in business and industry.* New York: John Wiley.

McGill, I., & Brockbank, A. (2004). *The action learning handbook: Powerful techniques for education, professional development, and training.* London: Routledge Falmer.

McLagan, P. (1996, January). Great ideas revisited. *Training & Development*, 60–65.

McNerney, D.J., & Brigins, A. (1995, June). Competency assessment gains favor among trainers. *HRFocus, 72*(6), 19.

Meckel, N.T. (1981, July). The manager as career counselor. *Training and Development Journal*, 65–69.

Merriam, S.B., & Caffarella, R.S. (1999). *Learning in adulthood: A comprehensive guide* (2nd ed.). San Francisco: Jossey-Bass.

Meyers-Levy, J. (1989). Gender differences in information processing: A selectivity interpretation. In P. Cafferata & A.M. Tybout (Eds.), *Cognitive and affective responses to advertising* (pp. 219–260). Lexington, MA: Lexington.

Mezirow, J. (2000). Learning to think like an adult. In J. Mezirow & Associates (Eds.), *Learning as transformation: Critical perspectives on a theory in progress* (p. 8) San Francisco: Jossey-Bass.

Mezirow, J. (1991). *Transformative dimensions of adult learning.* San Francisco: Jossey-Bass.

Mieszkowski, K. (1998, February-March). Get with the programs! *Fast Company, 13,* 28–30.

Mighty, E.J., & Ashton, W. (2003). Management development: Hoax or hero. *Journal of Management Development, 22,* 14–31.

Mignerey, J.T., Rubin, R.B., & Gorden, W.I. (1995). Organizational entry: An investigation of newcomer communication behavior and uncertainty. *Communication Research, 22,* 54–85.

Miles, R. (1965, July-August). Human relations or human resources? *Harvard Business Review, 148*–163.

Milkovich, G.T., & Anderson, J.C. (1982). Career planning and development systems. In K.M. Rowland & G.R. Ferris (Eds.), *Personnel management* (pp. 364–389). Boston: Allyn & Bacon.

Miller, R. (1994, April 4). New training looms. *Hotel and Motel Management, 26,* 30.

Mitchell, O.S. (1988, July). The relation of age to workplace injuries. *Monthly Labor Review,* 8–13.

Moen, P. (2001). Couples work/retirement transitions. *Social Psychology Quarterly, 64,* 55–71.

Moingeon, B., & Edmondson, A. (1996). *Organizational learning and competitive advantage.* Thousand Oaks, CA: Sage.

Morgan, G., & Ramirez, R. (1981). Action leaning: A holographic metaphor for guiding social change. *Human Relations, 37,* 1–28.

Morhman, S.A., & Mohrman, A.M. (1989). In A.M. Mohrman, S.A. Mohrman, G.E. Ledford, T.G. Cummings, & E.E. Lawler (Eds.), *Large scale organizational change* (pp. 35–47). San Francisco: Jossey-Bass.

Morrison, E.W., & Robinson, S.L. (1997). When employees feel betrayed: A model of how psychological contract violation develops. *Academy of Management Review, 22,* 226–256.

Moses, B. (1987, December). Giving employees a future. *Training and Development Journal,* 25–28.

Murray, F.T., & Murray, A.H. (1986). SMR forum: Global managers for global business. *Sloan Management Review, 27*(2), 75–80.

Murrell, A., Crosby, F., & Ely, R. (1999). *Mentoring dilemmas: Developmental relationships within multicultural organizations.* Mahway, NJ: LEA.

Naumes, W., & Naumes, M.J. (1999). *The art and craft of case writing.* Thousand Oaks, CA: Sage.

Nevis, E.C., DiBella, A.J., & Bould, J.M. (1995). Understanding organizations as learning systems. *Sloan Management Review, 36*(2), 73–85.

Newstrom, J.W., & Lengnick-Hall, M.L. (1991). One size does not fit all. *Training and Development Journal, 45*(6), 43–48.

Noe, R.A. (1986). Trainee's attributes and attitudes: Neglected influences on training effectiveness. *Academy of Management Review, 11*, 736–749.

Noe, R.A., & Wild, S.L. (1993). Investigation of the factors that influence employees' participation in development activities. *Journal of Applied Psychology, 78*, 291–302.

Novicevic, M., & Buckley, M. (2001). How to manage the emerging generational divide in the contemporary knowledge-rich workplace. *Performance Improvement Quarterly, 14*(2), 25–38.

Nunally, J. (1978). *Psychometric theory* (2nd ed.). New York: McGraw-Hill.

Odiorne, G.S., & Rummler, G.A. (1988). *Training and development: A guide for professionals.* Chicago: Commerce Clearing House.

Ogbonna, E., & Harris, L.C. (1998, Spring). Organizational culture: It's not what you think. *Journal of General Management,* 35–48.

Ohlott, P.J., Ruderman, M.N., & McCauley, C.D. (1994). Gender differences in managers' developmental job experiences. *Academy of Management Journal, 37*, 46–67.

Olsen, R.N., & Sexton, E.A. (1996, January). Gender differences in the returns to and the acquisition of on-the-job training. *Industrial Relations, 35*(1), 59–77.

Orndoff, K. (2002). Developing competencies. *Information Management Journal, 35*, 57–62.

Osigweh, C.A.B. (1986–1987). The case approach in management training. *Organizational Behavior Teaching Review, 11*(4), 120–133.

Otte, F.L., & Hutcheson, P.G. (1992). *Helping employees manage careers.* Upper Saddle River, NJ: Prentice-Hall.

Pask, G. (1988). Learning strategies, teaching strategies and conceptual or learning style. In R. Schmeck (Ed.), *Perspectives on individual differences, learning strategies and learning styles* (pp. 83–100). New York & London: Plenum Press.

Pasqueletto, J. (1989, June). An HRS marketing strategy. *Personnel Journal,* 62–71.

Patton, C. (1998, February). In proper conduct. *Human Resource Executive,* 30–32.

Patton, W.D., & Pratt, C. (2002). Assessing the training needs of high-potential managers. *Public Personnel Management, 31*(4), 465–484.

Payne, R.C. (1984, April). Mid-career block. *Personnel Journal,* 42–48.

Pereira, J. (1997, July 24). Leader of the pack in wilderness training is pushed to the wall. *Wall Street Journal,* A1, A6.

Peters, L.H., O'Connor, E.J., & Eulberg, J.R. (1985). Situational constraints: Sources, consequences, and future considerations. In G. Ferris & K. Rowland (Eds.), *Research in personnel and human resource management* (Vol. 3, pp. 79–114). Greenwich, CT: JAI Press.

Pfeffer, J., & Sutton, R.I. (2000). *The knowing-doing gap: How smart companies turn knowledge into action.* Cambridge, MA: Harvard Business School Press.

Phillips, J.J. (1997). *Return on investment in training and performance improvement programs.* Houston, TX: Gulf.

Phillips, J.J. (1996a). How much is the training worth? *Training & Development, 50*(4), 20–24.

Phillips, J.J. (1996b). ROI: The search for the best practices. *Training & Development, 50*(2), 43–47.

Phipps, P.A. (1996, March). On-the-job training and employee productivity. *Monthly Labor Review,* 3.

Pinder, C.C., & Schroeder, K.G. (1987). Time to proficiency following job transfers. *Academy of Management Journal, 30,* 336–353.

Porter, L.W., Lawler III, E.E., & Hackman, J.R. (1975). *Behavior in organizations.* New York: McGraw-Hill.

Powell, W.W., & Snellman, K. (2004). The knowledge economy. *Annual Review of Sociology, 30,* 199–220.

Ragins, B., & Cotton, J. (1999). Mentor functions and outcomes: A comparison of men and women in formal and informal mentoring relationships. *Journal of Applied Psychology, 84*(4), 529–550.

Raimy, E. (2002, January). Ladders of success. *Human Resource Executive,* 36–41.

Raimy, E. (1997, February). Knowledge movers. *Human Resource Executive,* 32–36.

Randolph, A.B. (1981, July). Managerial career counseling. *Training and Development Journal,* 54–55.

Rao, T.V. (2005). The new roles of an HRD manager. *IT people.* Retrieved October 19, 2005 from: http://www.expressitpeople.com/20040503/management2.shtml

Reber, R.A., & Wallin, J.A. (1984). The effects of training, goal-setting, and knowledge of results on safe behavior: A component analysis. *Academy of Management Journal, 27,* 544–560.

Recardo, R., & Jolly, J. (1997, Spring). Organizational culture and teams. *SAM Advanced Management Journal,* 4–7.

Reilly, R.R., Henry, S., & Smither, J.W. (1990). An examination of the effects of using behavior checklists on the construct validity of assessment center dimensions. *Journal of Applied Psychology, 43,* 71–84.

Revans, R. (1982). What is action learning? *Journal of Management Development, 1*(3), 64–75.

Robinson, D.G., & Robinson, J. (1995). *Performance consulting: Moving beyond training.* San Francisco: Jossey-Bass.

Robinson, S.L., & Morrison, E.W. (2000). The development of psychological contract breach violation: A longitudinal study. *Journal of Organizational Behavior, 21,* 525–546.

Rosen, R., & Digh, P. (2001). Developing globally literate leaders. *Training and Development, 5,* 70–81.

Rossett, A. (1999). Overcoming obstacles to needs assessment. *Training, 36*(3), 36, 38–40.

Rossi, P.H., Freeman, H.E., & Lipsey, M.W. (1999). *Evaluation: A systematic approach.* Thousand Oaks, CA: Sage.

Rothwell, W.J., & Kazanas, H.C. (2004). *The strategic development of talent* (2nd ed.). Amherst, MA: HRD Press.

Rousseau, D.M. (1995). *Psychological contracts in organizations: Understanding written and unwritten agreements*. Thousand Oaks, CA: Sage.

Rousseau, D.M., & Wade-Benzoni, K.A. (1995). Changing individual-organizational attachments. In A. Howard (Ed.), *The changing nature of work* (pp. 290–322). San Francisco: Jossey-Bass.

Rubis, L. (1998, April). Show and tell. *HR Magazine*, 110–117.

Saari, L.M., Johnson, T.R., McLaughlin, S.D., & Zimmerle, D.M. (1988). A survey of management training and education practices in U.S. companies. *Personnel Psychology, 41*, 731–743.

Sackett, P.R., & Mullen, E.J. (1993). Beyond formal experimental design: Toward an expanded view of the training evaluation process. *Personnel Psychology, 46*, 613–627.

Sahl, R.J. (1992). Succession planning drives plant turnaround. *Personnel Journal, 72*(9), 67–70.

Salopek, J.J. (2004, March). Leading indicators: Leadership development in action. *Training & Development, 58*(3), 16–18.

Sarasin, L.C. (1998). *Learning style perspectives: Impact in the classroom*. Madison, WI: Atwood Publishing.

Schein, E.H. (1996). Career anchors revisited: Implications for career development in the 21st century. *Academy of Management Executive, 10*(4), 80–88.

Schein, E.H. (1991). What is culture? In P.J. Frost, L.F. Moore, M.R. Louis, C.C. Lundberg, & J. Martin (Eds.), *Reframing organizational culture* (pp. 243–253). Beverly Hills, CA: Sage.

Schein, E. (1985). *Organizational culture and leadership*. San Francisco: Jossey-Bass.

Schilling, M.A., & Stennsma, H.K. (2001, December). The use of modular forms: An industry-level analysis. *Academy of Management Journal*, 1149–68.

Schinzler, P. (2001, March). Sharing the wealth. *Business Week e-Biz*, 36–40.

Schippman, J.S. (1999). *Strategic job modeling: Working at the core of integrated human resources*. Mahwah, NJ: Lawrence Erlbaum.

Schneer, J.A., & Reitman, F. (1990). Effects of employment gaps on the careers of M.B.A.'s: More damaging for men than for women? *Academy of Management Journal, 33*, 391–406.

Senge, P.M. (1990). *The fifth discipline: The art and practice of the learning organization*. New York: Doubleday.

Sheehy, G. (1977). *Passages: Predictable crises of adult life*. New York: Bantam Books.

Shelton, L., Sheldon-Conan, J., & Fulghum-Nutters, H. (1992). *Honoring diversity: A multidimensional learning model for adults*. Sacramento: California State Library Foundation.

Silver, H.F., & Hanson, J.R. (1986). *Teaching styles and strategies: Techniques for meeting the diverse needs and styles of learners*. Moorestown, NJ: Authors.

Sims, D.M. (2002). *Creative new employee orientation programs*. New York: McGraw-Hill.

Sims, R.R. (1998). *Reinventing training and development*. Westport, CT: Quorum Books.

Sims, R.R. (1990). *An experiential learning approach to employee training systems*. Westport, CT: Quorum Books.

Sims, R.R., & Sims, S.J. (Eds.). (1995). *The importance of learning styles: Understanding the implications for learning, course design, and education.* Westport, CT: Greenwood.
Skinner, B.F. (1953). *Science and human behavior.* New York: Macmillan.
Sleezer, C.M. (2004). The contribution of adult learning theory to human resource development (HRD). *Advances in Developing Human Resources, 6*(2), 125–128.
Sloan, D.B. (2000). Identifying and developing high potential talent: A successful management methodology. *Industrial and Organizational Psychologist,* 80–90.
Smith, C.B. (1988). Designing and facilitating a self-assessment experience. In M. London & E. M. Mone (Eds.), *Career growth and human resource strategies: The role of the human resource professional in employee development* (pp. 157–172). New York: Quorum Books.
Smith, R.M. (1982). *Learning how to learn: Applied theory for adults.* Atlanta, GA: Follett.
Smith-Jentsch, K.A., Jentsch, F.G., Payne, S.C., & Salas, E. (1996). Can pretraining experiences explain individual differences in learning? *Journal of Applied Psychology, 81,* 110–116.
Sommer, R.F. (1989). *Teaching writing to adults: Strategies and concepts for improving learner performance.* San Francisco: Jossey-Bass.
Soverwine, A.H. (1977, June). A mythology of career growth. *Management Review,* 56–60.
Spira, J.B. (2000). In praise of knowledge workers. *KM World, 14,* 1–3.
St. John, W.D. (1980, May). The complete employee orientation program. *Personnel Journal,* 373–378.
Spreitzer, G.M., McCall Jr., M.W., & Mahoney, J.D. (1997). Early identification of international executive potential. *Journal of Applied Psychology, 82,* 6–29.
Staats, E. (1977, January-February). Career planning and development: Which way is up? *Public Administration Review,* 73–76.
Starcke, A.M. (1996) Building a better orientation program. *HR Magazine, 41*(11), 108–114.
Stein, B.A., & Kanter, R.M. (1980). Building the parallel organization. *Journal of Applied Behavioral Science, 16,* 371–386.
Sternberg, R.J., & Gigorenko, E.L. (1997, July). Are cognitive styles still in style? *American Psychologist, 52,* 700–712.
Stevens, L. (1998, January). Streamlined training. *Human Resource Executive,* 44–46.
Stone, T.H. (1981). *Understanding personnel management.* Hinsdale, IL: Dryden Press.
Stroh, L.K., & Reilly, A.H. (1997). Loyalty in the age of downsizing. *Sloan Management Review, 38,* 83–86.
Stufflebeam, D., Foley, W., Gepart, W., Guba, E., Hammond, R., Merriman, H., & Provus, M. (1971). *Educational evaluation and decision making.* Itasca, IL: Peacock.
Suchman, E. (1967). *Evaluating research.* New York: Russell Sage.
Sullivan, R., & Miklas, D. (1985, May). On-the-job training that works. *Training and Development Journal, 39*(5), 118–120.
Sullivan, S.E. (1999). The changing nature of careers: A review and research agenda. *Journal of Management, 25,* 457–484.
Swanson, L. (1995b). *Learning styles: A review of the literature.* ERIC Doc. Service. No. ED387067.
Swanson, R.A. (1995a). Human resource development, performance is key. *Human Resource Development Quarterly, 6,* 207–213.

Swanson, R.A., & Arnold, D.E. (1996). The purpose of human resource development is to improve organizational performance. In R.W. Rowden (Ed.), *Workplace learning: Debating five critical questions of theory and practice* (pp. 13–20). San Francisco: Jossey-Bass.

Swanson, R.A., & Holton III, E.F. (2001). *Foundations of human resource development.* San Francisco: Berrett-Koehler.

Swanson, R.A., & Holton III, E.F. (1999). *Results: How to assess performance learning and perceptions in organizations.* San Francisco: Berrett-Koehler.

Tan, J.A., Hall, R.J., & Boyce, C. (2003). The role of employee reactions in predicting training effectiveness. *Human Resource Development Quarterly, 14*(4), 397–411.

Tannenbaum, S.I., & Woods, S.B. (1992). Determining a strategy for evaluating training: Operating within organizational constraints. *Human Resource Planning, 15,* 53–81.

Tannenbaum, S.I. (1997). Enhancing continuous diagnostic findings from multiple companies. *Human Resource Management, 36,* 437–452.

Thomas, H.D.C., & Anderson, N. (2002, December). Newcomer socialization tactics, information acquisition and attitudes. *Journal of Occupational and Organizational Psychology,* 423–437.

Thomas, J. (1985). Force field analysis: A new way to evaluate your strategy. *Long Range Planning, 18*(6), 54–59.

Thornton, G.C. (1992). *Assessment centers in human resource management.* Reading, MA: Addison, Wesley.

Tichy, N.M., & Charan, R. (1995, March-April). The CEO as coach: An interview with AlliedSignal's Lawrence Bossidy. *Harvard Business Review,* 69–78.

Toossi, M. (2004, February).Labor force projections to 2012: The graying of the U.S. workforce. *Monthly Labor Review,* 48–50.

Torraco, R.J., & Swanson, R.A. (1995). The strategic costs of human resource development. *Human Resource Planning, 18*(4), 10–29.

Towler, A.J., & Dipboye, R.L. (2001). Effects of trainer expressiveness, organization, and trainee goal orientation on training outcomes. *Journal of Applied Psychology, 86,* 664–673.

Toye, M. (1989). In S. B. Merriam & R. S. Caffarella (Eds.), *Learning in adulthood: A comprehensive guide.* San Francisco: Jossey-Bass.

Truby, M. (2001, January 7). Ford romances to prospects. *Detroit News.*

Tubre, T.C., & Collins, J.M. (2000). Jackson and Schuler (1985) revisited: A meta-analysis of the relationships between role ambiguity, role conflict, and job performance. *Journal of Management, 26,* 155–169.

Turnley, W.H., & Feldman, D.C. (1999). The impact of psychological contract violations on exit, voice, loyalty, and neglect. *Human Relations, 52,* 895–922.

Tyler, K. (2003, March). Find your mentor. *HR Magazine,* 89–93.

Tyler, K. (2000, May). Focus on training. *HR Magazine,* 94–102.

Tyler, K. (1998, May). Take new employee orientation off the back burner. *HR Magazine,* 49–57.

U.S. Department of Labor. (2001). *Glass ceiling report.* www.dol.gov.

Ulrich, D., Jick, T., & Von Glinow, M. (1993, Autumn). High-impact learning: Building and diffusing learning capability. *Organizational Dynamics,* 52–66.

Ulrich, D., & Smallwood, N. (2002, November 1). Global collaboration [Electronic version]. *New Straits Times.* Retrieved April 10, 2004, from http://80-global.factiva.com.proxygw.wrlc.org/en/arch/display.asp

Ulrich, D., Zenger, J., & Smallwood, N. (1999). *Results-based leadership: How leaders build the business and improve the bottom line.* Boston: Harvard Business School Press.

Van Maanen, J. (1978, Summer). People processing: Strategies for organizational socialization. *Organizational Dynamics,* 18–36.

Van Maanen, J. (1976). Breaking in: Socialization to work. In R. Dubin (Ed.), *Handbook of work, organization, and society* (pp. 67–130). Chicago: Rand McNally College Publishing.

Van Maanen, J., & Schein, J. (1979). Toward a theory of organizational socialization. In B. M. Staw (Ed.), *Research in organizational behavior* (Vol. 1, pp. 209–264). Greenwich, CT: JAI Press.

Vella, J.K. (1994). *Learning to listen, learning to teach: The power of dialogue in educating adults.* San Francisco: Jossey-Bass.

Vicere, A.A., & Fulmer, R.M. (1998). *Leadership by design.* Boston: Harvard Business School.

Vicere, A. (2000). Ten observations on e-learning and leadership development. *Human Resource Planning, 23*(4), 34–46.

Wanous, J.P. (1992). *Organizational entry* (2nd ed.). Reading, MA: Addison-Wesley.

Wanous, J.P. (1980a). *Organizational entry: Recruitment, selection, and socialization of newcomers.* Reading, MA: Addison-Wesley.

Wanous, J.P. (1980b). Effects of realistic job previews on job acceptance, job attitudes, and job survival. *Journal of Applied Psychology, 58,* 953–965.

Wanous, J.P., & Collela, A. (1989). Organizational entry research: Current status and future directions. In K.M. Rowland & G.R. Ferris (Eds.), *Research in personnel and human resources management* (Vol. 7, pp. 59–120). Greenwich, CT: JAI Press.

Ward, L. (1996, February 4). In the executive alphabet, you call them C.L.O.'s. *New York Times,* 12.

Warr, P., & Bunce, D. (2003). Trainee characteristics and the outcomes of open learning. *Personnel Psychology, 48,* 348–374.

Wasserman, S. (1994). *Introduction to case method teaching: A guide to the galaxy.* New York: Teachers College Press.

Watkins, K.E., & Marsick, V.J. (1995). The case for learning. In E. F. Holton (Ed.), *Academy of Human Resource Development Conference Proceedings.* Austin, TX: Academy of Human Resource Development.

Watkins, J.M., & Mohr, B.J. (2001). *Appreciative inquiry: Change at the speed of imagination.* New York: John Wiley.

Watson Wyatt Worldwide. (2004). *Phased retirement: Aligning employer programs with worker preferences—2004 survey report.* Washington, DC: Author.

Webb, W. (2003, January). Who moved my training?" *Training,* 1–4.

Wehrenber, S. (1989, August). Match trainers to the task. *Personnel Journal, 68*(9), 69–76.

Wehrenberg, S.B. (1987, April). Supervisors as trainees: The long-term gains of OJT. *Personnel Journal, 66*(4), 48–51.

Weinstein, C., & Mayer, R. (1986). The teaching of learning strategies. In M. Wittrock (Ed.), *Handbook of research on teaching*, (pp. 315–327). (3rd ed.). New York: Macmillan.

Wellens, R., & Rioux, S. (2000, May). The growing pains of globalizing HR. *Training & Development, 54*(5), 79–85.

Welsch, E. (2002, January). Cautious steps ahead: A slow economy means readiness assessments are back. *Online Learning,* 20–24.

Werner, J.M., O'Leary-Kelly, A.M., Baldwin, T.T., & Wexley, K.N. (1994). Augmenting behavior-modeling training: Testing the effects of pre- and post-training interventions. *Human Resource Development Quarterly, 5,* 169–183.

Werner, J.M., & DeSimone, R.L. (2006). *Human resource development* (4th ed.). Mason, OH: Thomson-SouthWestern.

Wexley, K., & Latham, G. (2002). *Developing and training human resources in organizations.* Upper Saddle River, NJ: Prentice-Hall.

Wexley, K.N., & Latham, G.P. (1991a). *Developing and training human resource in organizations* (2nd ed.). Glenview, IL: Scott, Foresman.

Wexley, K.N., & Latham, G.P. (1991b). *Developing and training human resources in organizations.* New York: HarperCollins.

Willis, S.L., & Dubin, S.S. (Eds.). (1990). *Managing professional competence: Approaches to career enhancement, vitality and success throughout a work life.* San Francisco: Jossey-Bass.

Winfred, Jr. A. et. al. (2003). Effectiveness of training in organizations: A meta-analysis of design and evaluation features. *Journal of Applied Psychology, 88*(2), 234–245.

Winterscheid, B.C. (1980, August). A career development system coordinates training efforts. *Personnel Administrator,* 28–32.

Work-Family Roundtable, The Conference Board. (1995, Spring), 1–9.

Wratcher, M.A., Morrison, E.E., Riley, W.L., & Scheirton, L.S. (1997). *Curriculum and program planning: A study guide for the core seminar.* Nova Southeastern University: Programs for Higher Education.

Ying, B. (2004, May). Can adult learning theory provide a foundation for human resource development? *Advances in Developing Human Resources, 6*(2), 129–145.

Yorks, L. (2005). *Strategic human resource development.* Mason, OH: South-Western.

Zand, D. (1974). Collateral organization: A new change strategy. *Journal of Applied Behavioral Science, 10,* 63–89.

Zemke, R.M. (1999, June). Don't fix that company! *Training,* 26–33.

Zemke, R. (1998, March). How to do a needs assessment when you think you don't have time. *Training, 35*(3), 38–44.

Zemke, R., Raines, C., & Filipczak, B. (1999, November). Generation gaps in the classroom. *Training,* 48–54.

Zemke, R., & Zemke, S. (1999, January). Putting competencies to work. *Training, 36*(1), 70–76.

Printed in the United States
206975BV00003B/46/A